The Theological Dickens

This is the first collection to investigate Charles Dickens on his vast and various opinions about the uses and abuses of the tenets of Christian faith that imbue English Victorian culture. Although previous studies have looked at his well-known antipathies toward Dissenters, Evangelicals, Catholics, and Jews, they have also disagreed about Dickens' thoughts on Unitarianism and speculated on doctrines of Protestantism that he endorsed or rejected. Besides addressing his depiction of these religious groups, the volume's contributors locate gaps in scholarship and unresolved illations about poverty and charity, representations of children, graveyards, labor, scientific controversy, and other social issues through an investigation of Dickens' theological concerns. In addition, given that Dickens' texts continue to influence every generation around the globe, a timely inclusion in the collection is a consideration of the neo-Victorian multi-media representations of Dickens' work and his ideas on theological questions pitched to a postmodern society.

Brenda Ayres, now retired from full-time residential teaching, currently teaches online for several universities. Besides the listing of publications below, her additional works can be found at Amazon, and they include her first book on Dickens *Dissenting Women in Dickens' Novels: The Subversion of Domestic Ideology* (Praeger, 1998). She published two other books by Routledge: *Victorians and Their Animals: Beast on a Leash* (2019) and *Animals and Their Children in Victorian Culture* (2020).

Sarah E. Maier is Professor of English and Comparative Literature at the University of New Brunswick. Besides the works listed below as coeditor and coauthor, she has published extensively on the Brontës; edited special issues on *Sir Arthur Conan Doyle*, *Neo-Victorian Considerations* and *Charlotte Brontë at the Bicentennial* as well as published articles on biofiction, neo-Victorian vampires, *Penny Dreadful*, transmedia adaptations; Anne Lister, and neo-Victorian narratives.

Brenda Ayres and **Sarah E. Maier** coedited and contributed chapters to the following: *Neo-Victorian Madness: Rediagnosing Nineteenth-Century Mental Illness in Literature and Other Media* (Palgrave, 2020); *Neo-Gothic Narratives: Illusory Allusions from the Past* (Anthem, 2020); *Animals and Their Children in Victorian Culture* (Routledge, 2020); and *Reinventing Marie Corelli for the Twenty-first Century* (Anthem 2019). The two cowrote *A Vindication of the Redhead: The Typology of Red Hair Throughout the Literary and Visual Arts* (Palgrave 2021) and will be publishing *Neo-Victorian Things: Re-Imagining Nineteenth-Century Material Cultures* with Palgrave in 2021 (adding Danielle Dove as coeditor).

Routledge Interdisciplinary Perspectives on Literature

137 T. S. Eliot and the Mother
Matthew Geary

138 Orientalism and Reverse Orientalism in Literature and Film
Beyond East and West
Edited by Sharmani Patricia Gabriel and Bernard Wilson

139 Narratives of Scale in the Anthropocene
Imagining Human Responsibility in an Age of Scalar Complexity
Edited by Gabriele Dürbeck and Philip Hüpkes

140 Figures of the Migrant
The Roles of Literature and the Arts in Representing Migration
Edited by Siobhan Brownlie and Rédouane Abouddahab

141 Commodifying Violence in Literature and on Screen
The Colombian Condition
Alejandro Herrero-Olaizola

142 The Theological Dickens
Edited by Brenda Ayres and Sarah E. Maier

143 Connecting Literature and Science
Jay A. Labinger

144 Migrating Minds
Theories and Practices of Cultural Cosmopolitanism
Edited by Didier COSTE, Christina KKONA, Nicoletta PIREDDU

For more information about this series, please visit: *www.routledge.com/Routledge-Interdisciplinary-Perspectives-on-Literature/book-series/RIPL*

The Theological Dickens

Edited by Brenda Ayres and
Sarah E. Maier

First published 2022
by Routledge
605 Third Avenue, New York, NY 10158

and by Routledge
2 Park Square, Milton Park, Abingdon, Oxon, OX14 4RN

Routledge is an imprint of the Taylor & Francis Group, an informa business

© 2022 selection and editorial matter, Brenda Ayres and Sarah E. Maier; individual chapters, the contributors

The right of Brenda Ayres and Sarah E. Maier to be identified as the authors of the editorial material, and of the authors for their individual chapters, has been asserted in accordance with sections 77 and 78 of the Copyright, Designs and Patents Act 1988.

All rights reserved. No part of this book may be reprinted or reproduced or utilised in any form or by any electronic, mechanical, or other means, now known or hereafter invented, including photocopying and recording, or in any information storage or retrieval system, without permission in writing from the publishers.

Trademark notice: Product or corporate names may be trademarks or registered trademarks, and are used only for identification and explanation without intent to infringe.

Library of Congress Cataloging-in-Publication Data
A catalog record for this book has been requested

ISBN: 978-0-367-74215-7 (hbk)
ISBN: 978-1-032-12283-0 (pbk)
ISBN: 978-1-003-15661-1 (ebk)

DOI: 10.4324/9781003156611

Typeset in Sabon
by Apex CoVantage, LLC

Brenda Ayres wishes to dedicate this book to

Rev. Roger H. Mentzer,

Pastor of Bethlehem United Methodist Church in Dallastown, Pennsylvania, from 2001 to 2021 who often "preached" Dickens from the pulpit;

and to all other Dickensian Congregants

Sarah E. Maier's dedication is

Always, always, with love for my Mom, my Dad, and my Daughter.

Contents

List of Figures ix
Acknowledgments x

Introduction: Dickens' Theology: A Hard Nut to Crack 1
BRENDA AYRES

1 "Rightly Dividing the Word of Truth" and Dickens' Non-Christian Theology 18
BRENDA AYRES

2 Consecrated Abomination: Pilgrimage and Churchyard Homage in Dickens' Novels 37
DANIEL STUART

3 Dickens and the Specter of Materialism: The Spiritual Significance of Ghosts in the Christmas Books and Ghost Stories 55
CHRISTINE SCHINTGEN

4 Dickens Demystified: The Jesuitical Journey of Ebenezer Scrooge: Through the *Spiritual Exercises of St. Ignatius of Loyola* 73
MARY-ANTOINETTE SMITH

5 "For Whom the Bell Tolls": Dickens' *Barnaby Rudge* 91
JULIE DONOVAN

6 "Gazing at All the Church and Chapel Going": Social Views of Religious Nonconformity in Dickens' Fiction 110
LYDIA CRAIG

viii *Contents*

7 Needful Things: Dickens, Social Justice, and
   the Meaning of Human Work   128
   SUSAN JOHNSTON

8 The Gospel of Modernity: Idolatry as the Road
   to Grace in *David Copperfield* and *Great Expectations*   149
   MARIE S. HENEGHAN

9 Unheavenly and Broken Homes in Dickens' Novels   168
   BRENDA AYRES

10 Ghosts of Dickens' Past: The Death of Judaism in
   Oliver Twist and *Our Mutual Friend*   192
   LINDSAY KATZIR

11 Theological Shifts in Dickensian Narratives Before
   and After Darwin's *Origin*: *Little Dorrit* and
   Our Mutual Friend   212
   AARON K. H. HO

12 Teeming City, Tangled Web: Dickens' Affinity
   With Darwin   228
   TONY SCHWAB

13 Theology of the Street: *Dickensian* Characters
   for the Twenty-First Century   246
   SARAH E. MAIER

Notes on Contributors   267
Index   271

Figures

4.1	The four "weeks" and themes of the *Spiritual Exercises*	76
4.2	*Spiritual Exercises of St. Ignatius*	79
5.1	George Cattermole, "The murderer arrested," *Barnaby Rudge*	98
9.1	Hablot Knight Browne (Phiz), Frontispiece, *David Copperfield*	172
9.2	Hablot Knight Browne (Phiz), "I make myself known to my aunt," *David Copperfield*	173
9.3	Hablot Knight Browne (Phiz), "Mysterious appearance of the Gentleman in small clothes," *Nicholas Nickleby*	181
9.4	Hablot Knight Browne (Phiz), "The children at their cousin's grave," *Nicholas Nickleby*	183
10.1	George Cruikshank, "Oliver introduced to the respectable Old Gentleman," *Oliver Twist*	197

Acknowledgments

The editors would like to thank the contributors to this volume: Lydia Craig, Julie Donovan, Marie S. Heneghan, Aaron K. H. Ho, Susan Johnston, Lindsay Katzir, Christine Schintgen, Tony Schwab, Mary-Antoinette Smith, and Daniel Stuart.

Brenda Ayres appreciates coeditor Sarah E. Maier for her continued friendship, brilliant ideas, passion for literature and writing, and acumen in editing.

Sarah E. Maier wants to thank the formidable Dr. Juliet McMaster, who introduced her to the magic of Dickens; she is fondly thought of sitting in her office among her many hand-sculpted versions of his characters. *Dickensian* reminds me of her. Her gratitude goes to Brenda Ayres—she makes her work better in every way across the miles; to Christine Coleman for decades of friendship; to Rachel Friars for neo-Vic enthusiasm; to Lars Stuijts for bookwormishness; to Patrick Young for curry and cookie breaks.

Introduction
Dickens' Theology: A Hard
Nut to Crack

Brenda Ayres

In a 1903 issue of *The Living Age*, its editor, Eliakim Littell, published a short article titled "Charles Dickens's Religion" which ended with "It is possible that this collection of [Dickens'] views on . . . religion may be of some interest and some use to-day" (187). Since then, a plethora of articles and books have explored this subject with seemingly little left to add.[1]

Nevertheless, this collection of essays, *The Theological Dickens*, offers fresh insights into the Inimitable's[2] vast and various opinions on the uses and abuses of the tenets of Christian faith that imbued his culture. Although previous studies have looked at his well-known antipathies toward Dissenters, Evangelicals, Catholics, and Jews, they have equally disagreed about Dickens' thoughts on Unitarianism or speculated on doctrines of Protestantism that he endorsed or rejected as articulated in his letters, articles, short stories, journalism, and novels. This collection of new perspectives on his various writings as well as modern interpretations of his writings address gaps in scholarship and unresolved illations in its investigation of Dickens' theological concerns. Next to Shakespeare, Dickens has received the greatest volume of literary criticism, and his texts continue to affect millions of readers of every generation around the globe, all of which warrants a scrutiny of the theological ideologies embedded and not so embedded in his texts, particularly as his works continue to be invoked via neo-Victorian adaptations for a twenty-first-century audience.

Brenda Ayres, the coeditor of *The Theological Dickens*, believes that Dickens' theology was not static throughout his life and that it does not serve Dickens scholarship to assume that what he believed in 1833 when he was writing *Sketches by "Boz"* was the same as when he strove to finish *The Mystery of Edwin Drood* (1870) before his death. Moreover, to locate his convictions and practices within any neat nomenclature as "Christian" and then "Anglican" and then "broad church,"[3] as many scholars have done, is equally unsuitable and misleading. In Chapter 1, "Rightly Dividing the Word of Truth," Ayres argues that *The Life of Our Lord* (written between 1846 and 1849) and his canon dispute the

DOI: 10.4324/9781003156611-1

notion that Dickens embraced Christianity as it is defined in the King James Bible and enumerated in sets of beliefs in foundational, ecumenical creeds. Ayres' is not the first to question Dickens' subscription to Christian doctrines, but previously published statements that did likewise, seem to have nil effect on a persistent general notion that Dickens was a model Christian and was even more influential in spreading the Gospel than was St. Paul. Dickens rejected the Old Testament as God's Word and declared that it had no place in the Bible. He acknowledged that people could and did do evil to each other, but he could not accept that a loving God would ever send anyone to a place called hell. He rejected Christ's statements about a final judgment. He believed that Christ was a good teacher and that his fellow Victorians should imitate His behavior. In this way, to Dickens, Jesus was a savior, but Dickens rejected the Christian doctrine that Jesus died on the cross for the propitiation of sin. Dickens did not believe in the concept of sin. By "sin," I refer to the Hebrew (*chatà*) in the Old Testament and the Greek (*hamartia*) in the New, with both meaning literally "missing the mark" and contextually "being separate" from God because there is no fellowship between unrighteousness and righteousness.[4] Although Dickens certainly understood that people did awful things to each other and deserved earthly consequences, he did not accept the Christian doctrine that sin separates one from God, and reconciliation is possible only through the saving grace of Christ (2 Cor 5:18). Further, Jesus was a son of God, just as we could be sons and daughters of God, but He was not the only begotten Son of God to Dickens. Neither did he believe that Mary was a virgin who conceived Christ through the Holy Spirit; thus, Dickens did not endorse either the Nicrene Creed (325 AD) or the Apostle's Creed (390 AD) both of which state the fundamental beliefs of Christianity. Through her theological investigation of *The Life of Our Lord*[5] and the Gospel through the eyes of children in Dickens' novels, Ayres' chapter challenges the widespread and longstanding faulty assumption that Dickens was a Christian if defined as "a follower of Jesus Christ."

John Forster claimed that once Dickens tenaciously clung to Established Church tenets, but "as time went on, he found himself able to accommodate all minor differences" between Anglicanism and tenets of other religions (1870, 59). A year prior to his death, Dickens requested that these words be included on his tomb: "I commit my soul to the mercy of God, through our Lord and Saviour Jesus Christ"; however, he added "I exhort my dear children humbly to try to guide themselves by the teaching of the New Testament in its broad spirit, and to put no faith in any man's narrow construction of its letter here or there" (quoted in Forster 1870, 60). Here again is Dickens' selectivity about Christianity; he endorses the New Testament, says nothing about the Old Testament, does not refer to the Bible which includes the Old Testament, and implies his rejection of "narrow" Christian dogma.

Dickens may have carved out his own theology with which he guided his life and of which he used to proselytize his children and readers, but his own theology failed to serve him when it came to the reality of death; his belief system simply could not support him when he faced, for example, the death of Mary Hogarth. Another indication of his inability to grasp and his dislike of the reality of death is found in the pervasiveness of gravesites and burial plots in his fiction. Few physical spaces in Dickens are more wretched than city cemeteries. Daniel Stuart, in Chapter 2, "Consecrated Abominations: Pilgrimage and Churchyard Homage in Dickens' Novels," undertakes this preoccupation but perceives a different aspect of Dickens' theology than his discomfort with death. Throughout his novels, workhouses, and slums are symbols of overcrowding and poverty while prisons expose Victorian squalor, but no place registers the author's contempt for the callous treatment of the poor as much as the unacceptably degraded burial plots for the poor or disadvantaged. As early as *Nicholas Nickleby* (1839), Dickens comments on the horror of such final resting places. Ralph Nickleby reflects on how "the uppermost coffin was within a few feet of the surface" where the dead are "parted from the living by a little earth and a board or two" (605). In *Bleak House* (1853), Dickens foregrounds the urban churchyard most prominently where Nemo's burial ground receives his most visceral reaction. Indignity in death after a miserable life seems to amplify the author's pen and churn his narrative toward resolution.

Similar instances occur outside the city to highlight this position. Poor or blighted souls such as Little Nell in *The Old Curiosity Shop* (1841) or Betty Higden in *Our Mutual Friend* (1865) are set to rest in desolate or isolated places. Dickens' treatments of gravesites are transitional spaces for catharsis and even spiritual experience for those still living. Homage is always paid to such sites in one way or another, emphasizing the need to honor the dead in order to sustain the living and promote a more charitable Christian ethic of collective well-being.

Aside from the starved who unwillingly chastised their flesh with fasting alongside the other forms of dying, corpses, and spirits that populate a Dickens novel, there are, of course, the rather corporeal or, more accurately, the corpulent whose flesh is a constant botheration for those hyper-religious souls like Mrs. Clennam, but apparently not so for the likes of devout Reverend Chadband. Recent criticism of Victorian literature has placed an emphasis on the body's materiality, a view of the body as a thing in a world of things. Rarely, if ever, do critics pause to consider whether this view of the body, which is undoubtedly present in novels such as *Our Mutual Friend*, is endorsed by the novel or whether the novel deploys strategies to question or to critique this view. Against the background of Dickens' stated belief in the human soul, and his view, shared with his mentor Thomas Carlyle, that the spiritual is greatly more important than the material in human life, society, and culture, Christine

Schintgen's chapter, "Dickens and the Specter of Materialism" (Chapter 3), suggests that *Our Mutual Friend* presents just such a critique as an anti-materialist novel that challenges and supersedes a fragmentary approach to the human body. *Our Mutual Friend* underlines the need to understand the human person as not just a body, but rather a body–soul composite. Dickens achieves this vision largely through satire on a body-obsessed culture, inscribing the ways in which this obsession leads to the fragmentation of the human person reflected in such absurdities as Silas Wegg's wooden leg and Mr. Venus' collection of human limbs. Exploring Dickens' personal writings, such as the book he wrote for his children, *Life of Our Lord*, Schintgen establishes that Dickens did in fact believe in the existence and immortality of the human soul, and then she investigates Dickens' ghosts in his Christmas books and ghost stories, arguing that Dickens wanted readers to be open to the actual spiritual existence of the ghosts within the context of the story, and that these spiritual entities served as reminders of an important truth: namely, that the spiritual realm is just as real as material existence.

Also interested in his inquest of the spiritual, Mary-Antoinette Smith declares that Dickens possessed a Christianity "of the broadest kind" while aligning him with a small "c" *catholicism* (derived from the Greek word καθόλου [katholou] meaning "universal"). Rather than debate Dickens' denominational allegiances, Chapter 4, "Dickens Demystified: The Jesuitical Journey of Ebenezer Scrooge through the *Spiritual Exercises of St. Ignatius of Loyola*" (2000 [1586]), locates within the context of the universal nature and appeal of Dickensian writings, a spiritual narrative such as *A Christmas Carol* (1843) that can be illuminated by unveiling its embedded catholicity as reflected by the evolutionary conversion of Ebenezer Scrooge. While Scrooge is typically associated with the Protestant-centered spiritual journeys of the main protagonists in *The Somonyng of Everyman* (1510) and *The Pilgrim's Progress* (1678), Smith presents a compelling case for a Jesuitical interpretation of his transformational trajectory via the structured outline of the "weeks" and "internal movements" of the Catholic-derived *Spiritual Exercises of St. Ignatius of Loyola* (written by the founder of the Society of Jesus [Jesuits] in 1548). Definitionally, the *Spiritual Exercises* serves as a guide with which Jesuits have led innumerable laypersons through a spiritual journey divided into four "weeks" or sections. This journey culminates in a confrontation in which the person undertaking the exercises is called upon to choose between the two standards of good and evil. These are the very "standards" with which the spiritually lapsed layman Scrooge comes to grapple from the time of his encounter with the ghost of Jacob Marley through his enlightening journeying with the Ghosts of Christmas Past, Present, and Yet to Come.

Usually antagonistic toward Roman Catholicism in his writing, Dickens does show some sympathy to Catholics when they are oppressed as he does in *Barnaby Rudge* (1841). Set amidst the Gordon Riots of June 1780, rebelling against Parliament's passing of the 1778 Catholic Relief Act, the novel stands as one of his most vivid engagements with religious events. Scholarship has noted its religious aspects, but there is a component that has not received any sustained critical examination and that is Dickens' use of bells. Chapter 5, "For Whom the Bell Tolls" by Julie Donovan, interprets the representation of bells as a framing narrative for the novel, not just as a convenient literary device but also as compelling witnesses to a changing society struggling to contend with the contiguity of Catholic and Protestant histories. First serialized in the short-lived periodical, *Master Humphrey's Clock* (1840–1841), Dickens' novel is introduced as Master Humphrey hears a resonant sound—the bell of St. Paul's. Extending from the soundscape of London to the village of Chigwell, Essex, another bell features at the beginning of *Barnaby Rudge*, where, in The Maypole Inn, a ghostly story (fittingly told by Chigwell's bell-ringer Solomon Daisy) recounts a murder that took place in The Warren, a nearby house owned by the Catholic Geoffrey Haredale. While bells are used for more secular purposes in The Maypole, the Catholic past might be said to reside within The Maypole itself because readers are told it was built during the days of Henry VIII. The Maypole also brings to mind the Queen of May, the Virgin Mary, celebrated in the month of May since medieval times. In Dickens' day, Britain was a Protestant nation and yet had not discarded remnants of a vanquished Catholic past. Furthermore, most of Dickens' characters in *Barnaby Rudge* are associated with bells, which register their moral standards.

Additionally, bells constantly appear as an integral part of the sonic environment of the country and the city, providing an inimitable means of expressing complex links between sound and culture. Finally, though lofty and old, bells also form part of the modern capitalist world; indeed, the bells of the old nursery rhyme, "Oranges and Lemons," speak to this in their questions about owing money and getting rich. Bells moved from monastic and church production to manufacture on a more industrial scale. The latter was epitomized in the Whitechapel Bell Foundry, which made Philadelphia's Liberty Bell. That famous bell is relevant to the mosaic of *Barnaby Rudge* because Lord George Gordon decried colonial policy, and the Protestant Association opposed the extension of Catholics' rights so that they could join armies that fought American Protestants.

In *Hard Times* (1854), bells do ring on Sundays but to the deaf ears of factory workers. The clanging of bells belonging to 18 denominations is the only attempt these churches make to reach out to weary laborers, that and through mandating attendance through an act of Parliament. In 1853, prior to serializing this industrial novel, Dickens visited Preston, Lancashire, a locale considered to have inspired the fictional depiction of smoke-filled Coketown. He describes Coketown's proliferation of indistinguishable Nonconformist churches that failed to support the frustrated workers. Divided and inaccessible, churches were constantly teaching infantilized and empty didactic moralism through books and tracts that left them were distracted from any humane usefulness because of their petty theological disputes, a portrait rendered in *Hard Times* (62). In this novel, Dickens makes an allusion to 1 Peter 1:6–7, "In this you greatly rejoice, though now for a little while, if need be, you have been grieved by various trials, that the genuineness of your faith, *being* much more precious than gold that perishes, though it is tested by fire, may be found to praise, honor, and glory at the revelation of Jesus Christ" (emphasis in original), when he says, "Coketown did not come out of its own furnaces, in all respects like gold that had stood the fire" (28). While this passing reference underscores the religious and financial poverties suffered by Coketown's lower strata, Dickens was evidently deeply troubled both as a social reformer and as an Anglican by Preston's many denominations. In fact, his initial concern may have been sparked by observing multiple recent and ongoing building projects for new churches appearing concomitant with strike demonstrations (Pollard 1882, 173).

More than 20 years later while visiting Preston in 1867, he specifically alluded again to its congregations in "George Silverman's Explanation." In what may be Dickens' most anti-dissenting sketch, the impact of Preston's judgmental theology on the poor coupled with the vindictive preaching of Brothers Hawkyard and Gimblet has painful adult consequences for an orphaned boy who constantly represses his desires to avoid being "a worldly little devil" (1868, ch. 3). In Chapter 6, "Gazing at All the Church and Chapel Going" (a phrase from *Hard Times* (28)), Lydia Craig contextualizes Dickens' repeated literary references to the industrialized, religious environment following his two visits to Preston. She concludes that Dickens considered the large presence of the city's Nonconformist churches and their failures to unify inhabitants as contributing to local unrest.

As for Dickens' attitude toward laborers and work as an ethic, his theology aligns with Scripture when he has Mr. Vholes (in *Bleak House*) quote Jesus: "The labourer is worthy of his hire" (1853, 489) from Luke 10:7, although Mr. Vholes' labor as being an honest endeavor is rather problematic. Victorian Britain evinced multiple lines of thought on work, and much of Dickens criticism has therefore focused on situating his discourses of labor and personhood in the context of Marxist thought, on the one hand, or on liberalism and its utilitarian perversions, on the other. In Chapter 7, "Needful Things: Dickens, Social Justice, and the Meaning of Human Work," Susan Johnston proposes, rather differently from prior criticism on Dickens, to read class and human work as they are represented in *Hard Times* and *A Christmas Carol* in the theological context which would, by the end of the nineteenth century, find its best known expression in Leo XIII's 1891 encyclical *Rerum Novarum* ("On the Condition of the Working Classes"), often taken as the first major document of modern Catholic social teaching. Dickens' social gospel, despite his reiterated antipathy for "Romishness," finds important echoes in *Rerum Novarum* and later works, resonances that suggest Dickens may be fruitfully read in a different intellectual tradition, outside the Marxist or liberal accounts of labor. Such a project does not read Dickens' theology to illuminate class and human work but rather uses human work to illuminate his idea of the modern subject in theological terms.

This communitarianism finds early expression in the work of Dickens, strengthened by what Jesus had to say about work, from which Johnston borrows for her chapter's title, "Needful Things." The story is in Luke 10 but is not included in Dickens' *The Life of Our Lord*. Jesus has come to visit his friends in Bethany when Martha complains that her sister Mary does not help her with the work necessary to provide hospitality to their guests but instead sits at the feet of Jesus and listens to him. Jesus says, "But one thing is needful: and Mary hath chosen that good part, which shall not be taken away from her" (42). "As ungenerous men will be ungenerous, as Christian men (by courtesy) will be unchristian, a Poor Law is indispensable in England," Dickens mused in *American Notes* (1842, 26). Denouncing the Poor House in *Oliver Twist* (1838) and speaking those infamous Malthusian words through Scrooge in response to the horrors of the Poor House, "If they would rather die . . . they had better do it, and decrease the surplus population" (1845 [1843], 14); Dickens' pen campaigned for better treatment of the poor.

After Dickens' first tour of America in 1842, he wrote to Dr. Cornelius Felton, a professor of Greek literature at Harvard and later the university's president:

> Disgusted with our established church, and its Puseyisms and daily outrages on common sense and humanity, I have carried into effect an old idea of mine, and joined the Unitarians, who would do something for human improvement, if they could, and who practise charity and toleration.
>
> (1843, 957)

Upon returning to England, he attended a few services at the Essex Street Chapel and then went to hear Rev. Edward Tagart's memorial service for Dr. Channing (Pope 1978, 37). Impressed with his sermon, Dickens purchased a pew for himself and his family at Tagart's Portland Street Unitarian Chapel. By the time he left on his tour of Italy in 1844, he had stopped attendance there and never returned. However, he did form a close friendship with the minister which would last until Tagart's death in 1858 (37) and would continue his friendship with Unitarians John Forster, Southwood Smith, W. J. Fox, Henry Morley, and Elizabeth Gaskell (37). Even though Robert Browning called Dickens "an enlightened Unitarian,"[6] Forster made this claim about Dickens: "Upon essential points he had never any sympathy so strong as with the leading doctrines of the Church of England" (1870, 59).

During the Regency, more than 200 churches were built in England (Altick 1973, 174). During that time, over 100 new religious periodicals appeared, and there were nearly 500 clergymen (Davidoff and Hall 1987, 78). By 1831 there would be 15,000 Anglican clergy, and by 1911, 23,000 (Mingay 1976, 148). These developments were a backlash against the "Regent's world of public entertainment and lax morality" (153), taking on an even more tangible and prolific form and force in the foregrounding of the home as a domestic ideal that protected inhabitants from the evil of the world. To most Victorians, the house was indeed a castled fortress that mirrored the biblical portrait of "sanctuary." Translated from the Hebrew, *miqdāš* refers to a physical place, one that is holy and contrasts with the world, a place for worship and peace. The word appears in the King James Bible 137 times, with this reciprocal promise in Exodus 25:8: "And let them make me a sanctuary; that I may dwell among them."

Such houses of sanctuary were an ideal and not a reality. Dickens is well known for his disgust with Evangelical cant, but he was also well aware of the brokenness of the Established Church which, like personal home dwellers, worshipped money instead of God and neglected in caring for people put into their charge by God. In 1823, 5300 out of 12,000 beneficed clergy did not reside in their parishes as they should have (Norman 1976, 6). The Bishop of Llandoff held 16 livings but visited his parishes only once in 34 years (Altick 206). Nearly 60 clerics below the rank of bishop enjoyed five or more livings, and nearly 4000 clerics had two to four livings each (206). One clergyman was paid for 50 years to minister to a non-existent parish called St Edmunds North; it had disappeared into the sea in the sixteenth century (206). There was much nepotism as well, as demonstrated by Archbishop Manner-Sutton who gave 7 of his relatives 16 benefices (Norman 508). Another archbishop left a million pounds to his elder son (508).

Clearly, ecclesiastical corruption and theology were struggles for Dickens, and his attitudes toward Unitarianism, Catholicism, Nonconformism, Anglicanism, and Judaism vacillated. Nonetheless, one conviction that constantly drove him was that Christians were supposed to be sympathetic to the poor, no doubt inspired by his own unforgettable childhood trauma with the family's financial crises that landed his father and family in prison. The persistent, carping criticism that he had toward all religions, except Unitarianism, was a failure to follow Christ's example to be charitable to the poor. It is because of this priority that Dickens approved of the Unitarian church in America because

> the poor have good reason to remember and bless it; for it befriends them, and aids the cause of rational education, without any sectarian

or selfish views. It is liberal in all its actions; of kind construction; and wide benevolence.

(1842, 66)

Although John Ruskin and Dickens were anything but friends, Dickens most likely agreed with Ruskin's complaint in *Unto This Last* (1881 [1860]) that Britain had become too greedy and selfish to follow the charity extolled by Christ in His parable of the Workers in the Vineyard, namely to provide a decent living wage for workers. Similarly, Dickens' good friend Thomas Carlyle accused Britain of worshipping Mammon—another biblical phrase[7] found in *Past and Present* (1843). Certainly, Dickens advocated for the poor but his theology about what caused the conditions of the poor and his perspective about idolatry might be as perplexing and ambiguous to readers and scholars as have been his theology about Unitarianism and utilitarianism.

Actually, Dickens despised religious dogma as is clear in his declaration: "Isms! Oh Heaven for a world without an ism."[8] Given the highly charged denouncement of idolatry and the bane associated with the word during the Victorian period, then Marie S. Heneghan's chapter on Dickens and idolatry further complicates an understanding of Dickens' theological ideologies. Chapter 8, "The Gospel of Modernity," scrutinizes Dickens' "simple" spiritually that he advocates through coming to the knowledge of self and discovering sincerity. He skillfully uses the biblical term of idolatry as a catalyst in moral and spiritual growth in the bildungsromane *David Copperfield* (1850) and *Great Expectations* (1881 [1861]). Heneghan presents Dickens' understanding of faith as a journey of persistent negotiation and idolatry as the rite to moral and spiritual maturity—the ultimate spiritual test—and a persistent negotiation. A deliberation of idolatrous attachments formed in Dickens' childhood identifies his belief that suffering is essential in personal growth and the negotiation of faith. His and anyone's faith journey never ends with a simple return to home or childhood but meanders through a pattern of a fractured parable (referring to the Prodigal Son in Lk 15:11–32) or "the Gospel of Modernity." The fractured parable follows a trajectory that does not end with God but with uncertainty; it is a story suited for the modern man in a post-Romantic world where redemption is no longer simple and yet remains anchored in biblical teachings from the four Gospels. In the Dickens' bildungsroman, faith is a journey marked by idolatry, which is the ultimate catalyst in discovering a new expression of faith in the modern world.

Dickens would not have considered himself an idol worshipper of money; nevertheless, solvency was a constant battle for him in his provision for numerous relatives and his ten children. Money, or the lack of it, must have felt like a curse. When little Paul Dombey asked his father, "What's money?" Dombey finally asserted that "Money caused us to be honoured, feared, respected, courted, and admired, and made us powerful and glorious in the eyes of all men" (1848, 42), certainly benefits that inspired Dickens to be a workaholic, but they were also motivators that purchased only misery for Dombey (and Dickens) and those dependent upon him. If Dickens had not been thusly motivated to produce as he did, which turned into a blessing for posterity, what a loss to the world that would have been.

Dickens knew all too well the reality of 1 Timothy 6:10: "For the love of money is the root of all evil." Unable to live within his means, John Dickens was incarcerated with his family, except for Charles, in the Marshalsea Debtors' Prison while his 12-year-old scholarly and sensitive son was forced to work 10-hour days at Warren's Blacking Warehouse. Then while the author gleaned fame and money, he constantly found himself in pecuniary straits in providing not only for his increasing family but also for his relatives and friends. Although Catherine Waters claims that Dickens saw himself as "a prophet of the hearth, and his contemporaries hailed his reputation as the purveyor of cozy domestic bliss" (2001, 120), most of the families in his novels are what we would consider dysfunctional. "The Victorians turned marriage into a creed and the home into a domestic shrine," Andrew St. George noted in his study of Victorian manners (1993, 85). Yet, scandalously, Dickens did separate from his wife, the mother of his ten children. George Newlin calculated that in all his novels, there are "149 full orphans, 82 with no father, and 87 with no mother, making a total of 318 full or partial orphans."[9] Chapter 9 by Brenda Ayres, "Unheavenly and Broken Homes in Dickens' Novels," surveys Dickens' fictional broken homes that illustrate the Victorians' failure to follow biblical tenets to prioritize family over material goods.

Money is also a major concern in *Oliver Twist*, as Lindsay Katzir argues in Chapter 10. With a long-time propensity to blame Jews for the evil temptations and consequences of money, most scholars have written about Dickens' following suit with anti-Semitism. They have long seen Fagin, from Charles Dickens' *Oliver Twist*, as a Jewish racial stereotype rather than as a critique of Judaism because in the novel, Fagin is irreligious. In "Ghosts of Dickens' Past: The Death of Judaism in *Oliver Twist* and *Our Mutual Friend*,"[10] Katzir suggests a reconsideration of Dickens' characterization of Fagin, arguing that he is an anti-orthodox caricature, secularized. Several modern adaptations of *Oliver Twist*, including *Oliver!*, the stage musical (1960); and *Oliver Twist*, the BBC miniseries (2007), attempt to render Fagin religious, a feature conspicuously absent from the original. Katzir explores how Dickens portrays Fagin as ritualistically devoted to wealth and gain, not unlike orthodox Judaism's reverence for texts and laws, thus reinforcing the anti-Semitic belief that Jews worship money. *Oliver Twist* concludes that such devotion is unsustainable, leading Fagin to the gallows without the support of London's Jewish community, a real-life fixture of the Victorian midcentury. Some scholars insist that Riah, from *Our Mutual Friend* (1865), functions as Dickens' revision of the anti-Semitic Fagin. That view comes from Dickens' correspondence with Eliza Davis, an Anglo-Jewish woman who complained to the famous author that Fagin was nothing but a contemptible stereotype.[11] Though Dickens' response to Davis shows some remorse,[12] Katzir disagrees with the prevailing scholarly view that Dickens' perspective of Jews and Judaism meaningfully changes from *Oliver Twist* to *Our Mutual Friend*. If Fagin represents the stereotype of the criminal Jew, Riah represents the stereotype of the shtetl Jew: sexless, effeminate, and domineered by others. This view of Jewish men was not uncommon in the literature of the latter half of the nineteenth century.

Next to Catholicism and Judaism, most Anglicans were threatened by Darwinism with its challenges to a literal interpretation of the Bible. Historically, the Christian Church has taught that the authoritative, infallible Word of God described a fixed creation, that God created Earth in just six days, with calculations that the Earth was less than 10,000 years old. All species were created by God, and current species are descendants of those that left Noah's ark. This understanding had been taught by the Church up until evolutionary theory infiltrated Western culture during the Age of Enlightenment. In 1794, Charles Darwin's grandfather, Erasmus Darwin, presented his theory of "common descent," that one species can give rise to new species over "perhaps millions of ages before the commencement of the history of mankind" (1801 [1794], 240). He also theorized that the strongest and most active of a species will propagate and pass on those strengths, thus articulating the idea that Herbert Spencer would encapsulate in the phrase "Survival of the Fittest" (1884 [1864], 444). In the early 1800s, French zoologist Jean-Baptiste Lamarck observed that when creatures had to adapt to the changes in their environment, these adaptations often became permanent and then were passed on to their offsprings (1801). Tumult erupted between the adherents of creationism and evolution, however, with the publication of Charles Darwin's *On the Origin of the Species* in 1859.

Dickens was not silent about his views on Darwin's theory. Darwinian scholars Gillian Beer (2000) and George Levine (1991) have famously compared narrative strategies between Dickens and Darwin: Both Victorian thinkers utilized chance and random entanglements over a period of time in their narratives. But Beer's and Levine's analyses pose serious chronological challenges since most of Dickens' oeuvre (except his last three novels) was completed before the publication of Darwin's *On the Origins of Species* in 1859. Levine explained away this analytic limitation through the mutual influence of the two Victorians as a moment of *Zeitgeist*, but perhaps further scrutiny is required in the influence. More accurately, one might ask how Darwinian evolutionary theories had affected Dickens' works and theological thinking by inspecting his pre- and post-Darwin novels, which is what Aaron Ho does in Chapter 11,

"Theological Shifts in Dickensian Narratives Before and After Darwin." Darwin professed to be agnostic in his autobiography although Levine, in a later book, *Darwin Loves You* (2006), surmises that he could neither come out as an atheist in the Victorian cultural climate nor publicly reject Darwin's theories. Instead, by following Victorian norms and protocols, Darwin manipulated the system so that his theories could be at least acknowledged. If Darwin's theories propagated an ambiguity over the existence of God, did Dickens accept the evolutionary science that would cast doubt on his Anglican beliefs or was he unaffected?

According to Philip Allingham, Dickens was familiar with evolutionary theories of his time (2014). Although there is no concrete evidence that Dickens had read *Origins* cover to cover, the book, along with other notable evolutionary studies such as Charles Lyell's *Geological Evidence of the Antiquity of Man* (1863), Comte de Buffon's (Georges-Louis Leclerc's) *Natural History* (1797–1807 [1749–1788]), Georges Cuvier's *Animal Kingdom* (1840 [1817]), and George Henry Lewes's *The Physiology of Common Life* (1859), was found on the shelves of his country home, Gads Hill Place. In addition, *All the Year Round*, a weekly journal in which Dickens personally sanctioned every story and review, published three technical reviews, published "anonymously" but were most likely by Edmund Saul Dixon (as Tony Schwab argues in the next chapter): "Species" (June 2, 1860), "Natural Selection" (July 7, 1860), and "Transmutation of Species" (March 9, 1861). In other words, Dickens was aware of some Darwin's theories. In this chapter, Ho uses *Little Dorrit* (1857) and *Our Mutual Friend* to investigate Dickens' theological understanding before and after the publication of Darwin's *Origins*.

Many portray Dickens as a religious sentimentalist indifferent to science, but with regard to Darwinism, he showed his open-mindedness and seemed to know intuitively that the evolutionary paradigm could not threaten his certainty that goodness, humility, and self-sacrifice, the values of Jesus, would remain eternal. How was Dickens able to engage with the Darwinian controversy without anger or doubt? Chapter 12, "Teeming City, Tangled Web: Dickens' Affinity with Darwin" by Schwab finds the answer in Dickens novels in their portrayal of human beings in a contest between good and evil. Dickens' protagonists are engaged in an everyday struggle, akin to Darwin's war of nature, to achieve goodness in the face of a social system antagonistic to Christian ideals. Focusing on *Oliver Twist* and *Bleak House*, Schwab points out that for his protagonists to flourish, Dickens must show how the London environment continually modifies them and then highlight their adaptations through instincts of survival and the aid of enlightened others who have their best interests in mind. In fact, evolution is evident in every character's response to the Victorian environment which varies from the maladaptive to the sublime. Dickens connects with today's evolutionary biology through his intuitive choice to make homeostasis, the ability to achieve equipoise between the internal and external environments, and the survival mechanism that represents the highest stage of Dickensian Man.

Dickens' novels have persevered into the present, carrying along with them, a mixed bag of theological perceptions. *The Theological Dickens* closes with Chapter 13, "Theology of the Street: Dickensian Characters for the Twenty-First Century." In it, coeditor Sarah E. Maier considers what contemporary readers and viewers of film adaptations of Dickens learn from his theological bents. If a kind of prophet of the people, then Dickens' journalism and novels give us insight into his theological positions in relation to the many creeds of Victorian culture. Maier concludes that it is in his belief of the common people, the vastly overcrowded, forgotten communities of characters where we find the divine in the everyday rather than as dogma put forward by the Anglican Church, Anglo-Catholics, or Evangelical followers or as to the shaming techniques of the Sabbatarian or Temperance movements. To that end, it seems inevitable that Dickens' views on children, widows, family, criminality, usury, and justice that abound in the mash-up *Dickensian* (2015–2016) reflect both the contextual views of Victorian time and our postmodern, neo-Victorian relation to the characters—like Oliver Twist, Fagin, the Barbary and Cratchit families, the Bumbles, Little Nell, Jaggers, and Miss Havisham—who intermingle under the watchful eyes of Inspector Bucket as they reflect to us theological and ethical questions of the Victorian past, and present, day.

Notes

1. See Keith Hooper's *Charles Dickens: Christian Faith, Angels, and the Poor* (2017) and Gary Colledge's two books, *God and Charles Dickens* (2012) and *Dickens, Christianity and "The Life of Our Lord"* (2009). Prior to these were Janet Larson's *Dickens and the Broken Scripture* (1985) and Dennis Walder's *Dickens and Religion* (1981).
2. From 1819 to 1821, when the family lived in Chatham in Kent, Dickens attended Mr. Giles Academy in Clover Land. He was taught and befriended by a young Baptist minister by the name of William Giles. Halfway through the publication of *Pickwick Papers* (1840 [1837]), Mr. Giles sent him a silver snuff-box with this inscription: "the inimitable Boz." (Forster 1908 [1872], 11). Ever since, Dickens often signed his name in letters to his closest friends as "the Inimitable" (Hogarth and Dickens 1893 [1882], 211).
3. The term "broad church" was not in vogue at the time of his writing of novels prior to 1840. Benjamin Jowett, Master of Balliol, heard it from poet Arthur Hugh Clough in 1848 ("Broad" 2021).
4. Throughout *The Theological Dickens*, unless indicated otherwise, scriptural references are from the Authorized Version or the King James Version of the Bible since that would have been what Dickens read.
5. Dickens wrote *The Life of Our Lord* for his children from 1846 to 1849. On the death of Sir Henry Fielding Dickens, the eighth of ten children sired by Charles Dickens, his will provided that if his wife and children agreed, *The Life of Our Lord* might be published, and it was in 1934 and in 1999.

6. In a letter to Elizabeth Barrett Browning, May 7, 1846 (1899 [1846], 2:136).
7. Matthew 6:24 and Luke 16:13: "Ye cannot serve God and mammon."
8. Letter to Mrs. Talfourd on April 27, 1844 in Tillotson (1977, 114).
9. Quoted in Waters (120) from Newlin (1995, 285).
10. Katzir's original title came from the fifth chapter of *Our Mutual Friend* when Jenny Wren calls to Riah, "Come back, and be dead." Jenny and Lizzie like to sit up on the roof where it is "tranquil" and "peaceful" like dead. Riah hears her soft voice like a song, saying "Come up and be dead! Come up and be dead!" (1876 [1865], 118).
11. Letter from Eliza Davis to Dickens on June 22, 1863 in Hartley (2012, 378n1).
12. Letter to Eliza Davis on July 10, 1863 in Hartley (377–78).

Bibliography

Allingham, Philip. "Darwin's *On the Origin of the Species* Reviewed in *All the Year Round*—and Introduction." *The Victorian Web*. 2014. www.victorianweb.org/science/darwin/dickens.html.

Altick, Richard. *Victorian People and Ideas: A Companion for the Modern Reader of Victorian Literature*. New York: W. W. Norton, 1973.

Beer, Gillian. *Darwin's Plots: Evolutionary Narrative in Darwin, George Eliot and Nineteenth- Century Fiction*. Cambridge: Cambridge University Press, 2000.

"Broad." *Oxford Reference*. In *Oxford Dictionary of Phrase and Fable*. Oxford: Oxford University Press, 2021. www.oxfordreference.com/view/10.1093/oi/authority.20110803095528510?rskey=GJaqlI&result=5.

Browning, Robert. *The Letters of Robert Browning and Elizabeth Barrett Barrett: 1845–1846*. Vol. 2. London: Smith, Elder, and Company, 1899. https://books.google.com/books?id=HPy_hm9XhVMC.

Carlyle, Thomas. *Past and Present*. 1843. London: Chapman and Hall, 1894. https://books.google.com/books?id=LEg3ILl18cAC.

Colledge, Gary. *Dickens, Christianity and 'The Life of Our Lord': Humble Veneration, Profound Conviction*. London: Continuum, 2009.

———. *God and Charles Dickens: Recovering the Christian Voice of a Classic Author*. Grand Rapids, MI: Brazos Press, 2012.

Cuvier, Jean Léopold Nicolas Frédéric (Georges). *Cuvier's Animal Kingdom*. 1817. London: William S. Orr and Company, 1840.

Darwin, Charles. *On the Origin of the Species by Means of Natural Selection. . . .* London: John Murray, 1859. https://books.google.com/books?id=jTZbAAAAQAAJ.

Darwin, Erasmus. *Zoönomia: Or, the Laws of Organic Life*. 1794–1796. Vol. 2, 3rd ed. London: Johnson, 1801. https://books.google.com/books?id=n848AAAAcAAJ.

Davidoff, Leonore, and Catherine Hall. *Family Fortunes: Men and Women of the English Middle Class, 1780–1850*. Chicago, IL: University of Chicago Press, 1987.

Dickens, Charles. *American Notes*. New York: Harper and Brothers, 1842. https://books.google.com/books?id=onI-WL7FpTAC.

———. *Barnaby Rudge: A Tale of the Riots of Eighty*. London: Chapman, 1841. https://books.google.com/books?id=rmgOAAAAQAAJ.

———. *Bleak House*. London: Bradbury, 1853. https://books.google.com/books?id=KlsJAAAAQAAJ.

———. *A Christmas Carol. In Prose. Being A Ghost Story of Christmas*. 1843. London: Chapman and Hall, 1845. https://books.google.com/books?id=MlMHAAAAQAAJ.

———. *David Copperfield*. London: Bradbury and Evans, 1850. https://books.google.com/books?id=NcsNAAAAQAAJ.

———. *Dombey and Son*. 1848. Philadelphia: Lea and Blanchard, 1848. https://books.google.com/books?id=dibZQA_tGLIC.

———. "George Silverman's Explanation." 1868. London: Chapman and Hall, 1905. In *"Hard Times" and Reprinted Pieces*, Vol. 15, edited by David Price, n.p., 2014. www.gutenberg.org/files/810/810-h/810-h.htm.

———. *Great Expectations*. 1861. Boston: Estes and Lauriat, 1881.

———. *Hard Times*. London: Bradbury, 1854. https://books.google.com/books?id=X9RVAAAAcAAJ.

———. Letter to Dr. Cornelius Felton. March 2, 1843. In *North American Review*, edited by George Harvey, 955–57. New York: North American Review Corporation, 1917. https://books.google.com/books?id=XVbI4r6B_boC.

———. *The Life of Our Lord, Written Especially for His Children*. 1934. n.p., 1999. https://onlinechristianlibrary.com/wp-content/uploads/2019/05/dickens_life.pdf.

———. *Little Dorrit*. London: Bradbury and Evans, 1857. https://books.google.com/books?id=XvpcAAAAcAAJ.

———. *Master Humphrey's Clock*. Paris: A. and W. Galignani and Company, 1841. https://books.google.com/books?id=DFsmAAAAMAAJ.

———. *Nicholas Nickleby*. London: Chapman and Hall, 1839. https://books.google.com/books?id=NdYNAAAAQAAJ.

———. *Old Curiosity Shop*. London: Chapman and Hall, 1841. https://books.google.com/books?id=2dUNAAAAQAAJ.

———. *Oliver Twist*. London: Bentley, 1838. https://books.google.com/books?id=Vz8JAAAAQAAJ.

———. *Our Mutual Friend*. 1865. New York: D. Appleton, 1876. https://books.google.com/books?id=5dkGcb-MGhsC.

———. *The Posthumous Papers of the Pickwick Club*. 1837. New York: J. Van Amringe, 1840. https://books.google.com/books?id=r2ooAAAAMAAJ.

The Dickensian. Written by Tony Jordan et al. 20 Episodes. Red Planet Pictures. Aired December 26, 2015–February 21, 2016.

Forster, John. *The Life of Charles Dickens*. Vol. 1. 1872. In *The Works of Charles Dickens*. Vol. 39. London: Chapman and Hall, 1908. https://books.google.com/books?id=lPdQAQAAMAAJ.

———. *The Life of Charles Dickens: 1842–1852*. Vol. 2. London: Chapman and Hall, 1870. https://books.google.com/books?id=olkDAAAAYAAJ.

Hartley, Jenny, ed. *The Selected Letters of Charles Dickens*. Oxford: Oxford University Press, 2012.

Hogarth, Georgina, and Mamie Dickens, eds. *The Letters of Charles Dickens: 1833–1870*. 1882. London: Macmillan and Company, 1893. https://books.google.com/books?id=ldPNLuqre-MC.

Hooper, Keith. *Charles Dickens: Christian Faith, Angels, and the Poor*. Oxford: Lion, 2017.

Ignatius of Loyola. *Spiritual Exercises of St. Ignatius of Loyola*. 1586. Translated by Paul Shore. New York: Vintage, 2000. http://libraries.slu.edu/digital/spiritual-journeys/ignatius.html.

Lamarck, Jean-Baptiste de Monet de. *Hydrogéologie, ou Recherches sur l'influence au'ont Les Eaux sur la surface du globe terrestre* . . . . Paris: Agasse, 1801. https://books.google.com/books?id=52eTDlD5llAC.

Larson, Janet. *Dickens and the Broken Scripture*. Athens, GA: University of Georgia Press, 1985.

Leclerc, Georges-Louis, Comte de Buffon. *Buffon's Natural History: Containing a Theory of the Earth, a General History of Man, of the Brute Creation, and of Vegetables, Minerals, &c &c*. 1749–1788. Translated by James Smith Barr. 10 vols. London: H. D. Symonds, 1797–1807.

Leo XIII [Vincenzo Pecci]. *Rerum Novarum* [On the Condition of the Working Classes]. 1891. Boston: St. Paul Editions, 1942.

Levine, George. *Darwin and the Novelists: Patterns of Science in Victorian Fiction*. 1988. Chicago, IL: University of Chicago Press, 1991.

———. *Darwin Loves You: Natural Selection and the Re-enchantment of the World*. Princeton; Oxford: Princeton University Press, 2006.

Lewes, George Henry. *The Physiology of Common Life*. 2 vols. Edinburgh: William Blackwood and Sons, 1859.

Littell, Eliakim. "Charles Dickens's Religion." *The Living Age* 236, no. 3054 (January 17, 1903): 184–87.

Lyell, Charles. *Geological Evidence of the Antiquity of Man*. London: John Murray, 1863.

Mingay, Gordon. *Rural Life in Victorian England*. London: Lund Humphries Publishing, 1976.

Newlin, George. "Characteristics and Commentaries, Tables and Tabulations." In *Everyone in Dickens: A Taxonomy*. Vol. 3. Westport, CT: Greenwood Press, 1995.

Norman, Edward R. *Church and Society in England, 1770–1970*. Oxford: Clarendon Press, 1976.

Oliver! Music and Book by Lionel Bart. West End, 1960.

Oliver Twist. Screenplay by Sarah Phelps. 5 episodes. Aired 2007. BBC.

Pollard, William. *A Hand Book and Guide to Preston*. Preston: H. Oakey, 1882. https://books.google.com/books?id=jxkPAAAAYAAJ.

Pope, Norris F. *Dickens and Charity*. New York: Columbia University Press, 1978.

Ruskin, John. *Unto This Last: Four Essays on the First Principles of Political Economy*. 1860. New York: John Wiley and Sons, 1881. https://books.google.com/books?id=59UWAAAAYAAJ.

Spencer, Herbert. *Principles of Biology*. 1864. Vol. 1. New York: Appleton, 1884. https://books.google.com/books?id=oY5IAAAAYAAJ.

St. George, Andrew. *The Descent of Manners: Etiquette, Rules, and the Victorians*. London: Chatto and Windus, 1993.

Tillotson, Kathleen, ed. *The Pilgrim Edition of the Letters of Charles Dickens, 1844–1846*. Oxford: Oxford University Press, 1977.
Walder, Dennis. *Dickens and Religion*. 1981. London: Routledge, 2012.
Waters, Catherine. "Gender, Family, and Domestic Ideology." In *The Companion to Charles Dickens*, edited by John O. Jordan, 120–36. Cambridge: Cambridge University Press, 2001.

1 "Rightly Dividing the Word of Truth" and Dickens' Non-Christian Theology

Brenda Ayres

The following encomium to Charles Dickens by G. K. Chesterton is widely quoted: "If ever there came among men what they call the Christianity of Christ, it was the message of Dickens" (1911, 249). Angus Wilson asserted that Dickens "thought of himself as centrally a Christian" (1976, 55) while Leo Tolstoy and Fyodor Dostoevsky referred to him as "that great Christian writer" (quoted in 55). Was Dickens a Christian? This question was frequently raised while Dickens was alive and even more so immediately after his death during the Victorian Period, a time which Sir Robert Ensor asserted to be "one of the most religious that the world has known" (1936, 137). Was "the message of Dickens" Christian? These are the two questions that I wish to raise in this chapter, without judgment of Dickens' character, while emphasizing the qualifications of "being Christian" and correcting some historical misnomers regarding Dickens.

The term "Christian" appeared during the first century AD in Antioch to refer to the disciples and believers or followers of Christ, as recorded in Acts 11:26. Additionally, Agrippa employed it with derision in Acts 26:28. Before being crucified head down, Peter encouraged "Christians" in their sufferings not to be ashamed of being called Christians (1 Pt 4:16)[1]. How does the Bible define a Christian? Who exactly is a disciple, believer, and follower of Christ?

A Buddhist is someone who adheres to the teaching of Buddha. A Mormon believes in following the example of Jesus Christ and being guided by the prophetic revelations of Joseph Smith. Muslims obey the teachings of Muhammad. Hindus attempt to obey *dharma*. The Jews are an ethnoreligious race that originated from the Israelites and Hebrews. Dickens described Christianity as showing love for Christ by remembering "the life and lessons" that He taught (*Life* 1999 [1934], 122). In reality, Dickens was selective about those lessons; he did not accept many things that Christ said (as will be discussed later). Besides, a Christian is not someone who simply follows the teaching of Christ, and neither is anyone born a Christian. Jesus Himself stipulated that His disciple "must deny himself, and take up his cross and follow Me" (Mt 16:24). Dickens

DOI: 10.4324/9781003156611-2

would have construed this injunction as putting someone else's interests before one's own, as in heeding the Golden Rule. Thus, "charity," touted as the greatest Christian virtue in 1 Corinthians 13:13, is the greatest "cardinal virtue" in *Nicholas Nickleby* (1839, 161). Just as Christ stated that "Greater love hath no man than this, that a man lay down his life for his friends" (Jn 15:13), so Dickens paralleled in *A Tale of Two Cities* with "The man who had come to lay down his life for him," (1859, 149) when he had Carton sacrifice his life for Darnay.

Indeed, "picking up the cross" does inhere the practice of charity and sacrificial love; however, to follow Christ requires much more than this and in fact suggests that the only possible way to give selfless, conditional, and pure love is sacrificing self at the cross and becoming born again as a new creature through the power and guidance of the Holy Spirit. Jesus said, "Verily, verily, I say unto thee, Except a man be born again, he cannot see the kingdom of God" (Jn 3:3). To be "born again" is mentioned in Article XV of the 39 Articles of the Anglican Church (Dickens' choice of religion). Dickens would have agreed that "being born again" is all about revelation about one's place in the universe in his/her obligation to treat others with the kind of benevolence that typified Christ's ministry on earth. He would not have conceded that being a Christian is a faith process that begins with accepting God's forgiveness of sin possible through the atonement of Christ, dying to sin, and then living with a new spirit that seeks to please God. In contrast, Dickens did not believe in sin, and his concept of Christianity is "emphatically one of works, not faith" (House 1965 [1941], 111).

The first point to consider about Dickens is his advocacy of following Christ's teachings while at the same time, incongruously, rejecting the divinity of Christ and rejecting Him as God's sacrifice through which one may receive propitiation for sin. In *The Life of Our Lord*, Dickens described Christ as "No one ever lived who was so good, so kind, so gentle, and so sorry for all people who did wrong, or were in any way ill or miserable, as He was" (1999 [1934], 17). Then he began the narrative of Christ's life with "There is a child born to-day in the city of Bethlehem near here, who will grow up to be so good that God will love Him as His own Son" (18). The implication here and throughout his other writings is that *because* Jesus was so good, He earned God's love and therefore God claimed Him as His son. The second implication is that if we try to be good, then we will also be sons and daughters of God. Neither is scriptural. Christ said, "For God so loved the world, that he gave his only begotten Son, that whoever believes in him should not perish but have everlasting life" (Jn 3:16). Jesus Himself claimed to be God's "only begotten Son"; therefore, if one is going to follow His teachings as Dickens advocated, one has no choice but to accept that Christ was God's "only begotten Son." According to Genesis 1, Elohim created the earth—when "Elohim" is a plural noun and does take a plural pronoun reference in Genesis 1:26, which Protestants interpret as the Trinity: God, the Son, and the Holy Spirit. Therefore, Jesus existed with God before He came to earth. Then in Revelation 13:8, the Scripture says that before God created the earth, God gave man the freedom to obey or disobey God even though He knew that man would elect to disobey; therefore, He and Jesus planned for Jesus to come to the earth to present Himself as the perfect sacrifice to cover the sins of man so that humans could have an unbroken relationship with a righteous God, and thus become sons and daughters even if they were sinful.

Furthermore, according to John 1:12, "But as many as received him, to them gave he power to become the sons of God, *even* to them that believe on His name" (emphasis in original). According to Christianity, people become sons and daughters of God not by doing good but by believing in Christ as their personal savior. A year before he died, Dickens wrote in his will that he wanted his epitaph to read:

> I commit my soul to the mercy of God through our Lord and Saviour Jesus Christ, and I exhort my dear children humbly to try to guide themselves by the teaching of the New Testament in its broad spirit, and to put no faith in any man's narrow construction of its letter here or there.
>
> (quoted in Forster 1870, 301)

Dickens often did refer to Christ as "Saviour" only because Christ "did such Good, and taught people how to love God and how to hope to go to Heaven after death" (1999 [1934], 38), but as Andrew Sanders has concluded, "for Dickens the only certain knowledge of heaven is based on what is learnt on earth" (1982, xii). In *The Life of Our Lord*, Dickens wrote: "Our Saviour meant to teach them by this, that people who have done good all their lives long will go to Heaven after they are dead" (63). Here, Dickens is not regarding Jesus as the Son of God who gave His blood as a final sacrament for the forgiveness of sin which allows believers than to be saved into a relationship with God, followed by being saved from eternal damnation. Instead, Dickens' Christ is the Savior because He modeled being good and doing good, and if we are and do likewise, we will be saved. Dickens assured his children that people who do bad things can also be saved as long as they "are truly sorry for it, however late in their lives, and pray God to forgive them, will be forgiven and will go to Heaven too" (1999 [1934], 63).

Dickens explains the transfiguration to his children when Christ went up a nameless mountain to pray. He is transfigured into a spirit that is visible to the disciples and is joined by Elijah and Moses. A voice comes from heaven that tells the disciples, "This is My beloved Son, in whom I am well-pleased; listen to Him!"[2] Although Dickens was and remained a member of the Church of England all his life and would have been expected to recite the Apostles' Creed as a part of the *Book of Common Prayer* (1662) during each service, he did not believe in its confession that Jesus was "the only Son of God" nor that His mother was a virgin, nor that "He will come to judge the quick and the dead."[3] Neither did he believe in the Nicene Creed that lists Christ as "the Son of God . . . the Only-begotten"[4] Both creeds enumerate the fundamental beliefs of Christianity. Dickens may have believed that Jesus could and did perform miracles and that divinity was accorded to Him in that way—as it could and is for Christians—but in short, Dickens believed that Christ was only a good man and moral teacher, and his teaching could save people by inspiring them to do good in this life.

C. S. Lewis addressed this very issue, considering it "foolish" for anyone to say that he/she is ready to follow Jesus "as a great moral teacher, but [not] accept His claim to be God." Lewis pointed out that if one believes in what Jesus said as only "a great moral teacher," then he or she must also believe that He was a "lunatic—on a level with the man who says he is a poached egg" or "the devil of Hell" because Jesus claimed to be *the* Son of God (2001 [1952], 52), and not just *a* son of God. "Let us not come with any patronizing nonsense about His being a great human teacher," Lewis insisted. "He has not left that open to us. He did not intend to" (52).

Lewis' definition of the word "Christian" was "one who accepts the common doctrines of Christianity" (xii). He did not specify what might be "the common doctrines," but later he defined "Christianity" as believing that "Christ was killed for us, that His death has washed out our sins, and that by dying He disabled death itself" (55). By "Christ," he emphatically asked the reader of *Mere Christianity* to understand that he was not referring to "simply something mental or moral" (63). Like Dickens, he concurred that if people were "to take Christ's advice" (about being kind, generous, humble, and forgiving), it would make a better world (155–56); however, Lewis noted that humans have never been very good about following the advice of Christ, Plato, Confucius, and so on, as evident of their behavior over the last 4000 years (156).

Dickens believed that we are all sons of God, but Lewis stipulated that there is a huge difference between being a son of God and being the "only begotten Son" of God. "God begets God," but God did not create God as He created man, Lewis remarked, iterating the Bible's statement that even before God created Earth, Jesus was with him (157–58). "That is why men are not Sons of God in the sense that Christ is" was Lewis' conclusion (158).

Besides Dickens' rejection of the divinity including His virgin birth, please note the first part of the title of this chapter, "Rightly Dividing the Word of Truth," taken from the King James Version of 2 Timothy 2:15: "Study to shew thyself approved unto God, a workman that needeth not to be ashamed, rightly dividing the word of truth." Timothy was not advocating the partition of the Bible into the Old and New Testaments that should be kept separate from each other. Neither did he suggest that the Bible could be carved up for readers to decide what parts to accept and reject, which would become a familiar practice of Dickens throughout his writings. A compound, the Greek for "dividing" is *orthotomeō*, which consists of *orthos* ("to straight or correct, from which we get "orthodontics" or "straightening the teeth") and *tomoteros* ("to cut or dissect"). This word appears only once in the New Testament in this passage in 2 Timothy and is translated as "dividing" only in the King James or the Authorized Version. In other Bible versions, it is translated as "accurately handling." Strong's Concordance defines it: "to *make a straight cut*, i.e., (figuratively) to *dissect (expound) correctly* (the divine message):—rightly divide."[5] The context of the Scripture is explained in verses 17 and 18, about two early Christians in Ephesus who were misrepresenting "truth" through their dissection of the Bible, and their false teachings were "spread[ing] like gangrene" (NIV), thereby "destroy[ing]" (NIV) or "undermining" (BSB) "the faith of some." By not "rightly dividing the Word of God," Dickens' misappropriation of Scripture has been just as dangerous to his readers.

In writing his fiction, Dickens explained to his fellow writer, Reverend David Macrae, in a letter: "All my strongest illustrations are derived from the New Testament: all my social abuses are shown as departures from its spirit." As for his characters who are "good people," "they are humble, charitable, faithful, and forgiving. Over and over again, I claim them in express words as with characters that express words as disciples of the Founder of our religion," meaning Christ.[6] When Dickens wrote his five Christian books, he insisted that they could not

> be separated from the exemplification of the Christian virtues and the inculcation of the Christian precepts. In every one of those books there is an express text preached on, and the text is always taken from the lips of Christ.[7]

Dickens deliberately infused his articles, short stories, and novels with Christian precepts but was selective about what parts of the Bible he accepted as truth, as indicated in the following excerpt from a letter to his son:

> But I most strongly and affectionately impress upon you the priceless value of the New Testament, and the study of that book as the one unfailing guide in life. Deeply respecting it, and bowing down before the character of our Saviour, as separated from the vain constructions and inventions of men, you cannot go very wrong, and will always preserve at heart a true spirit of veneration and humility. Similarly I impress upon you the habit of saying a Christian prayer every night

and morning. These things have stood by me all through my life, and remember that I tried to render the New Testament intelligible to you and lovable by you when you were a mere baby.[8]

Throughout his life, Dickens advocated the New Testament but repudiated the Old Testament. "Dickens makes no bones about being himself a selective reader of the Bible, an extremely patchy literalist," Valentine Cunningham argues in his article on Dickens and Christianity. Dickens "cheerfully absorbed contemporary critical ideas about the construction of the Old Testament text, its outdated science, its unreliable history, its archaic theology modified later through what was called 'progressive revelation'" (2008, 269). Dickens blamed "half the misery and hypocrisy of the Christian world" on its inclusion of the Old Testament as biblical truth.[9]

If Dickens accepted the New Testament as truth, then he should have accepted what Paul said in 2 Timothy 3:16 (which is in the New Testament): "All Scripture *is* given by inspiration of God, and *is* profitable for doctrine, for reproof, for correction, for instruction in righteousness" (emphasis in original). In Paul's day, there was no such thing as the New Testament. By "Scripture," Paul meant the Hebrew Bible, which included the 39 books of what is now called the Old Testament. Similarly, in Luke 24:44–45, Jesus said,

> These *are* the words which I spake unto you, while I was yet with you, that all things must be fulfilled, which were written in the law of Moses, and *in* the prophets, and *in* the psalms, concerning me. Then opened he their understanding, that they might understand the scriptures.

Jesus constantly quoted from the Jewish Scriptures (the Old Testament). Furthermore, Jesus believed that His own words were divinely inspired when He said, "Heaven and earth will pass away, but my words will never pass away" (Lk 21:33), but there were many truths that Jesus spoke that Dickens did not accept as truth.

I realize that to base truth on truth that claims itself as truth can raise a few eyebrows. To build an argument upon a major premise that is not a given or is an abstract or is not inarguable goes against Aristotelian logic. To say that such and such is true because the Bible says so, to a Christian, it is not saying that the truth is the truth, but to a nonbeliever, it is a logical fallacy, either hypostatization, reification, or rabbit reasoning. Christians reject alethic relativism and any postmodern self-contradictory theory that all truth is relative or arbitrary. Besides, postmodern views that state that there is no such thing as truth are self-contradictory because if truth is subject only to one's interpretation, then how can the very statement that truth is relative be true?

Regardless, to claim to be a Christian is to believe in Christ, and Christ believed in the Word of God as absolute truth. The New Testament quotes the Old Testament over 300 times (McGovern 1906, 311). There is much "good news" or gospel in Dickens, and refreshingly so; from a biblical viewpoint, there are also many contradictions and flaws in Dickens' "theology." Although embracing the New Testament as a spiritual guide has its merits, Christians are called to embrace the Old Testament as part and parcel of biblical truth. Indeed, one cannot read the New Testament without its myriad references to Judaic law and the words of the prophets. In one of the Gospels, Jesus said, "Think not that I am come to destroy the law, or the prophets: I am not come to destroy, but to fulfill" (Mt 5:17). Furthermore, Bible scholars have listed over 300 prophesies in the Old Testament that were fulfilled by Jesus' life. Saint Augustine explained it this way: "The new is the old concealed; the old is the new revealed" (1871 [426], 141). Augustine said that the sacraments in the Old Testament foretold God's promise to provide a savior, and the New Testament is about God's offer of salvation through Christ (1990 [390], 15).[10] In 1940, George Orwell described Dickens as a "Bible-Christian" (2009 [1940], 59), but since Dickens rejected the Old Testament as being part of God's Word, such an epithet is not appropriate.

Philip Collins was more specific in designating Dickens a "New Testament" or "Four Gospels" or "Sermon on the Mount" Christian (1963, 54), but this is also an inaccurate assessment of Dickens' theology. If Christians are to follow Jesus as Dickens suggested, then they are to believe what Jesus believed and said, namely, "I am the way, the truth, and the life. No one comes to the Father except through Me" (Jn 14:6). Jesus was not just about being kind to each other. More than once Dickens rejected the Old Testament because he did not like the idea of judgment by God or by Christ, but in every book in the New Testament, there are statements that assert that Jesus will judge the quick and the dead, and that there will be a final judgment day that will result in a separation of those who are "written in the Book of Life" bound for heaven and the others "thrown into the lake of fire" (Rv 13:8 and 20:15).[11] Dickens did say that Jesus would come someday to judge the world (1999 [1934], 118), but the assumption here and in his novels is that the bad will be punished on earth but no one would be sent to hell because God is too loving and kind to do that. Dickens also wrote that Jesus said that "He would rise from the grave, and ascend to Heaven, where He would sit at the right hand of God, beseeching God's pardon to sinners" (56). Now it is a biblical truth that Jesus is the "one mediator between God and men" in that He paid the ransom for sin (1 Tm 2:5–6), and He "is at the right hand of God, who also intercedes for us" (Rom 8:34), but to quote only these scriptures is to ignore the conditions of Acts 16:31: "Believe in the Lord Jesus, and you will be saved" and Romans 8:33 that Christ is making intercession for "God's elect."

When writing *God and Charles Dickens: Recovering the Christian Voice of a Classic Author*, Gary Colledge stated that his intentions were to let Dickens speak through his texts "so that we might hear Dickens the Christian" (2012, xi). He claimed that his study "convinced" him that Dickens "was a Christian and that he wrote unapologetically as a Christian" (xii). His purpose was "not simply to prove that Dickens was a Christian but in order that the Christian voice of one of the great literary geniuses of all time might be heard" (xii). He added: "Dickens was not a theologian, a biblical scholar, or a churchman"; he was just a "layperson, who thought seriously and deeply about the life of faith, following Jesus, and just what that should look like" (xii.).

It may be appealing to embrace a few of Christ's teachings like forgiving sin, turning the other cheek, showing kindness to all especially the underdog, and blessing the poor, but to ignore the wisdom of other scriptures that demand humble obedience to what may seem contrary to human nature is likely to result in confusion and bondage. One area, for example, that needs to be addressed about Dickens when considering his religious bents is his fascination with spiritualism, mesmerism, and other occult practices expressly forbidden throughout the entire Bible, but this is a matter beyond the scope of this chapter. The gaps in Dickens' "Christianity" were filled with theology and a spirituality that ran and continue to run counter to Christianity, in particular, his resistance to perceiving people as sinners and Christ as the redeemer of sin. Janet Larson could not find evidence in any of Dickens' writing that intimated that Dickens believed that we were sinners and needed salvation through Jesus Christ (1985, 11).

Despite Dickens' propagation of some biblical truth, he also disseminated "false teachings" that were palatable to a lot of readers but nevertheless failed to "divide" God's work correctly. Misrepresenting the truth is a falsehood, and it is more dangerous than telling a lie. It is like encouraging someone to pick up a coral snake, saying, "Oh, that pretty snake isn't going to harm you." Readers—particularly young people—are not mature enough and religiously well trained to discern the falseness and adulterated dogmas in *The Life of Our Lord* and Dickens' novels. Granted, Dickens specified that he had written *The Life of Our Lord* for his children and insisted that it not be published. Nevertheless, its rewrite of the Gospel of St. Luke and parts of Acts misrepresents the Bible and the biblical Christ.[12] Although I freely acknowledge Dickens as a literary giant and genius whose writing has done so much since Christ to better the world with his words, sympathetic characters, and emotive storytelling, I am alarmed that so many people during and since his time believe that he was a Christian and that all they have to do is follow his beliefs and teachings in his novels, articles, *A Child's History of England*,

and *The Life of Our Lord*, then they too will be Christians, they too will satisfy God's requirements for salvation, and they too will have done their bit to get into heaven.

Even if Dickens had never intended for *The Life of Our Lord* to be published, he was perfectly aware that his novels were his podium to preach his own theology. Reverend David Macrae charged Dickens with being too critical of Christians in describing only the hypocrites and not "any specimens of earnest Christianity to show that Christian profession may be marked and yet sincere" (quoted in Hartley 2012, 364n1).[13] Dickens replied that he did feel "a deep sense of . . . great responsibility" to create characters who exhibited "faint reflections of our great Master, and unostentatiously to lead the reader up to those teachings as the great source of all moral goodness" (Hartley 364), but he intended to avoid the pontificating rant and officious cant that he perceived as characteristic of Evangelicals. He detested Evangelicals, as he represented them in Pecksniff and Chadband, with their "bloated glory" (Kucich 1981, 211) and their "inflated diction, the ornate euphemisms, the self-striving egotism of hatred of these corrupters of language" and "preposterous style" (211). Their speech was full of "Latinate diction, convoluted syntax, endling rolling clauses, elaborate euphemisms, the redundancies, the addiction to adjectives—all help to render the prose inhumanly mechanical" (211). He held such "strong an objection to *mere* professions of religion, and to the audacious interposition of vain and ignorant men between the sublime simplicity of the New Testament and the general human mind to which our Saviour addressed it," that he made his objections clear in his novels.[14]

Upon learning of Dickens' death, although John Ruskin lamented the literary loss, he accused Dickens of reducing Christmas to "mistletoe and pudding" and rejecting the biblical aspects of Christ's birth, death, and resurrection.[15] Les Standiford has specifically asserted that Dickens was "the man who invented Christmas" (2008), an audacious claim in that Christmas was God's invention when He sent His only begotten son to Earth to be born as a man for the purpose of redeeming the lost. "Victorian England was religious," begins Owen Chadwick's *The Victorian Church* (1966, 1). Although most Victorians perceived themselves as Christians (Norman 1976, 9), according to the 1851 census, fewer than 50% were churchgoers, and that statistic included the Nonconformists who were avid attendees (Marsh 1969, 7). By the end of the century fewer than 15% of those in England were communicants (Norman 9).

Serialized in *Household Words* from January 1851 to December 1853 and then a part of the curricula in British public and many American schools well into the 1920s, Dickens' *A Child's History of England* has wielded an incalculable effect on forging cultural attitudes about religion in both nations. Christianity in this book was synonymous with Britain: To be British was to be Christian and, most specifically, Protestant.

As Chadwick put it, "The Englishman knew himself to be Protestant," one who was threatened by the 5–1/2 million Roman Catholic Irish who were controlled by Westminster (8). It did not have to do with doctrine or beliefs; it was a nationalistic assumption that the British way of life was God's way for humans to live and behave on this earth. It was also a major political concern: Would Britain's immediate neighbor, which was Ireland and was Britain's portal to the Atlantic, pay loyalty to Britain or Rome in the event of international conflicts?

Dickens wrote:

> Above all, it was in the Roman time, and by means of Roman ships, that the Christian Religion was first brought into Britain, and its people first taught the great lesson that, to be good in the sight of GOD, they must love their neighbours as themselves, and do unto others as they would be done by.
>
> (1870 [1852–1854], 7)

He continued:

> Kent is the most famous of the seven Saxon kingdoms, because the Christian religion was preached to the Saxons there (who domineered over the Britons too much, to care for what *they* said about their religion, or anything else) by AUGUSTINE, a monk from Rome. KING ETHELBERT, of Kent, was soon converted; and the moment he said he was a Christian, his courtiers all said *they* were Christians; after which ten thousand of his subjects said they were Christians too.
>
> (9–10; emphasis in original)

To say one is a Christian is not enough to be one; nonetheless, self-identification of the British as Christian satisfied Dickens' sense of history.

Dickens' major interest was to define Britain as a nation that did not accept the high church or Catholicism, meaning the Anglican practice of Catholic-like rituals. In his *History*, Dickens portrayed the Pope as a villain (House 56) and otherwise denounced Puseyites as "apes of Rome" (quoted in 56). "Church" for Dickens "was a national repository of good feeling," observed Humphrey House (47), and by "Church," he meant the Anglican Church, but one not polluted by Catholicism and Nonconformity. "I am sick of it," Dickens exclaimed to his friend M. de Cerjat (Hogarth and Dickens 1879, 257). After venting about doctrinal squabbles, he made this complaint:

> How our sublime and so-different Christian religion is to be administered in the future I cannot pretend to say, but that the Church's hand is at its own throat I am fully convinced. Here more Popery,

there, more Methodism—as many forms of consignment to eternal damnation as there are articles, and all in one forever quarrelling body—the Master of the New Testament put out of sight, and the rage and fury almost always turning on the letter of obscure parts of the Old Testament.[16]

Even though Dickens equated Anglican Christianity with Englishness, Ruskin was unhappy about how he and others bandied the term "Christianity." In his *Praeterita* Ruskin lamented that there were "numbers, even of the most intelligent and amiable people" who did not know the meaning of "Christianity" (171). "The total meaning was, and is," he began as he summarized the biblically based tenets of this Abrahamic religion:

> That God who made earth and its creatures, took at a certain time upon the earth, the flesh and form of man; in that flesh sustained the pain and died the death of the creature He had made; rose again after death into glorious human life, and when the date of the human race is ended, will return in visible human form, and render to every man according to his work. Christianity is the belief in, and love of, God thus manifested. Anything less than this, the mere acceptance of the sayings of Christ, or assertion of any less than divine power in His Being, may be, for aught I know, enough for virtue, peace, and safety; but they do not make people Christians, or enable them to understand the heart of the simplest believer in the old doctrine.
>
> (1907 [1885–1889], 171)

If "Christianity" is defined as the practice of following Christ, one of the most common misunderstandings of Christianity is the idea that salvation is possible solely by doing good works. If one is a Christian, then one should be doing good works as did Christ, but Humphrey House described Dickens' religion as "emphatically one of works, not faith" (1941, 111). Dickens defined Christianity for his children in *The Life of Our Lord*:

> TO DO GOOD always—even to those who do evil to us. It is Christianity to love our neighbor as ourself, and to do to all men as we would have done them Do to us. It is Christianity to be gentle, merciful, and forgiving, and to keep those qualities quiet in our own hearts, and never make a boast of them, of our prayers of our love of God, but always to shew that we love Him by humbly trying to do right in everything. If we do this, and remember the life and lessons of Our Lord Jesus Christ, and try to act up to them, we may

confidently hope that God will forgive us our sins and mistakes, and enable us to live and die in Peace.

(122)

This gospel of doing good is exactly what Dickens preached in his novels. Even though most of the excerpt derives from the New Testament, its "theology" bears significant gaps even if the text were written for children and not for adults. He wrote: "The most miserable, the most ugly, deformed, wretched creatures that live, will be bright Angels in Heaven if they are good here on earth" (1999 [1934], 33). Although his point was that God loves everyone and therefore we should also love everyone, a valid biblical truth, he makes three theological mistakes. First, according to the Bible, no one is saved simply by being good. There are dozens of statements in the New Testament that make this assertion, but Romans 3:23–25 is the most emphatic and concise:

> For all have sinned, and come short of the glory of God; Being justified freely by his grace through the redemption that is in Christ Jesus: Whom God hath set forth *to be* a propitiation through faith in his blood, to declare his righteousness for the remission of sins that are past, through the forbearance of God.
>
> (emphasis in original)

Second, angels are God's creations; people do not die and become angels. Psalm 8:5 and Hebrews 2:7 assert that God made humans "a little lower than the angels," and 1 Corinthians 6:3 says that we are to judge angels. Third, there is no hint here or in Dickens' novels that despite all our good efforts and good intentions, in God's eyes according to the Bible, our "righteous acts are like filthy rags," and by "filthy rags," the prophet Isaiah means those of a menstruous woman" (Is 64:6). Dickens was repulsed by the Calvinistic notion of "total depravity," which was touted by joyless, emotionally paralyzed people like Mrs. Clennam, and he did create many characters who did do good and sacrificially so, like Little Dorrit, little Nell, Ruth and Tom Pinch, the Cheeryble brothers, and Agnes Wickfield. Dickens seemed to reject those parts of the New Testament that describe our sinful natures and suggested that we are all very much like Paul who remarked: "For that which I do I allow not: for what I would, that do I not; but what I hate, that do I" (Rom 7:15). Many scholars have commented that after Mary Hogarth's death, Dickens had a hole in his heart which he tried to fill with characters who were good and pure, but they were fabrications of fiction; according to the Bible, the only person who ever lived who was purely good, without sin, was Jesus.

Even so, to regard people as hopeless reprobates is not how Christ saw people at all and is abhorrent for Christians to treat people as if they are. In fact, "Christians" like Mrs. Clennam, Miss Barbary, Mr. and Miss Murdstone, Mr. Honeythunder, and Reverends Chadband and Melchisedech Howler are unfortunate portrayals of Evangelicals, Methodist, and Anglican alike, as obnoxious, self-righteous Calvinists, when John Wesley himself repudiated Calvinism. Besides "total depravity" Dickens resented the other tenets of Calvinism, that is, "unconditional election," "limited atonement," "irresistible grace," and "perseverance of the saints," when they were exhibited by rapacious religious fanatics who depicted God as a capricious being that arbitrarily and inexorably created certain people to be saved and others to be damned to hell. *Bleak House's* Esther is a "moral guide" (Smith 1970, 11) in contrast to the Mmes. Jellyby, Pardiggle, Chadband, Snagsby; Miss Barbary; and Lady Dedlock. Dickens' son, Sir Henry Fielding Dickens, related that his father

> made no parade of religion, but he was at heart possessed of deep religious convictions. . . . What he did hate and despise was the cant of religion, of the Pecksniffs, Chadbands and Stigginses in life, and these he attacked with all the weight of his genius.
>
> (1934, 41)

Dickens disliked Evangelicals because many of them were Calvinists or were like the Calvanists in seeing only "corruption instead of goodness" in people (Oulton 2003, 37) and perceiving most people as "eternally doomed" (95). He accused Evangelicals of forcing damnation into "an alliance" with the New Testament, which accounted for "half the misery and hypocrisy of the Christian world."[17]

Gary Colledge deduced that Dickens was unwilling to "use God's wrath as a tool for coercing people into religion conversion or to characterize God by it" (2012, 74). Even though Dickens rejected damnation as hysterical conceit of the Evangelicals, he also resented those parts of the Bible that depicted God as a God of wrath and judgment. Just as many Calvinists "emphasized God's wrath almost to the exclusion of love and grace" (73), Dickens also emphasized God's love and grace to the exclusion of recognizing sin in the lives of people that required Christ's atonement and redemption. Except for the damning accusations of self-righteous and sadistic Evangelicals (like Miss. Barbary who told Esther that she should never have been born), Dickens rarely used the word, "sin" in his novels (House 112) or in *The Life of Our Lord* (Collins 59). Jesus was not just a good man and a teacher of morals; it is the position of even the Church of England, which Forster claimed Dickens to be ever faithful to (1870, 59), that Christ died on the cross for forgiveness of sins. This belief should cause Evangelicals to rejoice and live in joy, in contrast to the stern, negative behavior of Evangelicals that populate Dickens' novels. Biblically it also gives reason for people to own up to their sin, ask forgiveness from Christ for it, and ask for help from Him so as not to sin again. This recognition of sin and God's plan of redemption is a major gap in Dickens' theology. Dennis Walder came to the same conclusion, stating that Dickens

> believed in a conception of conversion which did not primarily involve an acceptance of Christ, or the innate sinfulness of man, but which *did* involve a spiritual transformation affirming a new consciousness of oneself and one's place in the universe.
> (1981, 113, emphasis in original)

Even if Dickens mocked and condemned the Evangelicals for their portrayal of a vindictive, Old Testament God, Larson reminds us that in Dickens' plots "starved innocents and good-hearted prostitutes" do suffer and die (1985, 67). Dickens recognized the Providence of God as he has Mr. Brownlow relate to Monks that it was a "stronger hand than chance" that rescued Oliver Twist (1838, 229). Logically extending the premise, Larson reasons that Nancy was killed by "a stronger hand than Sikes" (72). In her analysis of *Little Dorrit* (1857), Larson finds a "God" who is "malevolent, faceless, or indifferent—at best a *deus absconditus*" (247); however, this is a misreading of Dickens' understanding of Providence in that it fails to factor in the value of suffering that builds character and creates conviction that readers should be more "Christian" in regard to their treatment to each other. As Walder puts it, "Dickens' religion is always oriented towards society and social action" (141).

Dickens abhorred fire-and-brimstone preaching, and he in particular denounced it when forced on children as it was on Arthur in *Little Dorrit*. In a scene when Arthur is an adult sitting in a coffee house, he despises the ringing of the bells that are calling people to Sunday evening services. The bells themselves seem to say that no one will come, and indeed, at the time of the novel's serialization between 1855 and 1857, more than half of the population in England and Wales was not attending church (Clark 1962, 149). Although there are many reasons for this lapse in attendance that exceed the scope of this chapter, if going to church were similar to Arthur's experiences, there is no wonder that most people preferred to do something else on their day off. Dickens was a strong anti-Sabbatarian; he opposed restricting recreation on Sunday, and he was not much of a church goer (Collins 55); Colledge referred to him as the "reluctant churchman" (2009, 138). Arthur recalled just one "dreary" Sunday when he was

> scared out of his senses by a horrible tract which commenced business with the poor child by asking him in its title, why he was going to Perdition?—a piece of curiosity that he really in a frock and drawers was not in a condition to satisfy—and which, for the further

attraction of his infant mind, had a parenthesis in every other line with some hiccupping reference as 2 Ep. Thess. C. iii. V. 6 & 7.
(1857, 22)

These passages warn believers not to associate with people who are disorderly and to make sure they follow only those who are not disorderly. But Sunday also meant being "morally handcuffed to another boy" and marched three times a day to chapel to hear an "indigestible sermon" when he would rather have liked "another ounce or two of inferior mutton," which was deprived to him in order to mortify his flesh (43). Sundays turned Dickens' mother into a compulsive reader of the Bible which seemed to form "a fortification against sweetness of temper, natural affection, and gentle intercourse" (44). Dickens implied that Mrs. Clennam was this way because of her neurotic adherence to the Old Testament, and he thought it "monstrous" to threaten children with an "avenging and wrathful" God.[18] Mrs. Clennam "represents the perversity of adhering to Old Testament traditions in preference to the mercy of the New" (Larson 21).

Dickens was not just concerned that children were being hurt by such a portrayal of God. In a letter to the Baroness Burdett-Coutts about religious instruction at Urania Cottage, Dickens suggested that the focus should be on the New Testament because so much harm had already been done by Evangelicals to "this class of minds by the injudicious use of the Old."[19] The problem with many Evangelicals of Dickens' day, but not all of them, was their Calvinistic zeal to represent God as vindictive in order to scare people into better behavior. What Victorians were failing to do, both zealous Evangelicals and Dickens, was to present the Old and New testaments "in such a way as to make the meaning reciprocally revealed" (Zemka 1997, 131).

Rev. George Stott in 1869 said that Dickens wrote a "gospel of geniality" (224), and House described Dickens as practicing a "humanist kind of Christianity" (131). Indeed Dickens was very critical of those Christians who "talked the talk," but failed to "walk the walk" by preaching at the poor instead of tending to the needs of the poor. In *Bleak House* the apex of despicable Christians is Rev. Chadband as he presses down on the already downtrodden soul to listen to his "lessons of wisdom," even those who came every day to hear his discourses (1853, 191–92). In the same novel is that good Christian who is devoted to the support of nearly 200 families who are "educating" the natives of Borrioboola Gha while her own family suffered serious neglect (27–29, 234). If those two, along with Mrs. Snagsby who thinks that Jo is "a limb of the arch-fiend" (192), are not exemplary Christian hypocrites, then add to the mix the formidable Mrs. Pardiggle, "most distinguished for this rapacious benevolence" (71), and you have perfect examples of what a Christian should not be in just one novel.

How does one know if someone is a Christian? Jesus said, "You know them by their fruit" (Mt 7:16). Granted, we are all sinners, including Christians, but Christians are called to live a life of sanctification: When they sin, the Holy Spirit convicts them of it and then helps them repent—that is to stop sinning and living instead with a clean conscience in order to serve God (Heb 9:14). There have always been plenty of Christians and godly people who have not kept their marriage vows despite the Bible's command to keep the "marriage bed undefiled; for God will judge the sexually immoral and adulterers" (13:4). When Dickens began his affair with Ellen Ternan and perhaps with other women, when he separated from his wife of 20 years and ensured the publication of his rationale for changing his "marriage bed," and when he took their children from her, he may have asked God forgiveness and would have been forgiven. Yet, his publicizing his separation due to incompatibility not only shows a lack of penitence but it also smacks of arrogance and defiance of God's ways. Dickens actually gloated over his immoral behavior so that it is shocking to me that Michael Slater made this statement about the adulterous last years of Dickens' life: "During the five intervening years he had continued to be widely loved and revered not only as a great writer but *also as a great and good, truly, Christian man*" (2012, 32; emphasis added).

Lest I be counted as "officious" ("Charles Dickens" 1870, 29) as were several self-appointed arbiters who, upon Dickens' death, declared that he was not a Christian and questioned whether he did or will make it to heaven, I agree with Dr. Bellows who said, "If he was not a Christian, he was a glorious instrument of God's providence, and may shame, at the great account, many whose Christianity is unquestioned, but whose usefulness and worth are taken on trust" (quoted in 27). I am a great admirer of the Christian work Dickens did accomplish in his writing. As Bellows said, "Ah! What a godlike thing it is to shed so much self-forgetfulness and balm into the sore and tired hearty of humanity!" Dickens was indeed "a vindicator of the intrinsic worth of all human souls" (27).

I also agree with James Paton Ham who eulogized Dickens at his death in "The Christian Pulpit" by saying, we "may properly honour the memory of a man who has probably by his writings, done more than any other man to humanize society—to bridge over the abrupt, deep chasms which divide classes by those delicate touches of nature which make the whole world kin" (1870, 5–6). What I do challenge are the claims that Dickens was a Christian writer as if he rightly divided the Truth of the Bible.

Notes

1. Unless indicated otherwise, all scripture quotes will be from the King James Version or the New American Standard Bible.
2. The transfiguration happens in Matthew 17:1–8, Mark 9:2–8, and Luke 9:28–36. It is retold in 2 Peter 1:16–18. Dickens quotes Matthew 17:5 from the KJV in *The Life of Our Lord* (59).

3. The Apostle's Creed (309 AD) is a list of beliefs held by most denominations of Catholic and Protestants, drawn from the canonical gospels and the Old Testament, and were said to be inspired by the Holy Spirit was accepted in the fourth century by a synod in Milan.
4. The Nicene Creed was approved prior to the Apostles' Creed in 325 and 381, during the first two ecumenical councils, asserting the divinity of Christ and the Holy Spirit.
5. Strong, G3718 (2007, 1654).
6. In Dickens' letter to David Macrae, 1861, in Hartley (2012, 364).
7. Ibid.
8. Dickens' letter to Mr. Henry Fielding Dickens, October 15, 1868 in Hartley (425).
9. Letter to Frank Stone, December 1858 (Hogarth and Dickens 1893, 472–73)
10. In his exposition of Psalm 73:2.
11. Here are just a few biblical references in the New Testament about Christ's judgment: Matthew 25:31–46; John 5:22 and 27, 8:15–16, 9:39, and 12:47–48, Acts 10:38–42 and 17:31, Romans 2:16, 2 Corinthians 5:10, 2 Timothy 4:1, 1 Peter 4:5, 2 Peter 2:9, Hebrews 1:8, and Revelation 19:11.
12. Dickens combined the Gospels and a part of Acts and recounted them in this little book for his children. He began it in 1846, just when he also began to write *Dombey and Son*. When his great-great-grandson, Gerald Charles Dickens, gained consensus from the family to publish it in 1934, the publishers at Simon and Schuster said that Dickens' purpose for writing the "life and history of Jesus Christ" was to "champion[] the virtues of mercy and forgiveness" (1999 [1934], 5). The first edition "was syndicated in three hundred newspapers" and it was "the year's biggest bestsellers" (6).
13. Quoted in Hartley 364n1.
14. Dickens' letter to David Macrae, 1861, in Hartley (364).
15. Ruskin's letter to Charles Eliot Norton, June 17, 1870 (1909, 7).
16. William de Cerjat Esquire and his wife were good friends of Dickens with whom he visited. They corresponded nearly every Christmas (Ley 1919, 258). This letter was written on October 25, 1864 (Hogarth and Dickens 1879, 257–60).
17. Dickens' letter to Frank Stone, December 13, 1858 in Dexter (1938, 79).
18. Dickens' letter to Mrs. Godfrey, July 25, 1839 in Hartley (57).
19. Dickens' letter to Baroness Angela Burdett-Coutts of November 3, 1847 in Osborne (1932, 93).

Bibliography

Augustine of Hippo. "Book 16: *The City of God*." Vol. 2.426. In *The Works of Aurelius Augustine, Bishop of Hippo*, 104–64. Translated by Marcus Dods. Edinburgh: T. and T. Clark, 1871. https://books.google.com/books?id=OykMAAA AIAAJ.

———. *Expositions of the Psalms 73–98*. Vol. 4.390. In *The Works of Saint Augustine: A Translation for the 21st Century*. Translated by Maria Boulding and edited by John E. Rotelle. New York: New York City Press, 1990.

Chadwick, Owen. *The Victorian Church, Part 1: 1829–1859*. London: A and C Black, 1966.

"Charles Dickens and His Christian Critics." *The Examiner* 1 (November 1870): 19–20. https://books.google.com/books?id=wMRkk2nBgpMC.

Chesterton, G. K. *Appreciations and Criticisms of the Works of Charles Dickens.* London: Dent, 1911.

Clark, G. Kitson. *The Making of Victorian England, Being the Ford Lectures Delivered Before the University of Oxford.* Cambridge: Harvard University Press, 1962.

Colledge, Gary. *Dickens, Christianity and "The Life of Our Lord": Humble Veneration, Profound Conviction.* London: Continuum, 2009.

———. *God and Charles Dickens: Recovering the Christian Voice of a Classic Author.* Grand Rapids, MI: Brazos Press, 2012.

Collins, Philip. *Dickens and Education.* London: St. Martin's, 1963.

Cunningham, Valentine. "Dickens and Christianity." In *A Companion to Charles Dickens*, edited by David Paroissien, 255–76. Malden, MA: Blackwell Publishing, 2008.

Dexter, Walter, ed. *Letters of Charles Dickens, 1858–1870.* Vol. 3, 12 vols. Bloomsbury: Nonesuch, 1938.

Dickens, Charles. *Bleak House.* London: Bradbury, 1853. https://books.google.com/books?id=KlsJAAAAQAAJ.

———. *A Child's History of England.* 1852–1854. London: Chapman and Hall, 1870. https://books.google.com/books?id=aJ8uAAAAMAAJ.

———. *The Life of Our Lord: Written for His Children During the Years 1846 to 1849.* 1934. Introduction by Gerald Charles Dickens. New York: Simon and Schuster, 1999.

———. *Little Dorrit.* London: Bradbury and Evans, 1857. https://books.google.com/books?id=XvpcAAAAcAAJ.

———. *Nicholas Nickleby.* London: Chapman and Hall, 1839. https://books.google.com/books?id=NdYNAAAAQAAJ.

———. *Oliver Twist.* London: Bentley, 1838. https://books.google.com/books?id=Vz8JAAAAQAAJ.

———. *A Tale of Two Cities.* Philadelphia: T. B. Peterson and Brothers, 1859. https://books.google.com/books?id=4VQOAAAAQAAJ.

Dickens, Gerald Charles. "Introduction." 1934. In *The Life of Our Lord*, 7–13. New York: Simon & Schuster, 1999.

Dickens, Sir Henry Fielding. *The Recollections of Sir Henry Dickens.* London: Heinemann, 1934.

Dyson, A. E., and Angus Wilson. "Charles Dickens." In *The English Novel*, edited by Cedric Watts, 53–72. London: Sussex, 1976.

Ensor, Robert C. K. *England 1870–1914.* Oxford: Oxford University Press, 1936.

Forster, John. *The Life of Charles Dickens.* Vol. 2: 1842–1852. London: Chapman and Hall, 1870. https://books.google.com/books?id=olkDAAAAYAAJ.

Ham, James Panton. *Parables of Fiction: A Memorable Discourse on Charles Dickens.* London: Trübner and Company, 1870. https://books.google.com/books?id=meMQAAAAMAAJ.

Hartley, Jennifer, ed. *The Selected Letters of Charles Dickens.* Oxford: Oxford University Press, 2012.

Hogarth, Georgina, and Mamie Dickens, eds. *The Letters of Charles Dickens.* Vol. 1: 1833–1870. London: Macmillan and Company, 1893. https://books.google.com/books?id=GTvzdR5O44IC.

———. *The Letters of Charles Dickens.* Vol. 2: 1857–1870. New York: Charles Scribner's Sons, 1879. https://books.google.com/books?id=V-A5AAAAMAAJ.

House, Humphrey. *The Dickens World.* 1941. London: Oxford University Press, 1965.
Kucich, John. *Excess and Restraint in the Novels of Charles Dickens.* Athens, GA: University of Georgia Press, 1981.
Larson, Janet. *Dickens and the Broken Scripture*: Athens, GA: University of Georgia Press, 1985.
Lewis, C. S. *Mere Christianity.* 1952. New York: HarperCollins, 2001.
Ley, James William Thomas. *The Dickens Circle: A Narrative of the Novelist's Friendships.* New York: E. P. Dutton and Company, 1919.
Marsh, Peter T. *The Victorian Church in Decline: Archbishop Tait and the Church of England, 1866–1872.* London: Routledge, 1969.
McGovern, James Joseph. *Light from the Altar; or, The True Catholic in the Church of Christ.* Part 2. Chicago, IL: Catholic Art and Publication Office, 1906. https://books.google.com/books?id=b1kWAAAAYAAJ.
Norman, Edward R. *Church and Society in England, 1770–1970: A Historical Study.* Oxford: Clarendon Press, 1976.
Orwell, George. "Charles Dickens." *All-Art Is Propaganda: Critical Essays.* 1940. New York: Houghton Mifflin, 2009, 1–62.
Osborne, Charles C., ed. *Letters of Charles Dickens to the Baroness Angela Burdett-Coutts.* New York: E. P. Dutton and Company, 1932.
Oulton, Carolyn W. de la L. *Literature and Religion in Mid-Victorian England.* Basingstoke: Palgrave Macmillan, 2003.
Ruskin, John. *The Letters of John Ruskin.* Vol. 2: 1870–1889. Edited by E. T. Cook and Alexander Wedderburn. London: George Allen, 1909. https://books.google.com/books?id=bqSaAAAAIAAJ.
———. *Præterita.* Vol. 2: 1885–1889. London: George Allen, 1907. https://books.google.com/books?id=jqdHAAAAMAAJ.
Sanders, Andres. *Charles Dickens Resurrectionist.* New York: St. Martin's, 1982.
Slater, Michael. *The Great Charles Dickens Scandal.* New Haven, CT: Yale University Press, 2012.
Smith, Mary Daehler. " 'All Her Perfection Tarnished': The Thematic Function of Esther Summerson." *Victorian Newsletter* 38 (Fall 1970): 10–14.
Standiford, Les. *The Man Who Invented Christmas: How Charles Dickens's "A Christmas Carol" Rescued His Career and Revived Our Holiday Spirits.* New York: Crown Publishing Group, 2008.
Stott, George. "Charles Dickens." *The Contemporary Review, 1866–1900* 10 (February 1869): 203–25. http://ezproxy.liberty.edu/login?qurl=https%3A%2F%2Fsearch.proquest.com%2Fdocview%2F6652631%3Faccountid%3D12085.
Strong, James. *Strong's Exhaustive Concordance of the Bible.* Peabody, MA: Hendrickson Publishers, 2007.
Walder, Dennis. *Dickens and Religion.* London: Allen and Unwin, 1981.
Zemka, Sue. *Victorian Testaments: The Bible, Christology, and Literary Authority in Early-Nineteenth-Century British Culture.* Stanford, CA: Stanford University Press, 1997.

2 Consecrated Abomination
Pilgrimage and Churchyard Homage in Dickens' Novels

Daniel Stuart

Few physical spaces in Dickens are more wretched than cemeteries. Alongside ragged schools, workhouses, and slums that expose the harsh conditions of Victorian life, they serve as sites of exposure in the author's satire, a way to pour contempt on society for its neglect of the dead. In *Oliver Twist*, he describes churchyards where paupers were buried so that "the uppermost coffin was within a few feet of the surface" (Dickens 2008 [1838], 41). Again, in *Nicholas Nickleby*, graves are "raised a few feet above" street level with the dead "parted from the living by a little earth and a board or two . . . no deeper down than the feet of the throng that passed there every day" (1998 [1839], 802). Scrooge's burial plot in *A Christmas Carol* is "walled in by houses; overrun by grass and weeds, the growth of vegetation's death, not life; choked up with too much burying" (2008 [1843], 75). Dickens' own correspondence mirrors his fiction. Notes from *The Uncommercial Traveller* liken London churchyards to "great shabby old mignonette box[es]" where "rot and mildew and dead citizens formed the uppermost scent" (2008 [1860], 72–73). Churchyards, often overcrowded, are forever dismal, desolate places, always forgotten, and rarely reverenced as sacred or consecrated ground.

Such depictions deepen our understanding of Dickens' attitude toward the dead revealing his sadness over their plight and a desire for change. He is not alone in feeling this way. His prose reflects the consciences of the reading public who were likewise repulsed by the uncereminious overcrowding, rot, putrefaction, and disease; indeed, there is a spiritual quality to Dickens' use of gravesites beyond mere empathy or humanitarian issues. Throughout the Dickens canon, gravesites, cemeteries, and churchyards repeatedly become respected spaces that honor the dead while restoring the living. The act as pivotal points of lived experience, revealing a lasting bond, or "causal relationship," as David McAllister writes, "between the aesthetics of burial . . . and death's psychological hold over the minds of the living" (2020, 235).

Certainly, burial sites in Dickens can be seen as symbols central to the significance for a Christian afterlife. More poignantly for Dickens, however, they become meeting points, drawing characters together in

DOI: 10.4324/9781003156611-3

ways that are often unplanned, or the result of multiple plot strands being resolved. Dickens positions such spaces—Anglican churchyards primarily—in his stories as an actionable means of binding characters together to commemorate the deceased and also to awaken or revitalize the living. Frequently such sequences involve arduous travel or migration whereby the principal characters labor in long journeys or under duress, often with one or more members of the party dying at the site shortly after arrival.[1] These scenarios where individuals progress to such spaces, simultaneously or in succession, embody pilgrimages comprised of a cross section of society or otherwise indifferent members of the community. By repeatedly uniting and reuniting visitors at gravesites, often in unorthodox ways, Dickens demonstrates how churchyards realize their significance not as hypocritical memorials but as sites of mutual interest prompting acts of spiritual growth in those still above ground. Dickens does seek a spiritual significance with burial grounds, but he does so by integrating ideas about spiritual practices and religious ceremony, specifically identifying travel to gravesites in physical acts of consecration. Narratives such as *The Old Curiosity Shop* (2000 [1841]) and *Bleak House* (2003 [1853]) feature such forms of travel as secular pilgrimages in ways that reconceive the significance of churchyards and other burial sites as more than symbols or objects for satirical scorn. Dickens' use of churchyards indicates not only his pity for how the dead are housed but also his shared hope for renewal of the living.

Dickens scholars have long identified death and churchyards as deeply personal elements embedded in the author's fiction. Many see them as emblematic of Dickens' own religious conscience, one that valued kindness and benevolence over official doxology for personal redemption. In his book *Dickens and Religion*, Dennis Walder observes Dickens' deviation from a Christianity that is deeply attentive to sin and depravity, even traditional forms of worship. Disenchanted with organized religion's mismanagement of social problems, Dickens' works feature death—often of one undeserving of it. The plight and passing of someone with a "natural goodness of the heart" can redeem or transform the living (2007, 87). Andrew Sanders' *Charles Dickens Resurrectionist* similarly perceives death and churchyards as affirming Dickens' own "mystical faith," one that valued life continuing on "inspired by the virtuous example of the dead" (1982, 17, 87). Perspectives on Dickens' religion often refer to this theme of death having a revitalizing power for the living. Even in less religious terms, death to Dickens has an inevitable effect on the way people live their lives. Emily Steinlight's *Populating the Novel*, for example, perceives Dickens' churchyard scenarios as participating in an "emerging biopolitical order" keen to identify expendable, or "supernumerary" members of the population and expediting their disposal (2018, 17). Most note the significance of homage paid to the dead and dying having a source in the Dickens' personal religious conscience, further associating the idea of pilgrimage with a figurative significance with his own experience. None, however, see the implication of actual pilgrimages being an integral part of the Dickens gospel, one extending as theme and practice throughout his work.

Formal definitions of "pilgrimage" generally refer to religious-oriented journeys, undertaken by spiritually minded individuals to a holy or sacred place. The *Oxford English Dictionary* places its literary origins as far back as the fourteenth century where narratives like the *Book of Margery Kempe* (1500) or *The Canterbury Tales* (1400) mark its importance as a Catholic spiritual practice designed to pay homage or respect (2021). Notably it is also a verb used in the intransitive sense to identify the progressive action of wandering or traveling. Pilgrimage as a form of religious practice holds a figurative significance, especially as a theological metaphor. Long before Dickens, John Bunyan's *The Pilgrim's Progress* (2007 [1678]) used the idea for its allegory of spiritual progression and Christian discipleship. Even as a secular idea, however, the narrative element of a journey, quest, or action is self-evident. The form of the novel is one that accommodates pilgrimages. Physical progression is a central function of characters in picaresque and adventure narratives just as more introspectively themed journeys emerge in the bildungsroman.

Dickens was no stranger to the picaresque novels of the eighteenth century as well as the Bible, *The Canterbury Tales*, and *Pilgrim's Progress*. Steadily evolving within his fiction were elements of personal transformation, conflict, and confrontation with one's own mortality. Gravesites and religious symbolism likewise permeated the author's narratives. Pip in *Great Expectations*, for example, awakens to his own identity and origins in the churchyard housing his parents' remains. Indeed, the "first most vivid and broad impression of the identity of things" (Dickens 1998 [1861], 3) comes not from his sister, who later finds herself in that same plot beside "Philip Pirrip, late of this parish, and Also Georgiana, Wife of the Above" (3–4), but from the tombstones bearing the remains of his family. The images he forms from this "bleak place overgrown with nettles" (4) mirror the fancifully imagined "expectations" of his life: fabricated visions simultaneously obscure and ruinous that ordain his destiny. Though no mystical association marks the space as sacrosanct, the churchyard forever binds Pip's life and consciousness to the spot "among the graves" (4) where the fateful meeting with Magwitch initiates his path forward.

There are no intentional pilgrimages in Dickens. In the formal sense, at least, no one undertakes a religious or even secular expedition to a holy place. Allusions abound, however, to pilgrims' journeys and the sites they visit, and Dickens is keen on the idea as a metaphor. In *The Pickwick Papers* (1840 [1837]), Sam Weller satirically embarks on "pilgrimage to Dorking, to see his Mother-in-Law"; *Oliver Twist's* subtitle "the Parish Boy's Progress" is literally adapted from Bunyan's title; the same text is read by Nicholas and Smike in *Nicholas Nickleby* as they travel on "their daily pilgrimage through the world" (1998 [1839], 297). In *Bleak House*, Esther's narrative begins "A Progress" while *Little Dorrit*'s two sections each start with "fellow travellers" meeting for the first time (1857), then journeying together like Chaucer's party of Canterbury pilgrims.

Gravesites are not always dour places of death, satire, or solemnity. Death and burial are depicted, if ironically, in less sober contexts. *A Tale of Two Cities* (1859) features Jerry Cruncher, the grave-robbing "resurrection man" who "fishes" cadavers from churchyards around London and then sells to medical men (Dickens 1998 [1859], 188). In *Our Mutual Friend* the pretentious Fascination Fledgeby is depicted climbing a staircase as if "he might have been the leader in some pilgrimage of devotional ascent to a prophet's tomb" (Dickens 2016 [1865], 279). In the same novel, schoolmaster Bradley Headstone travels to an urban churchyard for his ill-fated proposal to Lizzie Hexam. The "raised bank of earth" where the dead are "conveniently and healthfully elevated above the level of the living" (395) provides him with the opportunity to claim his namesake, "lay[ing] his hand upon a piece of the coping of the burial-ground enclosure, as if he would have dislodged the stone" (397). Detective Dick Datchery wanders among the tombs in a Cloisterham churchyard in *The Mystery of Edwin Drood* where he finds Mr. Durdles harassing the headstones—"stoning the dead"—because "their final resting place is announced to be sacred" (2007 [1870], 214).

Not all such characterizations strive for allusion or irony. Certain incidents in *David Copperfield* (1850) prove very sincere; in fact, they lead us to believe that Dickens' association with pilgrimages has a reverential quality. Alone in Blundeston years after his mother's death, David occupies himself in "solitary pilgrimages" near his old home "recall[ing] every yard of the old road as I went along it, and to haunt the old spots, of which I never tired" (2011 [1850], 327). Inevitably, he finds himself at the churchyard where his parents are buried:

> The grave beneath the tree, where both my parents lay—on which I had looked out, when it was my father's only, with such curious feelings of compassion, and by which I had stood, so desolate, when it was opened to receive my pretty mother and her baby—the grave which Peggotty's own faithful care had ever since kept neat, and made a garden of, I walked near, by the hour. It lay a little off the churchyard path, in a quiet corner, not so far removed but I could read the names upon the stone as I walked to and fro, startled by the sound of the church-bell when it struck the hour, for it was like a departed voice to me. My reflections at these times were always associated with the figure I was to make in life, and the distinguished things I was to do. My echoing footsteps went to no other tune, but

were as constant to that as if I had come home to build my castles in the air at a living mother's side.

(327)

The episode has a spiritual resonance connected to David's present circumstances. An orphan who is alone in the world, he is still young and desirous of an elusive intimacy. His "haunt[ing] of old spots" includes and inevitably culminates in a space reserved for the dead. Only here is he moved by the "reflections" of his "pretty mother and her baby" to concerns about his present circumstances—"the figure I was to make in life" and "the distinguished things I was to do" (327). It is not the only time David is renewed, even invigorated, by his mother's memory nor is it the first time he associates his own livelihood with churchyard symbolism. Sequestered upstairs following the arrival of Miss Murdstone, David is "more shut out and alienated from [his] mother." He is nearly "stupefied," but for the "small collection of books" that "kept alive my fancy, and my hope of something beyond that place and time" (69). Curiously, he associates the experience with a churchyard, "of a summer evening, the boys at play in the churchyard, and I sitting on my bed, reading as if for life" (70). "Every foot of the churchyard," he recollects, "had some association of its own, in my mind, connected with these books" (328).

Episodes like the above foreground the continuous theme of churchyard homage. Rather, Dickens draws his characters to churchyards through indirect, often vague means as a way to honor the dead and connect the living to their identity. Such incidents further elucidate Dickens' foundational religious ethos, one that associated cherished memories of the deceased with a reinvigorated enthusiasm for life among the living. In 1837, a decade prior to the publication of *David Copperfield*, Dickens' sister-in-law Mary Hogarth died suddenly without warning (likely of an undiagnosed heart condition). Grief at her death was substantial, leaving the author emotionally shattered. The girl, only 17, had been a part of the Dickens household following the author's marriage to her sister Catherine. In the wake of her passing, he not only planned her funeral, penning her epitaph, but also paid for the plot in which she was buried with the intention of being placed beside her at his own death. Dickens relinquished the plan only when Hogarth's brother George died shortly after and the family wished him to be buried beside Mary. Dickens submitted to it, though not without some reluctance. In an 1841 letter to John Forster, he described his feelings:

> It is a great trial to me, to give up Mary's grave; greater than I can possible express. The desire to be buried next to her is as strong upon me now as it was five years ago; and I know (for I don't think there ever was love like that I bear her) that it will never diminish . . . I

cannot bear the thought of being excluded from her dust . . . I ought to get the better of it, but it is very hard.

(Hartley 2012, 89–90)

Mary's death was only a moment in the life of the author—she actually died in his arms—but she was never far from his consciousness. He was convinced her spirit was beside him at certain rapturous moments such as when he stood before Niagara Falls five years after her death. In his book *Charles Dickens in Love*, Robert Garnett associates Mary's presence with Dickens' "strongest religious feeling," noting that "indeed, she *was* his religion" (2012, 3). Even in death, Mary remained a fixture of his consciousness. Her memory, uncorrupted by age, was a tranquility that calmed his anxious heart for the remainder of his life. As ethereal as her presence was, however, her memory was one sustained through material as well as spiritual means, a form of beauty and purity awakening his soul to action. Mary's burial plot at Kensal Green cemetery was routinely frequented by Dickens. He also kept her ring on his finger as a keepsake, never removing it in the 33 years following her death, an object ensuring her memory would remain. Pilgrimages of the mind through memory as well as physical acts of homage procured an attachment to her earthly remains as well.

More than a few critics have commented on the deeply penetrating appeal Mary's death had for Dickens. In addition to Garnett's book detailing Dickens' relationship to Mary Hogarth, Albert J. Guérard's *Triumph of the Novel: Dickens, Dostoevsky, Faulkner* discusses Mary as Dickens' "idealized anima, the mother of the soul or ideal feminine" who "remained alive in a very special way for Dickens the Christian believer" (1982 [1946], 72). More recently, Claire Wood's book *Dickens and the Business of Death* claims Mary's sudden passing implanted permanent sensitivity in Dickens, not only to the "charged emotional reaction" of the event but also to the potential for exploitation—for "making money from death and the manipulation of emotion" (2015, 61–62). It is a telling insight into the way Dickens deals with death. He understands the deep, often tragic, emotional investment involved as mutual experience involving much more than an end to consciousness.

If Mary's memory provided religious inspiration, then it also formed a source of Dickens' creativity. She is the model for a number of his female characters ranging from *Oliver Twist's* Rose Maylie to Rosa Bud in *Edwin Drood*, who exhibit the class and character associated with Mary's youthful innocence. Many consider her the source for a number of his death and near-death narratives such as those of young Paul Dombey in *Dombey and Son* (1848) who dies as a child and *Bleak House's* Esther Summerson who nearly succumbs to deathbed illness. The most famous character modeled on Mary is one who not only shares her qualities but also enacts a manner of extended pilgrimage culminating in her own death. Little Nell is the youthful heroine in *The Old Curiosity Shop* who, together with her grandfather, flees to London and the lecherous Daniel Quilp for the provinces. The story is a kind of fable, even fairy tale, in which characters simultaneously pursue or plot against Nell and her grandfather as they travel from the home counties to the midlands. As well as allegorical in the sense of identifying Nell's progression as one of spiritual transcendences, it also identifies the pilgrim's journey to its endpoint—a church and churchyard—with a reconnection and renewal among the other characters.

In many ways, Nell's pilgrimage directly parallels *The Pilgrim's Progress*. The opening chapters cast little doubt on this when Nell recalls her fondness for Bunyan's text after going "forth from the city"[2]:

> There had been an old copy of the Pilgrim's Progress, with strange plates, upon a shelf at home, over which she had often pored whole evenings, wondering whether it was true in every word, and where those distant countries with the curious names might be. As she looked back upon the place they had left, one part of it came strongly upon her mind. "Dear grandfather," she said, "only that this place is prettier and a great deal better than the real one, if that in the book is like it, I feel that we are both Christian, and laid down on this grass all the cares and troubles we brought with us; never to take them up again."
>
> (2000 [1841], 123–24)

The pair journeys from London—their "City of Destruction" (Bunyan 2007, 17)—to places and experiences bearing striking similarities to ones in the Puritan epic. Harassed by an Apollyon in the form of Quilp, they visit "Vanity Fair," a racetrack where grandfather gambles away their meager savings. They row through a "Slough of Despond" (21)—a canal in the "Black Country" of the industrial midlands—to a factory town with its own "Doubting Castle" (150), a forge kept by a laborer whose Giant Despair-like routine tethers him to a hopeless life. They finally find respite with their schoolmaster, Mr. Marton, at his new abode in a rural village. It becomes their personal House Beautiful even amid Nell's decline and grandfather's descent into madness.

The village church where they spend their final days is an ancient ruin, "a very aged, ghostly place ... built many hundreds of years ago," which is now derelict. Yet it becomes a sacred space for Nell who naturally finds solace in the churchyard with its "antiquated graves" now "overgrown with grass" (354). Already at home among the dead, having slept cold nights near country cemeteries or amid Mrs. Jarley's corpse-like wax works, she finds the burying place a source of comfort and consolation even as her death becomes inevitable. Far from being morbid or even macabre, the mood is inspiring. The churchyard is rendered as much a garden as gravesite. Upon asking the children at play among the tombs about a freshly dug grave, the idea takes form: "She drew near and asked one of them whose grave it was. The child answered that that was not its name; it was a garden—his brother's" (398). The sexton, who is both gravedigger and gardener, affirms as much when he tells Nell his "works don't all moulder away and rot in the earth" (399). The ruined church edifice is so old that it doubles as a crypt where Nell feels equally "happy, and at rest" (402) among the vaults housing the dead. Indeed, everything is "so beautiful and happy" Nell feels it is "like passing from death to life; it was drawing nearer Heaven" (403). Her final days are spent contemplating the atmosphere—one "sacred to all goodness and virtue" (403)—from a spot amid the entombed and where, when she finally dies, she is laid to rest.

Nell's death has been mocked by critics, many of whom are fond of Dickens yet see the deathbed scenario as gratuitous. Oscar Wilde is said to have stated, "one must have a heart of stone to read the death of Little Nell without laughing" (Ellmann 1988, 441) and Aldous Huxley cites the incident as overreaching in its sentimentality, a "vulgarity in literature" (1930, 56). It is not an unfair criticism. The drawn-out demise of Nell seems farcical on the surface. Dickens' intent may have been to emphasize childlike purity, to imbue youthful innocence with its own sanctity, and perhaps preserve the memory of Mary Hogarth. Yet from the perspective of a moral or spiritual allegory, this can seem inadequate. Nell is not quite real enough to develop or undergo any revelation. Despite being forced into the trials of adult responsibility, she maintains her innocence and her character never transforms. There is no real change from the child she is at the beginning until the time of her death.

Nell's parallels to Mary Hogarth and relatively static quality as a character should not negate a more significant spiritual, even theological theme present in the text. Nell's pilgrimage not only mirrors Bunyan's Christian allegory of personal salvation experienced through suffering, worldly trials, and self-denial. It also draws together and restores members of that same sad, suffering world. Nell's pilgrimage is a shared journey, a sacrament enjoining fellow casualties of life along the way to an earthly—even earthy—paradise, a churchyard physically cultivated both for the consecration of the dead and for the blessing of living. The schoolmaster who had earlier helped Nell is reunited with her in the village; Grandfather Trent's estranged brother joins them. Kit and his rescuer and Mr. Garland, who had helped foil Quilp's nefarious plot, congregate at Nell's shrine in tribute. Local members of the village in all their forms gravitate there. They all gather: "decrepit age, and vigorous life, and blooming youth, and helpless infancy, poured forth—on crutches, in the pride of strength and health, in the full blush of promise, in the mere dawn of life—to gather round her tomb" (543).

The child's death, funeral, and burial are well attended. But it is the gravesite itself, in addition to her memory, that generates life around it. Of the vault where she lay, the narrator proclaims: "what was the death it would shut in, to that which still could crawl and creep above it!" (544). Dickens' idea of the sacredness of churchyards, or crypts in Nell's case, is that they produce a vitality all of their own. Individuals respond not only to the memory of the deceased but also to the character of the physical space accommodating the dead. As the sexton had previously pointed out to Nell, his caretaking of the churchyard is not only as a gravedigger but also as a gardener, literally to replenish and "plant the graves": "'tis a good sign for the happiness of the living. And so it is" (407). Nell agrees and, despite her diminishing health, she spends her remaining days aiding the sexton's efforts. Any bereavement she feels is for "those who die about us" and "are so soon forgotten" (409).

Following Nell's death the memory of her prompts the living into action: "for every fragile form from which [Death] lets the panting spirit free, a hundred virtues rise in shapes of mercy, charity, and love, to walk the world, and bless it . . . every tear that sorrowing mortals shed on such green graves, some good is born, some gentler nature comes" (544). Certain characters like Grandfather Trent's younger brother, the mysterious "Single Gentleman," spring into action following Nell's death. He is the one sincere penitent in the story who goes "forth into the world, a lover of his kind" (544). His "chief delight" is not only to do good works but also to re-enact Nell's pilgrimage, "to travel in the steps of the old man and the child (so far as he could trace them from her last narrative), to halt where they had halted, sympathise where they had suffered, and rejoice where they had been made glad" (554). The poor schoolmaster is likewise renewed, retaining a permanent post in the rural village and enriching the lives of his students. Once in despair over his poverty, he, like Nell before him, becomes "fond of his dwelling in the old churchyard" realizing himself "a *poor* schoolmaster no more" (553–54).

In *Literary Remains: Representations of Death and Burial in Victorian England*, Mary Elizabeth Hotz argues that funerals for Dickens help renegotiate the idea of communal virtue. More than fostering the "virtues of love, mercy, and charity and the capacity of survivors to voice their farewells," Nell's death and burial "allows for a reconsideration of social relationships" (2009, 78). For Dickens, death and homage to the dead force "society to reject its emphasis on individuals thinking for themselves as isolated persons whose relationships with others are determined by predation and greed" (78). It is easy to see the effects of Nell's death in the spiritual resolve of others like the schoolmaster whose selfless acts become a blessing to the village or to the Single Gentleman. Not all characters are redeemed by Nell's death, yet it is curious to see the theme of religious homage sustained in churchyard symbolism and Christian motifs. Grandfather Trent, already deranged by the time of the child's death, obstinately refuses to leave her burial plot. Holding vigil over Nell's grave, he clothes himself in his pilgrim's attire, intending to once again embark upon the pair's journey only to suddenly fall prostrate over the child's grave, "dead upon the stone" (548). Quilp's demise is quick and violent. His drowned body is found, "though not until some days had elapsed," only to "be buried with a stake through his heart in the centre of four lonely roads" (550). Nell's rogue brother, Frederick, a co-conspirator with Quilp, winds up dead in a Paris morgue where no one claims. His death is emblematic of the unredeemed, the profligate, and the wanton whose eternal resting place is not only questionable but whose earthly resting place is also void of any dignity, sacred or otherwise.

The Old Curiosity Shop foregrounds important aspects of Dickens' religion, one particular to the man who remained more or less a broad-church Anglican. His own Christianity was fondly professed though practiced with less frequency. He attended worship sporadically and never stayed too long with a single parish. In his biography of Dickens Forster asserts the author's adherence to Christianity and the [Church of England's] teaching on "essential points" (1892, 137). Dickens would also seem to be someone disenchanted by ritualistic forms of worship. Walder in *Dickens and Religion* writes how he connected empty repetitive practice to the despotism he saw in Catholic countries. And yet he was not immune to true spiritual feeling when it gripped him as it did upon the death of Mary. "He was doubtless stimulated by his surroundings" (11) and perceived that religious ceremony could be meaningful if enacted out of sincerity and purpose. His own repetitive practices and routine work ethic attest to a man committed to a religious form of discipline. There was also humanitarian part of him that identified Christian religious practice with charitable acts and social outreach.

Thus, while Nell's narrative remains heavily cloaked in symbol or religious gesture, its real religion—indeed its true gospel message—is one associated with personal relationships: how veneration of a cherished loved one can influence existing social bonds. The novel reveals Dickens' spirituality as a very personal one tied to religious practice involving private spaces and the material world. But such spaces, though stationary, are never inactive. Nell's pilgrimage, final destination, and ultimate burial plot not only integrate elements of homage and consecration, but her experiences also mark such an interaction as sacred; her life, death, and legacy literally sacralize the physical spaces—churchyard and crypt—she encounters. The spiritual within the physical exemplified the theological disposition abiding in a still youthful Dickens who had been devastated by the loss of a loved one yet remained committed to a life of forward action. It is the type of Christian message he wishes to disseminate, one that values the poor and innocent through mutual compassion, shared commemoration, and a resultant outpouring of benevolence.

Pilgrimage as an act of commemoration takes center stage in a more serious novel a decade following Little Nell's death. *Bleak House* involves the legacy of another downtrodden soul. This time the person in question is neither female nor young nor wholly innocent. Nemo's death, burial, and gravesite in the Tom-All-Alone's slum solidify Dickens' idea of dignity in death and churchyard homage. The cemetery where Captain Hawdon (known as Nemo) is buried is integral to the narrative in its connecting characters and advancing the plot; it articulates the author's understanding of how burial plots and monuments to the dead—urban churchyards in this case—extend beyond their fixed spaces. Nemo's final resting place is a focal point of the novel. The rotting corpses from the churchyard form the source of the fever that blights the city. Yet just as it disseminates poisonous disease, it attracts individuals suffering from deeper, more spiritual ailments, those with long-suffering emotional wounds. Pilgrimages in *Bleak House* are not quite as allegorical or sentimental as in *The Old Curiosity Shop* nor are they concentrated on a single person or scenario. Rather, individuals representing a cross section of the community descend on the toxic ground zero in spite of the disease to unintentionally consecrate the churchyard in ways that validate Dickens' ideas.

Surely Dickens is at his most rancorous in *Bleak House* regarding churchyard neglect. The state of London's gravesites had reached a nadir in the years prior to its publication when Edwin Chadwick's report on the sanitary conditions of urban cemeteries revealed a woeful lack of caretaking and civil oversight. "Burial grounds," according to Chadwick, were "morally offensive, and appear[ed] as physically dangerous in proportion to the numbers interred in them" (1843, 134). Dickens was a friend of Chadwick and championed the cause, his concern for the plight of the dead becoming a public outcry. An 1850 address to the Metropolitan Sanitation Commission spelled out his disgust: "this great sacrifice of human life is accompanied by an amount of physical degradation and mental depravity, which act as effective barriers to the inculcation either of social obligations or of Christian virtues" (Fielding 1977, 104).

Bleak House is a deeply intertextual novel steeped in biblical Scripture satirizing the churchyard. It is harshly critical of a Christianity that neglects the poor of the parish in favor of those persons farther away, a "telescopic philanthropy" (2003 [1853], 44) based on misguided zeal and self-righteousness. It can even seem to repudiate theological or traditionally Christian themes altogether, especially during the Nemo burial in the disease-ridden slum of Tom-All-Alone's where spiteful allusions to biblical or Anglican texts resonate. (Even the chapter heading of "Our Dear Brother" is drawn from the *Book of Common Prayer* as a sinister jest at parish funerary practices (1986 [1662], 112)). But though much of the book forces irony through the lens of religious tradition or ceremony, it models a type of experience through which ritualistic acts of religious duty may be perpetuated. Captain Hawdon may be an outcast, a literal nobody known to all as Nemo, but he is markedly at odds with the acquisitive and sanctimonious factions in midcentury Victorian society. His quiet benevolence is not overlooked, and notwithstanding his opium habit, the event of his death suggests a martyred figure. On the surface, it is a sacrifice emphasizing civic and social martyrdom for a cause, highlighting burial ground abuses and a need for sanitary reform. The bitter irony is that overcrowding of the cemeteries ensures that Nemo's carcass still abides in the world of the living. As Robert Lougy points out, Nemo is a liminal figure, or "corpse god" occupying a transitional space between life and death (2002, 480). The dynamic forms a particularly potent metaphor for personal legacies as well as the inability of civilization to contain the natural world. Nemo's undignified position is used by Dickens to expose disparity and also highlight how ecological detriment begets human endangerment. Even considering the dreadful sanitary crisis, however, his death and internment hold deeper implications for personal devotion.

Such a perspective is perhaps easy to overlook in the aggressive satire framing the burial. The focus is truly on the plight of the urban poor laid to rest through neglect and apathy only to "be raised in corruption" (that is, the contagion spreading from the rotting corpses). Dickens' mockery reaches its peak in the last few paragraphs with sardonic references to the spot as a "beastly scrap of ground which a Turk would reject as a savage abomination" (165). Further allusions to filth and contagion imply the diseased state of the graveyard and, following his burial, Nemo is explicitly described as the source of a lingering problem, an "avenging ghost at many a sick bedside" with "every poisonous element of death in action close on life" (165). A solitary mourner makes his way to the site, little suspecting the deadly poison arising from the tombs. It is Jo, the crossing sweeper, one of Dickens' orphans and another in a long line of unfortunate souls misused by the world. While his fate in the novel serves to indict the powers that be, his dedication to Captain Hawdon reveals how monuments to the dead receive validation through human attachment. His pilgrimage to the gravesite seems something of an afterthought, his "slouching figure" a poor excuse for a pilgrim. Jo's visit is the first of three visits, three vigils really, all framed as solemn moments of reverence. As an act of tribute, Jo adorns the site with some modest improvements. He "softly sweeps the step, and makes the archway clean" amid something like "a distant ray of light" which Dickens intends as his halo (165).

But more important than the sentiment are the implications for the surviving world, for the legacy among a still struggling humanity who turn their attention to death's monuments for solace. Like Antigone of the Greeks finding no greater glory than "to give [her] own brother a decent burial" (Sophocles 2007 [429 BC], 84), Jo the "rejected witness" knows no other destiny but to consecrate the grave of Captain Hawdon with his one worldly possession. Any reward for Jo's pious devotion to the gravesite does not seem to be in this life; the death of his friend presages an even sadder existence for Jo. Soon to be caught up in a web of scandal, treachery, and terminal illness, his tribulations will become even greater, his fortunes dimmer until the event of his own fever-induced death. His ties to the Hawdon gravesite affirm his own identity in these, his final days, even as they also lead to his own demise. For even without knowing the name of his friend, Jo knows the burial ground of he "who wos wery good to me" as a source of fulfillment until his dying breath (181).

The second visit to the gravesite highlights the misery of the setting, its grotesque features only outdone by its host neighborhood Tom-All-Alone's. The burial plot is vividly described and even depicted in the first of the two Phiz illustrations. The image wryly depicts Jo guiding the gaze of Lady Dedlock to the plot of her former lover nestled "among them piles of bones." Mentioning the coffin's elevation above the ground as "wery nigh the top," Jo comments on how they had "to stamp on it to get it in" (242–43). The scene is borderline macabre with its detailed look at the crypt of overcrowded coffins and their refuse, not to mention the rats scampering to and fro. Jo's casual expression betrays his station in life, one accustomed to despair and abandonment. It is an amusing contrast to Lady Dedlock who recoils in horror. Confused by her sense of "abomination," and at a loss to know whether it is "consecrated," "blest," or even "consequential ground," Jo nevertheless tends to the site after the ghostlike departure of his fellow mourner, again sweeping the archway "step and passage with great care" (243).

The exchange between Jo and Lady Dedlock plays a relevant role in binding both characters to the spot. Jo, on his deathbed later in the novel after losing the sovereign as well as his health, shares his final wish: to get to "that there berryin' ground" (677). Little suspecting the churchyard as the source of his plight, Jo remembers Hawdon's frequent reference to the pair's comparative poverty. With only moments to live, Jo confesses his one desire to Esther and the physician Alan Woodcourt: to tell Hawdon "that I am as poor as him now, and have come there to be laid along with him." The scene is remarkably pathetic. And after Jo dies Dickens uses his death to draw attention to the hardships suffered by those less fortunate. In the soliloquy that follows, he erupts in a tirade against Her Majesty, parliament, and those "Right Reverends and Wrong Reverends of every order" (677). The sardonic tone may convey the disparity between Jo and the privileged world. But overshadowed is yet another incident revealing Dickens' use of the gravesite's ability to attract people from all sectors of society.

The novel's final visit is a true pilgrimage. It is also the novel's most dramatic and drawn-out sequence, gradually interconnecting the narrative strands to provide closure to the plot as well as a final consecration of the gravesite. While themes of detection and pursuit dominate, a notable correlation to real pilgrimages—intentionally arduous, contemplative journeys—finds itself embedded in the text. Conviction and duty drive the wayfarers on, tributes are paid to the other symbolic spaces, and further religious or mythical imagery stresses the sober nature of the march forward. Lady Dedlock's flight is iconic. Quitting her home and marriage, she treks through the city in disgrace so that her progress strongly resembles a sort of penitent wandering. Likened to Cain in exile after his murder of Abel, she is perhaps more like the banished Oedipus blindly in search of her Colonus. It is not so much the imagery she evokes, however, as it is the places she visits and the commitment that draws her to them. These, too, are places of neglect, the people in them victims of abuse and self-righteous zealots. They not only hold narrative significance but also form points of interest as their own unlikely sacred spaces, or consecrated abominations. They are themselves singular as places where secrets long harbored become revelations imparted.

Following the same path, Esther and Alan Woodcourt, along with Inspector Bucket, informally pay tribute to these same spots. They even stop at another place reserved for the dead, a riverside wharf where victims of suicide have been "Found Drowned" (769). The progress from one location to another serves the purpose of illuminating truths to its travelers, a path of enlightenment embodying its own pilgrim's progress to the Nemo gravesite. Valuable information is obtained in the form of both clues and long-held secrets. But a greater thematic emphasis focuses on identity as it is oriented to sacred spaces. It is the attempt of characters like Esther and her mother to fully realize and reclaim their own identity amid neglected though personally redemptive locales. Such a quest for truth and resolution serves to strengthen the correlation between people and monuments as once again characters find purpose and meaning through demonstrative tributes to the dead. Lady Dedlock's need to be near the "poor burying ground" is not unlike Jo's final wishes. Her indication of the "place where I shall lie down," which "has been often in my mind," is the final clue in the pursuit (841). While it confirms her identity as Hawdon's lover and Esther's mother, in more spiritual terms, it is the place where she can unburden her guilt. Tormented by "terror and my conscience," she finds true solace in proximity to the plot of ground she once recoiled from. Arriving there plagued by illness and fatigue she collapses at the gate. As with Jo with his broom, she anoints the archway steps with her one instrument of homage—her "long dank hair"—before dying (844).

The Nemo burial ground may help relieve the conscience of those who grieve, but it has the power to reinstate an identity for those born as a "mother's shame." Esther, having always known she was illegitimate, now finds redemption at the churchyard. Her own pilgrimage to the gravesite is arduous, characterized by the wintry climate and late hours.

Her distorted sense of reality—"the unreal things were more substantial than the real" (842)—plagues her soul as she and her two escorts encroach upon the gravesite. In her confusion and near delirium, she mistakes the identity of the dead figure on the steps for another—believing it to be Jenny, the Brickmaker's wife—and it is debated whether she should be allowed to discover the truth. Once there, however, in the midst of both parents now deceased, her own identity is finally confirmed in fact as well as substance. Esther's entrance into and presence at the burial site spiritually consummates her own allegorical pilgrimage, one progressing from societal neglect to domestic respectability. In some ways the burial ground seems secondary, almost a prop or vague symbol amid the narrative significance. But this is to overlook how it highlights the way burial sites are sustained by lives still dependent on their legacy, how they become their own sacred spaces. The power of the Nemo gravesite is prolonged not so much by its own status or conditions, nor even by the foul, infectious legacy it bequeaths to those still living, but by the individuals still invested in the communal link it forges between the living and the dead. Such connections extend beyond on-site admiration to devoted, pious, and even arduous physical journeys made to realize the true value of such a bond.

As with the death of Little Nell, the final graveyard visit has been judged, even criticized for its excessive pathos. Just as the other gravesite homage moments reach for a determined purpose, the finality of the scene may overemphasize sentiment and emotion. It is not an uncommon critique of Dickens. D. A. Miller has pointed out that these "closural moments" in *Bleak House* repeatedly "end by producing a corpse, as though the novel wanted to attest, not just the finality, but also the failure of a closure that, even as it was achieved, missed the essence of what it aspired to grasp" (1989, 97). *Bleak House* is certainly "one of the most death-haunted novels in British literature" (Lougy 479), and Dickens' taste for generating sympathy through death seems to lend a moral determinism to his art. While the story may reach too far with its reliance on death, return visits echo the degree sacred spaces are acted into significance. Contrasting the Nemo gravesite is of course the "mausoleum in the park" where Lady Dedlock's remains are preserved. While it points out the disparity between Nemo's burial and her own, it is the soulless lack of resolution that diminishes her memory. Far from consecrating her legacy, the mausoleum can only serve as a source of gossip among the "world of fashion" who wonder that others interred alongside her "never rose against the profanation of her company" (970). The matter of her death "is all a mystery" (970). And though her memory is quietly kept by her pardoning husband, Sir Leicester, the same process of commemoration—an active, ambulatory tribute in pursuit of redemptive truth—cannot validate her memory with the same cathartic power.

52 *Daniel Stuart*

Certainly, there is retribution for a society that neglects its dead. In correlating the pestilence emerging from the burial ground with the infection of innocent victims, the narrative incorporates the Nemo episode to show how all societies are bound together. And in reuniting the scorned child—Esther Summerson—with her parents (Hawdon/Nemo and Lady Dedlock) at the gravesite, the story achieves closure and connection between the living and the dead. But Dickens' social satire and condemnation of churchyard neglect overshadow his purpose for granting gravesites a commemoration of their own. In his book *Symbolic Interactionism*, Herbert Blumer states that monumental ornaments or sacred spaces are not memorialized by their official status but depend on individuals and "the basis of the meanings that the [places] have for them" (1986, 31). Such is the case in *Bleak House* where the legacy of Nemo's gravesite, a woefully neglected urban churchyard, is commemorated into relevance. By repeatedly uniting and reuniting visitors there, by unorthodox though deliberate means in the manner of a pilgrimage, Dickens shows how memorials to the dead realize the individual's significance. The dead can truly communicate to the living, not by mystical revelation or even biological contamination, but by the broader scope of action their memories can authorize.

By means of pilgrimage, personal sacrifice, suffering, and respect for the dead, Dickens shows how memorials are truly begotten by actualized deeds of homage. It is a personal religious experience that embodies both Christian charity and the material world. Though the meaning embedded in these pilgrimages is never named as such, the author makes plain that the destination and the path taken toward it are of equal significance. It is not just an idle gesture by Dickens to arrange such excursions. The fact of the journey and all its methods of progress betoken the significance that burial sites engender. Consequently, Dickens perceives that "you will always have the poor among you" (Jn 12:8)—even after they die.

Notes

1. Churchyards in Dickens are invariably associated with death, but not always with funeral or burial. Ralph Nickleby passes by the gravesite of the "throng no deeper down than the feet of the throng" in *Nicholas Nickleby*, for example, on his way to commit suicide (1998b [1839], 802). In "The Convict's Return," an interpolated tale in *The Pickwick Papers* (1840 [1837]), the wayward son visits his longsuffering mother's grave only to cross paths with his abusive father, killing him accidentally. Deaths associated with travels to gravesites include *The Old Curiosity Shop* (2000 [1841]) and *Bleak House* (2003 [1853]), both mentioned in this chapter. *Barnaby Rudge* (1841) is another in which an individual's—Rudge Sr's—wandering about among the tombs literally resurrects him as a "ghost" thought to have been dead.
2. Dickens' use of *The Pilgrim's Progress* is more than a passing reference to the Puritan tradition. It is a transcription of Bunyan's fable in less orthodox terms,

emphasizing instead a natural goodness of the heart and grace bestowed through charitable benevolence. In eulogizing Nell in the context of Pilgrim's eternal journey, Dickens resituates the idea of a pilgrimage in less metaphorical terms, identifying Nell's death less with the promise of heaven and eternity than with a reaffirmation of grace and charity among the living. For further reading on Dickens, Christianity, and his ode to *The Pilgrim's Progress*, see Walder.

Bibliography

Blumer, Herbert. *Symbolic Interactionism: Perspective and Method.* Berkley: University of California Press, 1986.
The Book of Common Prayer. 1662. New York: The Church Hymnal Corporation, 1986. www.bcponline.org.
Bunyan, John. *The Pilgrim's Progress.* 1678. Chicago, IL: Moody Bible Institute, 2007.
Chadwick, Edwin. *Report on the Sanitary Condition of the Labouring Population of Great Britain. A Supplementary Report on the Results of a Special Inquiry into the Practice of Interment in Towns. Made at the Request of Her Majesty's Principal Secretary of State for the Home Department.* London: W. Clowes and Sons, 1843.
Dickens, Charles. *Barnaby Rudge: A Tale of the Riots of 'Eighty.* London: Chapman, 1841. https://books.google.com/books?id=rmgOAAAAQAAJ.
———. *Bleak House.* 1853. New York: Penguin, 2003.
———. *A Christmas Carol.* In *A Christmas Carol and Other Stories.* 1843. Oxford: Oxford University Press, 2008.
———. *David Copperfield.* 1850. New York: Penguin, 2011.
———. *Great Expectations.* 1861. Oxford: Oxford University Press, 1998.
———. *Little Dorrit.* London: Bradbury and Evans, 1857. https://books.google.com/books?id=XvpcAAAAcAAJ.
———. *The Mystery of Edwin Drood.* 1870. Oxford: Oxford University Press, 2007.
———. *Nicholas Nickleby.* 1839. Oxford: Oxford University Press, 1998.
———. *The Old Curiosity Shop.* 1841. New York: Penguin, 2000.
———. *Oliver Twist.* 1838. Oxford: Oxford University Press, 2008.
———. *Our Mutual Friend.* 1865. Oxford: Oxford University Press, 2016.
———. *The Posthumous Papers of the Pickwick Club.* 1837. New York: J. Van Amringe, 1840. https://books.google.com/books?id=r2ooAAAAMAAJ.
———. *A Tale of Two Cities.* 1859. Oxford: Oxford University Press, 1998.
———. *The Uncommercial Traveller.* 1861. Newcastle upon Tyne: Cambridge Scholars Publishing Classic Texts, 2008.
Ellmann, Richard. *Oscar Wilde.* New York: Vintage, 1988.
Fielding, Lawrence. *Speeches of Charles Dickens: 1843–1851.* London: Paramour Press, 1977.
Garnett, Robert. *Charles Dickens in Love.* New York: Pegasus, 2012.
Guérard, Albert J. *The Triumph of the Novel: Dickens, Dostoevsky, and Faulkner.* 1946. Chicago, IL: University of Chicago Press, 1982.
Hartley, Jenny, ed. *The Selected Letters of Charles Dickens.* Oxford: Oxford University Press, 2012.

Hotz, Mary Elizabeth. *Literary Remains: Representations of Death and Burial in Victorian England*. Albany: SUNY Press, 2009.

Huxley, Aldous. *Vulgarity in Literature: Digressions from a Theme*. London: Chatto and Windus, 1930.

Lougy, Robert E. "Filth, Liminality, and Abjection in Charles Dickens's *Bleak House*." *ELH* 69, no. 2 (2002): 473–500. www.jstor.org/stable/30032028.

McAllister, David. "Dickens's 'School of Affliction': Learning from Death in *Nicholas Nickleby* and *The Old Curiosity Shop*." *Victoriographies* 10, no. 3 (2020): 228–47.

Miller, D. A. *The Novel and the Police*. Berkeley: University of California Press, 1989.

"pilgrimage, n." *OED Online*. June 2021. Oxford University Press. www.oed.com.

Sanders, Andrew. *Charles Dickens Resurrectionist*. London: Palgrave Macmillan, 1982.

Sophocles. *The Theban Plays*. 429 BC. Translated by David Eagles. New York: Penguin, 2007.

Steinlight, Emily. *Populating the Novel: Literary Form and the Politics of Surplus Life*. Ithaca: Cornell, 2018.

Walder, Dennis. *Dickens and Religion*. London: Routledge, 2007.

Wood, Claire. *Dickens and the Business of Death*: Cambridge: Cambridge University Press, 2015.

3 Dickens and the Specter of Materialism
The Spiritual Significance of Ghosts in the Christmas Books and Ghost Stories

Christine Schintgen

Whatever reservations Dickens may have had about orthodox Christianity, he shared one of its fundamental premises, namely, a belief in the reality of the spiritual realm. Dickens viewed his society as excessively focused on the material to the neglect of the spiritual. In the Christmas books[1] and ghost stories, he labors to present specters and other spirits as actual spiritual phenomena that constitute a bold protest against the materialism so prioritized by Victorians, not just in the sense of obsession with their making of money and collecting of things (though they are that) but also in the broader sense of either rejection or neglect of the spiritual.

Attention to both physical influences and emotional realities have led critics to perceive the supernatural in these books as mere projections of the characters' minds and hearts and to see Dickens as constructing the narrative in a way that encourages such a reading. Louise Henson, for example, argues that Dickens was skeptical about the reality of ghosts. She grounds her argument in an 1848 review for *The Examiner* which Dickens wrote of a work by Catherine Crowe called *The Night-Side of Nature; or, Ghosts and Ghost-Seers*. Henson quotes an important statement by Dickens in which he asserts that many cases of supposed ghosts are "known to be delusions superinduced by a well-understood, and by no means uncommon disease"—that is, nervous excitement—or, he goes on to say, by that state which is "between sleeping and waking" in which our perceptions are unreliable (2004, 45). In a similar vein, Jen Cadwallader contends that Dickens' ghosts are "most commonly indications of his characters' troubled psyches," and "reflections of his ghost-seers' fractured selves" (2016, 51). She does allow that characters' tendencies to experience the supernatural may signal, in Dickens, their ability to achieve "greater spiritual insights" (54), but she does not fundamentally challenge the material basis of the ghosts asserted by Henson.

DOI: 10.4324/9781003156611-4

I wish to consider the possibility that in his Christmas books, Dickens was not reducing the appearance of ghosts to the psychological or the emotional, but instead was drawing attention to the reality of the spiritual world. Dickens uses narrative and literary devices to signal the idea that, at least in the story, the ghosts do have a real existence beyond the corporeal realm. Moreover, the centrality of the ghosts to the plot, and the extent to which they have a salvific role in the stories, underscores a key message in Dickens' works—that his society has become too caught up in the material (in both social and philosophical sense) and must return to an emphasis on the spiritual. Ghosts in the Christmas books are, then, important motifs representing the core of Dickens' commentary, both social and, ultimately, theological.

Theologically, ghosts have had a chequered history within Christianity. For Protestants, the Old Testament injunction against consulting spirits coupled with the view that ghosts constitute a demonic presence have typically held sway. During the English Reformation, the old Catholic belief in purgatory, whence ghosts were thought to appear, was abandoned and replaced with the idea that ghosts were tricks played by the devil to confuse people (Marshall 2002). Dickens' own Anglican upbringing would lead one to assume that he would take the Protestant view; however, the reality may be more complex. Although Dickens' writings generally demonstrate contempt and loathing for the Catholic Church, he also exhibits a fascination for, even an attraction to, Catholicism, as in his account of the magnetic allure of some of Italy's finest churches in *Pictures from Italy* (1846). In this travelogue, he is awestruck by Roman Catholic churches that attest to a deep attraction for Catholic expressions of "faith" (Eslick 2012, 356).[2] Moreover, in 1844, the year that Dickens spent with his family in Genoa, Italy, Dickens had an experience that was pivotal in both his relationship to Catholicism and his view of spirits. One September night Dickens had a dream in which his beloved but now deceased sister-in-law Mary Hogarth appeared to him as a spirit "in the guise of the Madonna" (quoted in Eslick's abstract 2011, n.p.). He questioned the spirit as to what the "True Religion" was and asked if "perhaps the Roman Catholic is the best?" and her response was, "for *you*, it is the best."[3]

Perhaps, as Matsuto Sowa puts it, "Dickens was a man who preached Protestantism while some of his imagination remained on the side of the Roman Catholic Church" (2014, 99). Or again, Mary Lutze may capture the paradox when she writes that

> Dickens's words betray his confusion about which true religious denomination was the right one. However, he seemed to resolve this conundrum by selecting religious beliefs that he accepted as true from various doctrines rather than accepting one specific creed or belief system.
>
> (2016, 99)

Either way, the idea that Dickens presented ghosts that draws from Catholic theology more than from evangelical or other Christian belief is a theoretically tenable position. Ghosts in Dickens, then, may plausibly be seen as visitations from a purgative realm in which the soul has escaped eternal damnation but must be cleansed of the vestiges of sin before being fit to enter the dwelling place of the blessed, and may assist souls on earth as a way of helping both themselves and the earthly souls achieve heaven. As such, they point to the ultimate importance of the spiritual realm; they are emblems of hope that their interlocutors' souls, too, may reach heaven, if they recognize the importance of the spiritual and make heaven and its laws their guide in life. Coming as it did in the fall of 1844, just months before the publication of Dickens' first Christmas book, the episode involving Mary Hogarth's spirit has special significance for this study. Ghosts are legion in Dickens' Christmas books.

In this chapter the idea of ghosts as visitations from purgatory will serve as a theological framework to allow the reader to view Dickens' ghosts as beneficent visitations rather than demonic ones.

A Christmas Carol

A Christmas Carol (1843) is of course the first and most famous of the Christmas books, but because it is dealt with extensively both in this volume and elsewhere, I will dedicate more space to the other ghost stories. There are two ways, however, in which *Carol* is a keynote for the other works. The first is the debt to Dickens' great friend and mentor Thomas Carlyle. In the 1830s and 1840s, Carlyle was concerned about the extent to which his society emphasized material reality to the exclusion of the spiritual realm. In *Sartor Resartus* (first published serially in 1833–1834), Carlyle strongly advocates not viewing the world in purely material terms. The fictional editor of the work greatly admires the imaginary Professor Diogenes Teufelsdröckh's philosophy of Transcendentalism, according to which there is a spirit at the heart of the universe that is not reducible to what we experience with our senses. Indeed, the editor opines that reflective readers, "in contradiction to much Profit-and-Loss Philosophy," will have concluded that "Soul is not synonymous with Stomach" (1984 [1836], 122). The editor communicates emphatically that despite the views of utilitarian philosophers, there is more to the world than simply matter. Dickens greatly admired Carlyle's works and was profoundly influenced by his outlook, as demonstrated by, for example, his dedication of his great novel excoriating industrial materialism, *Hard Times* (1854), to Carlyle. A commitment to emphasizing the need for a spiritual basis for any philosophy, whether personal or collective, is one way in which the influence of Carlyle on Dickens is felt.

Ebenezer Scrooge in *Carol* iterates the opposite of Carlyle's editor's maxim. In answer to the question posed by Jacob Marley's ghost as to why Scrooge doubts his senses, Scrooge replies: "Because . . . a little thing affects them. A slight disorder of the stomach makes them cheats. You may be an undigested bit of beef, a blot of mustard, a crumb of cheese, a fragment of an underdone potato. There's more of gravy than of grave about you, whatever you are!" (1845 [1843], 27). In other words, Scrooge insists that the tormented soul in front of him is nothing but the product of Scrooge's stomach. This reductionist materialist view directly opposes the wisdom of Dickens' mentor and, in the end, is shown to be flawed, as Scrooge has to overturn his whole worldview.

The other essential feature of *Carol* to consider is Dickens' literary strategies for depicting the incorporeal. The scene of the appearance of Marley's ghost in the opening "stave" of the story will again serve as a fruitful point for critical analysis. Dickens has two strategies for "placing" the spirits in relation to the physical: the metaphorical and the metonymic. The first involves having the spirit take the place of the physical. He employs this strategy in the first appearance of Marley's ghost in the knocker on the door to Scrooge's dwellings. He takes pains to tell the reader that there is nothing unusual about the knocker except that it is large (19). It is an ordinary physical object. But suddenly, not because of any strange hallucinations on Scrooge's part, and "without its undergoing any intermediate process of change," it was "not a knocker, but Marley's face":

> It was not in impenetrable shadow as the other objects in the yard were, but had a dismal light about it, like a bad lobster in a dark cellar. It was not angry or ferocious but looked at Scrooge as Marley used to look: with ghostly spectacles turned up on its ghostly forehead. . . . As Scrooge looked fixedly at this phenomenon, it was a knocker again
>
> (20)

We notice that although Marley's face is spiritual—"ghostly"—and charged with a supernatural aura, it takes the place of a physical reality and then cedes the space to the object again when it disappears. Here, the spiritual is described in physical terms, though with a different aspect.

When Scrooge is inside his lodgings, however, Dickens uses the second trope, metonymy, to create a sense of Marley's presence. The ghost is contiguous to the physical realities described in relation to it: "[Marley's] body was transparent; so that Scrooge, observing him, and looking through his waistcoat, could see the two buttons on his coat behind;" A little further on, Scrooge "mark[s]" the "very texture of the folded kerchief bound about its head and chin" (26). The space the ghost inhabits is vacant, but the physical objects emphasize his spiritual presence as they create a boundary around it with their concrete materiality.

The effect of these two tropes is to emphasize the extent to which the ghost is *not* material, using the strongest means available to a writer who after all must use description of material things to create his effects. The result is a radical sense of the supernatural, the otherworldly, and the incorporeal. This real spiritual presence is the catalyst for Scrooge's rejection of materialism, in both senses of the word, and ultimately for his care of the poor.

The Chimes

Dickens' next Christmas book, *The Chimes: A Goblin Story; or, Some Bells That Rang an Old Year Out and a New Year In* (1844), has a strong biographical connection to Carlyle. Dickens wrote to Forster that he particularly wanted Carlyle to preview *The Chimes* before publication because his own ideas about materiality aligned with what Dickens wanted to achieve in his own story.[4] As with *Carol*, in this story social commentary is achieved through the use of phantom figures, once again making the theological point that care of the oppressed is accomplished, not by denial of the spiritual, but precisely through heightened attention to it.

Whereas *Carol* is memorable for ghosts and spirits that appear in more-or-less human form, *The Chimes* is notable primarily for its granting of spirits to physical objects. The wind has a "ghostly sound" (3), and the church bells of the title have been "baptized by bishops" (4), as if they have souls. These bells, at first, have an unambiguously positive valence for Toby Veck, a poor "ticket-porter" or message carrier who awaits work on the steps of the church: when his beloved daughter Meg brings him what is for him a luxurious meal of tripe, the chimes ring, "[breaking] in like a grace," which emphasizes their spiritual associations, and Toby adds that they often seem to be saying "Toby Veck, Toby Veck, keep a good heart, Toby!" (23).

Later in the story, however, the meaning of the chimes is more complex. When Toby encounters a Member of Parliament, an alderman, and a rich man on New Year's Eve, their conversation drives home for Toby the idea that the poor of the city are worthless people. Further, Toby is distraught by a newspaper account of an impoverished woman who drowned herself and her young child. Toby concludes that poor people like himself must be bad by nature. The sound of the bells becomes correspondingly gloomier for him, evoking despair in his heart. When Toby next visits the church belfry, the chimes are "Shadowy, and dark, and dumb," and it is "barely possible to make out their great shapes in the gloom" (91), a description that is suggestive of the bells' spiritual nature, given their nebulous corporeality, but which also imbues them with a more solemn, even sinister sense compared to their appearance in the "First Quarter" of the book.[5]

At the end of the "Second Quarter" of the story, Toby "[sinks] down in a swoon" (91), and what follows, in the "Third Quarter," is a long, sustained passage presenting the bells with goblins and spirits emanating from them and uttering a dual message of chastisement and hope to Toby (chastisement for believing the lie that the poor are bad, and for hearing in the bells any disparagement of the poor). The passage is charged with the supernatural in an overdetermined, madcap, bizarre, and baroque manner. As the end of the novella reveals, everything that happens after the "swoon" could be a dream or hallucination from which he awakes or comes to his senses when the Bells ring once more and his daughter, Meg, admonishes him not to eat tripe again without consulting his doctor as he "ha[s] been going on" (167). Nevertheless, what happens between the swoon and the revival is significant for Toby in that it has changed his attitude toward life, himself, and others. Very much in the same vein as *Carol*, *Chimes* presents spiritual beings as pivotal in the moral transformation of the protagonist. We shall look first at how these spiritual beings are presented—what narrative strategies Dickens uses to evoke them—and then at their moral effects, in an attempt to demonstrate once again the precise significance of immaterial presences in the Christmas books.

To begin with, after the swoon, darkness turns to light, and the bell is "peopled with a myriad figures" (93). He hears a voice whispering, "Haunt and hunt him," and he sees a "Goblin sight" (93). The words "Haunt" and "Goblin" have sinister associations, alluding to a somber side to these immaterial beings. Now the tower "swarm[s]" with "dwarf phantoms, spirits, elfin creatures of the Bells" (93). In the description that follows, the focus is on activity; the spirits are "leaping, flying, dropping, pouring from the Bells without a pause" (94). Indeed, Dickens describes them as "violently active" (94). This characterization may surprise the reader as spirits are often thought of as serene and lifeless, whereas this description conveys the impression of life, and even of physicality, with references to their "tear[ing] their hair" and "howl[ing]" (94). A few lines later, however, the narrator tells us that "Stone, and brick, and slate, and tile, became transparent to him as to them" (94), which reminds us that their physicality is an illusion, a kind of metaphor for what they are. Indeed, the illusory nature of this materiality is highlighted by the sudden disappearance of the spirits as the Bells stop ringing: "As he gazed, the Chimes stopped. Instantaneous change! The whole swarm fainted! their forms collapsed, their speed deserted them; they sought to fly, but in the act of falling died and melted into air. No fresh supply succeeded them" (96). Dickens evokes the phantoms through physical references but then shows that they transcend corporality by having their analogously physical presence dissolve into thin air as if they had never been.

The spirits have not disappeared but merely migrated; now, in every Bell, there is "a bearded figure of the bulk and stature of the

Bell—incomprehensibly, a figure and the Bell itself" (96–97). This one short description is packed with significance in terms of Dickens' technique for representing the immaterial or, in effect, representing the unrepresentable. Dickens is again relying on information pertaining to the senses: each figure (spirit) is "bearded." In addition, the spirit is conveyed metonymically through association with something near it: "of the bulk and stature of the Bell" (96). But finally, there is a metaphoric trope here too: the figure *is* the Bell; there is substitution as well as contiguity. This double or triple imagery combines to produce the effect of rich signification and a mysterious (the word "mysterious" is used of the figures in the next paragraph) and paradoxical presence and transcendence at the same time.

The spirits' association with the Bells gives them immediate moral and religious significance; the Bells have already been shown to be important signs of hope for Toby. As has already been noted, when he "reads" the Bells as signifying despair, he is misreading them, and the same can be said, *a fortiori*, about the spirits behind/within/associated with the Bells. Although the spirits appear somber to him, their intention is benevolent: to restore hope in Toby's soul. They introduce him to a new spirit, the spirit of his child, Meg, who paradoxically is still alive as a grown woman, according to the vision (104–107). Under the guidance of the spirit of his child, the purpose of the visions is for Toby to learn not to judge the poor harshly when they are often driven to perform desperate acts due to their penury. Toby sees Meg as she would be years later, struggling to support a young infant by working every waking moment; her husband Richard has become corrupted by a drinking problem brought on by the delay in their marriage caused by fear-mongering social elites. Meg reaches such a pit of dejection that she is about to drown herself and her infant—the very crime of which a newspaper account led Toby to condemn the poor as "born bad." The vision portends his beloved and virtuous daughter being driven to desperate acts because of poverty and therefore he should not assume that the impecunious are evil. The story has a happy ending in that when Toby emerges from this vision, the tragic circumstances have been avoided; Meg is about to marry Richard, instead of opting for an injurious delay as in the vision, and there is every indication that they are about to embark on a happy life together (167–75). The spirits have convicted Toby to view the poor with compassion and mercy. This is the lesson that Dickens has for his readers.

Significantly, the story concludes with a New Year's wish from the narrator to the reader: "So may each year be happier than the last, and not the meanest of our brethren or sisterhood debarred their rightful share, in what our Great Creator formed them to enjoy" (175). This closing benediction connects the dots that Dickens has already implicitly linked together, namely, that the spiritual realm enters the human dimension, especially in its poverty-stricken form, to ennoble it and lift it up to the dignified position that the great spirit (God) has intended for it. Carlyle's idea that crude materialism debases, rather than rescues, the poor because it denies their dignity turns out to be crucial to a proper understanding of Dickens' outlook on the body/the material and the spiritual, and the relationship between the two. Thus, whereas there is a notion that Toby's vision may merely have been an illusion brought on by the consumption of too much tripe, the reader cannot escape the sense that on some spiritual level, the spirits of the Bells have a very real existence and that they have intervened to rescue Toby from his sick spiritual state, much as the ghosts of *Carol* redeemed Scrooge from his torpor of soul.

The Haunted Man and the Ghost's Bargain

This chapter will pass over *The Cricket on the Hearth: A Fairy Tale of Home* (1846 [1845]) though it does contain an interesting presentation of spirits, as well as *The Battle of Life: A Love Story* (1846) in favor of a consideration of Dickens' sustained use of a ghost in *The Haunted Man and the Ghost's Bargain* (1848). This final Christmas book represents a climactic return to the presence of the spiritual. The plot concerns Professor Redlaw, a man "haunted" by a past filled with grief, including for the death of a dear sister. Redlaw encounters a phantom version of himself who offers him the possibility of forgetting all memory of emotional ties and affections, and thus obliterating the pain associated with his memories. The professor accepts this offer only to discover that a life without memories of feelings is even more torturous than the suffering that these memories entail, for it results in his causing others with whom he comes in contact to lose their memories unwillingly, and it also leads him—and them—to lose the ability to sympathize with others. Through the influence of the benevolent Milly Swidger, he regains his memories and eschews forever the temptation that the phantom offered him to imagine that life would be better without the recollection and experience of suffering.

In this story, in contrast to the previous Christmas books, the ghostly figure seems at first to represent a force for ill rather than good. We must analyze both how Dickens represents this figure in the narrative, and what role this spirit plays in the story, especially in the context of his treatment of the spiritual overall in the Christmas books. Philip Allingham notes that in reference to this figure, Dickens uses the terms "'phantom' (36 times), 'shadow' (14 times), and 'shade' (5 times) much more often than 'ghost' (8 times) to describe this *döppelganger* [*sic*]" (2000). That Dickens does use the term "ghost," however, signifies that this phantom is of the same nature as the ghosts of Christmas Past, Present, and Future in *Carol*, and that it is an immaterial replica of the protagonist obviously complicates the sense in which it can be said to really exist. Still, Dickens takes pains to communicate that the phantom is not a mere figure of speech or fancy within the context of the story. It is true that the story opens with Mr. Redlaw sitting morosely in his inner chamber like a "haunted man"; we are told that someone might "by a very easy flight of fancy, [have] believed that everything about him took this haunted tone, and that he lived on haunted ground" (4), all of which does at first suggest such hauntedness as imaginary. Suddenly, however, a *real* ghostly presence intrudes:

> It is certain that no gliding footstep touched the floor, as he lifted up his head with a start, and spoke. And yet there was no mirror in the room on whose surface his own form could have cast its shadow for a moment; and, Something had passed darkly and gone!
> (10–11)

In contrast to the whimsicality of the metaphorical haunting, the real phantom has a more solid presence; it is a "Something" whose movement was definite and distinct. We find that the movement of this ghost is less frenetic than that of the spirits of the Bells in *The Chimes*. The phantom in the final story, apart from being "an awful likeness of himself [i.e., Redlaw]" (33), is described as "Ghastly and cold, colourless in its leaden face and hands, but with his features, and his bright eyes, and his grizzled hair," and it is said to come "into his terrible appearance of existence, motionless, without a sound" (33). The "leaden" face and hands, as well as the absence of motion or sound, make this specter appear much more somber, subdued, and forbearing than those of *Chimes*. The phrase "appearance of existence" insinuates that that although the ghost seems to have a material presence, this seeming is merely an illusion. The phantom could, theoretically, be a construct of Redlaw's fevered imagination, as Cadwallader argues (78–79); more likely, though, given the surprise Redlaw manifests upon noticing its apparition, it is a real spiritual presence that has adopted a chimerical material form. The phantom does "melt before him" after their conversation and therefore reinforces the sense of the illusory nature of his physical frame. That the bargain offered by the ghost actually comes into effect also demonstrates that he is no mere figment of the imagination.

The next question is what role this spiritual presence plays in the story. The fact that he dons the appearance of Redlaw can be explained by the way in which he uses his semblance to Redlaw's tragic younger self to stir up Redlaw's self-pity to the point of his desiring to enter into the ghost's bargain. That the bargain itself is ill-advised might cause the reader to see the phantom as an unkind presence in the story; indeed, the narrator refers in this scene to the phantom's "evil smile" and "glassy face" (42). Viewed in the context of the narrative as a whole, however, the ghost's actions can be understood in a more benign fashion. After all, it is through the adverse effects of the bargain that Redlaw comes to see sorrowful emotions—indeed, of suffering itself—as necessary if one is to have empathy for other people. At the end of Chapter 2, "The Gift Diffused," Redlaw exclaims, after having seen the soul-numbing effects of the destruction of sad memories on Philip Swidger and his son William:

> Phantoms! Punishers of impious thoughts! . . . Look upon me! From the darkness of my mind, let the glimmering of contrition that I know is there, shine up and show my misery! In the material world as I have long taught, nothing can be spared; no step or atom in the wondrous structure could be lost, without a blank being made in the great universe. I know, now, that it is the same with good and evil, happiness and sorrow, in the memories of men. Pity me! Relieve me!
> (133)

Detrimental as the ghost's bargain has been in terms of its immediate effects, in the long run it proves beneficial to Redlaw as it teaches him the need for acceptance of suffering as part of the great tapestry of life; what he knew to be true about the material world he now understands to apply to the spiritual realm as well. If we compare the role of the supernatural in *The Haunted Man* to that of the earlier Christmas books, then it is interesting to note that the protagonist's release from the spell cast on him by supernatural forces comes not from the forces themselves at the pleading of the protagonist, as in *Carol*, nor through the action of the lead character, as in *Chimes*, but through the benevolent influence of another character. Milly Swidger, who intuits that one must hold on to painful memories because they remind us to forgive our tormenters, achieves, through her altruism, a complete reversal of the spell for all the characters. This resolution powerfully conveys that the truths conveyed to us from the spiritual realm, far from directing our attention away from this world, remind us of the need for compassion toward, and self-sacrifice for, our fellow human beings.

The Ghost Stories

In addition to the Christmas books, Dickens wrote more than two dozen ghost stories. Some are contained within longer works, for example, the five ghost stories contained within Dickens' first complete novel, *The Pickwick Papers* (1840 [1837]). Others were published in his periodicals, such as the stories that he published yearly at Christmas time in *Household Words* (from 1850), and in *All the Year Round*. What we find in the ghost stories, as in his Christmas books, is a preoccupation with demonstrating that the spiritual world really exists—moreover, that the spiritual world is benevolent, and wants to help human beings. In "The Queer Chair," for example, a supernatural story in *The Pickwick Papers*, Tom Smart is assisted by a chair that transforms itself into an old man in preventing the comely landlady of the inn at which he is staying from succumbing to the advances of a tall man who is secretly married. The "strange, grim looking, high backed chair, carved in the most fantastic manner" (1983 [1836–1837], 40) wakes him at night and reveals that he knows all about Tom, from his penchant for punch to his fancying the landlady, of whom "the chair" declares himself to be the guardian. Indicating a pair of trousers in a cabinet, the old man announces that in a pocket of the trousers is a letter from the tall man's wife begging him to come home to her and their six little children.

Tom shortly falls back to sleep, and when he wakes up, he accuses himself of having a wild imagination for having believed the chair to have been a man. But he finds the trousers in the press with the letter just as the chair had described. In a brief space of time, he shares the letter with the widow, boots "Jinkins," the tall man, out the door, and secures the affections of the landlady, whom he marries a month later. The old man in the chair, while not a ghost in the conventional sense, is a supernatural being whose existence challenges the protagonist's notions of the reliably fixed nature of material reality (a chair is a chair), and the fact that this creature offers assistance to Tom, and indirectly to the widow, shows the positive value that Dickens ascribes to the spiritual realities that dwell beneath the surface of ordinary material objects.

In "A Christmas Tree," otherwise known as "Christmas Ghosts," or "Ghosts at Christmas," written in 1850 and published as Dickens' first annual Christmas story in *Household Words* (and later *All the Year Round*), Dickens looks back nostalgically at the traditions that shaped his experience of Christmas as a young boy. The early part of the piece teems with an abundance of material details such as the tree, presents, and a cornucopia of food. In describing the ornaments on the tree, for example, he spins a sentence of 219 words filled with concrete examples such as "teetotums, humming-tops, needle-cases, pen-wipers, smelling-bottle, conversation-cards, [and] bouquet-holders" (2021 [1850], 289). This random assortment of material things, which he calls a "motley collection of odd objects" (289), is part of a vast array of items that together create an impression of plenty, indeed, of a superabundance of items that appeal to the physical sense. All these ornaments, presents, and culinary treats are an inextricable part of the Christmas experience.

A later section of the story, however, has a contrasting focus on spiritual entities, namely, ghosts. Relating the English tradition of recounting ghost stories around the fire at Christmas time, Dickens piles on example after example of ghost narratives and clichés, the surfeit of supernatural beings matching or cancelling out the superfluity of physical objects in the earlier section. Dickens tells of a housekeeper in an old castle, betrayed by a cavalier in green, and intent on haunting his room centuries later; of a stain that will not come out of the floorboards in the spot where a lord once shot himself; of an orphan boy who haunts people who are doomed to die young, and so on. It is as if the oversupply of physical trinkets and delectable treats must be counterbalanced by a glut of supernatural elements that chasten the spirit and subdue the mind after the sensory excitement caused by the overload of physical stimuli.

Notably, the segue between the materialistic and the spiritualistic segments of the story is a familiar image: the Christ child. The narrator hears "Waits" or minstrels playing Christmas music and the associated scene set forth on the Christmas tree is that of "An angel, speaking to a group of shepherds in a field; some travellers, with eyes uplifted, following a star; a baby in a manger" (292). This picture, coming as it does right in the middle of the narrative, anchors both the plethora of physical images and the collection of ghost stories in the traditional Christmas manger scene. The miracle of the incarnation weds the bodily and the spiritual and keeps them in proper balance. Moreover, it redeems both the material, by presenting a soberingly quiet scene after the mad swirl of physical objects, and the spiritual, by presenting the reader with a morally meaningful and uplifting tableau, in contrast with the spooky supernatural that frightens and chastens without consoling. Perhaps this is the reason that Dickens returns to the image of Jesus at the end of the story:

> In every cheerful image and suggestion that the season brings, may the bright star that rested above the poor roof, be the star of all the Christian World! A moment's pause, O vanishing tree, of which the lower boughs are dark to me as yet, and let me look once more! I know there are blank spaces on thy branches, where eyes that I have loved have shone and smiled; from which they are departed. But, far above, I see the raiser of the dead girl, and the Widow's Son; and God is good! If Age be hiding for me in the unseen portion of thy downward growth, O may I, with a grey head, turn a child's heart to that figure yet, and a child's trustfulness and confidence!
>
> (295)

Christ, the "raiser of the dead girl," is, as they say, the "reason for the season," and it is to him that the speaker's eyes are lifted with hope. Whereas the physical gifts of Christmas pull the speaker earthward, the ghosts lift him beyond the physical, but in a way that is shifting and aimless, Jesus represents the stabilizing marriage of the two, the fixed star that gives the soul direction. Perhaps one intuits in this design something of the wisdom behind the very tradition of telling ghost stories on Christmas. Ghosts lift us out of the here and now to give us a taste of the supernatural; Christ fulfills that yearning by rooting it in our ordinary fleshly reality.

Caley Ehnes argues that Victorian writers used the Christmas story to connect contemporary social concerns with Christian values and traditions (2012). She focuses on Elizabeth Gaskell's "The Old Nurse's

Story," published in the Christmas edition of Dickens' *Household Words* in 1852, but Dickens also features prominently in her analysis. Ehnes' study is gratifying in that it recognizes the religious import of the ghosts in stories such as Gaskell's and Dickens', as well as the connection of the ghosts to Christmas but it does not quite go far enough in recognizing the spiritual value of the ghosts. In other words, it is not just the fact that ghosts are connected with religion and thereby reinvigorate the notion of Christmas with a religious thrust, but that ghosts are spiritual entities, and therefore by their very nature emphasize the spiritual over the material. In Dickens, these values intersect and mutually reinforce each other: ghosts are spiritual rather than material, and they benevolently point us in a good direction, away from obsession with material things (the fatal flaw of his society). This is especially so at Christmas, a time when we remember the Christ child, who reminds us of our spiritual home while at the same time paradoxically (and yet not paradoxically) calling to mind our duty to care for those materially less fortunate by detaching ourselves from material things so as to share with those in need.

Dickens' tradition of ghost stories at Christmas continues through to the end of his career. Perhaps his best-known Christmas story after *A Christmas Carol*, "The Signal-Man," appeared in the Christmas edition of *All the Year Round* in 1866, three-and-a-half years before his death. In this story a railway signal-man is haunted by a ghost that tries to warn him of impending disaster by crossing one arm across his face and waving violently with the other. When the signal-man describes the ghost the narrator quietly imagines the specter saying, "For God's sake, clear the way!" (1983 [1866], 303), but the narrator never voices these words. At the end of the story, when the signal-man has in fact been killed by an oncoming train, the conductor of the train says that as he was approaching he leaned out the window and cried, "For God's sake, clear the way" (309)—the very words the specter had uttered in the narrator's own imagination. This eerie coincidence, inexplicable by natural causes, is all the more striking in that the signal-man had studied natural philosophy—that is, physical science, the study of nature— as a young man, and was therefore aligned with science, reason, and empirical study. The very natural philosophy the signal-man was committed to fails to account for the circumstances of his own death, echoing Hamlet's famous pronouncement, "There are more things in heaven and earth . . . Than are dreamt of in your philosophy" (Shakespeare 1603, 1.5.167–68). The presence of ghosts once again signals the existence (and importance) of a reality beyond the material. In this case the ghost is perhaps not as clearly benevolent as the spirits in *Carol*, *Chimes*, "The Queer Chair," and others, since it does not rescue the central character from death, but it does at least appear to be attempting to warn the signal-man of his fate, and the sequence of events has the meritorious effect of enlightening the narrator (and the reader) as to the existence of forces beyond the natural that must be acknowledged and respected.

Séances

Famously, Dickens had a connection with supposed real-life ghosts through his attendance at séances, where ghosts were reputed have communicated with the living. In contrast to his treatment of fictional ghosts, Dickens seems to have taken pains to discredit these events on various occasions, for example in a series of articles in *Household Words* in the 1850s. One of these, "Well-Authenticated Rappings" (1858), is a satire on belief in séances. In this short, hilarious sketch, the narrator, clearly experiencing a nasty hangover, feigns a belief that "raps" on his head (throbbing from the hangover) are the communications of the spirit of a deceased person. The spirit eventually reveals its name to be "Port," causing the writer to

> lie prostrate, on the verge of insensibility, for a quarter of an hour: during which the rappings were continued with violence, and a host of spiritual appearances passed before his eyes, of a black hue, and greatly resembling tadpoles endowed with the power of occasionally spinning themselves out into musical notes as they swam down into space.
> (1983 [1858], 337–38)

The comical, over-the-top tone of the piece takes a jab at participants who, in séances, claim to have undergone similarly outlandish experiences. The fact that the episode is supposed to have taken place on December 26, thus the result of Christmas revelry, reinforces the sense of irony surrounding the spiritual, the ghostly, and things associated with Christmas. The narrator goes on to describe a second experience, this time on the second of January, which the reader understands to be heartburn, which he recounts as "rappings" in his stomach. These prove to be linked to "pork pie," as well as "Cape. Gamboge. Camomile. Treacle, Spirits of wine, Distilled Potatoes" (340). This litany of causes bears an uncanny resemblance to Scrooge's claim that the apparition of Ghost of Marley is likely to have been caused by "a fragment of underdone potato" and the like. It is almost as though Dickens is spoofing himself. It is possible that Dickens did not discount séances entirely: he continued as a member of the London Ghost Club of which he was a founding member in 1862 (though one of the main accomplishments of the Club was to expose the fraudulence of fake magicians). But he was more heavily invested in mesmerism than in any other paranormal activity, as his famous attempt to cure Mme Augusta de la Rue in Italy in 1844, as well as other episodes, attests. Perhaps Dickens, without discounting the possibility of the real existence of ghosts, was more interested in creating ghosts that are real within the confines of fiction, as reminders of the spiritual, than in flirting with ghosts one wishes to control for the satisfaction of one's curiosity. Moreover, Jennifer Bann, in her fascinating analysis of how spiritualism influenced the depiction of ghosts in ghost stories in the latter half of the nineteenth century and beginning of the twentieth, argues that ghosts in fiction became more active, powerful, and even physical after 1850 due to the impact of séances in which the ghostly hand would literally take control of its surroundings and effect material change (2009). It may be that Dickens, despite his profound interest in ghosts, was less enchanted with the ghost of the séance precisely because what attracted him most to specters, namely their spiritual nature, was increasingly downplayed within spiritualism in favor of beings who were more and more earthbound, rather than emphasizing the spiritual realm and the need to recognize that "the world and its desires pass away" (1 Jn. 2:17).

Conclusion

Dickens' lifelong preoccupation with ghosts and spirits, as seen in his Christmas books and ghost stories, is also reflected in his longer fiction, including *The Pickwick Papers* (1840 [1837]), as well as *Nicholas Nickleby* (1839). In Dickens' last completed novel, *Our Mutual Friend* (1876 [1865]), ghosts do not feature prominently, but the social critique of materialism that Dickens has been carrying out through his use of ghosts in the Christmas books and ghost stories finds its culmination in this *pièce de résistance*. Characters in this novel who embody a materialistic approach to life, such as Samuel Wegg and Rogue Riderhood, meet a miserable end, and those who value, or learn to value, the spirit over wealth and/or the flesh, such as John Harmon and Bella Wilfer, find abiding happiness. The influence of Carlyle and his anti-materialist philosophy can be traced throughout Dickens' *oeuvre*[6]; in the Christmas books and ghost stories it manifests itself primarily through the prevalence of ghosts that are real within the context of the narrative, of supernatural phenomena that cannot be explained by purely material causes. This spiritual message coexists with, and in a sense can be said to be the motivating force for, Dickens' often savage social critique. In Dickens' philosophy, and ultimately his theology, for a nation to truly care for the body, it must learn to recognize and appreciate that the body has a soul.

The Mystery of Edwin Drood (1870), famously never completed and published posthumously, provides an intriguing coda regarding the presentation of specters in Dickens' writings. In one sense, the novel is replete with ghosts, as references to ghostlike figures and hauntings abound. Rosa Bud approaches like an "apparition" (26); Mrs. Tisher moves through a room "like the legendary ghost of a dowager in silken skirts" (30); Jasper gives himself over to opium and "the Spectres it invokes at midnight"

(58); and Jasper "haunts [Rosa's] thoughts, like a dreadful ghost" (83), to cite just a handful of examples. The cathedral crypt, curated by Durdles with obsessive attention, tantalizes with its centuries-old corpses, but no spirits emerge from them (52–56). The only ghosts in *Drood* are figurative ones, as the society of Cloisterham fails to connect with its ancient, spiritual past. Cloisterham has literally given up the ghost. At the heart of the novel is Jasper and his sickly attachment to drugs and to a woman he disgusts. Dickens' final novel, *Drood* is perhaps also his most pessimistic, and his cynicism about the growing decadence of his society is signaled by the disappearance of the literal ghost, replaced by the specter of materialism.

Notes

1. From 1843 to 1848, Dickens published one book on a Christmas theme yearly in December (skipping a year in 1847), resulting in what became known as Dickens' "Christmas books." The five books are: *A Christmas Carol; The Chimes; The Cricket on the Hearth; The Battle of Life;* and *The Haunted Man.* In the 1850s and 60s, Dickens also produced special Christmas editions of his journals *Household Words* and *All the Year Round*, for which he wrote short Christmas stories, but the five "Christmas books" are distinct in that each was published under separate cover.
2. Eslick further investigates the attraction/repulsion dynamic in Dickens' relationship to Catholicism in "*Barnaby Rudge* and the Jesuit Menace" (2018), 153–65.
3. Quoted in Eslick (2011,1) from a letter from Dickens to his good friend and biographer John Forster in September 1844. See Forster (1873, 122–24; 124). In his unpublished doctoral thesis entitled "Charles Dickens: Anti-Catholicism and Catholicism," Eslick explores illuminating connections between this vision and the ghost of Marley in *A Christmas Carol*. For Eslick, the reference to Catholicism by the spirit of Mary Hogarth prepares the way, both for Dickens and for the reader, for an interpretation of *Carol* that situates Marley in purgatory (348). He presents convincing evidence for this reading, from the statement by Marley's ghost that he is on a mission to help Scrooge reform his life, which may be an argument against construing the ghost as a demon. Eslick references Shakespeare's *Hamlet* in *Carol* that draws an affinity between Marley and Hamlet Senior as visitors from a purgative realm who are bound by the "secrets of the prison-house" (2011, 81–105, 91).
4. See Rodger Tarr's "Dickens' Debt to Carlyle's 'Justice Metaphor' in *The Chimes*" for this reference and for further exploration of the connections between Carlyle (especially his 1840 work *Chartism*) and *The Chimes* (1972, 208–9).
5. For a more in-depth discussion of the spirituality of Dickens' references to bells, see Julie Donovan's chapter in this volume titled "For Whom the Bell Tolls": Dickens' *Barnaby Rudge*.
6. Barry Qualls has argued persuasively for evidence of Carlyle's influence on *Our Mutual Friend* in particular, citing a letter Dickens wrote to Carlyle a few months before starting this novel, in which Dickens declared himself to be "always reading you faithfully and trying to go your way" (1978, 199). The letter is dated April 13, 1863 and can be found in Dexter (1938, 3:348).

Bibliography

Allingham, Philip V. "The Last of Dickens's Five Christmas Books: *The Haunted Man and the Ghost's Bargain* (19 December 1848)." *Victorian Web*. November 28, 2000. www.victorianweb.org/authors/dickens/xmas/pva33.html.

Bann, Jennifer. "Ghostly Hands and Ghostly Agency: The Changing Figure of the Nineteenth-Century Specter." *Victorian Studies* 51, no. 4 (2009): 663–86.

Cadwallader, Jen. *Spirits and Spirituality in Victorian Fiction*. London: Palgrave Macmillan, 2016.

Carlyle, Thomas. *Sartor Resartus*. 1836. London: Dent, 1984.

Dexter, Walter, ed. *Letters of Charles Dickens*. Vol. 3. Bloomsbury: Nonesuch, 1938.

Dickens, Charles. *The Battle of Life: A Love Story*. London: Bradbury and Evans, 1846. https://books.google.com/books?id=mSkEAAAAQAAJ.

———. *The Chimes*. 1844. London: Chapman and Hall, 1845. https://books.google.ca/books?id=N6RbAAAAQAAJ&pg=PA5&dq=chimes+dickens&hl=en&sa=X&ved=2ahUKEwiCk_3ou-_tAhUoc98KHam4AoUQ6wEwA3oECAMQAQ#v=onepage&q=chimes%20dickens&f=true.

———. *A Christmas Carol. In Prose. Being A Ghost Story of Christmas*. 1843. London: Chapman and Hall, 1845. https://books.google.com/books?id=MlMHAAAAQAAJ.

———. "A Christmas Tree." *Household Words: A Weekly Journal* 2, no. 39 (December 21, 1850): 289–95. *Victorian Short Fiction Project*, edited by Ben Wagner. February 14, 2021. https://vsfp.byu.edu/index.php/title/a-christmas-tree/.

———. *The Cricket on the Hearth: A Fairy Tale of Home*. 1845. London: Bradbury and Evans, 1846. https://books.google.com/books?id=kykEAAAAQAAJ.

———. *Hard Times*. London: Bradbury, 1854. https://books.google.com/books?id=X9RVAAAAcAAJ.

———. *The Haunted Man and the Ghost's Bargain*. London: Bradbury and Evans, 1848. https://books.google.ca/books?id=riMEAAAAQAAJ.

———. *The Mystery of Edwin Drood*. 1870. New York: Hurd and Houghton, 1871.

———. *Nicholas Nickleby*. London: Chapman and Hall, 1839. https://books.google.com/books?id=NdYNAAAAQAAJ.

———. *Our Mutual Friend*. 1865. New York: D. Appleton, 1876. https://books.google.com/books?id=5dkGcb-MGhsC.

———. *Pictures from Italy*. Leipzig: Bernhard Tauchnitz, 1846.

———. *The Posthumous Papers of the Pickwick Club*. 1837. New York: J. Van Amringe, 1840. https://books.google.com/books?id=r2ooAAAAMAAJ.

———. "The Queer Chair." 1836–1837. In Haining, 36–47, 1983.

———. "The Signal-Man." 1866. In Haining, 299–309, 1983.

———. "Well-Authenticated Rappings." 1858. In Haining, 335–42, 1983.

Ehnes, Caley. "'Winter Stories—Ghost Stories . . . Round the Christmas Fire': Victorian Ghost Stories and the Christmas Market." *Illumine* 11, no. 1 (2012): 6–25.

Eslick, Mark. "Architectural Anxieties: Dickens's *Pictures from Italy*." *English: Journal of the English Association* 61, no. 235 (Winter 2012): 354–64.

———. "Chapter 10: *Barnaby Rudge* and the Jesuit Menace." In *The Oxford Handbook of Charles Dickens*, edited by John Jordan, Robert L. Patten, and Catherine Waters, 153–65. Oxford: Oxford University Press, 2018.

———. "Charles Dickens: Anti-Catholicism and Catholicism." PhD diss., The University of York, September 2011. https://core.ac.uk/download/pdf/40013315.pdf.

Forster, John. *The Life of Charles Dickens*. Vol. 2. London: Chapman and Hall, 1873.

Haining, Peter, ed. *The Complete Ghost Stories of Charles Dickens*. Toronto: Franklin Watts, 1983.

Henson, Louise. Chapter 2: "Investigations and Fictions: Charles Dickens and Ghosts." In *The Victorian Supernatural*, edited by Nicola Bown, Carolyn Burdett, and Pamela Thurschwell, 44–66. Cambridge: Cambridge University Press, 2004.

Lutze, Mary. "Swedenborg's Enduring Influence: The Resurfacing of Heaven and Hell in Dickens's *A Christmas Carol*." *The New Philosophy* 119, no. 1–2 (January–June 2016): 443–66.

Marshall, Peter. "The Disorderly Dead: Ghosts and Their Meanings in Reformation England." In *Beliefs and the Dead in Reformation England*. Oxford: Oxford University Press, 2002.

Qualls, Barry. "Savages in a 'Bran-New' World: Carlyle and *Our Mutual Friend*." *Studies in the Novel* 10, no. 2 (Summer 1978): 199–217.

Sowa, Matsuto. "Dickens and 'Mariolatry': Dickens's Cult of the Virgin Mary." *Bulletin of Christian Studies* 17 (2014): 97–126.

Tarr, Rodger L. "Dickens' Debt to Carlyle's 'Justice Metaphor' in *The Chimes*." *Nineteenth-Century Fiction* 27, no. 2 (September 1972): 208–15.

4 Dickens Demystified

The Jesuitical Journey of Ebenezer Scrooge: Through the *Spiritual Exercises of St. Ignatius of Loyola*

Mary-Antoinette Smith

This mystery is profound.

—Eph 5:32 (ESV)

Many analytical inquiries concerning Charles Dickens and religion have addressed the lacuna identified nearly 50 years ago acknowledging that "the Christian aspect of [his] work has been badly neglected... [although] it is in fact an absolutely essential part of his development as a novelist" (Wilson and Dyson 1976, 55). The pervasive mystery of the man, his religiosity, and its influence on his works, however, still remain unsolved. A. N. Wilson admits that his recent biography *The Mystery of Charles Dickens* is so titled "because, of all the great novelists, Dickens was the most mysterious" (2020, 6). The mystery thickens further when seeking to demystify the theological Dickens because of conflicting claims that he was "non-religious, anti-religious, antagonistic towards Christianity, [and] inconsistent in [his] religious beliefs" (Hanna 2013, 183); that he "was not much of a Christian... [and] his theology is always a little fuzzy at best" (Cox and Elliot 1975, 922); that his was the "voice of one who was neither theologian or biblical scholar nor churchman but a layperson, one who thought seriously and deeply about the life of faith, following Jesus, and just what that should look like" (Colledge 2012, xii), and more. While tempted amidst these disparate doctrinal perspectives to abort further inquiry and conclude along with Stephen Blackpool in *Hard Times* that "'Tis a muddle... 'Tis a' a muddle!" (Dickens 1854, 89), this analysis dares to probe the theological mystery of the man and his written matter.

Dickens' canonical enterprise reflects a religiosity that is richly interwoven with the spiritual and social action agenda of his divine exemplar, Jesus Christ, whose life he immortalized in *The Life of Our Lord*, written between 1846 and 1849 exclusively "for his own children. He set it down

DOI: 10.4324/9781003156611-5

in his own hand, for their eyes—and their eyes alone—to answer their questions about religion and faith" (1934, 3), explaining:

> My Dear Children, I am very anxious that you should know something about the History of Jesus Christ. For everybody ought to know about Him. No one ever lived who was so good, so kind, so gentle, and so sorry for all people who did wrong, or were in any way ill or miserable, as he was. And as he is now in Heaven, where we hope to go, and all to meet each other after we are dead, and there be happy always together, you never can think what a good place Heaven is, without knowing who he was and what he did.
> (11–12)

This gospel according to Dickens was "sacredly guarded as a precious family secret" (Simon and Schuster 7) until its posthumous publication in 1934. It is an invaluable compendium for unraveling the mystery of the author's moral view across the breadth of his writings—the canonical whole of which comprises a Dickensian *Summa Theologica* whose thesis can be found in his letter to David Macrae indicating:

> With a deep sense of my great responsibility always upon me when I exercise my art, one of my most constant and most earnest endeavours has been to exhibit in all my good people some faint reflections of our great Master, and unostentatiously to lead the reader up to those teachings as the great source of all moral goodness. All my strongest illustrations are drawn from the New Testament; all my social abuses are shown as departures from its spirit; all my good people are humble, charitable, faithful, and forgiving. Over and over again, I claim them in express words as disciples of the Founder of our religion.
> (Hartley 2012 [1861], 364)

Rather than wrangle within debates concerning Dickens' denominational and doctrinal allegiances and their impact on his writings, this chapter centers on connecting elements of catholicity in the *Spiritual Exercises of St. Ignatius of Loyola* (1548) with the contents of *A Christmas Carol. In Prose. Being A Ghost Story of Christmas* (1843).

The Case of the Dickensian Catholic Connection

> Then the mystery was revealed to [him] in a vision of the night.
> —Dn 2:19 (ESV)

Catholic convert and fellow writer G. K. Chesterton "did in effect claim that Dickens was at heart a Catholic" (Oddie 2012, n.p.). Dickens' adherence to Catholicism may be true given his visionary encounter with the Blessed Virgin Mary in 1844. He describes this mystical experience in a letter to his friend and first biographer, John Forster:

> Let me tell you of a curious dream I had . . . I was visited by a Spirit [that] . . . wore a blue drapery, as the Madonna might in a picture by Raphael . . . It was so full of compassion and sorrow for me . . . and I said, sobbing, "Oh! give me some token that you have really visited me!" "Form a wish," it said . . . "[A]nswer me one . . . question! . . . What is the True religion?" As it paused a moment without replying, I said . . . "You think, as I do, that the form of religion does Not so greatly matter, if we try to do good? or," I said, observing that it . . . was moved with the greatest compassion for me, "perhaps the Roman Catholic is the best? perhaps it makes one think of God oftener, and believe in him more steadily?" "For you," said the Spirit, full of such heavenly tenderness for me, that I felt as if my heart would break; "for you, it is the best!" Then I awoke, with the tears running down my face.[1]

While not positing an explicit espousal of Roman Catholicism from this mysterious Marian moment, this analysis attributes to Dickens a small "c" *catholic* (Greek: καθολικός/Latin: *catholicus*) connection. Connotatively it means "universal" and speaks to the universality and embedded catholicity within *A Christmas Carol*, a text typically aligned with such Protestant-centered conversion narratives as *The Somonyng of Everyman* (c. 1510) and *The Pilgrim's Progress* (1678). Making this [c]atholic connection broadens the explicatory range of *A Christmas Carol* beyond the limitations of the claim that it consists of just "two texts, the one that Dickens wrote in 1843 and the [culture-text] that we collectively remember" (Davis 1990, 4) to posit a third text wherein Scrooge's conversion unfolds in conjunction with the Catholic-derived *Spiritual Exercises of St. Ignatius of Loyola*.

Before further probing the mystery (*mysterium*) of this Dickensian [c]atholic connection, it is useful to recall the centrality of mysteries to the faith tradition wherein the mystery of faith (*mysterium fidei*) serves as the wellspring for many mysteries of the Catholic catechism. These include the divine mysteries of the Holy Trinity (*Sancte Trinitatis*), the Incarnation (*Incarnatio*), and the Holy Eucharist (*Sanctus Eucharistia*), as well as the mysteries of the Virgin Birth of Mary, the Resurrection of Jesus Christ, and the Holy Rosary (the five-part format of which shapes the analysis in the following), among others. Particularly relevant to *A Christmas Carol* are the mysteries of faith which are by definition "supernatural truths whose existence cannot be known without revelation from God and whose intrinsic truth, while not contrary to reason, can never be wholly understood even after revelation" (Stravinskas 2002, 526).

Scrooge's storyline aligns with these criteria with his four ghostly visitors serving as divine ambassadors through whom "mysteries [that] are above reason, not against reason" (526) unravel during his Jesuitical journey through the *Spiritual Exercises of St. Ignatius of Loyola*.

The Founder of the Society of Jesus and His *Exercitia Spiritualia Ignatij de Loyola*

> This is how one should regard [him], as [a] servant of Christ and steward of the mysteries of God.
>
> —1 Cor 4:1 (ESV)

The fully titled *Spiritual Exercises; chosen with a view to lead Man to conquer himself, to disengage himself from the fatal influence of evil afflictions, and, with his heart thus set free, to trace out for himself the plan of a truly Christian life* were composed between 1522 and 1524 by Íñigo López de Oñaz y Loyola (1491–1556), a sixteenth-century Spanish priest, theologian, and founder of the Society of Jesus [Jesuits] in 1534. He gave the *Spiritual Exercises* as privately held retreats prior to their publication in 1548. They have since served as a handbook for spiritual directors to guide exercitants through a sequenced program of prayer, meditation, and reflection which follows the life of Jesus from his conception through his death, resurrection, and beyond. Designed as a 30-day retreat, they are divided into "four weeks which comprise each an indefinite number of days, corresponding to what the ancients called the purgative, the illuminative, and the unitive ways" (1881, xviii). Along the way of these "weeks" exercitants strengthen their spiritual musculature, for "just as well-designed physical exercises can help improve and renew one's physical life, Ignatius believed that well-designed spiritual exercises can help improve and renew one's spiritual life" (Savary 2010, ix). In the process each exercitant is compelled to choose between the two standards of good and evil. These are the very "standards" with which Scrooge grapples in *A Christmas Carol* as he is companioned by his four "spirit-guides" ("ghostly" equivalents of Ignatian spiritual directors) through the four "weeks" and themes of the *Spiritual Exercises* as follows:

Ignatian Spiritual Exercises	Themes of the Evolutionary Journey	Dickensian Spirit-Guides
First Week	Sin and God's Mercy	Jacob Marley
Second Week	Scenes in the Life of Jesus	Christmas Past
Third Week	Paschal Mystery of Jesus	Christmas Present
Fourth Week	Resurrection	Christmas Yet to Come

Figure 4.1 The four "weeks" and themes of the *Spiritual Exercises*

As his nightlong evolutionary journey unfolds Scrooge exemplifies that exercitants "are called upon to use the faculties of their understanding and their heart. They come to act for themselves . . . [and] in acting they come . . . to exercise . . . their soul and its chief powers—the[ir] understanding and the[ir] will" (vii). Although Scrooge is not a typical exercitant following the month-long *Spiritual Exercises* program of daily prayer, scripture reading, meditation, contemplation, and meeting with a spiritual director, there are adaptive equivalencies reflected in his three-day-compressed-into-three-hours encounter with his four spirit-guides. Each guide serves as an emissarial spiritual "apostle" (*apostolicus*), that is, "one sent on an errand, a messenger" (*OED* 2021a), who accompanies him through transformative inner movements common to exercitants making an Ignatian retreat.

While there is no evidence that Dickens knew anything of the *Spiritual Exercises* when he authored *A Christmas Carol*, this analysis posits that the former offers an illuminating interpretive lens through which to view the protagonist's conversionary journey. Scrooge possesses the characteristics of an exemplary exercitant, including having the caliber of "courage" and "generosity" encouraged by the retreat as he bravely confronts his flawed past, present, and future-yet-to-come while traversing the mysteries of his spiritual sojourn.

The Mysterious Jesuitical Journey of Ebenezer Scrooge

> When you read this, you can perceive my insight into the mystery of Christ.
>
> —Eph 3:4 (ESV)

While G. K. Chesterton believed that the "mystery of Christmas [wa]s in a manner identical with the mystery of Dickens" (1911, 103), and that his "greatest work may yet prove to be the perpetuation of the joyful mystery of Christmas" (1929, 335), he also wondered how he "came to associate his name chiefly in literary history with the perpetuation of a half pagan and half Catholic festival" (1911, 103). That Dickens wrote innumerable yuletide stories is indicative of his affinity for the Nativity of the Lord. *A Christmas Carol*, however, is "not really just a Christmas story. More importantly, it is an Easter story, one of resurrection" (Davis 29). Given the span of the storyline, a more representative title might be *A Holy-Day [Holiday] Hymn. In Prose. Being A Ghost Story of Christmas through Easter*. From this vantage point Scrooge's journey parallels the full course of his Dickensian New Testament—*The Life of Our Lord*—in addition to having structural alignments with the *Spiritual Exercises of St. Ignatius*. This broader perspective expands the singularity of the storyline's association solely with "carols" sung exclusively during Christmas time to incorporate "hymns" sung across multiple liturgical seasons of the Catholic Calendar—including Christmas, Epiphany, Lent, Easter, Ascension, and Pentecost. The Easter connection is particularly relevant in that "Christ's resurrection took three days, and Scrooge's rebirth felt as if it took three days" (Davis 29). Along this wider continuum Dickens' story of conversion can be considered in homophonic terminology as a prose hymn by him (Dickens) in tribute to the life of Him (Jesus) that was secularly scripted for the salvation of him (Scrooge).

While Dickens serves as an authorial mystagogue (Latin: *mystagōgus*/ Greek: μυσταγωγός) of *A Christmas Carol*, that is, "a person who instructs initiates people in religious mysteries" (*OED* 2021d), Ignatius serves synonymously as an authorial hierophant (Latin: *hierophantēs*/ Greek: ἱεροφάντης) of his *Spiritual Exercises*, that is, as "[a]n official expounder of sacred mysteries" (*OED* 2021c). Both authors structurally format their respective texts as journeys wherein mysteries unravel, and there are parallels between both as our pilgrim-exercitant fictively (re)envisions events from his life in Dickens' novella while imaginatively traveling alongside Jesus from conception through resurrection through Ignatius' handbook. Use of imagination is a key Ignatian convention, particularly the practice of imaginatively inserting oneself into scriptural scenes

> to see with the eyes of Christ. That is why he has retreatants meditate on the events of Christ's life. He wants [them] to get inside Jesus, to become so immersed in the thoughts, words, emotions, and actions of Jesus that [they] know what it is to think and live like Jesus.
> (Savary 20)

Dickens similarly (re)inserts Scrooge into scenes in which he (re)imagines his past, present, and future life during his mystical sojourn. Whether "played out" as a fictive reliving of the life of Jesus or as the fictional account of a reforming miserly misanthrope, both storylines have parabolic primacy. This is especially true of *A Christmas Carol*, because Dickens "always had really only one goal as a novelist: He wanted his novels to be 'parables,' stories that would emphasize the teachings of Christ" (Timko 2005, 30). As a parabolic tale of conversion, *A Christmas Carol* is structurally divided into five chapters styled "staves" in homage to "carols" of the holiday season. These staves parallel five stages of the classic hero's journey (the call, the other, helpers and guides, treasure, transformation) while Scrooge's "schooling" aligns with the five elements of the Ignatian Pedagogical Paradigm (context, experience, reflection, action, evaluation). Referred to as "our pilgrim-exercitant" throughout this analysis, Scrooge's interior movements coincide with these quintipartite sets of elements while reflecting aspects of the Ignatian primer listed here as his mysterious journey unfolds through the *Spiritual Exercises of St. Ignatius*:

PRIMER OF KEY IGNATIAN CONCEPTS AND PRINCIPLES

Principle/Concept	Meaning/Significance	Scrooge as Pilgrim-Exercitant
Courage and Generosity	Foundations for entering the *Spiritual Exercises*	Despite first saying he would "rather not" launch his journey, he ultimately does so with courage and generosity
Loved Sinner	No matter how sinful, one is deeply loved by a benevolent God and caring others	He discovers through his four ghost visitations that he is worthy and beloved despite his sinful past
Cura Personalis	Meaningful "care for the whole person" is emphasized	Benefits from the kindly care of all four ghostly visitors
Use of Imagination	Practice of inserting oneself into scripture stories during meditation [this enhances spiritual journey and growth]	Imaginatively inserts himself into scenes of his past, present, and future which facilitate his deepening awareness and growth towards wholeness
Two Standards of Good and Evil	One must make the conscious choice to do good over evil in life	He uses discernment to navigate good vs. evil in his past, present, and future; he gradually chooses the "good" standard by the end of the story
Desolation/ Consolation	Life has a mix of hardships and graces; it is important to savor the consolations, especially during times of desolation	The "hard" Scrooge unwittingly experiences many desolations, which the "soft" Scrooge exchanges for consolations as he journeys towards integration
Examen [examination of conscience]	Ritual daily review practiced to holistically discern divine direction in one's life	Engages frequent *examens* as he discerns his way through his past, present, and future
Discernment	Deep thoughtful decision making	Exercises discernment and decision-making as he disassociates from his inordinate miserly attachments
Detachment	Indifference towards inordinate attachments	Develops healthy impartiality to assets and generously shares with others
Cultivation of the Whole Person for social justice activism	Wholistic self-development leading to taking social action for the common good	Successfully completes his formation as a whole person dedicated to a life of service by the end of the story
Ad majórem Dei glóriam	"For the greater glory of God" [Jesuit Motto]	Incorporates this sensibility into his life and livelihood after conversion

Figure 4.2 Spiritual Exercises of St. Ignatius

Mystery the First—The Annunciation: Or, the Call of the Christmas Curmudgeon

> For now [he] see[s] in a mirror dimly, but then face to face. Now . . . know[ing] in part; then [he] shall know fully, even as [he has] been fully known.
>
> —1 Cor 13:12 (ESV)

In "Stave I: Marley's Ghost" Scrooge receives his "call" to embark on his transformational journey. This "call" typically heralds a protagonist "on the brink of a great change . . . [and t]he summons can come from any source: a friend, a relative, a stranger, an alluring object, or an impulse within the characters themselves" (Schechter and Semeiks 1992, 7–8). Scrooge's call comes from his "other" in the ghostly form of his deceased business partner, Jacob Marley. Of all his spirit-guides, Marley is the one most like himself with "a close examination reveal[ing] that the two figures are one and the same" (8). In effect, "the two men had always been interchangeably one" (Newey 2016, 23) and, relationally, they form a Dickensian doppelgänger duo bridging the nether world of one with the present world of the other. Thus, when Dickens describes Scrooge, he is also describing Marley:

> Oh! But he was a tight-fisted hand at the grindstone . . . a squeezing, wrenching, grasping, scraping, clutching, covetous old sinner! Hard and sharp as flint, from which no steel had ever struck out generous fire; secret and self-contained, and solitary as an oyster. The cold within him froze his old features, nipped his pointed nose, shrivelled his cheek, stiffened his gait; made his eyes red, his thin lips blue; and spoke out shrewdly in his grating voice.
>
> (Dickens 3)

The only difference between them is that, while one still lives, his "other" is dead. Since dying unshriven Marley has been encumbered for seven years by a chain made of "cash-boxes, keys, padlocks, ledgers, deeds, and heavy purses wrought in steel" (25). Noticing, Scrooge tremblingly beseeches, "You are fettered . . . Tell me why?" (30). The ghost replies, "I wear the chain I forged in life . . . I made it link by link, and yard by yard; I girded it of my own free will, and of my own free will I wore it" (30).

As Scrooge's "other" Marley symbolically "represents precisely that dark, unlived, and generally unacknowledged part of the central character's personality, kept hidden away from the eyes of the world and often from the protagonist's own awareness" (Schechter and Semeiks 96). Determined that the same fate should not befall Scrooge, Marley explains, "I am here to-night to warn you, that you have yet a chance and hope of escaping my fate. A chance and hope of my procuring, Ebenezer." Scrooge confirms this benevolence saying, "You were always a good friend to me . . . Thank'ee!" But at the prospect of being "haunted . . . by Three Spirits" (Dickens 34) Scrooge stutters: "I—I think I'd rather not" (Dickens 34). Undaunted, however, Marley forewarns, "Without their visits . . . you cannot hope to shun the path I tread. Expect the first tomorrow, when the bell tolls One" (35). Underscoring Marley's coercive kindness is the Ignatian principle of *cura personalis* (care of the whole person) which he benevolently bestows upon his dear friend to propel him toward salvation.

Mirroring the thematic focus of *Sin and God's Mercy* during the First Week of the *Spiritual Exercises*, this encounter centers on three significant meditations of our pilgrim–exercitant. In the first he will reflect on the benevolence of God, in the second he will discern how his patterns of sin have obstructed his freedom in experiencing a loving relationship with the Lord, and in the third he will embrace the truth of being a "loved sinner" who is called by a loving creator to full humanity through following the exemplary path of the Jesus. This introductory process, known as the Principle and Foundation of the *Spiritual Exercises*, underscores that

> Man is created . . . to praise, reverence, and serve the Lord his God, and by this means to arrive at eternal salvation. All . . . objects . . . on the earth are created for the benefit of man, and to be useful to him, as means to his final end; hence his obligation to use [them] . . . according as the bring him nearer to that end. Hence we must above all endeavour to establish in ourselves a complete indifference towards all created things.
>
> (Ignatius 1881, 21–22)

Scrooge will discover the importance of detachment as he liberates himself from his miserly ways by the end of *A Christmas Carol*, and Marley's ghost represents the fundamental import of the "the Principle and Foundation serv[ing] as a kind of screening process" (Dyckman, Garvin, and Liebert 2001, 90) for his transformational journey. He is firm in establishing how critical it is for Scrooge to undertake and endure what lays ahead and, after succeeding in screening our pilgrim-exercitant into his "spiritual exercises" the specter retreats saying, "[l]ook to see me no more; and look that, for your own sake, you remember what has passed between us!" (Dickens 35). Our pilgrim-exercitant accepts his "call" and will embark on a journey of remembrance recall reflecting the Principle and Foundation being "intended to evoke a present or remembered experience [which] . . . 'grounds' a person in graced self-awareness and God-awareness, which is food for the journey" (Dyckman et al. 103–104).

Mystery the Second—The First Visitation (Spirit-Guide of Christmas Past)

> We were gentle among you.
> —1 Thes 2:7 (ESV)

In "Stave II: The First of the Three Spirits" the Ghost of Christmas Past appears as the premier helper spirit-guide for our pilgrim-exercitant. On the hero's journey "helpers and guides are . . . [f]igures who assist the protagonist along the difficult road . . . [and] through this unforeseen support, the main characters learn; they move on; they come closer to their goals" (Schechter and Semeiks 9). This first spirit-guide "is accompanied by theophany, a light that emanates from the head of the ghost" (Newey 173) and serves as initiator of Scrooge's enlightening journey. In response to his inquiry regarding "what business [has] brought him there" (Dickens 45), the spirit-guide replies, "Your welfare!" Noting Scrooge's resistance, the spirit-guide clarifies and commands, "Your reclamation, then. Take heed! . . . Rise! and walk with me" (45–46). In keeping with the cultivation of *cura personalis* common to Ignatian spiritual direction the spirit-guide's "voice was soft and gentle" (44) as it "gazed upon [Scrooge] mildly . . . [and had a] gentle touch" (47) while beckoning his hesitant pilgrim-exercitant to "'Bear but a touch of my hand *there*' . . . laying it upon his heart, 'and you shall be upheld in more than this!'" (46). They then embark on their travels back in time to Scrooge's childhood, his young adult employment with Mr. Fezziwig, and his loving, though failed, relationship with Belle.

The emotive impact of these visitations mirrors the internal movements of the Second Week of the *Spiritual Exercises* covering *Scenes in the Life of Jesus*. During this phase of the retreat exercitants imaginatively accompany Jesus from birth through his ministry and engage in discernment, which ultimately inspires choosing to do the Lord's work on earth. Although still in their infancy, Scrooge's interior movements are profound during this first visitation as he remembers many scenes he had blocked from his past. As he journeys with his spirit-guide, he recalls his boyhood practice of imaginative thinking to overcome his isolation at school. As previously indicated, the use of imagination is integral to Ignatian spirituality, and was inspired while the knightly Ignatius recuperated from a debilitating shattered leg injury incurred in 1521 during the Battle of Pamplona. Bedridden for months with access to only two books—one on the life of Jesus, the other one on the lives of the saints—Ignatius repeatedly re-read them and adopted the habit of imaginatively inserting himself into various scenes.

Scrooge's childhood survival habit of imaginatively inserting himself into literary works populated by his favorite protagonist–friends reflects

Ignatius' belief that God speaks to human beings as much through imagination as He does through their thoughts and memories. Although he endured much "desolation" while in school, Scrooge experiences "consolation" as he fondly recalls his intimate imaginative time with his childhood fictional friends—Ali Baba, Valentine, Orson, the Sultan's Groom, Robin Crusoe, Friday, and more. After re-experiencing several scenes from his past, Scrooge is so overcome by his memories that he begs, "Spirit! . . . remove me from this place . . . I cannot bear it! . . . Leave me! Take me back. Haunt me no longer" (Dickens 72). Having endured these necessarily painful memories from his past, our pilgrim exercitant returns home to await his next ghostly visitor with a paradoxical mix of reticence and anticipation.

Mystery the Third—The Second Visitation (Spirit-Guide of Christmas Present)

> Behold! I tell you a mystery. . . [and you shall] . . . be changed, in a moment, in the twinkling of an eye.
> —1 Cor 15:51–52 (ESV)

In "Stave III: The Second of the Three Spirits" Scrooge embarks on the leg of his journey paralleling the Third Week of the *Spiritual Exercises*. This "week" focuses on the Paschal Mystery of Jesus, including his last supper, passion, and death. Scrooge awakens from his previous night's wanderings wondering about his next helper spirit-guide and "being prepared for almost anything, he was not by any means prepared for nothing [as] . . . a strange voice called him by his name, and bade him enter. He obeyed . . . entered timidly, and hung his head before this Spirit" (Dickens 78). His evolutionary progress is evident because "he was not the dogged Scrooge he had been; and though the Spirit's eyes were clear and kind, he did not like to meet them. . . [although he gradually] reverently did so" (78). The ghost's evident benevolence facilitates Scrooge's now characteristic "courage" and "generosity" as he submits: "Spirit . . . conduct me where you will. I went last night on compulsion, and I learnt a lesson which is working now. To-night, if you have aught to teach me, let me profit by it" (Dickens 78). This phase of his journey has the harsh immediacy of Scrooge inserting himself into the "present" of his actual life wherein he visits to the holiday homes of his impoverished employee, Bob Cratchit, and his nearly estranged nephew, Fred. His spirit-guide also exposes him to the waifish figures representing "Ignorance" and "Want" of whom he asks: "Have they no reference or resource?" (120). These wanton figures, along with his emergent regrets regarding his treatment of Bob Cratchit's family and his deceased sister's son, provoke his thoughtful and remorseful contemplation. Befitting the experiential unfolding of the *Spiritual Exercises*, our conscience-stricken pilgrim-exercitant begins to juxtapose scenes from good works of the Lord with contrasting scenes of his own miserable miserly life. Comparisons reveal the harmful impact he has on those around him. Witnessing the consequences of his actions paves the painful path of his personal "passion" as it parallels the *Passion of Jesus* leading to his crucifixion. Although Scrooge will not suffer the same physical fate of the Lord, his passion–experience also ends in death—a symbolic one after which he will be born anew in the next phase of his journey.

Mystery the Fourth—The Third Visitation (Spirit-Guide of Christmas Yet to Come)

> For I want you to . . . reach all the riches of full assurance of understanding and the knowledge of God's mystery, which is Christ, in whom are hidden all the treasures of wisdom and knowledge.
> —Col 2:1–3 (ESV)

In "Stave IV: The Last of the Spirits," Scrooge obtains his "treasure" which on a hero's journey may be "a literal treasure, an actual object of great monetary value. . . [and it] is always a priceless *psychological gain*: an expanded consciousness, a saving insight" (Schechter and Semeiks 9). The foreshadowed grace of our pilgrim-exercitant's treasure beyond measure aligns with the Fourth Week of the *Spiritual Exercises,* which focuses on *Resurrection.* Scrooge admits upon meeting his third helper spirit-guide:

> Ghost of the Future! I fear you more than any spectre I have seen. But as I know your purpose is to do me good, and as I hope to live to be another man from what I was, I am prepared to bear you company, and do it with a thankful heart.
>
> (Dickens 123)

This more temperate pilgrim-exercitant thoroughly reflects the requisite "courage" and "generosity" of the *Spiritual Exercises* and, although fearful, he surrenders, saying: "Lead on! Lead on! The night is waning fast, and it is precious time to me, I know. Lead on, Spirit!" (123). This willingness bodes well for his imminent conversion as he bravely faces the transformative tribulations ahead.

Scrooge's final helper spirit-guide is the one most in keeping with the charism of "holy listening" in Ignatian spiritual direction because it remains utterly silent. When he appeals, " 'Will you not speak to me?' . . .

It gave him no reply" (123). This reciprocally rigorous "silence" demonstrates that

> spiritual directors, like all good teachers, need to live with the silence, not merely to endure it but to be comfortable with it. If [they] are to assist people in the work of knowing and being known, to define themselves authentically and spontaneously in relation to God and their world, then [they] must be willing to wait with [exercitants] and often to acknowledge that there are no words . . . [even though the s]ilence is rarely comfortable.
>
> (Guenther 1992, 79)

The synergistic silence between our pilgrim-exercitant and this spirit-guide prods him to probe within his inner mysteries for needful answers. Through his *examen* (examination of conscience) he learns the most vital lessons of his journey—the terrain of which facilitates his living into the significance of his Dickensian naming. His forename derives from the biblical scripture referencing the Eben-Ezer stone which Samuel erected and made sacrifice upon the evening before battling the Philistines: "[He] took a stone and set it up . . . named it Ebenezer, saying, 'Thus far the LORD has helped us'" (1 Sm 7:12 NIV). He and the Israelites subsequently won the fight. The name Ebenezer means "stone of help" and it is "[u]sed appellatively in religious literature in figurative phrases, alluding to the sentiment 'Hitherto hath the Lord helped us'" (*OED* 2021b). Because his surname bears phonetic resonance with the word "scourge," Dickens may have chosen it to reflect Scrooge's endurance of great suffering. As he undergoes the rigors of this phase of the *Spiritual Exercises*, he bravely burrows deep within the mires of his miserly ways and suffers agonizing afflictions and a thorough scourging. The result is that the "mean old Ebenezer Scrooge, whose first name chimes with 'squeezer' as well as 'geezer,' [and] whose last name is a combination of 'screw' and 'gouge'" (Atwood 2008, 87) begins to transform into his better self. His name has profound significance when he comes upon the "Eben-Ezer [tomb]stone" portending his unshriven death. So scourged is Scrooge that he counters its imminence with a powerful prophetic vow: "I will live in the Past, Present, and the Future. The Spirits of all three strive within me. I will not shut out the lessons they teach" (Dickens 151). Our pilgrim-exercitant beseeches his spirit-guide, "Oh tell me how I can sponge away the writing on this stone!" (151). His proactive and accountable phrasing affirms the integrity of his conversion-in-progress as he pleads, not that the decedent's name be *expunged*, but rather *sponged*. The baptismal sacramentality of sponging/scouring away the sins of his past foreshadows his emergence as a *tabula rasa* awash with the promise of rebirth.

This cemetery scene parallels the meditation in the *Spiritual Exercises* on the *Agony in the Garden of Gethsemane*. Mirroring the strife of Jesus, our pilgrim-exercitant, "[i]n his [own] agony . . . caught the spectral hand . . . it sought to free itself, but he was strong in his entreaty, and detained it. The Spirit, stronger yet, repulsed him" (151). This resistance reflects Ignatius' indication that during the latter days of Jesus' life the divine was hidden, as well as the fact that a spiritual director must be "an S.O.B. with a heart, when necessary. That was the precise role all of the Phantoms assumed, especially the Ghost of the Future, to give Scrooge the independence he needed" (Cusumano 1996, 44) for full conversion. Just as Jesus suffered the traumatic events of his Paschal Mystery as completely human sans divine intervention, Scrooge also undergoes his mystical experience with his "immovable as ever" (Dickens 151) silent spirit-guide as all alone as the Lord. Utterly surrendered and mirroring Jesus' supplicatory stance, he held "up his hands in a last prayer to have his fate reversed, [and] he saw an alteration in the Phantom's hood and dress. It shrunk, collapsed, and dwindled down into a bedpost" (151). Left to contemplate the complexities of his conversion Scrooge will soon awaken to find his "death" stone removed and himself unencumbered by his inordinate worldly attachments as prescribed in the *Spiritual Exercises*.

Mystery the Fifth—The Transformation and Transcension

> The mystery was made known to me by revelation . . . When you read this, you can perceive my insight into the mystery of Christ. . . as it has now been revealed.
>
> —Eph 3:2–4 (ESV)

In "Stave V: The End of It," our pilgrim–exercitant returns from his imaginative meditations and mystical wanderings are transformed. In this phase of the hero's journey

> characters are transfigured by the quest they have undertaken and completed. The[ir] lives . . . may be radically different from what they were before, or the protagonists may see everything differently: though the outward circumstances of their lives may seem the same, nothing they look at will be untouched by what they have been through. The ideal outcome of the hero's quest is a profound experience of rebirth and inner liberation—a renewed sense of life's limitless possibilities.
>
> (Schechter and Semeiks 9)

Having transcended his past misdeeds, Scrooge awakens from his ordeal recognizing, "Yes! . . . the Time before him was his own, to make amends in" (Dickens 152), while reiterating in supplication:

> I will live in the Past, the Present, and the Future! . . . The Spirits of all Three shall strive within me. Oh Jacob Marley! Heaven, and the Christmas Time be praised for this! I say it on my knees, old Jacob; on my knees!
>
> (152)

His transcendence transports him between the Ignatian dyadic polarities of consolation and desolation as he finds himself "laughing and crying in the same breath" (153) He is overjoyed with consolation to be alive with his bed curtains intact. Symbolically these coverings represent the cast-off winding sheet (shroud) of his dying unto his old self in exchange for the swaddling clothes of his newborn self. He euphorically exclaims, "I'm quite a baby. Never mind. I don't care. I'd rather be a baby. Hallo! Whoop! Hallo here!" (154). This grand celebratory moment represents "two births . . . that of Jesus, and that of the reborn baby Scrooge" (Atwood 171).

Rebirth, reformation, and resurrection are the primary points of the profoundly powerful experiences of both *A Christmas Carol* and the *Spiritual Exercises*, and

> to understand the titanic transformation that took place in Scrooge's wretchedly cold, dark life is to understand the power of even a miniscule amount of Christ's true light when it is allowed to enter our lives . . . It made all the difference for Scrooge.
>
> (Cusumano 29)

By the end of his conversionary journey our former Christmas curmudgeon achieves the Ignatian ideal of whole personhood and is prepared to enact social justice that is hallmark of the Jesuit tradition. A future of continued evolutionary formation, however, still remains ahead for Scrooge, whose lifelong success in sustaining his transformation depends on the wholistic merging of his life and moral view with that of his spiritual doppelgänger—Jesus Christ. Having completed the rigors of his "spiritual exercises" and vowing to live meaningfully "in the Past, the Present, and the Future," our pilgrim-exercitant is well prepared for the remainder of his life-long journey.

Poised at this penultimate point of the *Spiritual Exercises* Scrooge can say to the Lord

> at the end of the last week, 'Since thou hast given Thyself entirely to me, let me now belong wholly to Thee: take me; keep me!' *Suscipe,*

> *Do ine, universam mean libertatem!* If he says at first to Jesus Christ, as Jesus Christ Himself said to His Father, 'All Thine is mine;' he adds at the end, 'All that is mine is thine!' The gift is reciprocal, the exchange perfect, the transformation is complete.
>
> (Ignatius 1881, xx)

This exchange, known in popular parlance as the *Prayer of St. Ignatius*, states:

> Take, O Lord, and receive all my entire liberty, my memory, my understanding, and my whole will. All that I am, all that I have, Thou hast given me, and I give it back to Thee, to be disposed of according to Thy good pleasure. Give me only Thy love and Thy grace; with these I am rich enough.
>
> (236)

This prayer, also known as *The Suscipe*, sums up the life our pilgrim-exercitant lives out in his future who, as confirmed by Bob Cratchit at the end of *A Christmas Carol*:

> Scrooge was better than his word. He did it all, and infinitely more.... He became as good a friend, as good a master, and as good a man, as the good old city knew, or any other good old city, town, or borough, in the good old world.... His own heart laughed: and that was quite enough for him.
>
> (Dickens 165)

While embodying the merged purposes of the mystagogue and the hierophant of *A Christmas Carol* and *Spiritual Exercises*, respectively, our once misanthropic miser turned penitent pilgrim-exercitant realizes that "seeing oneself as a unique and precious creative act of God gives a joy that does not come from success or external validation" (Dyckman et al. 107). At "the end of it" this (slightly adapted) closing paragraph of the publisher's Preface to the 1881 edition of Ignatius' handbook serves equally for both authors in expressing the doctrinal desires of their two texts:

> May th[ese] book[s] be the means of making the teachings of the holy founder of the Society of Jesus [and the author of *A Christmas Carol*] better appreciated; may [they] ... conduce to the greater glory of God [*Ad majórem Dei glóriam*], to the honour of our Lord and Savior Jesus Christ, and the salvation of many souls!
>
> (Catholic Publication Society, xxv)

The inclusive universality of this aim is best summed up by Tiny Tim's affecting invocation: "God bless, Us, Every One!" (Dickens 166). Even though the elusive mystery of the theological Dickens remains unsolved, it is more significant to recognize in the end that the

> beauty and the real blessing of the story do not lie in the mechanical plot of it, [or] the repentance of Scrooge . . . they lie in the great furnace of real happiness that glows through Scrooge and everything around him; that great furnace, the heart of Dickens.
> (Chesterton 1989, 137)

His was a heart demonstrated by this analysis to have been a [c]atholic one committed to the universal transformation of all persons into seekers of the common good in keeping with the Ignatian ethos.

Note

1. Letter to John Forster, September 30 (?), 1844 in Hartley (143–44).

Bibliography

"apostle, n." *OED Online*. 2021a. Oxford University Press. https://www-oed-com.proxy.seattleu.edu/view/Entry/9427?rskey=NCXk4W&result=1.

Atwood, Margaret. *Payback: Debt and the Shadow Side of Wealth*. Toronto: House of Anansi, 2008.

Chesterton, G. K. "Charles Dickens." In *The Encyclopædia Britannica*, Vol. 24, edited by Gavin, James Louis, Franklin Henry Hooper, and Warren E. Cox, 331–35. New York: The Encyclopædia Britannica, 1929.

———. "Christmas Books." In *Appreciations and Criticisms of the Works of Charles Dickens*, 103–14. Whitefish: Kessinger Publishing, 1911. https://books.google.com/books?id=VWE6AQAAMAAJ.

———. Chesterton on Dickens. In *The Collected Works of G. K. Chesterton*, vol. 15. San Francisco: Ignatius Press, 1989.

Colledge, Gary. *God and Charles Dickens: Recovering the Christian Voice of a Classic Author*. Ada, MI: Brazos Press, 2012.

Cox, Don Richard, and Elliot L. Gilbert. "Scrooge's Conversion." *PMLA* 90, no. 5 (1975): 922–24.

Cusumano, Joseph D. *Transforming Scrooge: Dickens' Blueprint for a Spiritual Awakening*. Woodbury: Llewellyn Publications, 1996.

Davis, Paul Benjamin. *The Lives and Times of Ebenezer Scrooge*. New Haven, CT: Yale University Press, 1990.

Dickens, Charles. *A Christmas Carol. In Prose. Being A Ghost Story of Christmas*. London: Chapman and Hall, 1843. https://books.google.com/books?id=MlMHAAAAQAAJ.

———. *Hard Times: For These Times*. London: Bradbury & Evans, 1854. https://books.google.com/books?id=X9RVAAAAcAAJ.

———. *The Life of Our Lord*. New York: Simon and Schuster, 1934.

Dyckman, Katherine Marie, Mary Garvin, and Elizabeth Liebert. *The Spiritual Exercises Reclaimed: Uncovering Liberating Possibilities for Women*. Mahwah: Paulist Press, 2001.

"Ebenezer, n." *OED Online*. 2021b. Oxford University Press. https://www-oed-com.proxy.seattleu.edu/view/Entry/59180?redirectedFrom=Ebenezer.

Guenther, Margaret. *Holy Listening: The Art of Spiritual Direction*. Lanham: Cowley Publications, 1992.

Hanna, Robert C. "God and Charles Dickens: Recovering the Christian Voice of a Classic Author." *The Dickensian 109*, no. 490 (2013): 181, 183, and 116. ProQuest. http://ezproxy.liberty.edu/login?qurl=https%3A%2F%2Fwww.proquest.com%2Fscholarly-journals%2Fgod-charles-dickens-recovering-christian-voice%2Fdocview%2F1439821470%2Fse-2%3Faccountid%3D12085.

Hartley, Jenny, ed. *The Selected Letters of Charles Dickens*. Oxford: Oxford University Press, 2012.

"hierophant, n." *OED Online*. 2021c. Oxford University Press. https://www-oed-com.proxy.seattleu.edu/view/Entry/86833?redirectedFrom=hierophant+.

Ignatius, Saint. *Manresa: Or, the Spiritual Exercises of St. Ignatius, for General Use*. New York: Catholic Publication Society, 1881.

"mystagogue, n." *OED Online*. 2021d. Oxford University Press. https://www-oed-com.proxy.seattleu.edu/view/Entry/124629?redirectedFrom=mystagogue.

Newey, Vincent. *The Scriptures of Charles Dickens: Novels of Ideology, Novels of the Self*. London: Routledge, 2016.

Oddie, William. "The Night Dickens had a Marian Vision." *Catholic Herald*, February 15, 2012. https://catholicherald.co.uk/the-night-dickens-had-a-marian-vision/.

Savary, Louis M. *The New Spiritual Exercises: In the Spirit of Pierre Teilhard de Chardin*. Mahwah: Paulist Press, 2010.

Schechter, Harold, and Jonna Gormely Semeiks, eds. *Discoveries: Fifty Stories of the Quest*. Hoboken, NJ: John Wiley and Sons, 1992.

Simpson, J. A., Weiner, E. S. C, and Oxford University Press. *The Oxford English Dictionary*. 2nd ed. Prepared by J. A. Simpson and E. S. C. Weiner. Oxford: Oxford University Press, 1989.

Stravinskas, Peter. *Catholic Dictionary, Revised*. Huntington, IN: Our Sunday Visitor, 2002.

Timko, Michael. "Ebenezer Scrooge's Conversion." *UU World: The Magazine of the Unitarian Universalist Association* 19, no. 5 (Winter 2005): 80–84.

Wilson, Angus and A. E. Dyson. "Charles Dickens." In *The English Novel*, edited by Cedric Watts, 53–72. Eastbourne: Sussex Books, 1976.

Wilson, A. N. *The Mystery of Charles Dickens*. New York: Harper, 2020.

5 "For Whom the Bell Tolls"
Dickens' *Barnaby Rudge*

Julie Donovan

Set amid the Gordon Riots of June 1780, which disputed Parliament's passing of the 1778 Catholic Relief Act (to be identified later), Dickens' *Barnaby Rudge: A Tale of the Riots of Eighty* (1841) represents one of his most vivid engagements with religion. Scholarship has noted the novel's religious aspects, but there remains a lacuna—Dickens' use of bells—which deserves some critical and theological examination of Dickens' works.[1]

Barnaby Rudge was first serialized in the weekly periodical, *Master Humphrey's Clock*. When he introduces the novel, Master Humphrey notes "the voice of the deep and distant bell of St. Paul's as it struck the hour of midnight" (434). As he prepares to read the manuscript of *Barnaby Rudge*, Master Humphrey finds the bell's portentous sound fitting for the story that will unfold: "This . . . to be opened to such music, should be a tale where London's face by night is darkly seen" (434). The significance of bells in Dickens' novel is not confined to this opening remark but rather sustained as bells form a means of framing and punctuating his narrative. They not only represent distinctly religious objects but also serve more secular purposes that have, nevertheless, a religious provenance. Dickens has them ring to reflect the varied soundscape of his plot, to signal danger and celebration, to order servants around, and to act as moral arbiters. They propel the narrative, conveying the vagaries of a changing society struggling to contend with the contiguity of Catholic and Protestant histories.

Bells are massive, loud, technological creations, bound up in capitalist modernity. The memorable bells of the nursery rhyme "London Bells" (commonly known as "Oranges and Lemons") reflects this in their questions about owing money and getting rich: "When will you pay me? / Ring the bells at Old Bailey; /When I am rich, /Ring the bells of Fleetditch" (1815 [1794], 23–24).[2] That the churches in the rhyme are located in London reflects the city's commercial relevance, still potent today, as does the historical tradition of ringing a bell to signal the beginning of the trading day on the London Stock Exchange (a tradition adopted by the New York Stock Exchange on Wall Street).

DOI: 10.4324/9781003156611-6

Bells are also venerable and old. While there is no exact date available as to when bells were first used by the English church, there is evidence that points to large bells existing as far back as 750 AD; prior to that, portable handbells were more suitable for the then smaller, more disparate, and less established congregations (Walters 1977, 4) Initially, bells were the products of medieval monastic and church production, often cast at pits situated in a church or in its grounds; over time, they were manufactured on a more industrial scale, and centralized foundries became common when railways allowed easier transportation (175). The Whitechapel Bell Foundry in east London (which made Philadelphia's Liberty Bell) dates to 1570, and at the time of its closure in 2017, was said to be probably the oldest manufacturing company in Britain (216).

Master Humphrey's reference to St. Paul's bell reinforces an anomaly. Bells somehow managed to survive the Reformation with its discard and devaluation of Roman Catholic objects connected to worship; in fact, St. Paul's is notable for not being a Catholic church that was converted to Protestant use, such as were other well-known English cathedrals like Durham, Winchester, Canterbury, or York Minster. As a truly Protestant edifice completed in post-Reformation 1710, St. Paul's bell represents what was deemed acceptable from the old faith, because bells remained important instruments of Protestant ritual and expression (Marsh 2010, 467).[3] Peter Ackroyd describes the survival of bells as intrinsic to the London soundscape: "It might be surmised that the effect of the bells ended with the Reformation, when London was last a Catholic city, but all the evidence suggests that the citizens continued to be addicted to them" (2003, 71). If not addicted, then Dickens was at least deeply impressed by the way in which St. Paul's bell, and other bells, spoke to events in London and beyond.[4]

The continuous use of bells after the Reformation is examined by Christopher Marsh in *Music and Society in Early Modern England*, where he reports that the bell "gave English Protestantism of all shades something of a headache. How could its deeply customary sound and associations possibly be incorporated into the new religious order?" (2010, 467). Bells were successfully incorporated into the Protestant belief system, somehow evading the fate of other religious objects like rosaries, statues, and stained-glass windows deemed as detestable popish accessories. When Henry VIII died in 1547, his son, Edward VI, under the influence of the Archbishop of Canterbury, Thomas Cranmer, made more concerted efforts to remove Catholic objects from places of worship. Some bells were confiscated, and the Edwardian injunction of 1547 banned bells during church services, with the exception of a single bell to signify the imminence of a sermon (Brown 2017, 637). Larger bells were often not removed from churches. Since they were usually located beyond the visual range of onlookers, they probably presented less offense to Protestant eyes. As for Protestant ears, nothing else was as pragmatic for local functions such as indicating time, curfews, and sounding alarm in case of fire or attack (O'Regan 2016, 338). The latter meant that bells had been useful in fortresses and castles, though they still had a primarily ecclesiastical purpose (Creighton 2005, 26; Williams 1992, 23). Murray R. Schafer writes of the bell's capacity to act as an "acoustic calendar," observing how the church bell was preferable to the clock dial: "to see the dial one must face it, while the bell sends the sounds of time rolling out uniformly in all directions" (1977, 55). Bells were also clear communicators when there was no mass literacy. Even though Catholic traditions of baptizing bells and inscribing them with saints' names ended in favor of inscriptions of donors, bell manufacturers, or national events like St. George's Day, ensured that bells remained a loud yet somehow subtle link with England's Catholic past.[5] By the eighteenth century, how much bells remained paramount in the public imagination is demonstrated in one of the most popular poems of the era, Thomas Gray's *Elegy in a Country Churchyard*, which opens with a resonant line: "The curfew tolls the knell of parting day" (1827 [1751]). Gray's phrase indicates a practical purpose of bells—to control communities through curfews—but there was also represented a reassuring sense of regularity, common understanding, and social accord.

Because of the powerful contrasts in their sound registers, bells were versatile instruments. While the peal of bells joyously sounded the celebration of marriage, they could also sound the somber tones of grief, the latter so memorable that, as Marsh observes, "the passing bell and death knell provided one of England's most familiar sonic signatures" (474). Marsh suggests that bells essentially became a means of compromise, "metal mediators, filling the gap left by the saints" (478). Changes to the bell-ringing calendar came to reflect Protestant rather than Catholic victories. November 5, for example, marked the failed Gunpowder Plot to blow up Parliament (Cressy 1989, 141–70). Only Puritans thoroughly objected to the sound of bells as sinister popish sounds (Tombs 2016, 183). When the nineteenth century came around, it was observed that

> England is frequently said to be known as the Ringing Isle, from the fact that wherever the stranger or foreigner turns, or stays, in this land, he is sure to meet with the well-tuned bells, and well-timed changes, pealing forth from our venerable church towers and steeples.
> (Goslin 1881, 7)

Dickens was attuned to the familiar presence and sound of bells forming a distinctive part of the urban and rural soundscape; it was a presence that strongly appealed to his expansive imagination.

Following the *Master Humphrey* framing device featuring London's famous bell, the opening of *Barnaby Rudge* further establishes the bell as a frame of reference upon which Dickens will rely throughout his novel.

In the village of Chigwell, Essex, a bell features in a ghostly story, fittingly told by Chigwell's bell-ringer, Solomon Daisy. Sitting in the Maypole Inn, Daisy recounts a night when he was ordered to toll the passing bell for an old man recently deceased but was halted in his task: "At that minute there rang—not that bell, for I hardly touched the rope—but another!" (240). Edgar Allan Poe praised the power of this scene in his review of Dickens' novel: "The belfry man in the lonely church at midnight, about to toll the 'passing bell,' is struck with horror at hearing the solitary note of another, and awaits, aghast, a repetition of the sound" (1978 [1841], 218).[6] As the wind eerily carried the sound, Daisy considered the event some kind of haunting: "I had heard of corpse candles, and at least I persuaded myself that this must be a corpse bell tolling of itself at midnight for the dead" (Dickens 240). Daisy's likening of the bell to "corpse candles," flickering flames considered an omen of death, is borne out the next morning when Reuben Haredale, former owner of the Warren, is found murdered in his bed. In Reuben's hand, Daisy notes, "was a piece of the cord attached to an alarm-bell outside the roof, which hung in his room and had been cut asunder, no doubt by the murderer when he seized it" (240). The Haredales are a Catholic family, and the murder of its patriarch hastens the decline of the Warren from a valuable property in good condition to a dreary and dilapidated place, with "whole suites of rooms shut up and mouldering to ruin" (4). Reuben's brother, Geoffrey Haredale, who inherited the Warren, rues his family's decline: "We are a fallen house" (75). The bell that sounded his brother's death also sounds failing Catholic fortunes regarding ownership and wealth in Protestant England.

Geoffrey Haredale also owns the Maypole, a property in close proximity to the Warren; like the Warren, the Maypole has seen better days than its current "melancholy aspect of grandeur in decay" (291). Failing Catholic fortunes are further associated with the Maypole when the narrator divulges that it was built during the days of Henry VIII, whose break with the Catholic church entailed appropriating Catholic property. Local lore suggests that Henry's daughter, Elizabeth I, stayed at the Maypole, but there is another non-Protestant virgin queen also evoked by the inn's name. The Maypole brings to mind the Queen of the May, the Virgin Mary, celebrated in the month of May since medieval times (Warner 1976, 283). Despite the pagan provenance of maypoles, the church of the Middle Ages adapted to rituals around the maypole that often involved drinking and Morris dancing with bells (Morris dancers usually wear bells around their shins).[7] Chaucer's poem, *The Chance of Dice* (1440), refers to a maypole at Cornhill, London, which was higher than the adjacent church of St. Andrew Undershaft and was erected by its parishioners every year (Hutton 1996, 233). In a post-Reformation world, maypoles were more frequently viewed as encouraging debauched behavior. Evangelical Protestants were particularly inimical, and the Cornhill maypole was eventually "sawed up and burned after a preacher denounced it as an idol" (235). By the nineteenth century, Benjamin Disraeli encouraged May festivals as a symbol of social harmony. Keen to emulate what he saw as the social cohesion of the Middle Ages, John Ruskin also promoted May Queen celebrations (297). The potency of the simultaneously attractive and repellent pagan-Catholic past is memorably captured in Nathaniel Hawthorne's short story, "The Maypole of Merry Mount," which describes revelers around a maypole with "bells appended to their garment, tinkling with a silvery sound" (1832, 108). Even across the Atlantic Ocean, the religious past keeps ringing. Hawthorne's Puritan characters disapproved of the merry tinkling of bells, but Philadelphia's Liberty Bell would become a powerful symbol of the new Republic. John Pass and John Stow recast the bell after it cracked and had their names, together with a quote from Leviticus 25:10, inscribed on it: "Proclaim Liberty throughout all the land unto the inhabitants thereof" (Nash 2010, xi).

The action of *Barnaby Rudge* increasingly revolves around the Gordon Riots, spearheaded by the head of the Protestant Association, Lord George Gordon. While the protested Catholic Relief Act did not grant freedom of worship to Catholics or allow them to hold public office, it did seek to remove certain limitations in force since the seventeenth century through penal laws. Limitations on Catholic land ownership were to be relaxed, and Catholics were to be permitted preaching and publishing rights. The Catholic Relief Act also enabled Catholics to join the army by removing the requirement to take an oath of allegiance to the British crown, which had meant accepting the authority of the Church of England (Haywood and Seed 2012, 2). Gordon claimed that Lord North's government passed the Catholic Relief Act not out of compassion for Catholics, but for the purpose of using Irish and Highlander troops to fight American colonists, with whom Gordon sympathized as fellow Protestants battling injustice (Seed 2012, 82). Determined to stop any Catholic relief being passed at Westminster, Gordon garnered considerable support, encouraged in his successful opposition of Catholic relief in Scotland, where the government had to retreat from proposed reforms. Gordon repeated his protests in London, where a march to parliament was planned, a march that would present a petition of some 40,000 signatures (Haywood and Seed 1). After a peaceful start, the march descended into the Gordon Riots, which besieged London from June 2 to June 9, 1788, and which remain, to this day, one of the most serious disturbances that London has ever encountered.

John Bowen writes that the Gordon Riots revealed how "two of the major forces that shaped national policy were at work: the fear of insurrection and popular anti-Catholicism" (2003, xix). In the preface to *Barnaby Rudge*, Dickens declared that he had "no sympathy with the Romish church" (1866, viii). Yet popular anti-Catholicism as exhibited by the Gordon Riots is savaged by Dickens in his narrative as early on as in the preface, where he states "that it is begotten of intolerance and persecution; that it is senseless, besotted, inveterate, and unmerciful" (vii). At this stage in his writing career, Dickens did not concur with alarming cries against the encroaching power of Rome manifested in the Oxford Movement, which heightened following John Henry Newman's conversion to Catholicism in 1845 (Pattison 1991, 3). As time went on, however, anti-Catholicism does emerge in Dickens' work. In *Pictures from Italy* (1846) for example, Dickens notes a pair of Jesuits "slinking noiselessly about, in pairs, like black cats" (57). Dennis Walder writes that "it is too easy to place Dickens merely in terms of simple-minded anti-popery" (2007, 92). *Barnaby Rudge*, argues Walder, demonstrates "a liberal Protestant attitude towards Roman Catholics" (92). But Walder also concedes that in *Pictures from Italy* and in *A Child's History of England* (1851–1853), Dickens displayed "powerful antipathies towards the characteristic features of the Catholic religion" (93). In *Popular Anti-Catholicism in Mid-Victorian England*, Denis G. Paz calls *A Child's History of England* Dickens' "most sustained attack" (1992, 69) on Catholicism. The timing of Dickens' varying attitudes was no doubt related to the so-called Papal Aggression of 1850–1852, when Pius IX restored the Catholic hierarchy in England, appointing Nicholas Wiseman the Cardinal Archbishop of Westminster (Burstein n.d.). Dickens' reactionary views toward Catholicism are not present in *Barnaby Rudge*. Instead, Dickens' horror at both insurrection and rabid anti-Catholicism emerges through repeated descriptions of the rioters as a menacing mob, "the very scum and refuse of London" (1841, 220).[8] The portrayal of the rioters as detritus floating through the capital city reflects Dickens' abhorrence at what Patrick Brantlinger has called "grotesque populism" (2001, 61). In *Anti-Catholicism in Eighteenth-Century England*, Colin Haydon argues that Dickens' treatment of the rioters was no less than a demonization, building up into a "picture of anarchy and senseless violence," obfuscating how the Gordon Riots had, in fact, a "pattern of purpose, even of order, underlying the surface chaos" (1993, 228). In *Barnaby Rudge* the rioters blunder, fail, and die amid Dickens' outrage. All the while, bells mark not only their rise and fall but also the fates of everyone else caught up in the tumult.

As Dickens introduces the characters who either instigate, abet, or become caught up in the Gordon Riots as willing and unwilling actors, bells figure as registers of morality and as a means of calling out religious hypocrisy. The hero of *Barnaby Rudge*, Gabriel Varden, works as a locksmith, but he also fixes and maintains bells with which he has a harmonious relationship befitting his good-natured character; in many ways, Varden represents a Dickensian ideal—good but not sanctimonious, prepared to labor, but also ready to drink and socialize at the Maypole Inn "after a long day's work at locks and bells" (1841, 246). When Gabriel works, he makes sweet music: "clear as a silver bell, and audible at every pause of the streets' harsher noises"; in fact, "mothers danced their babies to its ringing" (169, 168). Gabriel patiently deals with his ridiculously self-important apprentice, Simon Tappertit, who gets embroiled in the Gordon Riots until he is saved by his master. Tappertit addresses his master in a way that shows how intrinsic bells are to Gabriel's identity: "This night, sir, I have been in the country, planning an expedition which shall fill your bell-hanging soul with wonder and dismay" (233). It may not be a coincidence that Gabriel shares his name with the archangel who was one of God's most important messengers.

As well as having a difficult apprentice, Gabriel has not been blessed in his choice of wife, Mrs. Varden, who describes her husband's drinking ale as a "Pagan custom, the relish whereof should be left to swine, and Satan, or at least to Popish persons" (37). Dickens mercilessly pokes fun at Mrs. Varden's anti-Catholicism. As a zealous reader of the "Protestant Manual," we are informed that Mrs. Varden, devoid of grace, is "most devout when most ill-tempered" (260). Her fickle moods and fervent anti-popery sentiments are aligned with bells, "performing, as it were, a kind of triple bob major on the peal of instruments in the female belfry" (272). Dickens' description reflects one of the changes in bell ringing, consisting of a set of bells rung in a fixed sequence (a bob minor is rung on six bells, a bob major on eight). The treble bob is a method in which bells have a dodging course (Goslin 26–27). Mrs. Varden is prone to lounging in bed for long periods of time due to alleged anxiety which does not seem to affect her appetite. She often orders "to be immediately accommodated with the little black tea-pot of strong mixed tea, a couple of rounds of buttered toast, a middling-sized dish of beef and ham cut thin" (1841, 260). Her evangelical theatrics form part of a double act she puts on with Miggs, the Vardens' servant, who adds to Mrs. Varden's noise with more anti-Catholicism and the inane repetition of her sister's address: "Golden Lion Court, number twenty-sivin, second bell handle on the right hand door post" (287). As a clanging duo, the pair dramatically contrasts with Gabriel's dulcet chimes.

How far Mrs. Varden and Miggs are from religious discernment is evidenced in their high estimation of the thoroughly hypocritical John Chester, the sly architect behind unrest that will besiege London streets, as he manipulates alternately naïve and thuggish Protestants to riot.

Mrs. Varden deems John Chester "a meek, righteous, thorough-going Christian," adding that "this gentleman is a saint" (91). Miggs calls Chester (not Gabriel) "an angel" (92). Dickens links Chester with a particularly secular adaptation of bell-ringing—to summon servants. After chastising and effectively abandoning his son, Edward, for wanting to marry the Catholic and insufficiently rich Emma Haredale, Chester gives his son a preemptory dismissal: "If you will do me the favor to ring the bell, the servant will show you to the door" (120). Chester rings the bell

98 *Julie Donovan*

again to inform Peak, his servant, that Chester will not be available for future calls from his son, and that no one should disturb him, "but the hair-dresser" (374).

The latter request is in keeping with the preservation of a man who appears in the most elegant fashions of the day, meticulously arranges his cravat in the mirror, and possesses all manner of luxurious items, such as a golden toothpick. Hablot K. Browne's illustration for this section of *Barnaby Rudge* depicts Chester with a bell on a table next to him, emphasizing Chester's facile need for proximity to the instrument that calls servants.

Beside the bell in the illustration is a book with the writings of Philip Stanhope, the fourth Earl of Chesterfield (Chester's almost namesake),

Figure 5.1 George Cattermole, "The murderer arrested," *Barnaby Rudge* (London: Chapman and Hall, 1841), 264

Source: https://books.google.com/books?id=rmgOAAAAQAAJ

whom Chester admires for his "captivating hypocrisy" (63).⁹ Chesterfield's *Letters to His Son on the Art of Becoming a Man of the World and a Gentleman* (1917 [1722]) reflects the unctuous worldliness Chester embodies. The illustration goes further by featuring a picture on the wall of a man holding a knife—a depiction of Abraham and Isaac from Genesis 22, which serves as an ironic contrast. God directed Abraham to offer his son, Isaac, as a sacrifice, but after Isaac is bound to an altar, a messenger from God stops Abraham because God now knows that Abraham feared His word. Abraham was tested for obedience, trust, and belief; the sacrifice was halted because Abraham had earned salvation. Chester pays no heed to God and sacrifices both his sons without compunction. That Chester is motivated by self-interest rather than by belief in God underscores the contrast with that picture of which he seems serenely obtuse. Abraham was rewarded for his sacrifice; the implication is that Chester will not be rewarded because he has the wrong motivation. As a further irony, Chester lives in Temple, an area of London around the Inns of Court where, Dickens' narrator observes, there remains "something of a clerkly monkish atmosphere" (13).¹⁰ Historically, an important part of the intellectual and cultural world of the Inns of Court was religion and religious toleration (Winston 2016, 35). In the circumstances, Chester appears an effete squatter who, rather than being summoned by bells to pay homage to God, sacrilegiously prefers to summon others with bells to pay homage to himself—a further blasphemy compounding the irony Dickens has already so lavishly applied.

The exchange with Edward is partially echoed in a scene with Chester's other, illegitimate son, Hugh, who becomes his father's dupe and a violent participant in the riots. As Chester luxuriates with a placid smile, he finishes his chocolate and proceeds to "ring the bell for more" (375). When Chester stays at the Maypole, he continues to be associated with the secularized, shallow summoning of bells to meet his every whim. John Willet, landlord of the Maypole, hears Chester loud and clear, "a smart ringing at the guest's bell, as if he had pulled it vigorously" (305). Nearby, at the Warren, Emma Haredale presents a contrast to Chester's requests; her gentle call for service—"Pray, ring, dear uncle" (78)—is for the compassionate purpose of providing refreshment for the exhausted and distressed Mary Rudge.

One of the most powerful passages in *Barnaby Rudge* describes how the sound of a bell strikes terror into the dormant conscience of Rudge Senior, the murderer of Reuben Haredale. Dickens' close friend and biographer, John Forster, called the scene "as powerful a picture as any in his writings of the inevitable and unfathomable consequences of sin" (1876, 164). Rudge had faked his own death and in doing so implicated Haredale's steward in the crime against his master. Returning to the Warren after years on the run, Rudge appears as ruthless as ever until he hears the tolling of a bell, which suddenly puts him into a somatic and psychic crisis. As he agonizingly reenacts the stabbing of Haredale, Rudge is, at last, stricken by guilt, fear, and delayed remorse:

> It was the Bell. If the ghastliest shape the human mind has ever pictured in its wildest dreams had risen up before him, he could not have staggered backward from its touch, as he did from the first sound of that loud iron voice. With eyes that started from his head, his limbs convulsed, his face most horrible to see, he raised one arm high up into the air, and holding something visionary, back and down, with his other hand, drove at it as though he held a knife and stabbed it to the heart . . . still, still, the Bell tolled on and seemed to follow him . . . pouring forth dreadful secrets after its long silence—speaking the language of the dead—the Bell—the Bell!
>
> (255)

In a paroxysm triggered by the bell, Rudge continues to hear it striking deep within his tormented body, even after its actual sound stops; it resembles the onslaught of a battalion of furies, ghosts, and avenging angels, all making way for the ultimate arbiter: "It ceased; but not in his ears." The knell was at his heart. No work of man had ever voice like that which sounded there and warned

> him that it cried unceasingly to Heaven. Who could hear that bell, and not know what it said! There was murder in its every note—cruel, relentless, savage murder—the murder of a confiding man, by one who held his every trust. Its ringing summoned phantoms from their graves . . . a hundred walls and roofs of brass would not shut out that bell, for in it spoke the wrathful voice of God.
>
> (255–56)

When Rudge's innocent son Barnaby is associated with bells, it is to describe how he artlessly sings and keeps time "to the music of some clear church bells" (237). Father and son play out their lives in dramatically different moral registers. Like Gabriel Varden, Barnaby is associated with a benevolent clarity of sound; in contrast, his father must answer to the deafening tolls of damnation. John Bowen has observed that in *Barnaby Rudge* Dickens "frequently uses Gothic motifs to tell a tale full of haunting, trauma, and uncanny repetition" (2000, 160). Bells as a Gothic element emerge in the crisis of Rudge Senior, but Dickens reworks the traditionally anti-Catholic aspects of the Gothic novel, often peopled by nefarious monks and wicked priests, to record Protestant wrongdoing.

In his other writings, Dickens expressed awareness of how the music of bells could be not only quite glorious but also, as in the case of Rudge Senior, quite terrible; bells had the capacity to ring out both heavenly and hellish sounds. Such is the case in *Pictures from Italy*, where Dickens recounts the incessant sound of church bells:

> a horrible, irregular, jerking, dingle, dingle, dingle. . . . The noise is supposed to be particularly obnoxious to Evil Spirits; but looking up into the steeples, and seeing (and hearing) these young Christians thus engaged, one might very naturally mistake them for the Enemy. (1846, 59)

That bells could affect Dickens' nerves is also recorded in Forster's *The Life of Charles Dickens*, when Forster describes Dickens' stay at the Palazzo Peschiere in Genoa. As Dickens tried to write, the city's enthusiasm for bell-ringing proved " 'maddening' . . . pouring into his ears, again and again, in a tuneless, grating, discordant, jerking, hideous vibration that made his ideas 'spin round and round till they lost themselves in a whirl of vexation 'and giddiness' " (Forster 384). John Schad observes that churches in Dickens' work notably feature sound, especially "the sheer ubiquity of the church bell," representing what Schad describes as "a subversive or subterranean force" (1996, 8). That force attacks Dickens' ears in Genoa, but it also captivates Master Humphrey at the midnight hour and reflects what he will read in *Barnaby Rudge*.

Dickens' experience of the hellish din in Genoa provided inspiration for his hopeful 1845 story, *The Chimes: A Goblin Story of Some Bells That Rang an Old Year Out and a New Year*. Dickens was glad to tell Forster that it was "a great thing to have my title, and see my way to how to work the bells" (384). *The Chimes* notes the survival of bells through the Reformation, although certain adaptations paid heed to the new Protestant order: "Centuries ago, these bells had been baptized by bishops—Henry VIII stopped that" (1844, 10). Dickens' hero, Toby Veck (Trotty), identifies with the stolid quality of the local church bells; they work through sleet and snow, just as Trotty does in his humble job as a ticket porter. In his bleakest moment, when life seems hardly worth living, Trotty imagines spirits emerging from the bells, bell spirits that reprimand Trotty for thinking himself worthless because he is poor and meek.[11] After Trotty swoons from the vision, he is awakened by bells chiming in the New Year, one that gives him renewed confidence in his Christian virtue and self-worth.

In *Barnaby Rudge* bells figure as an integral part of the sonic environment of both the country and the city, providing an inimitable means of expressing complex links between sound and culture. George Delamere Cowan described the effect of bells on Dickens quite well: "From their lofty pulpits, church bells expounded to him daily, hourly, the grandest homilies on human life, compelling him to recognize in each cadence floating and eddying in the air above a something infinitely beyond a fugitive melody" (1876, 380). Bells also marked territory; this could be sacred, Christian territory, or bells ringing to honor events that shaped national identity, as in *Barnaby Rudge*, where the peal of bells celebrates "the anniversary of the king's birthday" (241). Even in cases like the latter, bells remained essentially religious in people's minds because their sound usually came from churches.[12] Such iconic status was attainable, even in noisy cities, because of the literal as well as the symbolic power of bells, what Torsten Wissman has described as "the use of sound in the expression of power in the urban environment" (2016, 136). Schafer writes of the capacity a church bell had to maintain social cohesion as it formed a "centripedal sound; it attracts and unifies the community in a social sense, just as it draws man and God together" (54). Even in the face of a Protestant modernity that had sought to reject the medieval world view in favor of rationalism, the sound of bells struck at something profoundly human, spiritual, and primal.

Over time, bells retained their usefulness as a means to sound alarm, which Dickens puts to great use in *Barnaby Rudge* since bells mark the drama, danger, and death caused by the Gordon Riots. When Dickens describes the sacking of Lord Mansfield's house, he notes a rioter "ringing Lord Mansfield's dinner-bell with all his might" (323). Lord Mansfield, Lord Chief Justice, became a target in the actual Gordon Riots because of his pro-Catholic stance, which was said to have influenced the king (Ditchfield 2002, 101–102). When the mayhem of the rioting eventually dies down in *Barnaby Rudge*, bells punctuate the eerie silence descending on London; they also seem to sound that God has been watching all the time:

> the noises in the streets became less frequent by degrees, until silence was scarcely broken save by the bells in church towers, marking the progress—softer and more stealthy while the city slumbered—of that Great Watcher with the hoary head, who never sleeps or rests.
> (385)

Judgment does come for the rioters, with scaffolds and gibbets constructed for their execution, a grim prospect made more imminent as the "prison bell began to toll" (388). As John Plotz puts it, "Die rioting and you die justly, Dickens suggests" (2000, 6). In *Dickens and Religion* Walder argues that Dickens took *Barnaby Rudge* "as an opportunity to express his hatred of religious intolerance and oppression, and to urge the need for a positive, counteracting force of goodwill based on reason and common sense" (2007, 92). As moral arbiters and as the soundtrack to his text, Dickens makes bells insistent commentators on the perils of ungodly riot.

When the rioters of *Barnaby Rudge* leave London to wreak more havoc on outlying areas, they approach the Warren and ring at bells while beating at the house's iron gates. The rioters turn the orderly

Maypole Inn into an "infernal temple . . . some ringing the bells till they pulled them down, others beat them with pokers till they beat them into fragments" (251). Gone is the peaceful scene with bells that greeted Haredale when he returned from London to the Warren: "a clear, calm, silent evening, with hardly a breath of wind to stir the leaves, or any sound to break the stillness of the time, but drowsy sheep-bells tinkling in the distance" (411). Solomon Daisy, the bell ringer, re-emerges during the rioting scenes at Chigwell, both as witness to extraordinary events and as comforter to the traumatized John Willet (even though Solomon himself weeps when he sees the destruction done to the Maypole). Solomon ultimately becomes a figure of reason and consolation, one who represents bell ringing in its orderly, legitimate function of passing time and marking events in a Christian community. Dickens had in mind that the humble and slightly comic character of Daisy would attain a modestly heroic stature during the course of *Barnaby Rudge*. Writing to Forster, Dickens stated his intention. Daisy was "meant to be one of those strong ones to which strong circumstances give birth in the commonest minds" (161). Dickens' decision might be why the bellringer's rather whimsical surname of Daisy is counteracted by the Christian name of Solomon which brings to mind the biblical king gifted with wisdom.[13]

Dickens might have been inspired by a real-life Solomon Daisy he encountered in his travels; in a letter to Forster, Dickens imparted as much: "Chigwell, my dear friend, is the greatest place in the world. . . . Such a delicious old inn opposite the churchyard . . . such beautiful forest scenery—such an out of the way, rural place, such a sexton!" (161). The Solomon Daisy of *Barnaby Rudge* witnesses Haredale grapple with Rudge Senior, and helps Haredale apprehend and bind the villain. Dickens was insistent in a letter to the novel's illustrator, George Cattermole, dated August 6, 1841, that the drawings for this scene feature a bell and Solomon Daisy:

> I want—if you understand—to show one of the turrets laid open—the turret where the alarm-bell is . . . and among the ruins (at some height if possible) Mr. Haredale just clutching our friend, the mysterious file, who is passing over them like a spirit; Solomon Daisy, if you can introduce him, looking on from the ground below.
> (Hogarth 1882, 50)

It is fitting that the bell ringer features in this dramatic scene, finally seeing in the flesh the imagined ghost of his oft-told story of the night when Reuben Haredale was murdered.

Barnaby Rudge demonstrates Dickens' awareness of bells ringing out secular and commercial callings as well as religious and spiritual ones in the novel's sub-plot concerning Joe Willet. When Joe leaves the Maypole after having argued with his domineering father, he goes to the Black Lion pub in London where he meets a recruiting sergeant. To encourage Joe to sign up, the sergeant tries to entice him with alcohol, summoning the bartender with a bell: "Here—let me give the bell a pull, and you'll make up your mind in half a minute, I know" (112). Joe worries that if he is noticed he will be further plied with drinks: "If you pull the bell here, where I'm known, there'll be an end to my soldiering inclinations in no time" (112). After Joe enlists, he walks through Islington and onto Highgate, recalling a fabled character: "but there were no voices in the bells to bid him turn. Since the time of the noble Whittington, fair flower of merchants, bells have come to have less sympathy with humankind" (254). As the story goes, in Highgate, on his departure from London, voices in the bells entreated Richard (Dick) Whittington to return to seek his fortune. He became a merchant and Lord Mayor of London.[14] Joe regrets that cynical bells no longer speak to the humble individual experience: "Wanderers have increased in number; ships leave the Thames for distant regions, carrying from stem to stern no other cargo; the bells are silent; they ring out no entreaties or regrets; they are used to it and have grown worldly" (254). Joe yearns not only to be free from his father but also for the love of Dolly Varden; if the bells had called him back, he would have listened.

Although *Barnaby Rudge* has not enjoyed the same success and critical acclaim accorded to many of Dickens' other novels, Dickens was justifiably proud of his achievement, confiding to Forster that "I was always sure I could make a good thing of Barnaby, and I think you'll find that it comes out strong to the last word" (163). Part of the novel's strength lies in the ways that bells reverberate through the text in complex and multivalent ways. Two of the titles Dickens had in mind before he decided on *Household Words* and its successor, *All the Year Round*, were "English Bells" or "Weekly Bells" (Bledsoe 2012, 73). His thinking reflects the idea of bells as supremely capable of demanding attention and spreading messages. As some of the most effective communicators in *Barnaby Rudge*, bells convey a society in flux, a society with an established Protestant identity that still contends with the echoes of its Catholic past.

Notes

1. For scholarship concentrating on religion in *Barnaby Rudge*, see the following: Robert Butterworth, (2016, ch. 9), Mark Eslick (2018), Denis Paz (2006), Dennis Walder (2007, ch. 4), and Judith Wilt (2001).
2. A more commonly known ending to the line is "Shoreditch" rather than "Fleetditch." The rhyme first appeared in print in the first anthology of nursery rhymes titled *Tommy Thumb's Pretty Song Book* (1794) by Nurse Lovechild, published by Mary Cooper in London. Cooper was the earliest publisher of children's books.

3. St. Paul's bell was a familiar reference for Dickens, appearing in *Our Mutual Friend* (1876 [1865]), *Great Expectations* (1866 [1861]), *Martin Chuzzlewit* (1868 [1844]), *David Copperfield* (1850), and *Little Dorrit* (1857).
4. See Cornelia Pearsall (1999, 382) for an account of the Duke of Wellington's funeral which was marked by the organized ringing of bells across Britain. See James Vernon (1993, 70–72; 199) for the use of bells to celebrate the swearing into office of new mayors, as well as the use of bells as a familiar instrument used by town criers to make announcements and spread news.
5. See Thomas North (1888, 9), Margaret Aston (2015, ch. 5); and Chiara Bertoglio (2017, 376).
6. Poe also wrote a longer review that appeared in *Graham's Magazine* in February 1842.
7. See Bruce Smith (1999, 141–42), Arthur George (2020, 121–33), Ken Dowden (2000, 119), and Ronald Hutton (1996, 223).
8. For an argument that *Barnaby Rudge* is predominantly about anti-Catholicism rather than Chartism, see Paz (2006, 9).
9. For an intriguing reading of Chester as a Jesuitical character, see Judith Wilt (2001).
10. John Donne, whose Meditation XVII from *Devotions Upon Emergent Occasions* (1923 [1624]) forms part of this essay's title, lived from 1592 to approximately 1596 in Lincoln's Inn, one of the Inns of Court. Donne was born a Roman Catholic but became an Anglican around 1600–1601. He was appointed dean of St. Paul's Cathedral in 1621. See David Colclough 2004.
11. For an argument that Dickens' inspiration for *The Chimes* came from Friedrick Schiller's poem, "Song of the Bell" (1837 [1798]), see Michael Slater (1970). For the case that *The Chimes* inspired Edgar Allan Poe's poem, "The Bells" (1881 [1748], see Burton Pollin (1998).
12. For scholarship examining the territorial aspects of bells see Alain Corbin (2004, 187).
13. The stories of Solomon are in the Bible's Old Testament: 2 Samuel, 1 Kings, and 2 Chronicles.
14. Dickens' fondness for the Dick Whittington story is discussed in Jay Clayton (2010, 35).

Bibliography

Ackroyd, Peter. *London: The Biography*. London: Anchor, 2003.
Aston, Margaret. *Broken Idols of the Reformation*. Cambridge: Cambridge University Press, 2015.
Bertoglio, Chiara. *Reforming Music: Music and the Religious Reformations of the Sixteenth Century*. Berlin: De Gruyter 2017.
Bledsoe, Robert Terrell. *Dickens, Journalism, Music: Household Words and All the Year Round* London: Continuum, 2012.
Bowen, John. "Introduction." In *Barnaby Rudge*, edited by John Bowen, xiii–xxxiv. London: Penguin, 2003.
———. *Other Dickens: Pickwick to Chuzzlewit*. Oxford: Oxford University Press, 2000.
Brantlinger, Patrick. "Did Dickens Have a Philosophy of History? The Case of *Barnaby Rudge*." *Dickens Studies Annual* 30 (2001): 59–74.

Brown, Christopher Boyd. "Music." In *The Oxford Handbook to the English Reformations*, edited by Ulinka Rublack, 621–42. Oxford: Oxford University Press, 2017.
Burstein, Miriam. "The 'Papal Aggression' Controversy, 1850–52." In *Romanticism and Victorianism on the Net*, edited by Dino Franco Felluga, n.p., n.d. *BRANCH: Britain, Representation, and Nineteenth-Century History*. www.branchcollective.org/?ps_articles=miriam-burstein-the-papal-aggression-controversy-1850-52.
Butterworth, Robert. *Dickens, Religion, and Society*. Houndmills: Palgrave Macmillan, 2016.
Chesterfield, the Earl of [Philip Domer Stanhope]. *Letters to His Son on the Art of Becoming a Man*. 1722. New York: The Chesterfield Press, 1917.
Clayton, Jay. "The Dickens Tape: Affect and Sound Reproduction in *The Chimes*." In *Dickens and Modernity: Essays and Studies*, edited by Juliet John, 19–40. Cambridge: D. S. Brewer, 2010.
Colclough, David. "John Donne." In *Oxford Dictionary of National Biography*. 2004. https://doi.org/10.1093/ref:odnb/7819.
Corbin, Alain. "The Auditory Markers of the Village." In *The Auditory Culture Reader*, edited by Michael Bull and Les Back, 187–92. Oxford: Berg, 2004.
Cowan, George Delamere. "Charles Dickens on Bells." *Belgravia* 28 (February 1876): 380–87.
Creighton, O. H. *Castles and Landscapes: Power, Community, and Fortification in Medieval England*. London: Equinox, 2005.
Cressy, David. *Bonfires and Bells: National Memory and the Protestant Calendar in Elizabethan and Stuart England*. Berkeley: University of California Press, 1989.
Dickens, Charles. *Barnaby Rudge: A Tale of the Riots of' Eighty*. London: Chapman and Hall, 1841. https://books.google.com/books?id=rmgOAAAAQAAJ.
——. *The Chimes: A Goblin Story of Some Bells That Rang an Old Year Out and a New Year In*. London: Bradbury and Evans, 1844. https://books.google.com/books/about/The_Chimes.html?id=-RtIAQAAMAAJ.
——. *David Copperfield*. London: Bradbury and Evans, 1850. https://books.google.com/books?id=NcsNAAAAQAAJ.
——. *Great Expectations*. 1861. London: Chapman and Hall, 1866. https://books.google.com/books?id=Sb8NAAAAQAAJ.
——. *Little Dorrit*. London: Bradbury and Evans, 1857. https://books.google.com/books?id=XvpcAAAAcAAJ.
——. *Martin Chuzzlewit*. 1844. London: Chapman and Hall, 1868. https://books.google.com/books?id=V7zgTtWMj5IC.
——. *Master Humphrey's Clock*. Paris: Baudry's European Library, 1841. https://books.google.com/books/about/Master_Humphrey_s_Clock.html?id=e3AQPuMxUAUC.
——. *Our Mutual Friend*. 1865. New York: D. Appleton, 1876. https://books.google.com/books?id=5dkGcb-MGhsC.
——. *Pictures from Italy*. London: Bradbury and Evans, 1846. https://books.google.com/books/about/Pictures_from_Italy.html?id=ZtgNAAAAQAAJ.

———. Preface to *Barnaby Rudge*. London: Chapman and Hall, 1866, v–ix. https://books.google.com/books?id=BK4QAAAAYAAJ.

Ditchfield, G. M. *George III: An Essay in Monarchy*. Houndmills: Palgrave Macmillan, 2002.

Donne, John. "17. Meditation." 1624. In *Devotions Upon Emergent Occasions*, edited by John Sparrow, 96–8. Cambridge: The University Press, 1923.

Dowden, Ken. *European Paganism: The Realities of Cult from Antiquity to the Middle Ages*. New York: Routledge, 2000.

Eslick, Mark. "*Barnaby Rudge* and the Jesuit Menace." In *The Oxford Handbook of Charles Dickens*, edited by John Jordan, Robert L. Patten, and Catherine Waters, 153–65. Oxford: Oxford University Press, 2018.

Forster, John. *The Life of Charles Dickens*. Vol. 1: 1812–1847. 2 vols. London: Chapman and Hall, 1876. https://books.google.fm/books/about/The_Life_of_Charles_Dickens0.html?id=5qzj5JZ7R9YC&hl=en&output=html_text.

George, Arthur. "May Day: Beltane Fires and the May Queen-Goddess." In *The Mythology of America's Seasonal Holidays" The Dance of the Horae*, 121–33. Cham: Palgrave Macmillan, 2020.

Goslin, Samuel B. *First Steps to Bell Ringing: Being an Introduction to the Healthful and Pleasant Exercise of Bell-Ringing*. London: John Warner and Sons, 1881. www.gutenberg.org/files/53022/53022-h/53022-h.htm.

Gray, Thomas. *Elegy in a Country Churchyard*. 1751. In *The Works of Thomas Gray, ESQ.*, edited by William Mason, 399–403. London: J. F. Dove, 1827. https://books.google.com/books/about/The_works_of_Thomas_Gray_with_memoirs_of.html?id=TMgIAAAAQAAJ.

Hawthorne, Nathaniel. "The Maypole of Merry Mount." 1832. In *Nathaniel Hawthorne: Representative Selections, with Introduction, Bibliography, and Notes*, edited by Austin Warren, 107–18. New York: American Book Company, 1934. https://babel.hathitrust.org/cgi/pt?id=mdp.39015011342196&view=1up&seq=204&q1=aypole%20of%20merry%20mount%20Nathaniel%20hawthorne.

Haydon, Colin. *Anti-Catholicism in Eighteenth-Century England*. Manchester: Manchester University Press, 1993.

Haywood, Ian, and John Seed. *The Gordon Riots: Politics, Culture, and Insurrection in Eighteenth-Century Britain*. Cambridge: Cambridge University Press, 2012.

Hogarth, Georgina, and Mamie Dickens, eds. *The Letters of Charles Dickens*. Vol. 1: 1833–1855. 2 vols. London: Chapman and Hall, 1882. https://babel.hathitrust.org/cgi/pt?id=hvd.hwjmcu&view=1up&seq=7&q1.

Hutton, Ronald. *Stations of the Sun: A History of the Ritual Year in Britain*. Oxford: Oxford University Press, 1996.

"London Bells." 1794. In *Tommy Thumb's Song Book, for All Little Masters and Misses*, edited by Nurse Lovechild, and published by Mary Cooper, 24–25. Glasgow: Lumsden and Son, 1815. https://archive.org/details/tommythumbssongb00loveiala/page/22/mode/2up.

Marsh, Christopher. *Music and Society in Early Modern England*. Cambridge: Cambridge University Press, 2010.

Nash, Gary B. *The Liberty Bell*. New Haven, CT: Yale University Press, 2010.

North, Thomas. *English Bells and Bell Lore*. Leek: T. Mark, 1888. https://catalog.hathitrust.org/Record/007839588.

O'Regan, Noel. "Music and the Counter-Reformation." In *The Ashgate Research Companion to the Counter-Reformation*, edited by Alexandra Bamji, Geert H. Jansen, and Mary Laven, 337–54. London: Routledge, 2016.

Pattison, Robert. *The Great Dissent: John Henry Newman and the Liberal Heresy*. Oxford: Oxford University Press, 1991.

Paz, Denis. G. *Dickens and Barnaby Rudge: Anti-Catholicism and Chartism*. Monmouth, Wales: Merlin Press, 2006.

———. *Popular Anti-Catholicism in Mid-Victorian England*. Stanford, CA: Stanford University Press, 1992.

Pearsall, Cornelia D. J. "Burying the Duke: Victorian Mourning and the Funeral of the Duke of Wellington," *Victorian Literature and Culture* 27, no. 2 (1999): 365–93.

Plotz, John. *The Crowd: British Literature and Public Politics*. Berkeley: University of California Press, 2000.

Poe, Edgar Allan. *The Bells*. 1748. Philadelphia: Porter and Coates, 1881. https://books.google.com/books?id=duqE1STiJ.

———. Review of *Barnaby Rudge*, by Charles Dickens. *Philadelphia Saturday Post*. May 1, 1841. In *Poe: Essays and Reviews*, edited by Gary Richard Thompson, 218–24. New York: The Library of America, 1978.

Pollin, Burton. "Dickens's 'Chimes' and its Pathway into Poe's 'Bells'." *The Mississippi Quarterly* 51, no. 2 (Spring 1998): 217–31.

Schad, John. "Dickens's Cryptic Church: Drawing on *Pictures from Italy*." In *Dickens Reconfigured: Bodies, Desires, and Other Histories*, edited by John Schad, 5–21. Manchester: Manchester University Press 1996.

Schafer, Murray R. *The Soundscape: Our Sonic Environment and the Tuning of the World*. New York: Knopf, 1977.

Schiller, Friedrich. *Schiller's Song of the Bell*. 1798. Translated by Samuel A. Eliot. Boston: Perkins and Marvin, 1837. https://books.google.com/books?id=on8N4KCT3CcC.

Seed, John. "'The Fall of Romish Babylon Anticipated': Plebeian Dissenters and Anti-popery in the Gordon Riots." In *The Gordon Riots: Politics, Culture, and Insurrection in Eighteenth-Century Britain*, edited by Ian Haywood and John Seed, 69–92. Cambridge: Cambridge University Press, 2012.

Slater, Michael. "Carlyle and Jerrold into Dickens: A Study of *The Chimes*." *Nineteenth-Century Literature* 24, no. 4 (March 1970): 506–26.

Smith, Bruce R. *The Acoustic Sound of Early Modern England: Attending to the O Factor*. Chicago, IL: University of Chicago Press, 1999.

Tombs, Robert. *The English and Their History*. New York: Vintage, 2016.

Vernon, James. *Politics and the People: A Study in English Political Culture c. 1815–1867*. Cambridge: Cambridge University Press, 1993.

Walder, Dennis. *Dickens and Religion*. New York: Routledge, 2007.

Walters, Henry Beauchamp. *Church Bells of England*. Wakefield: EP Publishing, 1977.

Warner, Marina. *Alone of All Her Sex: The Myth and the Cult of the Virgin Mary*. Oxford: Oxford University Press, 1976.

Williams, Ann. "A Bell-house and a Burh-geat: Lordly Residences in England before the Norman Conquest." In *Anglo-Norman Castles*, edited by Robert Liddiard, 23–40. Woodbridge: Boydell Press, 1992.

Wilt, Judith. "Masques of the English in *Barnaby Rudge*." *Dickens Studies Annual* 30 (2001): 75–94.
Winston, Jessica. *Lawyers at Play: Literature, Law, and Politics at the Early Modern Inns of Court, 1558–1581*. Oxford: Oxford University Press, 2016.
Wissman, Torsten. *Geographies of Urban Sound*. New York: Routledge, 2016.

6 "Gazing at All the Church and Chapel Going"
Social Views of Religious Nonconformity in Dickens' Fiction

Lydia Craig

Charles Dickens was a lifelong Anglican and social reformer, unlike the residents of Coketown, who on Sundays "lounged listlessly, gazing at all the church and chapel going, as at a thing with which they had no manner of concern" (1854a, 28). He abhorred evangelical outreaches of any kind that blamed the poor for their own misery and suffering. Temporarily attending a Unitarian church in the early 1840s, Dickens found a faith that avoided stringent doctrines and revered the earthly example of love and self-sacrifice set by Jesus Christ. Eventually, he returned to the Established Church in the same decade, attracted by broad church Anglicanism, a permissive movement that shared Unitarian belief in tolerance and social charity. When Dickens visited the town of Preston, Lancashire, in 1854 to cover an industrial strike ongoing since 1853 and to gain material for his upcoming novel, he unexpectedly found his attention straying from social unrest to the plentiful and multiplying ecclesiastical denominations standing idly by as the workers suffered. Offended that Nonconformist churches chiefly led misguided moral campaigns directed at the poor, rather than offering them spiritual comfort, Dickens reviewed their lack of social impact with the judgmental "eighteen denominations" of industrial Coketown (1854a, 28). Though socio-economic and educational aspects of this novel have received most critical attention, its largely overlooked spiritual subplot bears witness to the galvanizing spectacle of what the author interpreted as ineffectual and even deleterious evangelical cant. In this novel and in "George Silverman's Explanation" (1868), written after a subsequent 1867 visit to Preston, Dickens constructs responsive allegories of working-class individuals Stephen Blackpool and George Silverman reaching theosophic faith and redemption through by-passing aloof and hypocritical evangelical representatives of Nonconformist and Anglican Churches. Threatening such denominations with spiritual irrelevancy, Dickens urges reappraisal of the true social mission of the Christian church, which should be to love and comfort those in distress.

DOI: 10.4324/9781003156611-7

Unitarian Principles and the Preston Strike (1853–1854)

Throughout his career, Dickens objected to the "puritanical" tone often adopted by Calvinists and Evangelicals of both Nonconformist and Anglican persuasions who saw the poor as projects and problems rather than human beings. As early as 1836, Dickens had opposed Sabbatarianism, declaring the poor had a right to enjoy their one day of respite in the tract *Sunday Under Three Heads* (1836), a position reiterated in *A Christmas Carol* (1843). When Scrooge expresses his belief that the Spirit of Christmas Present would support closing businesses to observe the Sabbath day, he is met with the stern reply, "There are some upon this earth of yours . . . who lay claim to know us, and who do their deeds of passion, pride, ill-will, hatred, envy, bigotry, and selfishness in our name, who are as strange to us and all our kith and kin, as if they had never lived. Remember that, and charge their doings on themselves, not us" (stv. 3). Separating the lower-class ministry of the so-called evangelical Christians from that of Christ, Dickens saw that Evangelicals in the Calvinist, Methodist, and even Anglican traditions often mingled calls for repentance to both young and old with unfeasible imperatives to relinquish all worldly amusements. Valentine Cunningham states, "What Dickens finds amiss with these child-abusing, sin-and-judgment obsessives is that they are stuck fast in the Old Testament, are imperceptive about the New Testament's rewritings of the Old, the Christian dispensation's abolition of Judaic law" (2008, 268). Religious intolerance for wrong-doing or human weakness, Dickens believed, had an alienating effect upon those who might otherwise be receptive to the Christian message and pursue lifestyle changes. Consequently, he realized that the actions and attitudes of social reformers could attract the poor to faith, and just as surely drive them away.

Resenting Evangelicals often distracted Dickens from censuring other civic and social authorities who might more accurately be blamed for the continuing troubles of the British poor, and his critiques remained unsoftened by nuance or attention to the end result of various charities. Historically, Evangelicals "engaged not only in evangelism but in a self-consciously civilizing mission to reclaim the disreputable in town and country. In England the urban working classes were the most common targets of evangelical zeal" (Hempton 1994, 156). In many cases, their campaigns exerted a positive social effect in various cities, especially in response to unexpected disasters (Johnson 2020, 164). Unsatisfied with the results of charity, Dickens demanded compassion and understanding from those dispensing it to the poor, a viewpoint he promoted by creating literary teaching moments intended "to liberate human beings from selfishness and to direct empathy outward" (Metz 2019, 83). Five main characteristics of Dickens' religious belief have been established by

Robert Butterworth that stress the close association in the author's mind between faith and compassionate social advocacy:

> He is alert to and well-informed about developments in religion in his time; in taking a practical approach, against a theological background, to Christianity, he is primarily concerned with its moral teaching; he is impatient with theological, denominational or other disputes when they are a distraction from, or irrelevant to, the promotion of Christian moral values; he takes an interest in such debates only when he sees them as furthering the promotion of Christian morality; and he sees that morality as having a social, and not merely personal, dimension.
>
> (2017, 5)

Bettering society and the condition of fellow humans not only represented a spiritual duty to Dickens, but it was also a privilege, a belief he evidently felt that Evangelicals did not share as they adjured the poor to avoid sin and improve their lives through sober living and respectability.

Seeking a faith that stressed and revered the sacrificial earthly example of good works set by Jesus Christ rather than rules and regulations, Dickens became increasingly frustrated with the Established Church's mistaken religious priorities. Debate over the Tractarian or Oxford Movement exposed a dangerous ideological rupture between high-church advocates, who took inspiration from the ceremonies and doctrines of Roman Catholicism, and low-church adherents or Evangelicals (Brown and Nockles 2012, 2). Correspondingly, Dickens' interest in Unitarianism in the early 1840s was due to exasperation, as Gary Colledge claims, with "petty bickering and quarreling over ecclesiastical minutiae within the Anglican Church" and interest in the "positive social action" performed by many Unitarians (2011, 87). He and his family attended Essex Street Chapel and then Little Portland Street, the chapel of his friend Reverend Edward Tagart (Colledge 85; Slater 2009, 214). Although some Victorians deemed the denomination the nonbeliever's last refuge, Julie Melnyk observes, "For many, however, Unitarian beliefs offered a religious faith reconcilable with reason and a religious community that acknowledged human spirituality and sought social improvement" (2008, 40). Though he continued to share social interests with Unitarians like Elizabeth Gaskell and James and Harriet Martineau, toward the end of the decade, Dickens had returned to the Established Church, finding broad church Anglicanism a movement far more tolerant of theological differences, as its name implies.[1] What is clear, however, is that Dickens could become spiritually outraged on behalf of the English poor in the belief that they were being harassed or disregarded by representatives of Christianity to the extent of altering his place of worship.

Evangelicalism in its judgmental form touched a chord that motivated him to write against what he interpreted as fatal misunderstanding of the earthly purpose of the church, to serve the disadvantaged and inspire them with Christian hope. When on Friday, January 27, 1854, Dickens took a train from London to Preston to observe and report on the industrial strike ongoing since May 1853, he entered an overwrought environment featuring extreme poverty, class warfare, and religious Nonconformity. Explicitly, Dickens hoped to gauge the level of tension between workers insisting on a ten per cent wage increase, and masters, who had closed down mills to prevent vital donations from employed workers reaching strikers, a tactic known as a "lock-out." Lodging at the Old Bull Hotel with friend and journalist William Henry Wills, he emerged daily to examine posted literature and ongoing events, favoring capturing personal impressions over "material facts" (Butterworth 1991, 129, 134). Publishing his account in the article "On Strike" in *Household Words* on February 11, Dickens stated, "Neither by night or day was there any interruption to the peace of the streets ... I traversed the streets very much, and was, as a stranger, the subject of a little curiosity among the idlers; but I met with no rudeness or ill-temper" (Dickens 1854b, 557).[2] Both walking among the people and secretly gleaning inspiration for an industrial plot, the novelist absorbed the general aspect of Preston itself, a town visually distinct not only for its smoky atmosphere and drear buildings but also for its plethora of church buildings, ranging from lofty cathedrals to dingy rented chapels in side streets.

When Dickens left the inn on Saturday morning and walked down aptly named Church Street toward the town center, he encountered a dizzying array of 30-odd churches in a town with a traditionally robust Nonconformist presence.[3] On the right of the Old Bull Hotel was St. John's Minster, the official Anglican parish church, which was located on an ecclesiastic site occupied since early Christian times. With its dilapidated building and tower demolished in April 1853 and interior subsequently stripped, the church was not open to its congregation ("Re-Building," 1853, 5). At that time, it was being rebuilt and renovated, though the project undertaken by Edwin Hugh Shellard at a cost of over 6000 pounds would not conclude until 1855. Plentiful Anglican alternatives appeared; left at the Park Road fork stood St. Paul's Church and St. Mary's Church rose on the right. Well before he reached Park Lane as he walked north, Dickens would spy the Sisters of Charity convent, school, and Roman Catholic cathedral, St. Ignatius Church, erected in 1836 and boasting the first spire in Preston. Left and opposite, at the corner of Upper Walker Street, was the Wesleyan Chapel. If Dickens strayed back toward the inn, into the maze of roads behind Church Street, then he spied a Baptist Chapel at the corner of Queen Street and Leeming Street, and another Roman Catholic Chapel on Silver Street (Rapkin 1852). Continuing to "traverse," he would discover churches of multiple doctrines and faiths under construction or newly established. These included All Saints' Church, built by Evangelicals on the plot between Walker Street and Elizabeth Street and St. Walburge's off Pedder Street, a massive Roman Catholic church constructed between May 1851 and August 1854 by London architect Joseph Aloysius Hansom. Following a church schism among Particular Baptists, Zoar Chapel had recently opened in a new brick building on Regent Street, Avenham (Hewitson 1869, 192–96). With so many options, it appeared that Preston churchgoers were spoiled for choice.

While church bells tolled the next morning, Dickens observed the populace streaming not through the doors of cathedrals or chapels, but into Preston's Cock Pit, a decaying gaming amphitheater located directly behind St. John the Evangelist at Stoneygate and Lennox Street. According to William Pilkington, the Cock Pit, which could be rented for a nominal fee, "was the recognised arena of teetotalists, politicians, theologians, socialists, Mormonites, and infidels. All manner of questions were thrashed out here" (1894, 21).[4] Joining the immense crowd inside, Dickens listened to a bombastic speech by strike leader Mortimer Grimshaw before slipping away, overcome by the stifling heat of closely packed bodies. It did not escape his notice that strikers were spending their "only day of leisure" on business (Dickens 1854b, 556). Later, on Monday, church remained on Dickens' mind as he stood in Chadwick's Orchard among the strikers, who commenced their meeting with the Chartist hymn, "Assembled beneath thy broad blue sky," stanzas of which were quoted in both the *Preston Chronicle's* account of the event and Dickens' article published a week later ("Assembled," 1849, 132). Rather than worship beneath the arched roof of a cathedral, the people gathered in a red-brick courtyard, their situation eloquently mirroring the fancy of the religious song. Disused, within sight of the people singing outside, stood The United Methodist Free Church, well known as "the ugliest chapel in Great Britain and Ireland" and erected in 1831 by the Protestant Methodist denomination (Hewitson, 132). As with the Cock Pit meeting, Dickens could spare only enough time to register immediate impressions before heading to the train station ("Wages" 1854b, 3).[5] Besides the strikers' grim determination, Dickens took away the impression of a town filled with multiple churches of various faiths, which were wholly unconnected to working-class citizens.

Theosophical Faith in *Hard Times*

Though Dickens' middle-class view of the civic responsibility of municipal authorities, philanthropists, and businessmen to undertake philanthropy for the lower classes often smacked of Victorian neo-feudalism, he resented the same infantilizing impulse when adopted by religious organizations. Nonconformist Joseph Livesey and the other "Seven Men of Preston" originated the Temperance Movement in 1832, encouraging working-class men to take a pledge of total abstinence from alcohol (Turner-Bishop 2003, 383). A social advocate "deeply suspicious of all ascetic impulses and the will to impose them on others," Dickens portrays this and other evangelical outreaches in *Hard Times* as mistimed and oppressive, symptomatic of the cultural rupture between Coketown's churches and the populace ("Evangelical religion" 2011 [1999], 234). Instead of working together to improve the lives of the poor, the 18 denominations "incessantly scratched one another's faces and pulled one another's hair by way of agreeing on the steps to be taken for their improvement—which they never did" (Dickens 1854a, 58; bk. 1, ch. 8). Differing theologically in "every other particular, conceivable and inconceivable (especially inconceivable)," as Dickens puns, the churches share the belief that their charitable objects are "a considerable population of babies" who cannot be allowed to "wonder," or seek truth for themselves (59). Evangelicalism turns churches into denigrating bullies stripping the last piece of dignity from mill hands. Regulation and proscription are the order of the day:

> Then came the Teetotal Society, who complained that these same people *would* get drunk, and showed in tabular statements that they did get drunk, and proved at tea parties that no inducement, human or Divine (except a medal), would induce them to forego their custom of getting drunk.
>
> (28; ch. 5)

Instead of offering religious guidance, the town's 18 denominations demonize questionable activities such as drinking, opium smoking, and dancing that make industrial labor bearable.

Admittedly, Dickens had scrutinized Preston at an inopportune time when strikers logically prioritized union meetings over religious service; however, contemporary statistics supported his belief that the denominations, including evangelical Anglicans, were not attracting earnest congregants. According to the Census of Great Britain, taken two years prior on Sunday, March 30, 1851, Preston had an attendance rate of 16% at the traditional morning service peak, well below the nearly 22% and 26% reported from the much more populous cotton towns of Manchester and Leeds. Contrastingly, London's over two million inhabitants registered a church attendance rate of just under 20%. Numerically, Preston appeared to be in spiritual decline. Furthermore, the overwhelming majority of churchgoers in Dickens' London attended Church of England parishes, but Preston's Roman Catholics, swelled by Irish immigration, outnumbered Anglican attendees by a factor of two; the latter were also outstripped by the total number of Nonconformists who made it to church (Census of Great Britain 1854 [1851], 95, 97, 102). In reacting with sarcastic dismay to the prevalence of Nonconformists and apparent disinterest in Anglican church attendance, and by linking the two phenomena, Dickens evinced the typical Victorian reaction to the census, a significant subject of debate after its publication. Clive D. Field notes, "Whatever the statistical reality may have been, the characteristic reaction to the census results of most church leaders and the religious public was that church-going was far too low" (2019, 39). Witnessing the lower-class's absence from worship in Preston, Dickens blamed the moral reform movements for alienating them.

Culturally as unfamiliar with the industrial region's thriving religious diversity as with northern dialects, Dickens predictably attributed what he saw as evidence of the workers' growing secularism to the Nonconformist and Anglican evangelicalism he had long detested. By alluding to a biblical passage encouraging persons contending with "heaviness through manifold temptations" to expect heavenly riches after the earthly refining of their Christian faith, the narrator exposes a spiritual emergency ongoing in Coketown (1 Pt 1:5–7)[6]:

> No. Coketown did not come out of its own furnaces, in all respects like gold that had stood the fire. First, the perplexing mystery of the place was, Who belonged to the eighteen denominations? Because, whoever did, the labouring people did not. It was very strange to walk through the streets on a Sunday morning, and note how few of *them* the barbarous jangling of bells that was driving the sick and nervous mad, called away from their own quarter, from their own close rooms, from the corners of their own streets, where they lounged listlessly, gazing at all the church and chapel going, as at a thing with which they had no manner of concern.
> (Dickens 1854a, 28; bk. 1, ch. 5)

No refinement of faith through suffering occurs for the workers because the Coketown denominations fail to offer encouraging guidance and compassion to those encountering trials and tribulations. Instead of confronting their errors in ministry, churches seek to legally enforce attendance, petitioning Parliament to "make these people religious by main force" (25). If Christian worship can be legislated, then the spiritual value of free will deteriorates, rendering evangelical assistance merely another form of oppression in addition to the conditions imposed by mill owners. In a town filled with scattered denominations placing little emphasis on God, Coketown's people must look elsewhere for spiritual support as Dickens demonstrates with the troubled religious experiences of Stephen Blackpool.

Enabled by a prophetic dream, an earthly angel, and communion with nature, this Coketown power-loom weaver achieves a theosophic faith, representing the most significant spiritual journey undertaken by any Dickens character. Speaking of *Hard Times* as a whole, Dennis

Walder has dismissed the religious impact of the novel, insisting that it "gathers up and reinforces Dickens' repugnance toward Benthamite reductionism and his faith in Christian charity across class divisions, but does not add significantly to the evolving shape of his beliefs" (2012 [1981], 145). Acknowledging Stephen as a "martyr," Anne Smith finds his "prospects of paradise" an irritating distraction from the novel's unresolved class inequalities, overlooking the ecclesiastical negligence also at issue (1972, 168). Lost in the conventional details of a worker longing to escape his alcoholic wife prior to the Matrimonial Causes Act (1857) is the mystic quality of Stephen's dawning religiosity which is occurring outside ecclesiastical influence. Church and state alike provide no aid for him in his dilemma, but rather work in conjunction to damn him. Outraged at Stephen's desire for a marital separation, the factory owner Josiah Bounderby rebukes his employee, affecting to believe "the express object of his visit was to know how he could knock Religion over, and floor the Established Church" (Dickens 1854a, 217; bk. 2, ch. 8). Primarily using the local parish church clock as a timekeeper, Stephen associates this Anglican building with judgmental Old Testament theology promulgated by Evangelicals. Watching by his wife's bedside, Stephen dreams he stands inside the church, preparing to marry a woman he loves before a congregation of acquaintances, when a "tremendous light" interrupts the ceremony:

> It broke from one line in the table of commandments at the altar, and illuminated the building with the words. They were sounded through the church, too, as if there were voices in the fiery letters. Upon this, the whole appearance before him and around him changed, and nothing was left as it had been, but himself and the clergyman.
> (100–1; bk. 1, ch. 13)

Though the commandment is not specified, given Stephen's predicament in regard to his affection for fellow textile worker Rachael, it is likely the seventh, "Thou shalt not commit adultery" (Ex 20:14).

Expelled from the church without his bride and deprived of the friendly congregation, Stephen is damned, compelled to endure the loathing of his community for the sin he attempted to commit. He becomes the despised focus of

> a crowd so vast, that if all the people in the world could have been brought together into one space, they could not have looked, he thought, more numerous; and they all abhorred him, and there was not one pitying or friendly eye among the millions that were fastened on his face.
> (Dickens 1854a, 101; bk. 1, ch. 13)

When the burial service is read and his industrial loom rises like a scaffold, Stephen experiences instantaneous descent into a spiritual and physical void: "In an instant what he stood on fell below him, and he was gone" (101). Foreshadowing his exclusion from the community of Coketown workers due to his refusal to participate in their strike and the false accusation of theft that renders him a wanted man, this dream warns Stephen that the Evangelical church will not pity or succor his misery. Awakening to what becomes a Christ-like ordeal of temptation and persecution, Stephen nearly allows his wife to commit suicide with poison, an act prevented at the last moment by the interference of Rachael, a fellow mill-hand who figures as an angel of mercy and redemption. Claiming that she is an "Angel," the repentant weaver tells her, "Thou changest me from bad to good. Thou mak'st me humbly wishfo' to be more like thee, and fearfo' to lose thee when this life is ower, and a' the muddle cleared awa'. Thou'rt an Angel; it may be, thou has saved my soul alive!" (104; bk. 1, ch. 13). Echoing Psalm 30:3, "O Lord, thou has brought up my soul from the grave: thou hast kept me alive, that I should not go down to the pit," Stephen sees Rachael, whom he has pictured previously with a halo, or "glory" shining about her head, as facilitating his salvation by preventing his self-wrought damnation.

Generously, Rachael assumes the church's role as guide, directing Stephen's thoughts to the great rewards believers like her dead sister enjoy in heaven. Distracted by his love for her, Stephen mistakenly adores Rachael, kneeling and kissing the hem of her dress, though she rejects his homage: "Angels are not like me. Between them, and a working woman fu' of faults, there is a deep gulf set" (104). Yet, Stephen is consoled by the thought that she will walk with him in heaven, the narrator explaining, "As the shining stars were to the heavy candle in the window, so was Rachael, in the rugged fancy of this man, to the common experiences of his life" (105). Leaving Coketown after Bounderby fires him, Stephen angrily returns to refute accusations of theft, only to experience the physical and spiritual plummet of his dream into the Old Hell Shaft. Wandering on a Sunday out into the country "over-arched by a bright blue sky," the novel's moral heroines Rachael and Sissy Jupe stumble upon spiritual truth when they discover Stephen, mortally wounded (313, bk. 3, ch. 6). He ecstatically points out a literal star which has enabled him to commune directly with nature and the divine in a process wholly unmediated by church or theology. Believing it is the Star of Bethlehem which led the Three Wise Men to "Our Savior's home," Stephen explains to Rachael that this new spiritual guide has left him at peace with all former enemies: "It ha' shined upon me," he says reverently,

> in my pain and trouble down below. It ha' shined into my mind. I ha' lookn at't and thowt o' thee, Rachael, till the muddle in my mind have cleared awa, above a bit, I hope. . . . In my pain an' trouble,

lookin up yonder,—wi' it shinin on me—I ha' seen more clear, and ha' made it my dyin prayer that aw th' world may on'y coom toogether more, an' get a better unnerstan'in o' one another, than when I were in't my own weak seln.

(322–23; bk. 3, ch. 6)

Imagining he and the rescuers carrying him across the fields are following the star, Stephen dies. The narrative reiterates what the expiring man just testified: "The star had shown him where to find the God of the poor; and through humility, and sorrow, and forgiveness, he had gone to his Redeemer's rest" (322–23; bk. 3, ch. 6).

Critique of the Coketown denominations in *Hard Times* led to contemporary alarm over Dickens' rancor against Evangelicals and distrust of religious figures. Prominent examples of his dislike for the social misuse of Christianity include drunken Nonconformist teetotaler Mr. Stiggins in *The Pickwick Papers* (1840 [1837]) and Seth Pecksniff, Evangelical villain of *Martin Chuzzlewit* (1986 [1844]), while just previously, in *Bleak House* (1853), Dickens had ridiculed foreign mission projects and heartless evangelizing of the alcoholic and wretched poor. Remarking, "Nearly all portrayals of Dickens' religious characters and ministers are parodic caricatures of self-important or self-obsessed hypocrites," Christian Dickinson insists that in the latter novel, "The Church appears throughout the novel as a shadowy presence," counterbalanced by Esther Summerson's kindness (2018, 352). Similarly, *Hard Times* had shown the divided denominations opposing vice to be spiritually ineffectual in contrast to the ministrations of one compassionate Christian and a star. Reviewing the novel, a critic for *The British Quarterly Review* protests,

> In this story, again, as in all his works, Mr. Dickens has his characters of great moral beauty, but care seems to be taken that this beauty of character shall come into existence, not only apart from any religious influences, but in circumstances most alien to such influences. His best condition of humanity is a condition without religion, a condition that does not need religion.
>
> (*"Hard Times"* 1854, 582)

Ironically, the confusing distinction between true Christianity and the church appeared to allow for the insidious possibility of secularism. Concerned that readers would learn through this novel to distrust "everything religious" as "cant and hypocrisy," the reviewer demanded, "But are we all to become atheists, practically at least, if not avowedly, because the world has its hypocrites in religion, as in everything besides?" (582). Though the sight of Preston's empty and diverse churches had given rise to Dickens' most provocative literary exploration of Christianity, the author's diatribe against Evangelicals distracted from the spirituality of Stephen's redemption.

Redemption Through Self-Sacrifice

Near the end of Dickens' life, Preston's ecclesiastical environment again inspired reflection on the legacy of evangelicalism to the Lancashire poor. In 1867, Dickens arrived in Preston to perform a reading of "Doctor Marigold's Prescriptions" (1865) at the Theatre Royal on April 25. Despite collapsing from exhaustion and relinquishing the remainder of the farewell reading tour on the urgent orders of physicians, Dickens soon penned a new condemnation of evangelicalism in "George Silverman's Explanation," a three-part short story serialized in American periodical *The Atlantic Monthly* (January–March 1868) and in *All the Year Round* (February 1868). Previous reading tours in August 1856 and December 1861 had brought Dickens back to Preston, a town he loathed as the "nastiest" place he knew of, yet on these prior occasions he was not inspired to write a narrative set unabashedly in Preston of a poor orphan beset by hypocritical Calvinist Evangelicals.[7] Confused by its themes and timing, critics have interpreted this work as a strange aberration, when they consider it at all. Attributing its impetus to Dickens' fee of 1000 pounds received from *The Atlantic Monthly*, Andrew Lang commented, "Otherwise the little paper is inexplicable. Dickens' dislike of Dissent comes out even more strongly than in Mr. Chadband, Stiggins, and the Shepherd . . . But there is nothing of interest to be said about George Silverman" (1905, xiii). Rather than representing a mere financial calculation, the story was motivated by the author's serious reflection on religious dissent provoked by his irritated perception that Preston's denominations continued to proliferate with no observable effect on the appalling condition of the town's poor just recovering from the Cotton Famine (1861–1865) (Waugh 1867, 24). Now, a Free Gospel Chapel was housed in Ashmoor Street, and a Presbyterian Chapel established in the theatre of Avenham Institution for resident and immigrating Calvinists. The new Roman Catholic Church of St. Thomas of Canterbury and the English Martyrs had completed major construction on old Gallows Hill. Among several rebuilt ecclesiastical buildings was the Orchard Chapel, which had been torn down and rebuilt as the United Methodist Free Church (Hewitson 1869). Concerned for the spiritual welfare of working-class children taught to fear worldliness, Dickens decided the subject warranted attention.

Consequently, Dickens sought a historical exploration of Preston's Nonconformity, which took the author mentally and physically back to Lancashire's dissenting past and working-class resistance occurring long before the Victorian era. Allegedly, Dickens consolidated the story's outline prior to his physical breakdown as he trekked between Preston and Blackburn and visited the ruins of the old manor house, Hoghton Towers. For him, as an opponent of Sabbatarianism, this seven-mile walk represented a pilgrimage to the site where King James I favorably received a petition from the Lancashire working classes asking for permission to pursue secular diversions after Sunday worship (Roby 1829, 84). In consequence, ministers were ordered to read the *Book of Sports* (1617) from the pulpit, though Puritan successfully resisted doing so in 1618 (Parker 2002, 139–40). Writing to Wills on September 2, 1867, Dickens confided that the narrator's uncanny voice came to him as he toured the ruins:

> I am glad you see a certain unlikeness to anything in the American story. Upon myself it has made the strangest impression of reality and originality!! And I feel as if I had read something (by somebody else), which I should never get out of my mind!!! The main idea of the narrator's position towards the other people was the idea that I *had* for my next novel in A.Y.R. But it is very curious that I did not in the least see how to begin his state of mind until I walked into Hoghton Towers one bright April day.[8]

Inside desolate and vermin-infested Houghton Towers, young George hides, agonizing over his apparent spiritual wickedness and wondering, "How not to be this worldly little devil? how not to have a repugnance towards myself as I had towards the rats?" (Dickens 1868, ch. 5) As an adult, George associates the building with the monarch in question, but seems woefully ignorant of the relevancy of its past history to his own predicament. Like a sad refrain, he repeats, "What did I know then of Hoghton Towers?" (Dickens 1868, ch. 5). Rather than renew his own denunciation of Nonconformist evangelicalism and its continuing prohibition against earthly desires, Dickens now presents "testimony" from the spiritually abused Preston poor.

Stephen Blackpool's experience of evangelical indifference and judgment hinders his access to true faith, but George's narrative confirms that abusive evangelicalism unfairly condemns the poor for wanting anything. According to Peter Merchant and Catherine Waters,

> It is often said that Dickens 'doesn't believe in original sin.' Clearly the use made of the doctrine by contemporary evangelicalism, in which the natural corollary of original sin is infant depravity, never ceases to arouse his outrage and his ridicule.
>
> (2016, 58)

So deeply have constant evangelical accusations of worldliness become embedded in the minds of Preston's working classes that young George's basic needs are classed as a species of wicked selfishness:

> A worldly little devil was mother's usual name for me. Whether I cried for that I was in the dark, or for that it was cold, or for that I was hungry, or whether I squeezed myself into a warm corner when there was a fire, or ate voraciously when there was good, she would

> still say, "O, you worldly little devil!" And the sting of it was, that I quite knew myself to be a worldly little devil. Worldly as to wanting to be housed and warmed, worldly as to wanting to be fed, worldly as to the greed with which I inwardly compared how much I got of those good things with how much father and mother got, when, rarely, those good things were going.
>
> (Dickens 1868, ch. 3)

Even after his parents die of fever, apparently in the cholera epidemic of 1832, George continues to be accused of worldliness. A new guardian, Brother Verity Hawkyard, dins the epithet into George's soul, as do the members of Hawkyard's congregation in Preston, including the vindictive Brother Gimblet. Though he is told that his late grandfather, Brother Parksop, was a member of this Calvinist denomination, George cannot overcome his dislike of their "prolix addresses, their inordinate conceit, their daring ignorance, their investment of the Supreme Ruler of heaven and earth with their own miserable meannesses and littlenesses" (Dickens 1868, ch. 6). Over time, he comes to see them as being "no better than the rest of the human family" and, in fact, generally worse. Still, he continues to pathologically guard against his own potential sin.

Evangelicalism's insistence on the illegitimacy of all desire has warped George's ability to differentiate between self-interest and selfishness. When he asks after the status of his late grandfather's property, Hawkyard calls him worldly, causing the lad to fall silent under the familiar rebuke. Harry Stone pronounces, "Thus the iron circle of action and reaction, of misunderstanding and morbid guilt is early formed. And even more tragically, this pattern becomes the motivating and self-reinforcing of all his future struggles to do good" (1958, 88). Wrongly fearing he will infect his foster family with his parents' illness, George protects them by avoiding their companionship, a deprivation doubling as penance. Several years later, accurately surmising from a sly remark of Gimblet's that Hawkyard has stolen his rightful inheritance, George repents of his suspicions and allows the matter to drop lest he be accused of greed. Becoming an Anglican clergyman against the wishes of the Preston brethren, who deplore his "sin of worldly-mindedness" in seeking religious employment, George leaves their chapel "with an aching heart and a weary spirit," marveling that his noblest actions could be so misinterpreted (Dickens 1868, ch. 6). Another opportunity arises to disprove the charge when he accepts a North Devonshire living from Lady Faraway, only to fall in love with her talented daughter, Adelina. While in *Hard Times* affection for Rachael guides Stephen to faith, evangelical guilt prevents George from participating in "relationships of personal love" (Bock 1987, 121). He muses, "in imagination I took advantage of her noble trustfulness, took the fortune that I knew she must possess in her own right," and resolves, "No! Worldliness should not enter here at any cost" (Dickens 1868, ch. 8). Though Adelina's reciprocal affection justifies their union, George cannot allow himself to marry an heiress and risk further religious rebuke.

Paralleling Stephen's spiritual rapture, George does manage to attain peace through acquiring faith outside of church or theology as he performs an act of self-sacrifice for Adelina, as he believes. Like the Preston weaver gazing on a star, George also acquires a theosophic faith through nature, though his divine message derives from the rising sun on the summer morning of his love's wedding day to another. Perceiving this magnificent scene, the clergyman feels his anguish resolving:

> The tranquillity upon the deep, and on the firmament, the orderly withdrawal of the stars, the calm promise of coming day, the rosy suffusion of the sky and waters, the ineffable splendour that then burst forth, attuned my mind afresh after the discords of the night. Methought that all I looked on said to me, and that all I heard in the sea and in the air said to me, Be comforted, mortal, that thy life is so short. Our preparation for what is to follow has endured, and shall endure, for unimaginable ages."
>
> (Dickens 1868, ch. 9)

Heavenly happiness does not ensue immediately as in Stephen's case, with George undergoing further persecution by the bride's mother, who believes he has performed the wedding ceremony in return for significant monetary compensation from the heiress's new husband (ch. 8). Cast out of the living and ecclesiastically reprimanded, George slowly recovers his public reputation, but never escapes the impact of an evangelical upbringing. He concludes his explanation, still anxious that future readers ascertain that he cannot be a "worldly little devil," having relinquished the earthly rewards of fortune, affection, and livelihood. In an abrupt departure from the ecstatic death of Stephen, which positively circumvents corrupt ecclesiastical entities, Dickens presents George's brief shining moment of theosophical faith as paling besides the anguish of remaining constricted for life by longstanding evangelical regulation of the desires of the Lancashire poor.

Conclusion

Greater knowledge of what Preston represented to Charles Dickens in a spiritual, as well as industrial, sense can clarify the author's belief in extending charity without judgment or conditions to industrial workers. Witnessing the town's strong Nonconformist presence during the 1853–1854 industrial strike caused him to accuse its multiple denominations of unpardonable blindness in seeking to improve working-class morals by criticizing leisure activities rather than spiritually ministering to socioeconomic distress. To promote his ideal of Christian civic duty and rejection of prohibitive evangelicalism, Dickens created literary illustrations in *Hard Times* and "George Silverman's Explanation" of the spiritual harm Preston's poorest might endure through ecclesiastical alienation and theological persecution. Believing faith to be attainable without the restraining influences of denomination and dogma, as in the case of Stephen Blackpool, Dickens also became increasingly aware during his 1867 visit that for centuries Preston's poor had experienced behavioral constraints from Nonconformist religious authorities. In composing the dismal tale of George Silverman's renunciations, he remained cognizant of the possibility that those alienated by evangelicalism could attain theosophical faith. However, he also remarked upon the damage that could be spiritually and mentally wrought upon the impoverished through oppressive religious judgment. What Dickens proposed should be done to correct the situation was not entirely delineated in these texts, but his mysterious references to what Hoghton Towers should mean to a poor boy from Preston offers a clue. By 1867, he may have come to interpret the nonattendance of the working classes in 1851 not as mere secularism, but rather as a justifiable religious "strike" in the rebel spirit of their Early Modern ancestors.

Notes

1. Whether Dickens should be interpreted as an Anglican or Unitarian during this period, and to what extent he rejected or embraced the ideologies of either, remains an unresolved debate (Colledge 2011, 85–88).
2. Dickens was so determinedly "incognito" that he possibly dyed his "luxurious" mustache "jet-black"; despite his efforts, his brief presence at various strike meetings was observed and reported in advance of the publication of "On Strike" in a prominent local newspaper (*Preston Chronicle* 3.).
3. Although Preston's citizens numbered just below 70,000 in the 1851 Census of Great Britain, in contrast to London's two million inhabitants, the town accommodated similarly diverse religious factions and faiths (Snell and Ell 2000, 219). Preston contained 29 places of worship, 10 being Church of England, with 4 Roman Catholic, 3 Wesleyan Methodist, and the rest belonging to various dissenting sects (Census of Great Britain 1854 [1851], 128).
4. Every week, the strikers met here and in another place of public meeting, Chadwick's Orchard, as Dickens would have easily ascertained from townsfolk during his perambulations or from perusing the *Preston Chronicle* the morning after his arrival ("Wages" January 1854a, 3). At some point during this trip, Dickens had purchased newspapers at the Preston railway station (Dickens and Hogarth 1879, 196) as can be inferred from a letter to W. H. Wills (December 13, 1861).
5. Dickens may not have spent much time at strike meetings. The *Preston Chronicle* stated with unmerciful precision, "Mr. Dickens was a spectator at this meeting also, for about ten minutes. He left Preston for London the same evening by the 4.50 express train" ("Wages" 1854b, 3).
6. 1 Peter 1:5–7 (KJV).

7. Dickens and Hogarth (1879, 321) from letter to Mamie Dickens (February 1, 1867).
8. Dickens and Hogarth (1893, 629–30; emphasis in original) from letter to W. H. Wills (September 2, 1867).

Bibliography

"Assembled 'Neath the Broad Blue Sky." In *Democratic Hymns and Songs*. London: J. Barker, 1849.
Bock, Carol A. "Miss Wade and George Silverman: The Forms of Fictional Monologue." *Dickens Studies Annual* 16 (1987): 113–26.
Brown, Stewart J., and Peter B. Nockles, eds. *The Oxford Movement: Europe and the Wider World*. Cambridge: Cambridge University Press, 2012.
Butterworth, Robert D. "Dickens the Journalist: The Preston Strike and 'On Strike'." *The Dickensian* (1991): 129–38.
———. *Dickens, Religion, and Society*. New York: Palgrave Macmillan, 2017.
Census of Great Britain. 1851. London: George Routledge and Company, 1854.
Colledge, Gary. *Dickens, Christianity and 'The Life of Our Lord': Humble Veneration, Profound Conviction*. London: Continuum, 2011.
Cunningham, Valentine. "Dickens and Christianity." In *A Companion to Charles Dickens*, edited by David Paroissien, 255–56. Oxford: Blackwell, 2008.
Dickens, Charles. *Bleak House*. London: Bradbury, 1853. https://books.google.com/books?id=KlsJAAAAQAAJ.
———. *A Christmas Carol. In Prose. Being a Ghost Story of Christmas*. London: Chapman and Hall, 1843.
———. "George Silverman's Explanation." *The Atlantic Monthly* 21, nos. 123–35 (January–March 1868). Boston: Ticknor and Fields. In *Hard Times and Reprinted Pieces*, edited by David Price, Vol. 15. London: Chapman and Hall, 1905.
———. *Hard Times*. London: Bradbury and Evans, 1854a. https://books.google.com/books?id=03RFjIVjBoMC.
———. *Martin Chuzzlewit*. 1844. Harmondsworth: Penguin, 1986.
———. "On Strike." *Household Words* 8, no. 203 (February 11, 1854b): 553–59.
———. *The Posthumous Papers of the Pickwick Club*. 1837. New York: J. Van Amringe, 1840. https://books.google.com/books?id=r2ooAAAAMAAJ.
Dickens, Mamie, and Georgina Hogarth, eds. *The Letters of Charles Dickens: 1857 to 1870*. New York: Charles Scibner's Sons, 1879. https://books.google.com/books?id=V-A5AAAAMAAJ.
———. *The Letters of Charles Dickens*. Vol. 3. London: Macmillan, 1893. https://books.google.com/books?id=GTvzdR5O44IC.
Dickinson, Christian. "Neither High-Church, Low-Church, nor No-Church: Religious Dissatisfaction and Dissent in *Bleak House*." *Dickens Studies Annual* 49, no. 2 (2018): 349–77.
"Evangelical religion." In *The Oxford Companion to Charles Dickens*. 1999. Edited by Paul Schlicke, 233–34. Oxford: Oxford University Press, 2011.
Field, Clive D. *Periodizing Secularization: Religious Allegiance and Attendance in Britain, 1880–1945*. Oxford: Oxford University Press, 2019.

"'Hard Times.' Unsigned review of *Hard Times*, by Charles Dickens." *British Quarterly Review* 20, no. 40 (October 1, 1854): 581–82.

Hempton, David. "Evangelicalism in English and Irish Society, 1780–1840." In *Evangelicalism: Comparative Studies of Popular Protestantism in North America, the British Isles, and Beyond, 1700–1990*, edited by Mark A. Noll, David W. Bebbington, and George A. Rawlyk, 156–76. Oxford: Oxford University Press, 1994.

Hewitson, Anthony (as "Atticus"). *Our Churches and Chapels*. Preston: The Chronicle Office, 1869.

Johnson, Alice. *Middle-class Life in Victorian Britain*. Liverpool: Liverpool University Press, 2020.

Lang, Andrew, ed. *The Works of Charles Dickens*. New York: Charles Scribner's Sons, 1905.

Melnyk, Julie. *Victorian Religion: Faith and Life in Britain*. Westport, CT: Praeger, 2008.

Merchant, Peter, and Catherine Waters. *Dickens and the Imagined Child*. London: Taylor and Francis, 2016.

Metz, Nancy Aycock. "The Tremendous Potency of the Small": Dickens, the Individual, and Social Change in a Post-America, Post-Catastrophist Age." In *Charles Dickens as an Agent of Change*, edited by Lena Steveker and Joachim Frenk, 75–84. Ithaca, NY: Cornell University Press, 2019.

Parker, Kenneth L. *The English Sabbath: A Study of Doctrine and Discipline from the Reformation to the Civil War*. Cambridge: Cambridge University Press, 2002.

Pilkington, William. *Facts About the Origin of the Teetotal Principle and Pledge*. Preston: Steam Printing Office, 1894.

Rapkin, J. *Map of Preston*. Illustrated by H. Winkles. London: The London Printing and Publishing Company Limited, 1852.

"Re-Building of the Parish Church." April 16, 1853. *Preston Chronicle and Lancashire Advertiser*. British Newspaper Archive. www.britishnewspaperarchive.co.uk/viewer/BL/0000099/18530416/017/0005.

Roby, John. *Traditions of Lancashire*. Vol. 1. London: Longman, Rees, Orme, Brown and Green, 1829.

Slater, Michael. *Charles Dickens*. New Haven, CT: Yale University Press, 2009.

Smith, Anne. "The Martyrdom of Stephen in *Hard Times*." *The Journal of Narrative Technique* 2, no. 3 (1972):159–70.

Snell, K. D. M., and Paul S. Ell. *Rival Jerusalems: The Geography of Victorian Religion*. Cambridge: Cambridge University Press, 2000.

Stone, Harry. "Dickens' Tragic Universe: 'George Silverman's Explanation'." *Studies in Philology* 55, no. 1 (1958): 86–97.

Turner-Bishop, Aiden. "Livesey, Joseph (1794–1884)." In *Alcohol and Temperance, A History: An International Encyclopedia*. Vol. 1, edited by Jack S. Blocker, David M. Fahey, and Ian R. Tyrrell, 383. Santa Barbara, CA: ABC-CLIO, 2003.

"The Wages Movement." January 28, 1854a. *Preston Chronicle and Lancashire Advertiser*. British Newspaper Archive. www.britishnewspaperarchive.co.uk/viewer/BL/0000099/18540128/008/0003.

———. February 4, 1854b. *Preston Chronicle and Lancashire Advertiser. British Newspaper Archive*. www.britishnewspaperarchive.co.uk/viewer/BL/0000099/18540204/009/0003.

Walder, Dennis. *Dickens and Religion*. 1981. New York: Taylor and Francis, 2012.

Waugh, Edwin. *Home-Life of the Lancashire Factory Folk During the Cotton Famine*. London: Simpkin, Marshall, and Company, 1867.

7 Needful Things
Dickens, Social Justice, and the Meaning of Human Work[1]

Susan Johnston

> The joys and the hopes, the griefs and the anxieties of the men of this age, especially those who are poor or in any way afflicted, these are the joys and hopes, the griefs and anxieties of the followers of Christ. Indeed, nothing genuinely human fails to raise an echo in their hearts.
> —Paul VI (1965, sec. 1)[2]

> The Marxist claims him as "almost" a Marxist, the Catholic claims him as "almost" a Catholic, and both claim him as a champion of the proletariat (or "the poor," as Chesterton would have put it).
> —George Orwell (1981 [1946], 48)

Decades of careful criticism has accumulated around *Hard Times* and the great synecdoche through which Charles Dickens gestures toward the dehumanization of the factory workers "generically called 'the Hands' " (1996 [1854], 99). This critical reception examines the working class in historical, epistemological, political, and affective or emotional terms, from contemporary reviews that condemned the novel's "unreasonable exaggerations and unnatural characters" ("Historical" 1854, 277) to George Gissing (1898) and George Orwell's ideological critiques which turn on the novelist's ignorance of, and distaste for, the working classes.[3] Christopher Barnes (2004) is in some ways a successor to Orwell, treating the novel as an investigation—and critique—of systems of power and of systems *as* power while others, following Philip Collins' lead in "Dickens and Industrialism" (1980), are primarily concerned with what Dickens knew and when he knew it.[4]

Mary-Catherine Harrison blends the affective with the political in contending that Dickens' realism depends on synecdochal models of characters deployed to evoke empathy and direct it outward to the really suffering (2008, 268). Here she is complicating, for example, Martha Nussbaum's oft-cited claim in *Poetic Justice* that novel reading in general and the reading of *Hard Times* in particular "both exemplifies and

DOI: 10.4324/9781003156611-8

cultivates abilities of imagination that are essential to the intelligent making of such assessments, in public as well as private life" (1995, 52). For Nele Pollatschek (2013), who reads this empathic imagination through the novel's scriptural allusions, it takes on a specifically Christian character. Jennifer Gribble contends that Dickens works to "restore the marginalized discourse of Christianity, rewriting the parable of the Good Samaritan" (2004, 427) who "acts counter-culturally, effecting a decision about the meaning of self, other and moral action the novel affirms as the proper ground of all moral action and communal well-being" (439). In revisiting the figure of the "melancholy mad elephants" to compare the brutalized and passive workers with the violence and unpredictability of other forces, Tamara Ketabgian (2003) focuses on the disciplinary power of factory work's repetition.

Despite this critical history, the bulk of *Hard Times* criticism has continued what Katharyn Stober calls its overemphasis on the "destructiveness of fact" (2012, 129) and focused on the ways in which the utilitarianism and unbridled capitalism in the novel deform its "worker ant[s]" (134). Yet at the heart of this representation is an understanding of work, as well as of the person who performs it. Victorian Britain evinced multiple lines of thought on the subject, as Catherine Gallagher (2008 [2006]) has ably shown,[5] and much criticism on Dickens has therefore situated his discourses of labor and personhood in the context of Marxist thought, on the one hand, or utilitarianism and liberalism, on the other. This chapter proposes, rather differently, to read human personhood and human work as they are represented in *Hard Times* in the nineteenth-century Catholic and Anglo-Catholic theological context, best known through Leo XIII's 1891 encyclical *Rerum Novarum* ["On the Condition of the Working Classes"] and unpacked through successive twentieth-century iterations of Catholic social teaching. This approach may be surprising, for Dickens' own spiritual autobiography would not unveil much hidden attraction to Catholicism, whether of the Anglican or the "Romish" kind. And here I must echo Janet Larson's demurral at the outset of *Dickens and the Broken Scripture*: "Let it be said at once that this book is not an attempt to reclaim Dickens for Christianity" (2008 [1985], xi)—or, for that matter, for Catholicism. Instead I wish to illuminate the novel's idea of the worker in theological terms, that is to say, as a *person*, revealed through action (John Paul II 1979 [1969], 11). In this way, I hope to show that restoring a theological vocabulary to our critical lexicon will illuminate that subject in terms of the ineradicable personhood Dickens claims for it.

Although Dickens' anti-Catholicism is well documented, Mark Eslick has convincingly demonstrated that the vagaries of Dickens' religious biography were rooted not in faltering belief but in a disgust for "doctrinal controversy" and for ritualism (2011, 12, 15) that nearly equaled his disgust for Puritanism's anti-sensualism and for hypocrisy. The

Tractarians, like the Catholic Church, saw their rituals and liturgies as fundamentally connected to their sacramentalism and rooted in a theology of personhood unmarred by the distaste for the material world Dickens excoriated. Simon Skinner has gone a long way toward redressing views, like Dickens', of the Oxford Movement as invested in smells and bells at the expense of both charity and justice, proposing such figures as Thomas Mozley, Samuel Bosanquet, and John Henry Newman as advancing social commentary that both shook up older high-church views and enabled a newly robust social criticism (Ketabgian 1999, 201). In taking up a theology of the person that distinguishes the Tractarian and Catholic views, I am, first, following Skinner's account of Anglo-Catholic social criticism. Second, I am recognizing Eslick's understanding that the modes and tropes of anti-Catholicism so widespread in Victorian England were figures both of desire and of the self-critique of the liberal Anglicanism that captured Dickens' "Christian[ity] of the broadest kind."[6] My focus here is on the theology of the work of art, what Julia Lupton terms "a form of thinking" and thus "a speculative turning away from both nature and culture in their infinite variety to thought in its singular capacity to cut through the local habitations of lived experience" (2006, 147). I hope, however, to situate this account rather broadly in nineteenth-century social theology.

In *The Body Economic*, Gallagher identifies a significant shift at the start of the nineteenth century from a measure of "ultimate value" by the transcendent and spiritual to one of "organic 'Life' itself," a shift that "made human sensations—especially pleasure and pain—the sources and signs of that value" (3). *Hard Times*, situated after this shift, is not concerned with "factory hours . . . pollution, unemployment, class conflict, unsympathetic masters, or even the cash nexus" (62–63); rather, its concern is with "labor itself in its repetitious invariability" (63). Recognizing that "in *Hard Times*, monotonous work by itself makes people unhappy" (63), Gallagher contrasts Dickens with other early Victorian writers, who pursued "self-expression and self-realization through work . . . with a quasi-religious fervor" (64). Where Thomas Carlyle stressed the nobility of work, then, Dickens aligned rather surprisingly with Jeremy Bentham, for whom labor was pain, to be balanced against the pleasure of the wealth thus created (65–66). In Gallagher's account, "when Dickens blames Coketown's unhappiness on its severe workfulness, when he figures the spirit of the town as animal vitality bent into ceaseless rhythmic motion, he unwittingly adheres to Bentham's view" (66).[7] Gallagher here extends the view of industrial work as fundamentally deformative even to Sleary's horse riding (76–80), noting the labor entailed by keeping the people "amuthed" (Dickens 78).

Gallagher's emphasis on a Benthamite view of labor is in contradistinction to three other strands of thought on work and the worker in the nineteenth century which, though themselves tangled and contradictory, will also serve to orient us in the sea of Victorian political thought. The first of these is the liberal Protestant notion, which Charles Taylor traces to the French and American upheavals he calls "the founding revolutions of the eighteenth century" (1989, 215). Those revolutions proposed not just liberty but also fraternity and equality, and in so doing "exalted man as producer, one who finds his highest dignity in labour and the transformation of nature in the service of life" (215). At the same time, a strand of Christian thought was coming to the fore, one that embraced personal salvation by eschewing those hierarchies that Reformation theologians had felt were implied by the veneration of the sacred and doctrines of mediation that gave the Church, and thus religious life, a special role in drawing the laity closer to God (215–17). If, as in this view,

> the Church is the locus and vehicle of the sacred, then we are brought closer to God by the very fact of belonging and participating in its sacramental life. Grace can come to us mediately by the Church, and we can mediate grace to each other, as the lives of the saints enrich the common stock on which we all draw. Once the sacred is rejected, then this kind of mediation is also. Each person stands alone in relation to God: his or her fate—salvation or damnation—is separately decided.
>
> (216)

For Taylor, this new "affirmation of ordinary life" (14) entailed that a "full human life is now defined in terms of labour and production, on one hand, and marriage and family life, on the other" (213). The tension between the emergent and the residual notions appears in *Hard Times*, where the affirmation of ordinary life is indeed visible but so too is the view of mediating grace it apparently superceded, sometimes indeed in the same figures; Sissy Jupe, daughter of the horse riding, brings "a wisdom of the Heart" into the Gradgrind home, thus redeeming both Louisa and her father (Dickens 248), and the factory worker Rachael, who cares for Stephen Blackpool's drunken wife and saves her from accidental poisoning, is hailed by Stephen as "an Angel" who "changest [him] from bad to good . . . and hast saved [his] soul alive!" (123; Gribble 436).

It should be clear that there is more at stake in this strand of thought than the Protestant work ethic Max Weber (2002 [1905]) described. As Ruth Danon notes, "the myth of vocation," which so permeates our "work-centered culture . . . cannot be described simply in Weberian terms. The Protestant work ethic does not explain the expectations people have that they be made happy by their work" (2020 [1985], 2). Here, Danon anticipates Gallagher's account of the shifting locus of value. As part of the affirmation and new dignity of ordinary life, work came to have a dignity of its own. What is more, *meaningful* work acquired the capacity to confer this dignity on the worker. "Work," says Danon,

> is, ideally, a vocation. It can be chosen and chosen well, directed from within. Such well-chosen work is meaningful work, infusing our lives with significance. . . . It involves a person directly with the production of necessities, but does not limit a person to that. This work leads to the spiritualizing of all experience. Finally, meaningful work is joy-producing. One's happiness and one's work are inextricable.
>
> (14)

Such a view, of course, takes labor as inalienable, as did Karl Marx (2009 [1932]), the contours of whose argument are likewise familiar. Under capitalism, the worker sells—alienates—what ought to be inalienable, his labor; his role in production is therefore rendered invisible by the owner of the means of production, who owns the fruits of that labor. Indeed we see in Dickens' excoriation of the factory-owning middle class and their contempt for the Hands and their "piece-work" (110), which dignifies them neither through the money it makes nor its own essential nobility, the perils of such views. Where labor and its fruit are brought to the same level, the level of the thing, Marx contends that "the worker sinks to the level of a commodity and becomes indeed the most wretched of commodities; that the wretchedness of the worker is in inverse proportion to the power and magnitude of his production" (sec. 22). Where liberalism's understanding of the power to transform the world through labor ultimately gives us an idea of the human self as *agent*, Marxism's more pessimistic, and more Romantic, account sees that self as *subject*. This is an altogether more passive view, and one in which the world may be said to work on the self and to forge it, rather than the other way around.[8] It is from this Marxian perspective on the self that Patricia E. Johnson and others have read Stephen Blackpool as the creature of the factory system (1989, 129; Ketabgian 651). Jean Bethke Elshtain rightly criticizes the "econometric and materialistic doctrines" derived from such views and have formed so much modern reflection on the human subject because they "either obliterate the human subject or offer a reductionistic, thin treatment of the human subject because they fail to credit human agency and free will" (2002, 16) which leads both to Stephen's refusal to join the union and to the deathbed epiphany that "showed him where to find the God of the poor" (Dickens, 293). Elshtain might equally have remarked on the cavalier disregard for an intractable world that informs liberalism's overemphasis on the capacity of human agency to transform that world. But both liberalism and Marxism perceive the dignity of human work as inhering in the work itself and posit forms of work that will confer dignity on the human subject; I am arguing that Dickens deplores this view, though the extent of his disagreement becomes clear only from quite a different perspective on human work.

Though the third perspective shares much with these accounts, it proposes that the dignity of work is conferred on it by the human being who performs it, and not the other way around. In remarking the "inner affinity between the old Protestant spirit and modern capitalist culture" (6), Weber was surprised by its relative absence among Catholics. Ultimately, of course, this affinity is what he perceives as the narrow utilitarianism of capitalism, where it is "the duty of the individual to work toward the increase of his wealth, which is assumed to be an end in itself" (11).[9] The Catholic view of both work and wealth, however, is rather a different one. In *Rerum Novarum*, Leo XIII emphasized work as fundamental to creation, but distinguished this exertion from that of animals through that reason "which renders a human being human, and distinguishes him essentially from the brute" (sec. 6). John Paul II, reading *Rerum Novarum* from the perspective of the "acting person" noted earlier, understands work as "a 'transitive' activity, that is to say an activity beginning in the human subject and directed towards an external object" (1981, sec. 4). Thus does he claim that *"the proper subject of work continues to be man"* (sec. 5; emphasis in original). It is here that this third strand of thought distinguishes itself. In Catholic social teaching, meaningful work does not confer dignity *on* the human person, for dignity inheres *in* the human person. It is prior to work. Thus, though "man is destined for work and called to it, in the first place work is 'for man' and not man 'for work'" (sec. 6). John Paul II continues,

> pre-supposing that different sorts of work that people do can have greater or lesser objective value . . . each sort is judged above all by *the measure of the dignity* of the subject of work, that is to say the person, *the individual who carries it out.*
>
> (sec. 6)

Contrary to Bounderby's view of the bare life of the Hand, then, Stephen's value is infinite, as is Bounderby's own.

Laborem Exercens, like the other anniversary encyclicals, not only testifies to the interpretive consensus, that reads *Rerum Novarum* as central to the modern Catholic understanding of work and the person, but also demonstrates the continuity of modern Catholic social teaching from Leo XIII's *Rerum Novarum* onward.[10] This continuity is not surprising, for *Rerum Novarum* itself developed its themes of the dignity of the person, the misery and just claims of the worker, the perils of antagonism between capitalism and labor, and the twin stumbling blocks of liberalism and socialism through the interpretation of Christian scripture and the theological patrimony of the church, and through the influence of former Tractarians like Cardinal Manning.[11] Rather, the degree to which

Dickens, antipapist and afflicter of the comfortable, anticipates and concurs with Catholic thought around these themes suggests interesting affinities between his social theology, that of the despised Tractarians, and what would become the social teaching of the Catholic church.

Leo XIII begins by noting the troubling disappearance of the old trade guilds over the course of the eighteenth century so that "by degrees it has come to pass that working men have been surrendered, isolated and helpless, to the hardheartedness of employers and the greed of unchecked competition" (1891, sec. 3). This parlous state of affairs, he remarks, accounts for the attraction of workers to socialism, which at least proposes a remedy through the abolition of private property and the equal distribution of wealth and benefits. Such a remedy, however, poses an insult to the dignity of the worker equally with his freedom, for he is "master of his own acts" (sec. 7); if the abolition of private property deprives man of a motive for work, as Leo XIII proposed (sec. 7–10), it would likewise deprive him of his personal vocation, the capacity to express and fulfill himself through work (John Paul II 1991, sec. 6). This theology of work resembles the view of meaningful work Danon has outlined until Leo XIII notes that the "personal" dimension of work is accompanied by a "social" dimension, through its connection both to the good of the family—which precedes the state—and to the good of the state (sec. 12–14). In this way, work is separate from the striving of beasts, for though they share with the human animal the need "to exert oneself for the sake of procuring what is necessary for the various purposes of life, and first of all for self-preservation" (sec. 44), they cannot confer dignity on that striving through the dignity that is essentially their own, as does the human person. There is, in other words, an anthropology at the heart of *Rerum Novarum*, one in which, as John Paul II would later say, the human person is "irreducible" (1993b [1975], 210) to tool, to commodity, or to mere idea.

Significantly, this resistance to utilitarianism in *Hard Times* is largely spoken in Christian terms (Kidder 2009, 424), terms which reclaim the Hands as the work of God and in so doing contend for their essential humanness and dignity. What is more, that very humanness is understood as heir to the spiritual longing that is our birthright, whether it is, like Louisa's wistful yearning, for "all the inappreciable things that raise [life] from the state of conscious death . . . the graces of my soul . . . the sentiments of my heart . . . the garden that should have bloomed once, in this great wilderness" (Dickens 1996 [1854], 240–241) or, like Stephen Blackpool's hunger, "to work hard in peace, and do what he felt right" (274). Martha Nussbaum sees Dickens' "Fancy" as the grounding capacity of the imagination that lets us enter into the deeply human lives of others (1995, 26–27), yet as Paulette Kidder points out, this warmly sympathetic view is nonetheless cold to that "spiritual longing toward a dimension of transcendent mystery" that remains for so many the foundation of that deeply human life (420). To read Louisa and Stephen's aspirations in this way, as rooted in a Judeo-Christian tradition and symbolism and as arching toward a divine mystery as well as the mystery of the human person, Kidder suggests, "need not lead—as Nussbaum believes it does—to a belief that the struggles of this world are unimportant" (425). Such a view is possible only if we understand the idea that Christians are aliens in this world very gnostically indeed. Nor does the grace Stephen finds in the stars above Old Hell Shaft (Dickens 292) render insignificant the injustices that have marred his life. Contrary, then, to Nussbaum, Kidder reiterates the value of that "faith in a source of love that grounds our longing for a better world, and the grace that supports our capacity for hope and forgiveness" (425). Here we may, I think, take the Pastoral Constitution on the Church in the Modern World (*Gaudium et Spes*) quite seriously, despite its twin disabilities of belatedness and Romishness: "The Church . . . teaches that a hope related to the end of time does not diminish the importance of intervening duties but rather undergirds the acquittal of them with fresh incentives" (Paul VI, sec. 21).[12] *Gaudium et Spes* here echoes Leo XIII's insistence that

> [in] either must it be supposed that the solicitude of the Church is so preoccupied with the spiritual concerns of her children as to neglect their temporal and earthly interests. Her desire is that the poor, for example, should rise above poverty and wretchedness, and better their condition in life; and for this she makes a strong endeavor.
> (sec. 28)

In other words, the eschatological character of Christian hope does not preclude work in this world. Rather, it insists upon it as part of the work through which the "acting person" (John Paul II 1979 [1969]), intelligent and free, seeks to conform himself to the transcendent world which awaits him.[13] This is so, I propose, despite the emphasis some Christian schools of thought have placed on faith over works, for it is precisely this distinction that fires Dickens' journalistic desire to afflict the comfortable and remind them again of their duty to "teach [the poor] and relieve them if you can" (Dickens 1934, 28).

Thus far, I have outlined this theology of the person in its best-known form, despite its belatedness. Tractarian social theology, however, preceded both *Rerum Novarum* and Dickens. Thomas Mozley, bemoaning "The Religious State of the Manufacturing Poor" (1840) complained that the "tall chimneys" of the factories "have supplanted or surpassed the heaven-directed spires of our forefathers" (337).[14] Simon Skinner calls Mozley's text "a sustained onslaught against the corrosive effects of the new capitalism, and the displacement of the spiritual by commerce and manufacture" (206). A crucial part of Mozley's jeremiad is mounted against the erasure of the concrete person by the monstrous machinery of industrialism:

> The steam-engine is a monster of productiveness, which laughs at the slow industry of thousands, beats them away from their petty handicrafts, and compels them to minister humbly to its own giant evolutions. It is a new and enormous calculus, which reduces almost out of count, or sight, or thought, the moral units of which society is composed. It levels distinction, making the clever and the foolish, the strong and the weak, the father and the child, all one as good as another.
>
> (334)

For Dickens too, the steam engine that "worked monotonously up and down" creates "people equally like one another, who all went in and out at the same hours, with the same sound upon the same pavements, to do the same work, and to whom every day was the same as yesterday and tomorrow" (1996 [1854], 60). For Mozley the new capitalism forges "men that look to numbers, physical strength, combination, visible means, success, and such temporal matters" (335). Dickens likewise found

> the relations between master and man were all fact, and everything was fact between the lying-in hospital and the cemetery, and what you couldn't state in figures, or show to be purchaseable in the cheapest market and saleable in the dearest, was not, and never should be, world without end, Amen.
>
> (61)

Where Mozley laments at length the falling away of the laboring classes from church and even chapel, Dickens remarks it almost as an aside, but both men share a concern that everything human or divine is increasingly crowded out the "severely workful" (60). "The mill," says Mozley,

> is the only refuge of poverty, the only centre of hope, or rather despair, the hard service, the house of bondage, the furnace of Egypt, the heavy burden, the galling yoke, the mill-stone about the neck of the manufacturing poor. They cannot help themselves: hard though its terms be, they must come to it or starve. It is their church, the only rock on which all the temporal expectations of myriads are built.
>
> (338)

The Tractarian Mozley saw little solution but the restoration of that "church authority" that once "raised the temporal condition of the poor, and [gave] them a real dignity and independence, a just feeling of united strength and mutual support unknown to heathen antiquity" but whose waning

> has gone far to undo the blessing, and made the poor more hopeless, more helpless, more friendless, more at the mercy of precarious benevolence . . . and, worst of all, still more widely severed from intercourse of heart and mind with the wealthy and educated classes.
> (338)

As the *British Quarterly Review* remarked, *Hard Times* does not suggest the need for any "religious influences" ("Our Epilogue" 1854, 582) despite its reliance on seemingly untethered Christian ones. Like Mozley, however, Dickens here laments a form of communion and of personhood whose dwindling has dehumanized the working poor, both in rendering them as the generic mass of "Hands" and in erasing the "unfathomable mystery," which lies "in the meanest of them, for ever" (104).

The early 1840s saw the repeated publication of Tractarian essays and fiction addressing the social ills of the new industrialism. Thus, for example, Francis Paget's *The Warden of Berkingholt* (1843) echoes Dickens' critique of the New Poor Law in *Oliver Twist* (1838), as indeed do Frederick Oakeley's sermons on "The Dignity and Claims of the Christian Poor" (Skinner 212), and the industrial hellscape of Coketown is anticipated by William Gresley's *Colton Green* (1846): "a confused mass of chimneys vomiting forth volumes of black smoke, blazing furnaces, glowing coke hills, heaps of ashes around the pit mouth, steam engines plying their incessant work, and other signs of human drudgery" (quoted in Skinner 206). Just as Dickens sought a solution to these ills in individual acts of charity, the Tractarian social critics asserted the value of parochial experience and a concomitant local custodialism of the poor and vulnerable, though marked by a strong note of nostalgia for the social harmony of England's imagined past (Skinner 207–208). While their view was paternalist, it was also fraternal and communitarian, insisting on the shared brotherhood and dignity of man, and many of these Tractarians carried this view with them when they departed from the Anglican Communion for the Roman Catholic Church. Henry Manning, later Cardinal Manning, lived out this view as he mediated the London Dock Strike of 1889, and his contributions to Leo XIII's thinking on the worker question are widely acknowledged (Hughes 1941, 226). For such figures, as for Dickens, the gravest social ill of the new industrialism and the work it entailed lay not in the alienation of labor but in how the relations of that work render us alien to each other. In what remains, I will take up this mystery of the alien subject, treating the neglected Hand, Stephen Blackpool, in terms of his estrangement both from his fellows and from the world itself.

Dickens introduces him thusly:

> among the multitude of Coketown, generically called "the Hands,"— a race who would have found more favour with some people, if Providence had seen fit to make them only hands, or, like the lower creatures of the seashore, only hands and stomachs—lived a certain Stephen Blackpool, forty years of age.
>
> (99)

The substance of Dickens' critique is the de-humanization of the worker, who is synecdochically reduced to a spare part.[15] Elsewhere I have argued that "the key-note" (Dickens 60) of the novel is not, as Patricia Johnson suggested, the economic–utilitarian dependence on fact-based rationality manifested through the factory and its metonym, fact (130), though this is clearly central. Rather, that note is the consequence of this materialist conception for our view of the other,[16] that working-class other whom Dickens seeks to erect, *pace* Josiah Wedgewood, as both man and brother.[17] Thus Dickens' Coketown, with its interchangeable streets and its interchangeable Hands, lets the reader, like Bounderby, see the workers as an undistinguished mass. It need hardly be said that this is not the sameness of recognizably shared humanity on which the reformists of the nineteenth century depended, however naively, but of cogs in the great machinery of fact: "So many hundred Hands in this Mill; so many hundred horse Steam Power" (Dickens 104). The synecdoche of the Hand emphasizes that the laborers are interchangeable insofar as they can be imagined as without that psychological depth which is a key feature of the discourse of rights. As Nussbaum points out, "dehumanize the worker in thought, and it is far easier to deny him or her the respect that human life calls forth" (1995, 34). The humanity the reader shares with the workers, who like us are "deliberating subjects with complex loves and aspirations and a rich inner world" (34), is, for Nussbaum, the central point of Dickens' sense of the ineffable mystery of the human person. She sees his critique as an appeal to go beyond the visible,[18] and to contemplate the irreducible and *individual* mystery of selfhood.

Such a mystery is Stephen Blackpool, Coketown hand. Trapped in a loveless marriage to a bestial and drunken wife, caught up in a therefore hopeless longing for Rachael, outcast by his fellow laborers because he refuses to join the union, framed by Tom Gradgrind for a bank robbery, Stephen Blackpool remains, to a considerable degree, a cipher:

> Old Stephen might have passed for a particularly intelligent man in his condition. Yet he was not. He took no place among those remarkable "Hands," who, piecing together their broken intervals of leisure through many years, had mastered difficult sciences, and acquired

a knowledge of most unlikely things. He held no station among the Hands who could make speeches and carry on debates. Thousands of his compeers could talk much better than he, at any time. He was a good power-loom weaver, and a man of perfect integrity. What more he was, or what else he had in him, if anything, let him show for himself.

(1996 [1854], 99–100)

Here we see the tension between the monotony of the visible and the theological view of the person as both unique and uniquely valuable. Stephen is, as Dickens takes care to insist, ordinary, though he is also extraordinary, as are all human creatures, "unfathomable myster[ies]" (104), "awful unknown quantities" (105), because they are animated by human souls:

It is known, to the force of a single pound weight, what the engine will do; but, not all the calculators of the National Debt can tell me the capacity for good or evil, for love or hatred . . . or the reverse, at any single moment in the soul of one of these its quiet servants, with the composed faces and the regulated actions.

(104)

Dickens' emphasis here on the idea of the soul, as the animator of an inner and spiritual life, is as much a part of the claim to juridical personhood being advanced through the nineteenth century on behalf of women and laboring men as is the claim to an innate capacity for reason and virtue. Yet soul, reason, and virtue may all be deadened by the ceaseless work of "the melancholy mad elephants" (104) as Dickens terms the awful machinery of the mills so that the whole world appears to Stephen "awlus a muddle" (102).[19]

Elshtain, in "Work and Its Meanings," reminds us that the modern constructions of human life and work "demand that people busy themselves at every moment with utility-maximizing tasks driven by self-interest" (17). Such busy-ness recalls, of course, Aristotle's assertion that "the money-maker's life is in a way forced on him" (1985 [340 BC], 1.6.1096a6) in the sense that it has an external origin, "the sort of origin in which the agent or victim contributes nothing" (2.9.1110x). Such a life is slavish, even animal, because it mistakes the means to life for the ends of life. Bounderby, the mill owner, views the work of his Hands this way: as the all-encompassing task for which and to which human beings are fitted merely as tools. He advises Stephen "the only thing you have got to do, is to mind your piece-work" (Dickens 110). This piecework produces in Stephen "the old sensation . . . which the stoppage of the machinery always produced—the sensation of its having worked and stopped in his own head" (100), which breaks down the boundaries between machine and machine worker. To Bounderby, Stephen is fundamentally inhuman, falling in and out of gear like the looms and the wheels of his mill (cf. 105), but throughout the novel, this confusion of person and thing is condemned as "unnatural" (60, 99), part of the perverse busy-ness of Coketown.

Leo XIII likewise sees such busy-ness as perverting natural justice. Like *Hard Times* itself, his *Rerum Novarum* is a response to the effects of the Industrial Revolution (Naughton 1992, 16). And like *Hard Times*, it condemns "the cruelty of men of greed, who use human beings as mere instruments for money-making" (Leo XIII sec. 42), even as it insists on the worker's duty to refuse such slavishness: "No man has in this matter power over himself. To consent to any treatment which is calculated to defeat the end and purpose of his being is beyond his right; he cannot give up his soul to servitude" (sec. 40). The rest from labor that *Rerum Novarum* insists on for Sundays and holy days, for example, is necessary that we "forget for a while the business of his everyday life" (para. 41), a concern that the Tractarians shared in arguing not just for Sunday church-going but for recreation and amusement.[20]

Dickens' Coketown is a world without rest:

> exactly in the ratio as they worked long and monotonously, the craving grew within them for some physical relief—some relaxation, encouraging good humour and good spirits, and giving them a vent—some recognized holiday, though it were but for an honest dance to a stirring band of music—some occasional light pie in which even M'Choakumchild had no finger—which craving must and would be satisfied aright, or must and would inevitably go wrong, until the laws of the Creation were repealed.
>
> (Dickens 63)

It is particularly interesting that the anti-Sabbatarian Dickens invokes Creation here, with its own counsel to rest, though in emphasizing recreation over rest or worship he seems to concur with the Markan view of the matter, that "the Sabbath was made for man, not man for the Sabbath" (2:27). Or, as Dickens' immortal Sleary says, "people mutht be amuthed. They can't be alwayth a learning, nor yet they can't be alwayth a working, they an't made for it" (1996 [1854], 310).

For what, then, are we made? What is the "needful thing"? I want to suggest that *Hard Times* is not a critique of work in favor of the "fancy" or leisure we may take to be "another thing needful," but of the despotism which would keep the worker from it. In this sense, we may say that we are made to be unfettered, free. This is, of course, freedom *to* work rather than freedom *from* work, for labor is increasingly recognized as part of the human condition, and the Dickens of *Hard Times* shows us no other state. Indeed, Stephen Blackpool embodies an ethos that seems to anticipate *Rerum Novarum*'s insistence on the worker's duty to

> fully and faithfully perform the work which has been freely and equitably agreed upon; never to injure the property, nor to outrage the person, of an employer; never to resort to violence in defending their own cause, nor to engage in riot or disorder; and to have nothing to do with men of evil principles.
>
> (sec. 20)

For it is Stephen, "th' one single Hand in Bounderby's mill, o' a' the men theer, as don't coom in wi' th' proposed reg'lations" (Dickens 172), who stands against the union for reasons of his own, and who claims sovereignty over those reasons. He tells his "Men and Brothers," "I mak no complaints o' bein turned to the wa', o' being outcasten and overlooken from this time forrard, but hope I shall be let to work. If there is any right for me at aw, my friends, I think 'tis that" (174). Nor is Stephen diminished by his work; John Paul II's *Laborem Exercens* reminds us that

> *Work is one of the characteristics that distinguish* man from the rest of creatures, whose activity for sustaining their lives cannot be called work.... Thus work bears a particular mark of man and of humanity, the mark of a person operating within a community of persons.
>
> (1981, pref.; emphasis in original)

Such a view is, of course, profoundly counter-cultural, both in Dickens' time and in our own, not just because it opposes the antagonistic view of human community emphasized by Romantics like Rousseau and Marx but because it rejects as inept and misleading the worldly view that either idolizes work as the primary means to fulfillment or rejects it altogether in the pursuit of leisure without limit. We may therefore say that Bounderby has it precisely wrong when he tells Stephen that the only thing he has to do is mind his piece-work, for such instruction makes Stephen merely the tool of the subject, work, and *"the proper subject of work continues to be man"* (John Paul II 1981, sec. 5; emphasis in original). Or to put it another way: work was made for man, not man for work, and this is the right Stephen claims when he asks to be "let to work" (Dickens 174).[21] For his fellow workers as for Bounderby, Stephen's views are "unhallowed" (111); Dickensian and Catholic teaching alike identify the tyranny of "common cause" over "private feeling" (175). For such common cause can become the quiet despotism over conscience that Stephen both acknowledges and regrets: "I know weel that if I was a lyin parisht i' th' road, yo'd feel it right to pass me by, as a forrenner and stranger" (173). It is striking that Stephen invokes here the parable of the Good

Samaritan. For Jennifer Gribble, who sees "th[is] parable's narrative of redemptive love" as giving the novel "its ethical bearings" (427), the unexpectedness of the Samaritan, both as the loving neighbor and the neighbor who should be loved, lays bare "habitual constructions of identity" that have become "barriers to viable community and genuine self-knowledge" (431). Moreover, and more importantly to my conclusions here, the parable highlights what Gribble calls "the simplified self-identity with which [we] model a scaled-down life": Gradgrind's utilitarianism, Bounderby's myth of origin, Stephen Blackpool's piece-work (432). Such a parochial sense of identity is inimical to the brotherhood for which Stephen longs when he defends those who have cast him out as "true to one another, faithfo' to one another, 'fectionate to one another, e'en to death" (Dickens 179). Yet these fraternal bonds are fungible, no more the key to an expansive selfhood than the radical and deformed atomism of Josiah Bounderby. No accident, then, that Bounderby, the master, makes common cause with his disaffected men by casting Stephen Blackpool out of work. Nor is it an accident that Stephen's accident—he falls down a disused mine called the Old Hell Shaft—foregrounds the social and human failures of his masters:

> I ha' fell into a pit that ha' been wi' th' Fire-damp crueller than battle. I ha' read on 't the public petition, as onny one may read, fro' the men that work in pits, in which they ha' pray'n and pray'n the lawmakers for Christ's sake not to let their work be murder to 'em, but to spare 'em for th' wives and children that they loves as well as gentlefok loves theirs.
>
> (291–92)

Stephen recognizes that the conditions of work may so readily become so degraded that our labor renders us less than human, rather than, as it ought, *more* human (John Paul II 1981, sec. 9). Gribble draws our attention to his death scene, lit by the star which shone on him alone in the mine shaft, as "emblematic of the redemptive love that now envelops the outcast and reaffirms the bonds of community in which he has believed" (438). It also matters that it is this star which at last clears "awa t' muddle" (Dickens 292) because "the star had shown him where to find the God of the poor; and through humility, and sorrow, and forgiveness, he had gone to his Redeemer's rest" (293).

Gribble is right, of course, to emphasize the "bonds of community" to which Stephen is restored. I said at the outset that the person is revealed through action, as John Paul II would have it (1979 [1969], 11); now let me say it is clear from Stephen's fate that the action which reveals our humanity is what John Paul II calls "participation" (1993a, 200): it is acting together with others that reveals our capacity for personhood. Such participation is oriented both to our own good and to the common good; each, again, is infinitely valuable, and so to be participation our actions must affirm the humanity of the other as well as ourselves. This is the notion of action undergirding the Catholic conception of human work, which means work as it reveals to us the "irreducible dignity of human persons" (Elshtain 23; John Paul II 1993b) but cannot be substituted for it.

Not without reason, Dickens has been criticized for taking a "reactionary" position in this novel, "choosing to laugh at, rather than critically encourage, the Victorian task of developing public policies and facilities for education, health, and safety" (Law 1996, 18). Yet it is, I hope, clear that a theological vision of *Hard Times* may help us to understand his reaction here, for it is not against the social or the common good that he writes. For Dickens, the absence of what John Paul II would later present as a personalist vision of the human person means social action must inevitably go wrong. Seen in this way, Stephen's death is not a tragedy, but a victory. Faithful in his work even when his master and his fellows were faithless, Stephen has at last found the rest he sought; not the self-indulgent leisure without limit which leads Tom Gradgrind—or the seducer, Harthouse—astray, but the rest from labor which preserves it as a creative activity and an expression of human dignity (John Paul II 1981, sec. 25). Is this rest a kind of quietism, as Nussbaum might suggest, a substitution of the transcendent for the amelioration of this world (2003 [2001], 590)? It might seem that way, for even the practical views of *Rerum Novarum* are overtaken by the assertion that "when we have given up this present life, then shall we really begin to live. . . . He has given us this world as a place of exile, and not as our abiding place" (Leo XIII sec. 21). In this view, it is not surprising that only in death does Stephen enter fully into life. It may be, as Nussbaum suggests, that we "must ultimately choose between regarding this world as merely provisional and regarding it as a scene of significant struggles" (2003 [2001], 590), but this view is only coherent if, like so many modern literary scholars but *unlike* Dickens or the Christian social thought he seems to share, we assume that our spiritual hunger, and its fulfillment, are illusions. If it is not, though, then we are the stewards not only of eternal souls but also of the things which pass away, and "after this our exile" must show that we have used them rightly.

Notes

1. Conceived and written during the pandemic, this piece would have been impossible without the help of Archer and Campion Library staff, especially Kelly Jackman and Elaina St. Onge, and the staff of the Archdiocese of Regina, who made critical material from the archives available to me during the lockdowns, especially Brett Salkeld, Tasha Toupin, Eric and Melissa Gurash, and Amanda Trainor. Special thanks to Kathryn Nogue for providing a scholarly community in hard times.

2. From *Gaudium et Spes*, which literally translates as "Joy and Hope." Throughout, I adopt the Latin titles of papal encyclicals, and give the English short titles in brackets on first use in the text and in the bibliography. Here for instance, the short title would be "The Church in the Modern World." The Latin names are customarily taken from the first two words of the text, while the short titles denote the subject. Official vernacular titles appear in the bibliography.
3. Edmund Wilson, by contrast, remarks that "in his novels from beginning to end, Dickens is making the same point always: that to the English governing classes the people they govern are not real. It is one of the great purposes of Dickens to show you these human actualities who figure for Parliament as strategical counters and for Political Economy as statistics; who can as a rule appear only even in histories in a generalized or idealized form" (Wilson 1961 [1941], 23).
4. See also Bodenheimer (2010).
5. But see also Danon (2020 [1985]).
6. Quoted in Eslick (11) from Newsom (2000, para. 1).
7. Efraim Sicher suggests, differently, that even if *Hard Times* does not dispute Adam Smith's capacious understanding of labor and laborers ("useful bodies"), as "a novel of *individual* growth and imagination [it] is surely working against Bentham's felicific calculus, which regards society as an *aggregate*" determining their own interest and that of "the greatest number" (2011, 315).
8. In generic terms, the first gives us realism, the second naturalism, though this is a subject for another occasion.
9. Weber took this view as uniquely modern, but we see evidence of it as early as Aristotle's critique of "busy-ness" and the acquisitive life in *Nicomachean Ethics*; mistaking the means of life for its ends, the citizen in thrall to the acquisitive life is shut out from what he terms the good life (2.9.1110a1–3). I've addressed this point elsewhere (Johnston 2001, 113–34 and 135–4).
10. See the "anniversary encylicals": Pius XI's 1931 *Quadragesimo Anno* [Forty Years After: Reconstructing the Social Order], John Paul II's 90th anniversary letter, *Laborem Exercens*, and finally his 1991 *Centesimus Annus* [On the Hundredth Anniversary of *Rerum Novarum*].
11. But see Michael Walsh (2012) for a debunking of the "myth" that Rerum Novarum is the foundation of Catholic Social Teaching, both because of its robust opposition to socialism and to the trade unions it proposes to replace with voluntary fraternities of workers. Such voluntarism is a keystone of modern Catholic social teaching. See, for example, Benedict XVI's 2009 *Caritas in Veritate* [Charity in Truth].
12. See Nussbaum: "The image of heaven as a place of self-sufficiency, and a place of beatitude in the sense of an end to mourning, cannot ultimately be reconciled with the idea of ongoing compassion for human life" (2003 [2001], 590). There is a strong counter-argument to be made that Dickens' attack on the bureaucrats of practical progress—of drains, and the monitorial system which made increased access to education possible, etc.—is in fact emblematic of precisely the otherworldly disdain for this-worldly charity that Nussbaum deplores. Proof against it lies in the religious charities, including the Anglican sisterhoods, that Dickens supported, especially those to do with "fallen women."
13. See also John 23: "Hence, though the Church's first care must be for souls, how she can sanctify them and make them share in the gifts of heaven, she concerns herself too with the exigencies of man's daily life, with his livelihood

and education, and his general, temporal welfare and prosperity" (1961, sec. 3).
14. I am deeply indebted to Simon Skinner's "Liberalism and Mammon" (1999) for drawing my attention to Tractarian social criticism.
15. John R. Reed argues that Dickens consistently "exchange[s] human and non-human, animate and inanimate traits within his narratives. So humans lose some of their humanity and become wooden like trees, or dark and forbidding like caves, while chairs and buildings take on the ability to speak or to become ill and infirm" (2007, 15). See also Van Ghent (1950).
16. I do not mean to suggest that Johnson hasn't taken these consequences seriously; indeed, her treatment of Stephen and Louisa as the real "coke," both fuel and waste product, of the factory system, is a strong one. Johnson is primarily concerned with economic systems, however, where I am interested in the political consequences of the utilitarian view of the other.
17. Here I depart from the critical tradition noted by Stephen Spector, which indicts Dickens for his failure to depict the psychological depth and interiority of industrial workers convincingly (1984, 365–66). If Stephen and Rachael remain psychologically alien, and I agree that they do, I contend that this is Dickens' *subject* more than it is his *failure*.
18. Spector, on the other hand, takes these same lines as implicating Dickens himself, contending that Dickens' knowledge, observation, and reportage are all governed by the tyranny of the visible and therefore by the same facts he condemns (375).
19. See Ketabgian for an account of the tension between affective depth and shallowness in Blackpool and the machines.
20. See Skinner (207–10).
21. "Working for gain is creditable, not shameful, to a man, since it enables him to earn an honorable livelihood; but to misuse men as though they were things in pursuit of gain, or to value them solely for their physical powers—that is truly shameful and inhuman" (Leo XIII, sec. 20).

Bibliography

Aristotle. *Nicomachean Ethics*. 340 BC. Translated by Terence Irwin. Indianapolis: Hackett, 1985.

Barnes, Christopher. "*Hard Times*: Fancy as Practice." *Dickens Studies Annual* 34 (2004): 233–58.

Benedict XVI [Josef Ratzinger]. *Caritas in Veritate [Encyclical on Integral Human Development in Charity and Truth]*. 2009. The Holy See. *Papal Archive*. www.vatican.va/content/benedict-xvi/en/encyclicals/documents/hf_ben-xvi_enc_20090629_caritas-in-veritate.html.

Bodenheimer, Rosemarie. *Knowing Dickens*. Ithaca: Cornell University Press, 2010. http://ebookcentral.proquest.com/lib/uregina/detail.action?docID=3138006.

Collins, Philip. "Dickens and Industrialism." *Studies in English Literature, 1500–1900* 20, no. 4 (1980): 651–73. https://doi.org/10.2307/450376.

Danon, Ruth. *Work in the English Novel: The Myth of Vocation*. 1985. Routledge Library Editions: Eighteenth Century Literature. New York: Routledge, 2020.

Dickens, Charles. *Hard Times, for These Times*. 1854. Edited by Graham Law. Peterborough: Broadview Press, 1996.

———. *The Life of Our Lord, Written for his Children During the Years 1846 to 1849*. 1934. New York: Simon and Schuster, 1984. *Internet Archive*. https://archive.org/details/lifeofourlordwri011897mbp/page/n7/mode/2up.

Elshtain, Jean Bethke. "Work and Its Meanings." *Logos: A Journal of Catholic Thought and Culture* 5, no. 4 (2002): 15–24. https://doi.org/10.1353/log.2002.0049.

Eslick, Mark. "Charles Dickens: Catholicism and Anti-Catholicism." PhD diss., University of York, 2011. *CORE*. https://core.ac.uk/download/pdf/40013315.pdf.

Gallagher, Catherine. *The Body Economic: Life, Death, and Sensation in Political Economy and the Victorian Novel*. 2006. Princeton: Princeton University Press, 2008.

Gissing, George. "Dickens' Portrayal of the Working Class in *Hard Times*." 1898. In *Hard Times: An Authoritative Text, Contexts, Criticism*, edited by Fred Kaplan and Sylvère Monod, 3rd ed., 356–57. Norton Critical Editions. New York: W. W. Norton, 2001.

Gresley, William. *Colton Green: A Tale of the Black Country*. London: J. Masters, 1846. https://books.google.com/books?id=szRkAAAAcAAJ.

Gribble, Jennifer. "Why the Good Samaritan Was a Bad Economist: Dickens' Parable for Hard Times." *Literature & Theology* 18, no. 4 (2004): 427–41.

Harrison, Mary-Catherine. "The Paradox of Fiction and the Ethics of Empathy: Reconceiving Dickens's Realism." *Narrative* 16, no. 3 (2008): 256–78.

"Historical and Miscellaneous Reviews." *The Gentleman's Magazine* 42 (1854): 274–79. *HathiTrust Digital Library*. https://babel.hathitrust.org/cgi/pt?id=pst.000068790837&view=1up&seq=291.

Hughes, Philip. "England's Reception of *Rerum Novarum*." *Blackfriars* 22, no. 254 (1941): 226–31. www.jstor.org/stable/43811979.

John XXIII [Angelo Roncalli]. *Mater et Magistra [Encyclical on Christianity and Social Progress]*. 1961. The Holy See. *Papal Archive*. www.vatican.va/content/john-xxiii/en/encyclicals/documents/hf_j-xxiii_enc_15051961_mater.html.

John Paul II [Karol Wojtyla]. *The Acting Person*. 1969. Translated by Andrezj Potocki. Boston: D. Reidel, 1979.

———. *Laborem Exercens [Encyclical on Human Work on the Ninetieth Anniversary of Rerum Novarum]*. 1981. The Holy See. *Papal Archive*. www.vatican.va/content/john-paul-ii/en/encyclicals/documents/hf_jp-ii_enc_14091981_laborem-exercens.html.

———. *Centisimus Annus [Encyclical on the Hundredth Anniversary of Rerum Novarum]*. 1991. The Holy See. *Papal Archive*. www.vatican.va/content/john-paul-ii/en/encyclicals/documents/hf_jp-ii_enc_01051991_centesimus-annus.html.

———. "Participation or Alienation?" In *Person and Community: Selected Essays by Karol Wojtyla*, translated by Theresa Sandok, 197–207. Catholic Thought from Lublin, Vol. 4. New York: Peter Lang, 1993a.

———. "Subjectivity and the Irreducible in the Human Being." In *Person and Community: Selected Essays by Karol Wojtyla*, translated by Theresa Sandok, 209–17. Catholic Thought from Lublin, Vol. 4. New York: Peter Lang, 1993b.

Johnson, Patricia E. "*Hard Times* and the Structure of Industrialism: The Novel as Factory." *Studies in the Novel* 21, no. 2 (1989): 128–37.

Johnston, Susan. *Women and Domestic Experience in Victorian Political Fiction*. Westport, CT: Greenwood Press, 2001.

Ketabgian, Tamara. "'Melancholy Mad Elephants': Affect and the Animal Machine in *Hard Times*." *Victorian Studies* 45, no. 4 (2003): 649–76. https://doi.org/10.1353/vic.2004.0025.

Kidder, Paulette. "Martha Nussbaum on Dickens's *Hard Times*." *Philosophy and Literature* 33, no. 2 (2009):417–26.

Larson, Janet L. *Dickens and the Broken Scripture*. 1985. Athens, GA: University of Georgia Press, 2008.

Law, Graham. Introduction to *Hard Times, for These Times* by Charles Dickens. Edited by Graham Law, 7–28. Peterborough: Broadview Press, 1996.

Leo XIII [Vincenzo Pecci]. *Rerum Novarum [Encyclical on Capital and Labor]*. 1891. The Holy See. *Papal Archive*. www.vatican.va/content/leo-xiii/en/encyclicals/documents/hf_l-xiii_enc_15051891_rerum-novarum.html.

Lupton, Julia Reinhard. "The Religious Turn (to Theory) in Shakespeare Studies." *English Language Notes* 44, no. 1 (2006): 145–49.

Marx, Karl. "Estranged Labour." In *Economic and Philosophic Manuscripts of 1844*. 1932. Translated by Martin Milligan. 1959. Moscow: Progress Publishers, 2009. *Marxists Internet Archive*. www.marxists.org/archive/marx/works/1844/manuscripts/preface.htm.

Mozley, Thomas. "The Religious State of the Manufacturing Poor." *The British Critic and Quarterly Theological Review* 28 (1840): 334–71. *HathiTrust Digital Library*. https://hdl.handle.net/2027/njp.32101064461997.

Naughton, Michael. *The Good Stewards: Practical Applications of the Papal Social Vision of Work*. Lanham: University Press of America, 1992.

Newsom, Robert. "Religion." *Oxford Reader's Companion to Dickens*. Oxford: Oxford University Press, 2000. Electronic edition, *Oxford Reference*, 2011.

Nussbaum, Martha C. *Poetic Justice: The Literary Imagination and Public Life*. Boston: Beacon Press, 1995.

———. *Upheavals of Thought: The Intelligence of Emotions*. 2001. Cambridge: Cambridge University Press, 2003.

Orwell, George. "Charles Dickens." In *A Collection of Essays*, edited by George Orwell, 48–104. 1946. Orlando: Harcourt Brace/Harvest, 1981.

"Our Epilogue on Books." *British Quarterly Review* 20 (1854): 580–98. *HathiTrust Digital Library*. https://babel.hathitrust.org/cgi/pt?id=nyp.33433081647616&view=1up&seq=587.

Paget, Francis. *The Warden of Berkingholt; or, Rich and Poor*. Oxford: John Henry Parker, 1843. https://books.google.com/books?id=ns05GHiH5AQC.

Paul VI [Giovanni Montini]. *Gaudium et Spes [Pastoral Constitution on The Church in the Modern World]*. 1965. The Holy See. *Papal Archive*. www.vatican.va/archive/hist_councils/ii_vatican_council/documents/vat-ii_const_19651207_gaudium-et-spes_en.html.

Pius XI [Achille Ratti]. *Quadragesimo Anno [Encyclical on the Reconstruction of the Social Order]*. 1931. The Holy See. *Papal Archive*. www.vatican.va/content/pius-xi/en/encyclicals/documents/hf_p-xi_enc_19310515_quadragesimo-anno.html.

Pollatschek, Nele. "'Discard the Word Fancy altogether!': Charles Dickens's Defense of Ambiguity in *Hard Times*." *Dickens Quarterly* 30, no. 4 (2013): 278–87.

Reed, John R. "Dickens and Personification." *Dickens Quarterly* 24, no. 1 (2007): 3–17.
Sicher, Efraim. "Dickens and the Pleasure of the Text: The Risks of *Hard Times*." *Partial Answers: Journal of Literature and the History of Ideas* 9, no. 2 (2011): 311–30. https://doi.org/10.1353/pan.2011.0021.
Skinner, Simon. "Liberalism and Mammon: Tractarian Reaction in the Age of Reform." *Journal of Victorian Culture* 4, no. 2 (1999): 197–227. https://doi.org/10.1080/13555509909505990.
Spector, Stephen J. "Monsters of Metonymy: *Hard Times* and Knowing the Working Class." *ELH* 51, no. 2 (1984): 365–84. https://doi.org/10.2307/2872950.
Stober, Katharyn. "'Another Thing Needful': A New Direction in *Hard Times* Criticism and Pedagogy." *Victorians : A Journal of Culture and Literature*, no. 122 (2012): 129–35. *Gale Literature Resource Center.* https://link.gale.com/apps/doc/A316458792/GLS?u=vic_liberty&sid=bookmark-GLS&xid=8ef1401b.
Taylor, Charles. *Sources of the Self: The Making of the Modern Identity.* Cambridge, MA: Harvard University Press, 1989.
Van Ghent, Dorothy. "The Dickens World: A View from Todgers'." *Sewanee Review* 58 (1950): 419–38.
Walsh, Michael. "The Myth of Rerum Novarum." *New Blackfriars* 93, no. 1044 (2012): 155–62. https://doi.org/10.1111/j.1741-2005.2011.01473.x.
Weber, Max. "The Protestant Ethic and the 'Spirit' of Capitalism." 1905. In *The Protestant Ethic and the Spirit of Capitalism and Other Writings*, edited and translated by Peter Baehr and Gordon C. Wells, 1–202. New York: Penguin, 2002. Kindle edition, 2014.
Wilson, Edmund. "Dickens: The Two Scrooges." 1941. In *The Wound and the Bow: Seven Studies in Literature*, 1–93. London: Methuen and Company, 1961.

8 The Gospel of Modernity
Idolatry as the Road to Grace in *David Copperfield* and *Great Expectations*

Marie S. Heneghan

> I told her I should die without her. I told her that I idolised and worshipped her.
> —*David Copperfield* (1868 [1850], 345)

> I, trembling in spirit and worshipping the very hem of her dress; she, quite composed and most decidedly not worshipping mine.
> *Great Expectations* (1868 [1861], 227)

Idolatry and worship are important tropes in Charles Dickens' two well-known bildungsromane *David Copperfield* (1868 [1850]) and *Great Expectations* (1861). Committing idolatry was a serious moral issue for Victorians, and it is a sin referred to in the Bible as a people's turning away from God to other gods for fulfillment;[1] in spite of idolatry's presence in these novels, it has remained decidedly underexplored in Dickensian scholarship since Victorian studies is often primarily concerned with contemporary concerns—reading contemporary concerns into Victorian culture (Perkin 2009, 8). While religion in the period has always been an important topic in Victorian scholarship, and, by consequence, Dickensian scholarship, the "crisis of faith" narrative has been favored, one in which religion declines and is replaced by secularism. Its prevalence should not seem surprising since two of the most influential studies in nineteenth-century literature delineate the narrative of religious decline in the nineteenth-century literature, which include J. Hillis Miller's *Disappearance of God* (1963, 209) and M. H. Abrams' *Natural Supernaturalism* (1971, 13). In the last two decades, scholars have attempted to correct this view, including Russell J. Perkin (5) and Timothy Larsen, who note the dominance of the "crisis of faith" narrative as a particularly overdetermined aspect of religion in the Victorian period (2007, 18). God is absent, or at least inaccessible, in both Miller's and Abrams' interpretations, and this propensity is also present in Dickensian scholarship and the bildungsroman genre.

DOI: 10.4324/9781003156611-9

The majority of critics' interpretation of *David Copperfield* and *Great Expectations* do not consider the spiritual development as a matter of growth, but rather, growth emerges in the tension between the cultural system, or society, that constrains the individual and the individual's ability to discover true selfhood in a larger social order (Lowe 2012, 405; Moretti 2000, 185); this partiality is also evident in the readings of the bildungsroman genre since its emergence is seen as "both representative and symbolic of modernity" (Kuehn 2018, 26). Robyn Gilmour does not accept this view (1979, 141), and, along with Alan Barr (2007, 63) and William T. Lankford (1979, 454), he argues that *David Copperfield* idealizes childhood, and the past has great agency to shape the present. Spirituality is not commonly associated with the bildungsroman, however, and even those, such as Barr, who take the role of suffering into account, do not see this as a spiritual conclusion, but as a journey to moral and physical maturity (66). Recently, however, religion has become a subject of interest in Dickensian literary studies, and both Susan Colón's (2012, 97) and Janet Larson's readings of Dickens as parabler locate contradictory biblical patters, as well as secular and religious tensions in his bildungsroman (1985, 5).

In this chapter, I examine idolatrous experience in Dickens' bildungsromane as portraying direct, unmediated forms of faith, and, as I argue in a previous paper, idolatry has clear links to both British revivalism and more primitive forms of worship which reflects a broader cultural turn to simpler, direct forms of faith (Heneghan 2018, 55–56). Since the idolatrous experience is similar to the revivalist experience of God, it can be the road to true faith (61–63). In Dickens, access to God is possible in a simple spirituality unmitigated by liturgy which he perceived as humanly ordained hindrances to God.[2] Dickens strips this liturgy in the idolatrous experience, and spirituality is possible outside the church, external to the traditional framework of Christianity. The concern for Dickens is the heart and, drawing on New Testament tenets, the legitimacy of his protagonists' goodness is tested according to the goodness of their hearts, not their good works. Idolatrous worship originates in the desires of the heart, and idolatry reveals the true motives of David and Pip's hearts that seek their own justification in performing good works. Dickensian Christianity is well known as the social gospel of doing good, but I argue that these novels explore the difficulty of truly being good, of possessing hearts overflowing with goodness that are evidenced in good works.

Idolatry is traditionally understood as a transgressive trope, one that represents the worship of idols (Vejvoda 2000, 4; Carens 2015, 242). In the Victorian period, idolatry was inseparable from the anti-Catholic sentiment prevalent in the nineteenth-century Britain since British Protestants perceived themselves beyond the worship of physical vestments and statues (Peschier 2005, 25; Vejvoda 2000, 298). The King James Bible, however, identifies a much more nuanced notion of idolatry as a sin originating from the desires of the human heart, and the apostle Paul refers to idolators as those whose hearts are "darkened" (Rom 1:21).[3] Rooted in the heart, idolatry is centered on desire; as Alison Searle argues in her article on *Jane Eyre* and idolatry, this "sin" is first about love and the heart's desire (2006, 39). In this chapter, idolatry is also found in the human heart, concerned with the inner life, and inseparable from spiritual growth, including a process of transformation that leads both protagonists on a journey to grace via idolatry. Idolatry is central to the spiritual awakenings of David and Pip because it sets up a relationship between worship and the outpouring of the heart, which reflects (rather than rejects) the transformative faith revealed at the end of the bildungsroman.

The idolatrous experience, as it appears in Dickens, is a postsecular phenomenon, and in both novels, idolatry extends even beyond this intensity, to the core of existence, directing all other desires. Pip's trembling before Estella, and David's belief that he "should die" without Dora, constructs idolatry as an illogical, emotionally intense experience, inseparably linking and mutually reinforcing the relationship between desire and spiritual awe (230, 394). If God no longer directs desire in the idolatrous experience, then the idol replaces this function, and this proposes a postsecular conception of religion, a religion of the heart capturing imagination and desire outside structural liturgy. Postsecularism was developed by the philosopher Charles Taylor to explain the rise of modernity in the West, which is not posited as a narrative of subtraction but one of replacement (2007, 26, 543). Taylor acknowledges a drastic shift in the conditions of belief and argues that something else replaces the idea of moral and spiritual aspiration toward flourishing (26). Idolatry conveys the replacement strategy that seeks to discover spiritual flourishing apart from God through obtaining a spiritual experience of an immanent being. In the nineteenth-century context, postsecularism in literature is identified as the immanent (the natural) existing alongside the transcendent (the supernatural) in a common frame (Rectenwald 2016, 7). The immanent is transformed in the idolatrous experience with transcendent import, signaled by emotional intensity; the experience itself is a paradox since spiritual possibilities are present in the presence of an immanent (natural) being.

This paradoxical relationship between the immanent and the transcendent is evident in both *David Copperfield* and *Great Expectations*. Even though, for instance, Estella is an immanent being, Pip's experience of her is illogical and indivisible from its spiritual possibilities—all which are involuntary. Profound emotion is also the marker of the spiritual in the nineteenth century.[4] Estella is, in other words, Pip's religion. Here, religion moves beyond liturgies in the postsecular framework and is redefined as a religion of the heart (as distinct from the church or other religious institutions), "an embodied, material, liturgical phenomenon that shapes our desire and imagination before it yields doctrines and beliefs" (Smith 2012, 161). If God no longer directs desire in the idolatrous experience, then the idol replaces this function, both the secular and the religious exist in terms of their relationship to emotional intensity. David, for example, associates Dora with fiction and imagination, with the inner life; she is: "a Fairy, a Sylph" and it is an uncontrollable passion, even a sexual excitement (Dickens 317), as Robert Garnett argues (1997, 220). Idolatry in the Dickensian bildungsroman captures the protagonists' imagination and desire, directing all other desires and, in this relationship of consumption, a struggle is initiated to a divine grace, which culminates in a faith of accepting divine grace or rejecting it because simplicity is no longer possible (as is the case with Pip).

Idolatry is a trope Dickens employs in his direct reading of scripture and his critiques of those whose hearts lack grace and unconditional love, which are the cornerstones of Dickensian Christianity. Good works that do not proceed from a pure heart are a central concern in both *David Copperfield* and *Great Expectations,* and Dickens reprimands citizens whose "charity" exists for the sake of "patronage and power" in an article titled "Charity at Home" for *All Year Around* (1866, 287). Dickens' desire for people's pockets to touch "through their hearts" promotes a spirit of good works and generosity as the outpouring of the heart (287). The spirit of humility gives generously to all as the result of the heart's goodness; he interprets scripture in a simple and literal manner: "God resisteth the proud, but giveth grace to the humble" and grace can only come to the humbled heart (Jas 4:6). Scripture also states that grace is the gift that God extends to humankind but it is not separated from personal transformation and, again, Dickens presents an elementary understanding of the scriptures, one accessible to his Protestant readers:

> For the grace of God that bringeth salvation hath appeared to all men, Teaching us that denying ungodliness and worldly lusts, we should live soberly, righteously, and godly, in this present world; Looking for that blessed hope, and the glorious appearing of the great God and our Saviour Jesus Christ; Who gave himself for us, that he might redeem us from all iniquity, and purify unto himself a peculiar people, zealous of good works.
>
> (Ti 2: 11–14)

In this case, God's grace is a gift, but it is evidenced in a people "zealous of good works" (Ti 2:14). Both David and Pip may desire to do good works, but these do not proceed from the unconditional love foundational to grace, but to serve their own ends. David believes that his pure heart and "earnest" intentions justify good works completed for a conditional end—to mold his idol's (Dora's) mind (561). Pip's good deeds are provisional and they are performed with the aim of obtaining absolution from his corrupted expectations. His good deed toward Herbert Pocket, for instance, is performed to put Pip's mind "much more at rest" (379). Convicted of their provisory good deeds, David and Pip learn that good works can only be true if the heart is brimming with unquestioning love, which is only possible through the acceptance of divine grace—a simple faith. The bildungsroman is thus a pilgrimage in which redemption is contingent on welcoming divine grace through ideals of faith—characters whose good deeds proceed from their hearts.

Creating a heart that understands grace is a pilgrimage marked by suffering, and idolatry is essential to this journey in the Dickensian bildungsroman. The bildungsroman is a novel of growth and development, a pilgrimage similar to the famous early novels of development through trials, such as *The Pilgrim's Progress* (1678) by John Bunyan. Growth and development are achieved through trials presented to Christian in *The Pilgrim's Progress*, as well as in biblical stories, and these trials eventually lead to God (Soni 2007, 132). Similarly, in the Dickensian bildungsroman, idolatrous worship instigates suffering since the idol cannot satisfy the spiritual fulfillment sought by the worshipper; the suffering that springs from the dissatisfaction of unfulfillment is a catalyst for personal growth, humbling the worshipper's heart to receive the Gospel that can provide full satisfaction.

David and Pip's fraught views regarding good deeds and grace are shattered by the suffering that accompanies idolatry. When David loses his beloved idol, Dora, his pilgrimage through the continent leads him back to Agnes through whom he can accept divine grace. Joe Gargery, as the novel's Christian ideal, convinces Pip of the need for grace in his life, but Pip cannot accept this unconditional love since his idolatrous love for Estella has marred his heart. The resolution of the struggle between works and faith throughout both novels is thus contingent on accepting the workings of grace and relying on the ideal, as opposed to God himself, as renumeration. In this fractured parable, idolatry can be the road to faith—a journey to grace—but this divine grace is conditional; grace cannot be obtained if the heart has not been transformed through suffering, once again affirming the paradoxical yet indivisible relationship between idolatrous worship and transcendent spirituality.

Dickens and Christianity: The Workings of Grace

The vision of faith crafted in Dickens' novels is a Christian vision, one that legitimately explores the issues of living according to grace in the modern world. Grace is not an aspect generally accepted as a Dickensian view of Christianity and faith since it appears to be separate from good works and bound to religious dogma which Dickens abhorred (Walder 1981, 141; Butterworth 2016, 5). His aversion to dogma has encouraged scholars to apply a Christian vision solely concerned with good deeds to his work, a secularized focus, which is what is known as the social gospel: "putting social good works before credal content and demands" (Cunningham 2008, 258).[5] Christianity becomes about good works, not grace, and it is widely accepted that Dickens valued New Testament precepts and measured society according to how it upheld these Christian values which he saw as the source of all moral goodness (Gribble 2018, 590).

Evidence of Dickens' belief in the teaching of Christ also comes from *The Life of Our Lord* (1996 [1934]), which demonstrates how serious Dickens was in the religious instruction of his children (Colledge 2009, 7). In his examination of this text, Gary Colledge focuses on good deeds, but this extract from *The Life of Our Lord* upholds a Dickensian view of the importance of a compassionate heart, coupled with good deeds: "For everybody ought to know about Him. No one ever lived, who was so good, so kind, so gentle, and so sorry for people who did wrong" (Dickens para. 1). Dickens' vision of doing good always is not separated from divine grace, and he explores this in his own vision of Christianity outside the confines of a Church; both *David Copperfield* and *Great Expectations* uphold a practical theology grounded in biblical precepts, one that engages with issues of accepting divine grace, what I term the workings of grace, a simple faith legitimized by the heart.

Joe Gargery and Agnes Wickfield: Models of Faith

Dickens advocates a gospel in which good works cannot be separated from credal content because they need to be evidence of the heart's love. The workings of grace are outworked in the ideals of faith, and these characters embody the divine embrace of unconditional love. The religious ideals reflect Dickens' view of God as a God of grace; he believed it "monstrous" to hold God up to children as a "wrathful God" who will punish them for what they did wrong in this life (Hartley 2012, 93). Although good deeds are the fundamental evidence of Christianity, the ideal model of faith in Dickens is not solely one that does good for others, but one whose heart overflows with unqualified love. Grace is the cornerstone of the Gospels since it is the outpouring of God's *agape* love for his people "to the praise and glory of his grace, wherein he hath made us accepted in the beloved. In whom we have redemption through his blood, the forgiveness of sins, according to the riches of his grace" (Eph 1:6–7).[6] Grace is defined as a love given to the undeserving, a love that does not expect reciprocity.

Agnes Wickfield in *David Copperfield* and Joe Gargery in *Great Expectations* possess hearts brimming with unrestricted love, never considering themselves, but only seeking the good of David and Pip. Agnes never wavers in her love, but only seeks the good of David, as he tells her when he proposes: "If only you had been more mindful of yourself, and less of me ... my heedless fancy never would have wandered from you" (613). Joe also only thinks of Pip when he is endowed with great fortune, rejecting any sum offered to him, telling Jaggers that money can be no compensation for the "loss of the little child" (135). True Christianity is faith "which worketh by love" and the selfless love that both Agnes and Joe embody locates them as the ideals (Gal 5:6).

As the scriptures indicate, unequivocal love is only possible in a heart with no ostentations—a humble heart. Both Agnes and Joe are workers for good because their goodness is inseparable from the core of their existence. Joe's actions are transparent, a direct result of his heart, as Biddy tells Pip:

> how Joe loved me, and how Joe never complained of anything—she didn't say, of me; she had no need; I knew what she meant—but ever did his duty in his way of life, with a strong hand, a quiet tongue, and a gentle heart.
>
> (274)

Joe's good works are not separate from his heart, but as Biddy indicates, his gentle heart is his defining feature. Similarly, Agnes is "good and true," which David attributes to the core of her being, as an "Angel," rather than good works, with a calming influence (190, 258, 265, 299, 363, 596, and 599). Aside from the inherent goodness of Agnes and Joe, however, it is in the comparison with the protagonists that Dickens positions both these humble characters as the ultimate Christian model to follow.

Even though David's inadequacy of Agnes' divine love is proved in the novel through constant comparison, it does not separate him from her love, furthering a biblical theology of grace, which comes to the humble in heart (Jas 4:6). Agnes embodies general Victorian gender norms and Dickens' womanly ideal of Coventry Patmore's the *The Angel in the House*; in the poem "Love at Large," the Angel is elevated above all: "No liken'd excellence can reach/Her, thee most excellent of all" (Patmore 1854, 25). She is the natural priest, with the capacity to be closer to God than man (Slater 1983, 307). David calls her "far superior in character and purpose" (300) and "my better Angel" (306), as well as the guide that prevents him from doing wrong. He wishes to strike Uriah Heep, but resists, remembering "the entreaty of Agnes" (310). The deficiency, rather than creating a gulf between David and Agnes, draws them nearer to each other since David acknowledges his shortcomings as his means to Agnes. He asks her to accept him as husband "on no deserving of mine, except upon the truth of my love for her" (692). David thus comes to realize that his shortcomings grant him access to grace.

Pip's shortcomings, in contrast to David, create a distance between him and Joe that remains unpassable and Pip has to lay aside his pride and snobbery (Buckley 1974, 53). Pip questions the goodness of his heart the night before he departs from the forge, in terms of his posture of superiority toward Biddy and Joe. Pip believes himself good for offering to stay overnight at the forge, and he notes how it pleases Joe, and he feels he "had done rather a great thing in making the request" (272). The good deed is transactional in Pip's heart, giving him leverage to count himself as good. Pip writing about his past, however, posits Joe as a more admirable contrast. When Pip speaks with Biddy about the good he can do for Joe, it does not spring from a pure, unmitigated love but as a means to educate Joe and elevate him to his own station which he is convinced casts him as Joe's superior. He tells Biddy, "Joe is a good fellow—in fact, I think he is the dearest fellow that ever lived—but he is backward in some things" (142). His offer to help Joe is, in truth, a means to assert his own superiority, which Biddy suggests in response to Pip's suggestion. Pip is aware of his "virtuous and superior tone" as he accuses Biddy of jealousy (143). Here, Pip's pride seems most apparent and the swelling of his pride, more so than his rise of fortune, alienate him from Joe (Moore 2012, 330). Because of his pride, Pip, unlike Joe, makes insincere promises, which Biddy observes: "are you sure that you will come to see him often?" (260). Even though Pip's pride drives him to express shock, "this is a bad side of human nature" (143), Pip reveals that he does not fulfill his promise; he departs the forge, suggesting a separation from Joe, describing the mists as he departs: "If they disclosed to me, as I suspect they did, that I should not come back, and that Biddy was quite right, all I can say is—they were quite right too" (278). Because of Pip's pride, his own shortcomings magnify the distance he experiences as the narrator writing about his past, and he does not recognize his weakness as his access to grace but rather as the agent of estrangement from grace.

David Copperfield: The Test of the Pure Heart

David and Pip learn to question the motives of their inner life and idolatry, thus humbling their hearts to receive grace from God. Idolatry in *David Copperfield* is rooted in emotion and intense feeling integral to the spiritual growth of the protagonist. Early in his autobiography, David attempts to justify his childish attachment to Dora from his first encounters with her, couching it in irrationality, as an intense experience beyond his control: "There was no pausing on the brink; no looking down, or looking back; I was gone, headlong before I had sense to say a word to her" (274). The experience of Dora consumes David's entire being and he is disarmed, "steeped in Dora. I was not merely over head and ears in love with her, but I was saturated through and through" (334). He also explicitly associates his love for Dora with Exodus 20, as the worship of a graven image, an idolatrous worship: "it was a fine morning, and early, and I thought I would go and take a stroll down one of those wire-arched walks, and indulge my passion by dwelling on her image" (277).[7] Jerome Buckley does not perceive these early encounters in a positive light, in spite of David's youthful pleasure, and locates dark overtones that signal a *naiveté*, leaving David defenseless (39). David's inability to control his worship of Dora attests to a darker overtone in the novel, and, in spite of David's rapture in his early encounters with Dora, he soon realizes the errors of his "undisciplined heart."

David justifies his "undisciplined heart" by extracting immanent tenets from transcendent truths in scripture, which suggests that idolatry encourages introspection of the heart's true motivations. Although David acknowledges his worship of Dora as "an unsubstantial, happy, foolish time!" (345), idolatry can be justified in the postsecular reading of Dickens, if it comes from a pure heart, as David notes that "there was purity of heart" in his love for Dora (277). His idolatrous heart can thus be forgiven because he loves Dora with a heart with no pretensions: "if I did any wrong, as I may have done much, I did it in mistaken love, and in my want of wisdom. I write the exact truth" (458). Sincerity, in this case, is a transcendent precept that draws on the Gospels: "blessed are the pure in heart; for they shall see God," which is used for an immanent purpose (Mt 5:5). Dickens interprets these passages literalistically, however, and the proud cannot see God. His theology critiques the heart convinced of its own purity, without the evidence of good works, which is tested when David's idol, Dora, disappoints his expectations of fulfillment.

The idolatrous journey compels David to a Gospel-centered acceptance of Dora. David initially does not embrace Dora, and his treatment of her crushes her spirit, convincing her that "you must be sorry that you married me" (451). David's superiority complex in worldly related matters and housekeeping echoes, as James Kincaid argues, Murdstone's treatment of David's mother, particularly his attempts to form her mind to his "entire satisfaction" (1971, 190). His brief step into his stepfather's role ceases when David's intentional good deeds of teaching Dora reveals an acceptance of Dora that is inherently conditional on her performance as a wife, on her changing her childish ways to perform as his wife. The first step in David's journey to grace is ceasing to attempt forming his child-wife's mind and to love her unconditionally just as his beloved Agnes loves him. His aunt's remonstrance stresses the need for this in David's narrative of growth "it will be your duty, and it will be your pleasure . . . to estimate her (as you chose her) by the qualities she has, and not by the qualities she may not have" (452). The indicator of a good heart, as Betsy Trotwood states, is to "estimate her by the qualities she has," and to value others in spite of what one perceives as their unworthiness.

David thus faces the self-seeking nature of his good deeds toward Dora, which are shown to be illegitimate because his true motives are not to love her wholeheartedly. In humbling himself, and ceasing to view himself as superior to Dora, David learns the Gospel-centered value of grace in his struggle to love Dora: "It remained for me to adapt myself to Dora; to share with her what I could, and be happy; to bear on my own shoulders what I must" (595). Garnett perceives David's act as a false acceptance since his dissatisfaction with her remains, which eventually kills her (607). David's dissatisfaction is essential to his spiritual growth, however, and the suffering he experiences in this disquiet forms an unconditional love central to the act of grace he extends—of quietly accepting his own disappointment. Through suffering, through bearing "the toils and cares of our life" (458), David's insincere good deeds are revealed to him, and his idolatrous worship of Dora is pivotal to his transformation and his final journey to grace.

Great Expectations: Transactional Good Works

Pip's first experience of idolatry is the opposite of grace, a conditional, nonreciprocal love that directs all his desires and instills pride into his heart. *Great Expectations*, in particular, emphasizes the suffering that Pip undergoes during his initial experience of Estella, which arouses violent feelings in young Pip, driving him to kick "the wall, and took a hard twist at my hair; so bitter were my feelings" (59). The idol, as opposed to the love of God, directs all desires in the idolatrous experience which is why his first encounter of Estella shifts his experience of all things, reflecting a postsecular conception of religion. His former life is no longer adequate, and pride has invaded his humble beginnings: "I wished Joe had been rather more genteelly brought up, and then I should have been so too" (58). Indeed, Estella's defining feature is her pride, and when Pip first meets Estella, her beauty and pride are the first features he notices about her, and he tells Miss Havisham "I think she is very proud" (57). Here, as Matthew Taft argues, Pip begins to understand himself in terms of his value in the market and to be loved by Estella he must reproduce himself in "grander form," creating a ceaseless desire for more (2020, 1975). Estella subsumes Pip's existence, and the rest of his journey strives toward the goal of attaining material wealth and status. Beyond conscious deliberation, his idolatry for Estella dislocates his existence, as Pip is aware when he sees her once again as a young man, noting that "it was impossible" to separate her "presence from all those wretched hankerings after money and gentility" and impossible to separate her "from the innermost life of my life" (227).

The economy of value exchange is embedded in the entire narrative of *Great Expectations* since the story of Pip's expectations is indistinguishable from his self-narrative (Grass 2012, 635). Portable property and material wealth are significant themes in the novel, but the economy Sean Grass describes implicates Pip's spiritual growth as well, specifically his potential to receive grace. Pip's idolatrous attachment is more damaging in comparison to David, and his spirit is marred by the toxicity of his worship of Estella, since his attempt to do good and reverse his squandered expectations cannot be separated from an economy of value exchange. Redemption comes at a price, but not the unconditional love associated with Joe; instead, Pip is convinced he is capable of engineering redemption. As such, his act of goodwill in securing employment for Herbert is transactional and serves as a hope of absolution. Pip confesses to Wemmick that Herbert had given advantages to him by his society and he had "ill repaid them," which suggests a necessity for repayment (285). He describes helping his friend obtain a partnership at Clarriker and Co. as "the only good thing I had done, and the only completed thing I had done, since I was first apprized of my great expectations" (404). Taft perceives Pip's good deed as an act that changes the economy-exchange relationships between the characters in the novel into an economy in service to others (2020). Pip, however, stands to gain from his act of service and explicitly tells his readers of the deed as a recompense for his squandered expectations. Pip's desire to give hope to Herbert suggests a transformed heart; yet, he remains unable to grasp the workings of grace in life, hinging all hope of pardoning on his ability to do good: "I did really cry in good earnest when I went to bed, to think that my expectations had done some good to somebody" (289). Here, Pip is convicted of his inadequacy of receiving grace, which suggests that grace is still accessible to the protagonist, since the humility of the sinner resides in his heart, and he certainly acknowledges his own shortcomings more readily than David (Buckley 53). Although Pip possesses humility, the accessibility to grace is contingent on a heart humbled by suffering. The final step in the gospel of modernity is accepting grace, and the reality of faith in the modern world attests to the inaccessibility of grace and unqualified love in a world lacking simplicity.

The Fractured Parable: A Postsecular Conclusion

At the conclusion of the idolatrous journey, suffering teaches both David and Pip of the need for grace in their lives, though the access to grace varies considerably for the two protagonists. The final journey to grace needs to include the sinner's acceptance of unconditional love, which Pip struggles to receive, and David readily accepts through Agnes. In the fractured parable, not everyone is redeemed by grace, and redemption remains uncertain to varying degrees in both texts and thus is the key distinction of the Dickensian bildungsroman from narratives such as *The Pilgrim's Progress*.

The final part of *David Copperfield* displaces the protagonist, and his certainty of his own sincerity and pureness of heart faces the ultimate test. Performing a discursive critique of idolatry, Dickens extinguishes David's most significant idolatrous attachment; Dora's death tests the legitimacy of David's sincerity and sends him on a biblical journey in the wilderness.

On this journey, the protagonist experiences a baptism of suffering that serves a purpose-driven conclusion. His suffering is so immense that he believes he "should die. Sometimes, I thought that I would like to die at home; and actually turned back on my road" (577). He describes proceeding "restlessly from place to place, stopping nowhere . . . I had no purpose, no sustaining soul within me, anywhere" (578). David mourns the loss of innocence here, which is why many scholars suggest that the novel idealizes childhood (Barr 66; Gilmour 141). More than a loss of innocence, however, Dickens furthers a coherent theology in the final step of David's journey; his worship of Dora does not solely lead to him to lament the loss of innocence, but it also leads to less self-assurance and a greater acceptance of grace.

David reaches Agnes at the end of his suffering in the wilderness, which initiates his final period of spiritual growth before he discovers redemption, but this redemption does not lead directly to God; David cannot reach God but relies on the grace of his Angel, a figure in the immanent frame, for redemption. God can only be reached via a proxy of the divine in the fractured parable and Agnes is vital to this connection; she also tends to be seen as essential in David's journey.[8] Agnes expresses Dickens' feminine ideal as the natural priest, as Michael Slater argues, with a closer position to God, and is a source of encouragement: "everyone who knows you, consults with you, and is guided by you" (1983, 302). Since Agnes is the icon of feminine virtue, David's reasons for taking her as his wife are religious, rather than romantic because of her otherworldliness (Garnett 226). David gains salvation through Agnes because he learns to cast aside his egocentricity and David's final redemption occurs when he loses himself in her (Bandelin 1976, 611). Agnes is thus his way to salvation, which he dramatically declares at the conclusion of the novel. The path to redemption is simpler for David because he understands the workings of grace more readily than Pip, and eagerly accepts Agnes as his justification:

> thinking of her, pointing upward, thought of her as pointing to the sky above me, where, in the mystery to come, I might yet love her with a love unknown on earth, and tell her what the strife had been within me when I loved her here.
>
> (600)

David's sentimental expression of dependence on Agnes is contingent on her immediacy—her presence in the here and now; yet, through her David also is aware of his failings and the necessity for grace, which is based on New Testament teachings on grace. Agnes encapsulates the mystery to come as well as an immediacy; she is the tangible, Christ-like figure for the immanent frame.

The idolatrous journey in *David Copperfield* concludes with accepting grace via the representation of the divine, outside any structured liturgy. As the everyday representation of the divine, Agnes embodies a postsecular salvation, furthering a spirituality confined to the immanent frame. Her position as the Angel in the House can seem absurd in its devoted idealism; however, Dickens employs this role to explore the workings of grace. Couched in Victorian gender roles, the icon of feminine virtue offers salvation, and David's dramatic emphasis on her as his salvation seems farcical, though to David, his reliance on her is the ultimate remuneration. Gareth Cordery is skeptical of David's transformation in marrying his "sister-angel," but this is part of Dickens' view of Christianity, relying on fellow creatures, both men and women, as the representatives of divine grace and redemption (2008, 372). It is a tenet of Christianity that Cunningham and Colledge describe, one of transformation, but also one that accepts New Testament values and the necessity for grace to be shown to sinners.[9] Cordery is not entirely incorrect in his critique of David's reliance on Agnes, but he measures this reliance on her for redemption according to David's own ability to be good. The scandal of grace is the acceptance of sinners, and David eagerly accepts Agnes after the chastisement of his idolatrous journey, as his road to faith; she is the virtuous ideal for David to look to outside any structural liturgy, and, similar to Joe, she is his avenue to the divine in her simplistic qualities. This simplicity is based on a domesticated form of Christianity outside the confines of the Church. David's access to grace takes the form of immanent salvation, through Agnes, and Christianity becomes about accessing grace for happiness on earth, domestic angel.

Similar to David, Pip endures a baptism of suffering at the conclusion of his journey and is convicted if his idolatrous heart when Joe tends to him during his illness. Joe's acts of service, along with his sincere heart, promote the simple faith of the blacksmith. Joe remains by Pip's bedside, and, for Joe, the acts of goodwill toward his once-ungrateful old apprentice comes from the overflow of his "innocent heart" (458). Pip describes his own suffering in fragments, and: "that I suffered greatly, that I often lost my reason, that the time seemed interminable" is what Pip can recall of this time (450). Suffering is coupled with grace, and Pip remains unable to accept the divine grace extended to him through Joe: "O Joe, you break my heart! Look angry at me, Joe. Strike me, Joe. Tell me of my ingratitude. Don't be so good to me!" (451). Joe's grace humbles Pip's heart to seek forgiveness and to understand the need for grace in his life. Lawrence Dessner critiques Joe's simplicity in this pivotal passage and does not see it as an act of forgiveness, since Joe does not seem aware of any wrongs being committed against him (1976, 444). Pip's process of recovery does reveal a consciousness in Joe, however, and he becomes "a little less easy with me" in the apprehension that Pip will inevitably pluck "myself away" (458). When Pip attempts to apologize, Joe once again shows an awareness of Pip's past rejection of him, "dear sir, what have been betwixt us—have been" (459). Pip's illness thus is the final catalyst in his personal growth, and he is aware of suffering's significance in his journey, telling Joe "I feel thankful that I have been ill" (459). As a representative of the God the Father, Joe continues to show grace when he repays Pip's creditors, and Joe's gracious act compels him to return home, seeking to leave "arrogance and untruthfulness further and further behind" (465).

Pip's return to the forge, the place of his childhood and the sanctuary of humble Joe, represents his hope of redemption through a marriage to Biddy—his childhood love. Pip's hope in marrying Biddy is his final attempt to rewrite his disappointed expectations, and he is convinced that her love "will make me a better man for it, and I will try hard to make a better world for you" (460). Catherine Waters interprets Pip's desire to marry Biddy as an act that allows Pip to liken himself to the prodigal's son when he returns home (1997, 169), and, to Buckley, the conclusion is a reclaiming of Pip's "spiritual integrity" (46). The return, however, presents another disappointment. Pip's heart, in one of these final tests, is marred, and has not been transformed entirely; instead, Pip experiences inadequacy and cannot accept the divine grace extended to him. He thus desires to repay Joe:

> I shall never rest until I have worked for the money with which you have kept me out of prison, and have sent it to you, don't think, dear Joe and Biddy, that if I could repay it a thousand times over, I suppose I could cancel a farthing of the debt I owe you, or that I would do so if could!
>
> (467)

Pip demonstrates his rejection of divine grace through his attempt to monetize it; yet, at the same time, he exhibits a heart of humility in his acknowledgment that grace cannot be repaid. One of the fundamental verses about grace tells believers that "my strength is made perfect in weakness," which is why the apostle Paul rejoices in his weakness "that the power of Christ may rest upon me" (2 Cor 12:9). Pip is aware of the grace offered by Joe, but this grace remains inaccessible to him in seeking to remedy the wrongs he has committed. In spite of Pip's own feelings of unworthiness, he still admires Joe deeply and prizes him as the ideal of his life.

There is a simultaneous moment of biblical forgiveness and estrangement in the concluding parts of *Great Expectations*, all of which accumulate to the postsecular spirit of transcendent import into the immanent in the form of possible reconciliation. Pip and Estella sit in front of Satis House, marred by the world, unable to regain their child-like simplicity, but a transcendent hope remains in the form of Gospel-centered forgiveness. God is not, as Barry Qualls argues, unknowable in *Great Expectations* (1982, 90), but found in this fractured parable of forgiveness. Pip does not remember the wrong as Estella asks for forgiveness and tells her "we are friends" (472). Even though Pip has suffered irreparable damage from his worship of Estella, his readiness to extend unconditional love to her demonstrates a heart transformed by suffering as well as a heart that will continue in its pilgrimage. As Andrew Saunders argues, a sense of hope is present in Pip's interaction with Estella, particularly because the narrative has been developing a steady progress toward an end where Pip is reconciled to "strengths and weaknesses of his character" (2008, 27). The mending suggested between him and Estella, added to Pip's posture of humility, suggests his journey of faith will continue.

The gospel of modernity is not the social gospel: It portrays the true inner reality of the heart—the desire for one's own edification. It is a gospel-focused message that considers credal content as furthered by good works, and it is also one that accepts uncertainty as part of faith which is why Pip's redemption is not lost. Receiving divine grace in Dickens' fractured parable comes through paradox: a spiritual experience of an immanent being. This immanent spirituality dislocates the protagonists and drives them to reflect on their heart's true motives. Final redemption is only possible to those willing to acknowledge their shortcomings as their passport to divine grace, but it does not remain unattainable, if only the heart sees its own inadequacy as its entry into grace.

Notes

1. Kathleen Vejvoda (2003, 241), citing Exodus 20:32).
2. Dickens possessed what Dennis Walder calls a radical Protestant view, which perceived rituals, liturgies, and creeds as obstacles to serving one's fellow human beings (1981, 10).
3. Since Dickens would have been familiar with the King James Version, all biblical references in this chapter will be taken from that version.
4. In his study of John Stuart Mills' autobiography, Timothy Larsen considers other literature from the nineteenth century, and concludes that spiritual despair and crisis are not indications of a loss of faith but can be spiritual precisely due to their intense implorations (2018, 46).
5. Good works has been the basis of scholars' approach in Dickensian Christianity. Gary Colledge interprets *The Life of Our Lord* as evidence of Dickens' Christianity, which is about following the example of Jesus in performing good works (7). Robert Butterworth argues that Dickens was interested in Christianity only if it can provide a true moral outworking, which stresses good works (5). Dickens' Christianity, as noted by Walder, is driven by societal action and care for the poor—the social gospel (141).
6. The apostle Paul discusses addresses those who believe they can be redeemed through obedience to the Law and not through submitting to Christ: "Behold, I Paul say unto you, that if ye be circumcised, Christ shall profit you nothing . . . For we through the Spirit wait for the hope of righteousness by faith.

For in Jesus Christ neither circumcision availeth any thing, nor uncircumcision; but faith which worketh by love" (Gal 5: 2–6).
7. When God warns the Israelites against idolatry, it is referred to as a "graven image, or any likeness of any thing that is in heaven" (Ex 20:4).
8. Robert Garnett suggests that that the novel should be seen a process through which David achieves Agnes (1997, 215). Conversely, Carl Bandelin reads Agnes as David's salvation through which he loses himself to find himself in her (1976, 611).
9. Cunningham views Dickens' vision of Christianity as a broad New Testament one grounded in good works shown to one's fellow creatures (261). The New Testament is also viewed by Colledge as the basis of Dickensian Christianity, though good works is placed above credal content (7).

Bibliography

Abrams, Meyer H. *Natural Supernaturalism: Tradition and Evolution in Romantic Literature*, New York: W. W. Norton, 1971.

Bandelin, Carl. "David Copperfield: A Third Interesting Penitent." *Literature, 1500–1900* 16, no. 4 (1976): 601–11. www.jstor.org/stable/450277.

Barr, Alan P. "Mourning Becomes David: Loss and the Victorian Restoration of Young Copperfield." *Dickens Quarterly* 24, no. 2 (2007): 63–77. https://web-b-ebscohost-com.ezp01.library.qut.edu.au/ehost/detail/detail?vid=17&sid=08dd445d-b04e-4f84-81fd-799dd406d17c%40pdc-v-sessmgr05&bdata=JnNpdGU9ZWhvc3QtbGl2ZSZzY29wZT1zaXRl#AN=25223491&db=afh.

Buckley, Jerome H. "Dickens, David and Pip." In *The Bildungsroman from Dickens to Golding*, edited by Jerome H. Buckley, 28–62. Harvard: Harvard University Press, 1974, De Gruyter. https://doi.org.ezproxy.library.uq.edu.au/10.4159/harvard.9780674732728.

Bunyan, John. *The Pilgrim's Progress*. 1678. London: Penguin Classics, 2008.

Butterworth, Robert. "Dickens's Engagement with Religion." In *Dickens, Religion and Society*, edited by Robert Butterworth, 1–25. London: Palgrave Macmillan, 2016. https://doi-org.ezproxy.library.uq.edu.au/10.1057/9781137558718_1.

Carens, Timothy L. "Subversive Fantasy and Domestic Ideology." *Nineteenth-Century Literature* 7, no. 2 (2015): 238–66. www.jstor.org/stable/10.1525/nl.2015.70.2.238.

Colledge, Gary. "An Easy Account of the New Testament." In *Dickens, Christianity and Humble Veneration, Profound Conviction*, edited by Gary Colledge, 1–20. London: Bloomsbury Academic, 2009. http://dx.doi.org/10.5040/9781474211338.ch-001.

Colón, Susan E. "'The Agent of a Superior': Stewardship Parables in *Our Mutual Friend*." In *Victorian Parables*, edited by Susan Colón, 93–120. London: Bloomsbury Academic, 2012. http://dx.doi.org/10.5040/9781474211581.ch-005.

Cordery, Gareth. "David Copperfield." *A Companion to Charles Dickens*, edited by David Paroissien, 369–79. New York: Blackwell, 2008.

Cunningham, Valentine. "Dickens and Christianity." In *A Companion to Charles Dickens*, edited by David Paroissien, 255–76. New York: Blackwell, 2008.

Dessner, Lawrence Jay. "*Great Expectations*: 'The Ghost of a Man's Own Father.'" *PMLA* 91, no. 3 (1976): 436–49. www.jstor.org/stable/461693.
Dickens, Charles. "Charity at Home." *All the Year Around* 15, no. 362 (March 1866): 286–88. *ProQuest British Periodicals*, https://search-proquest-com.ezproxy.usq.edu.au/docview/7807122.
———. *David Copperfield*. 1850. New York: Books, Incorporated, 1868. https://books.google.com/books?id=NcsNAAAAQAAJ.
———. *Great Expectations*. 1861. London: Chapman and Hall, 1868. https://books.google.com/books?id=G6dZAAAAYAAJ.
———. *The Life of Our Lord*. 1934. *Our Favourite Books*. 1996. www.ourfavouritebooks.co.uk/downloadindiv/dickens/The%20Life%20of%20Our%20Lord.pdf.
Garnett, Robert R. "Why Not Sophy? Desire and Agnes in *David Copperfield*." *Dickens Quarterly* 14, no. 4 (1997): 213–31.
Gilmour, Robin. "Dickens, Tennyson, and the Past." *The Dickensian* 79, no. 389 (1979): 130–42. *ProQuest*, https://search.proquest.com/openview/4c1e04adeeab01a808f6e1a22a36e006/1?cbl=1818261&pq-origsite=gscholar.
Grass, Sean. "Commodity and Identity in *Great Expectations*." *Victorian Literature and Culture* 40, no. 2 (2012): 617–41. https://doi.org/10.1017/S1060150312000137.
Gribble, Jennifer. "Dickens and Religion." *The Oxford Handbook of Charles Dickens*, edited by John Jordan, Robert L. Patten, and Catherine Waters, 582–96. Oxford: Oxford University Press, 2018. https://doi.org/10.1093/oxfordhb/9780198743415.013.40.
Hartley, Jenny, ed. *The Selected Letters of Charles Dickens*. Oxford: Oxford University Press, 2012. https://ebookcentral.proquest.com/lib/qut/detail.action?docID=886543.
Heneghan, Marie S. "The Post-Romantic Way to God: Self-Worship in *Wuthering Heights*." *Australasian Journal of Victorian Studies* 22, no. 1 (2018): 53–65. https://openjournals.library.sydney.edu.au/index.php/AJVS/article/view/11596.
Kincaid, James. *Dickens and the Rhetoric of Laughter*. Oxford: Clarendon Press, 1971.
Kuehn, Julia. "*David Copperfield* and the Tradition of the Bildungsroman." *Dickens Quarterly* 35, no. 1 (2018): 25–46. https://doi.org/10.1353/dqt.2018.0002.
Lankford, William T. "'The Deep of Time': Narrative Order in David Copperfield." *ELH* 46, no. 3 (1979): 452–67. JSTOR. www.jstor.org/stable/2872690.
Larsen, Timothy. *Crisis of Doubt: Honest Faith in Nineteenth Century England*. Oxford: Oxford University Press, 2007. https://doi.org/10.1093/acprof:oso/9780199287871.001.0001.
———. "Vanity and Vexation of Spirit." In *John Stuart Mill: A Secular Life*, edited by Timothy Larsen, 45–53. Oxford: Oxford University Press, 2018. https://doi.org/10.1093/oso/9780198753155.003.0004.
Larson, Janet. *Dickens and the Broken Scripture*. Athens, GA: University of Georgia Press, 1985. https://books.google.com.au/books?id=z_xBwQkYXjMC&printsec=frontcover&source=gbs_ge_summary_r&cad=0#v=onepage&q&f=false.

Lowe, Brigid. "The *Bildungsroman.*" In *The Cambridge History of the English Novel*, edited by Robert L. Caserio, and Clement Hawes, 405–20. Cambridge: Cambridge University Press, 2012. https://doi-org.ezproxy.usq.edu.au/10.1017/CHOL9780521194952.

Miller, J. Hillis. *The Disappearance of God: Five Nineteenth-Century Writers*. Cambridge: Belknap, 1963.

Moore, Ben. "'When I went to Lunnon Town Sirs': Transformation and the Threshold in the Dickensian City." *Dickens Quarterly* 29, no. 4 (2012): 336–49. *EBSCOhost*.

Moretti, Franco. Preface to *The Way of the World: The Bildungsroman in European Culture*. Translated by Albert Sbragia, v–xiii. London: Verso, 2000.

Patmore, Coventry. *The Angel in the House*. Edited by Henry Moley. London: Cassell and Company, 1854. *Gutenberg Project Ebook*. www.gutenberg.org/files/4099/4099-h/4099-h.htm.

Perkin, Russell J. "Introduction: The Victorian Book of Life." In *Theology and The Victorian Novel*, edited by Russell J. Perkin, 3–30. Montreal: McGill-Queen's University Press, 2009. https://ebookcentral-proquest-com.ezproxy.library.uq.edu.au/lib/uql/detail.action?docID=3332145.

Peschier, Diana. *Nineteenth-Century Anti-Catholic Discourses: The Case of Charlotte Brontë*. Basingstoke: Palgrave Macmillan, 2005.

Qualls, Barry. "Transmutations of Dickens's Emblematic Art." In *The Secular Pilgrims of Victorian Fiction*, edited by Barry Qualls, 85–138. Cambridge: Cambridge University Press, 1982.

Rectenwald, Michael. *Nineteenth-Century British Secularism*. London: Palgrave Macmillan, 2016. *ProQuest Ebook Central*, https://ebookcentral-proquest-com.ezproxy.library.uq.edu.au/lib/uql/detail.action?docID=4441537.

Sanders, Andrew. "Great Expectations." In *A Companion to Charles Dickens*, edited by David Paroissien, 422–32. New York: Blackwell, 2008.

Searle, Alison. "An Idolatrous Imagination? Biblical Theology and Romanticism in Charlotte Brontë's 'Jane Eyre'." *Christianity and Literature* 56, no. 1 (2006): 35–61. https://doi.org/10.1177/014833310605600104.

Slater, Michael. "The Womanly Ideal." In *Dickens and Women*, edited by Michael Slater, 301–72. London: IM Dent and Sons, 1983.

Smith, James K. A. "Secular Liturgies and the Prospects for a 'Post-Secular' Sociology of Religion." In *The Post-Secular in Question: Religion in Contemporary Society*, edited by Philip S. Gorski, David Kyuman Kim, John Torpey, and Jonathan VanAntwerpen, 159–84. New York: New York University Press, 2012. https://muse.jhu.edu/book/20733.

Soni, Vivasvan. "Trials and Tragedies: The Literature of Unhappiness (A Model for Reading Narratives of Suffering)." *Comparative Literature* 59, no. 2 (2007): 119–39. www.jstor.org/stable/40279364.

Taft, Matthew. "The Work of Love: *Great Expectations* and the English Bildungsroman." *Textual Practice* 34, no. 12 (2020): 1969–88. https://doi.org/10.1080/0950236X.2020.1834700.

Taylor, Charles. *A Secular Age*. Cambridge, MA: The Belknap Press, 2007.

Vejvoda, Kathleen M. "The Dialectic of Idolatry: Roman Catholicism and the Victorian Heroine." PhD diss., University of Texas, 2000. https://search-proquest-com.are.uab.cat/docview/304626026.

———. "Idolatry in *Jane Eyre*." *Victorian Literature and Culture* 31, no. 1 (2003): 241–61. Cambridge Journals Online. https://doi.org/10.1017/S1060150303000123.

Walder, Dennis. "The Social Gospel: *David Copperfield* and *Bleak House*." In *Dickens and Religion*, 140–69. New South Wales: George Allen and Unwin, 1981.

Waters, Catherine. "Great Expectations." In *Dickens and the Politics of Family*, edited by Catherine Waters. 150–74. Cambridge: Cambridge University Press, 1997.

9 Unheavenly and Broken Homes in Dickens' Novels

Brenda Ayres

Like most Victorians, Dickens believed that a home should be more than just a place of shelter; it represented something much more holy and holistically essential. The "home" and the "house"—not always the same thing—figure significantly in Christian theology and even more so in Victorian Christian theology and, by extension, Dickens' theology. Home should be a state of existence among others with tightly formed bonds of love called "family," and for Dickens, this was rarely restricted to just a nuclear family. Dickens believed in the Golden Rule—"Therefore all things whatsoever ye would that men should do to you, do ye even so to them" (Mt 7:12). It is the major theme in every single one of his novels and short stories. He taught it to his children in the retelling of Christ's parable of the Good Samaritan in his *The Life of Our Lord*, concluding: "Be compassionate to all men. For all men are your neighbours and brothers" (1999 [1934], 71). In his novels, Dickens placed the socially marginalized into homes that offered safety, sanctuary, provision, peace, health, and happiness through close-knit relationships forged because of reciprocal needs and care for each other. Still, most of the homes throughout his novels and short stories are broken and their families dysfunctional. Many of them illustrate the Victorians' failure to follow biblical tenets to prioritize family over material goods.

In his study of Victorian manners, Andrew St. George deduced that the greatest fear of the mid-Victorians was "the idea of the non-home: the street, the workhouse, and the shame of not belonging" (1993, 101). In her preface to *The Complete Home*, Julia McNair Wright, a bestseller in 1870, wrote:

> Between the Home set up in Eden, and the Home before us in Eternity, stand the Homes of Earth in long succession. It is therefore important that our Homes should be brought up to a standard in harmony with their origin and Destiny.
>
> (1879, 3)

DOI: 10.4324/9781003156611-10

However, Dickens learned quite early in his life that no matter how necessary and desirable a home was to one's protection from a brutal world, it was often elusive and unstable, more like a house built on sand as Jesus describes in Matthew 7:26, or else—whether one's personal residence or the house of God—it was often broken. Home for most Victorians was *not* heaven on earth.

Before social mobility became possible for a greater number of people in England because of the Industrial Revolution, in the sixteenth and seventeenth centuries landed gentry comprised no more than one-tenth of 1% of the population (Ragland 1978, 42). By the end of the eighteenth century, the landed elite tallied barely over 1% (Henry 2002, 312). Their palatial houses were coveted and passed from one generation to the other through the law of primogeniture mandating that only the firstborn son would inherit an intact estate. The Enclosure Act of 1773 removed the right of commoners' access to about 7 million acres of land, which then became legally owned by manorial lords. While a person might be given a grand estate for political reasons and service to the Crown, the majority of British citizens counted themselves fortunate just to have a roof over their head even if that roof would never belong to them. Most were tenants who were susceptible to the whims of the lords of the manor. Ninety percent of Britain's land belonged to landowners and gentry (Mingay 2002, 143) and slumlords. Only 2% of the population or about 27,000 families did not have to work and were considered the upper class (Brown 1985, 7).

Not until the emergence of the middle classes, especially in the Victorian period, could most people purchase homes that would give them economic and political status. Nothing was so snug and inviting as a charming cottage in the countryside with thatched roof, ivy, and roses embracing white-plastered walls or else a three-story brownstone in the city with a top floor that housed servants. Further, by 1841, London was the largest city in the world with the greatest quantity of houses (Pritchard 2003, 180). In 1823 Sir Henry Rowley Bishop, an English composer, composed the song "Home! Sweet Home!"

The house has always been a status symbol in Britain, but it became much more than that for the burgeoning middle class in the nineteenth century. With the Great Reform Act of 1832, for the first time in the history of Britain, small landowners, tenant farmers, tradespeople, and other householders (including some lodgers) who paid at least 10 pounds in rent qualified men to vote. The act denied the vote to most of the industrial cities where people could not afford property but instead were two-to-three families of factory workers crammed into single rooms (Altick 1973, 44). Also disenfranchised were the Irish; in 1831, 20,000 of them "lived" in Manchester basements (Woodward 1962, 10). Such "homes" did not even have windows because until 1851, there was a tax imposed on them (44). On the average, 40 families shared one privy and a tap (44), and it was not unusual for a Spitalsfield house to hold seven people per room (Reader 1964, 64). And then there were the hideous, shameful workhouses, with 40 of them in London alone (Davidoff and Hall 35).

By midcentury, most of the rising middle class could afford a home in the suburbs (Altick 13) and hire at least two maidservants, a horse, and a groom (Young 1951 [1934], 104); 82% of the servants worked in middle-class households (Davidoff and Hall 388), and there were over 121,000 domestic servants in London alone by 1851 (Young (1951, 32). "The severe ethical style of the Victorians," Laura Brown surmised, "with its emphasis on hard work, the home, and strict morality, was largely a middle-class phenomenon" (20). A comfortable, fully furnished house with a profusion of bric-a-brac and servants was the dream of many a Victorian, but material acquisition became the order of the day often to the sacrifice of the well-being of the family. No matter how ornate, the house was more oft than not, a broken home. "The goal of all the bustle of the market place," Leonore Davidoff and Catherine Hall theorized in *Family Fortunes: Men and Women of the English Middle Class, 1780–1850*, was to provide a proper moral and religious life for the family," with a focus on preparing for "immortality and a heavenly home" (1987, 21). The reality was that most Victorians focused on the "market place" and not on the "moral and religious life for the family"—a criticism that permeates Dickens' novels.

Dickens was born in a respectable brick house on 387 Mile End Terrace in Landport, Portsea,[1] entirely appropriate for a father who was a clerk in the Navy Pay Office if he did not overspend on entertaining and attempting to be ornately genteel. John Dickens and his family—except for Charles—were removed from that happy home to the Marshalsea Debtors' Prison for failure to pay the baker's bill of 40 pounds and 10 shillings. His son would fictionally replicate this crisis with William Dorrit who was detained, with his family, in the Marshalsea for 23 years because he could not pay a debt of 400 pounds. Such situations were all too common and untenable for people who, because of their incarceration, could not labor to liquidate debt. The Dickenses were in prison for three months while Charles, like Amy Dorrit and David Copperfield (1850), worked to pay for the family's food and clothing. At the age of 12, Dickens took lodging with a family friend, one elderly, impecunious Elizabeth Roylance who, "with a few alterations and embellishments," became that "ogress of the castle and child-quellor" (Dickens 44), Mrs. Pipchin in *Dombey and Son* (1848; Forster 1892, 11). Later Dickens would be joined by his family in those tiny lodgings. Neither place would be a home because the family could not remain intact, and the father could not provide for them financially which John Dickens, like Mr. Dorrit, was unable to do until he came into an inheritance.

Acquisition of sufficient funds will be a driving curse for David Copperfield, one that will taint his home and first marriage, as happened to many Victorians and Dickens' characters like Ralph Nickleby, Mr. Dombey, and Jonas Chuzzlewit. For the famous author, it was a constant struggle to take care of his own growing family as well as relatives and friends. On the very first page of the novel, Dickens relates that Copperfield is born with a caul, which is the inner lining of the amnion amniotic sac that probably wrapped about his face. To be born with one is very rare and considered a lucky talisman especially appealing to sailors because it was thought to protect them from drowning (Cumming 1908, 220). David's caul was advertised in the newspapers for sale (5), which indicates that Mrs. Copperfield was strapped for money.

The house in which David is born is called Rookery, and, as Betsey Trotwood disdained to observe, it was exactly a name that her impractical nephew would choose in that although he hoped the cottage would have rooks (4–5) that usually are in abundance when they have access to arable land and pasture for food, the Copperfield house had no productive land and therefore no rooks. H. K. Browne (Phiz) illustrated the house (frontispiece), making it look like a comfortable country cottage with its clinging vines, diamond pane windows, and Aunt Betsey's nose pressed against those windows. One night Peggotty is embroidering a scene of a lovely little house with a thatched roof where in a distance sits St. Paul's Cathedral "(with a pink dome)" (19), intimating that all was well in the Copperfield home under God's protection on earth, represented by St. Paul. But insolvency does indeed make a house impractical and unsafe.

David's tranquil home and whole world crumble when his mother marries the austere Mr. Murdstone who pirates his home and relocates him to "a crazy old house with a wharf of its own . . . overrun with rats," where he would put labels on wine bottles (111). The ten-year-old boy will live in lodgings by himself but has the benefit of being befriended by the Micawber family (112–13).

Unable to bear the drudgery of factory work (as was Dickens), he makes his long trip to Dover to find refuge with Great-Aunt Betsey. Her cottage is also charming with an abundance of hollyhocks as tall as the house. It is Dickens' ideal home, and Betsey is his ideal Christian. She is one of the sheep instead of a goat, as per Matthew 25 when Jesus said that one is truly blessed and will

> inherit the kingdom prepared for you from the foundation of the world: For I was an hungry and ye gave me meat: I was thirsty, and ye gave me drink: I was a stranger, and ye took me in: Naked, and ye clothed me: I was sick, and ye visited me: I was in prison, and ye came unto me.
>
> (34–36)

Figure 9.1 Hablot Knight Browne (Phiz), Frontispiece, *David Copperfield* (London: Bradbury and Evans, 1850), Frontispiece

Source: https://books.google.com/books?id=GlgJAAAAQAAJ

Unheavenly and Broken Homes 173

Figure 9.2 Hablot Knight Browne (Phiz), "I make myself known to my aunt," *David Copperfield* (London: Bradbury and Evans, 1850), 137
Source: https://books.google.com/books?id=GlgJAAAAQAAJ.

Aunt Betsey had to support herself at a time when paying jobs for women were very limited. She took in Mr. Dick, rescuing him from the asylum, raised David, and often gave money to her ne're-do-well husband who did not live with them.

On both sides of the Atlantic, "family" and "home" were often interchangeable words in the nineteenth century. In 1851, Rev. Joseph A. Collier wrote *The Christian Home: Or Religion in the Family,* which won a monetary prize ($175) by the Board of Publication of the Presbyterian Church. It begins with "The Family!" and continues with these "delightful association . . . inwoven with the tenderest thoughts and emotions of the human heart": "The loved home, the cheerful fireside group, the fond tones of a mother's voice, the sweet dependencies of childhood, the interchange of confiding sympathies, the community of joys and griefs, of hopes and fears" (8). "Home" is not just a space; it is an experience, a shared humanity that seeks to support its members. To exist and be effective, "home" is "thoroughly pervaded by those holy principles that ally us to Divinity," such as not just a "mother's gentle voice," but one "linked with memories of childhood's prayers, and the heart's first thoughts of heaven" (8). She "seems an angel of the household, alluring us to the skies" (8). The "home"—the "family," he asserts, is an "oasis in the desert, a garden in the wilderness" in a "sin-desolated world." It is a "type of heaven" (8).

Dickens does offer his ideal in several of his novels, but *Martin Chuzzlewit* will suffice to argue that the heavenly home was possible only because it was inhabited by the Angel in the House, as Coventry Patmore called her in his best-selling poem by that name. Although the poem was not published until 1850, and Dickens' *Martin Chuzzlewit* was published as a book in 1844, the deification of the housewife and mother was already articulated in print. Mrs. Sarah Ellis, in her best-selling *Wives of England,* argued "At home it is but fitting that the master of the house should be considered as entitled to the choice of every personal indulgence" (1846 [1843], 100). Thomas Carlyle said that he

> never doubted but the true and noble function of a woman in this world was, is, and forever will be, that of being a Wife and Helpmate to a worthy man, and discharging well the duties that devolve on her in consequence as mother of children and Mistress of a Household— duties high, noble, silently important as any that can fall to a human being" which makes her the "Queen of the World."[2]

Dickens' notion of the Angel in the House, though, would be more accurately called "the doll in the house," the making of which is one of the thematic and plot developments in *Barnaby Rudge* (1841) with the maturation of Dolly Varden; however, the ideal is Ruth Pinch in *Martin Chuzzlewit,* "Pleasant little Ruth! Cheerful, tidy, bustling, quiet little ruth! No doll's house ever yielded greater delight to its young mistress, than little Ruth derived from her glorious dominion over the triangular parlour and the two small bed-rooms" (1868 [1844] 374). This description begins Chapter 39 with its subtitle referring to "domestic economy" and its chapter's short title of "A Born Housewife." From supposedly her point of view, to be her brother's housekeeper awarded her great "dignity!" and "implied the utmost complication of grave trusts and mighty charges" (374).

Her brother Tom is not the only one besot by the cheerful housekeeper; John Westlock instantly realizes that she will be an ideal wife and so begins that romance. What a contrast is this to the house of which Mercy (also known as Merry) Pecksniff is to become mistress where there is anything but mercy or merriment. What else can be expected when one marries a man like Jonas—whose first learned word was "gain" and second, "money"—who was taught to look at everyone as property and viewed his own parent

> as a certain amount of personal estate, which had no right whatever to be going at large, but ought to be secured in that particular description of iron safe which is commonly called a coffin, and banked in the grave.
>
> (76)

The "old-established firm of Anthony Chuzzlewit and Son" sits in "a very narrow street . . . where the brightest summer morning was gloomy." The house is "a dim, dirty, smoky, tumble-down, rotten older house," and not only was this a place to transact business but this was also the residence of Jonas and his parent (111).

As John Reed has observed, the Victorian home for Dickens should operate through and generate good virtues that could not be found in mercenary London. They were missing in the "home" that Magowitch (of *Great Expectations* (1861)) tried to gain outside of prison, and failed; that Author Clennam (of *Little Dorrit* (1857)) desired all his life and could find only within the Marshalsea; that John Harmon (of *Our Mutual Friend* (1865)) was able to create with Bella only once she could overcome the hegemonical pressure to prioritize "appearance" over reality (Reed 1975, 226–227). "It is, in fact, surprising to discover how very much of nineteenth-century English literature," Reed concludes in his *Victorian Conventions,*

> despite its praise of home and family, really depicts broken homes, and contentious familiars; how often young people in the narratives of the time find themselves in a world hostile to their noblest instincts, a world governed by their implacable parents and infiltrated by seditious siblings.
>
> (476)

To the Victorians, "home" was interchangeable with "family" and "heaven." Such conflation is biblical and reflects God's notions of health, happiness, and sanctuary for His people who live in a world that "is not my home"—as several nineteenth-century hymns pronounced such as, "I've left the land of death and sin . . . to seek a home on High" because "This world is not my home,/This world is but a wilderness" are the words to one hymn, based on Hebrews 13:14 (Harrod 1891, 590–91). A similar song was popular in the nineteenth century in the Cumberland Mountains, the southeast portion of the Appalachian Mountains in the United States, with the same title and with the description of the world outside the home as a "howling wilderness" (Barton 1898, 449). The song has allusions to the 40-year trek of the Israelites in the "wilderness" after having been delivered from bondage in Egypt (Ex. 12) en route to Canaan, "the promised land" (Ex. 33), one flowing with milk and honey (Ex 3:17). "Canaanland," as conveyed in several African-American spirituals, is synonymous with "heaven." Still popular today is a hymn also with the same title that states "I'm just a passing through," that the treasures are in heaven, and the "angels beckon me from heaven's open door" (Brumley 2006 [1936], 461). These lines come from Jesus' exhortation to lay up treasures in heaven instead of treasures on earth that can be destroyed by moth and rust (Mt 13:19).

The symbolism of "house" (and by extension "home," "family," and "heaven") so infuses *Bleak House* (1853) that the word "house" appears more than 500 times.[3] The title of the novel indicates the lack of hope and heaven in one's earthly home. At one time known as Peaks' House, which certainly suggests an image more positive than "Bleak," it has been owned by a great uncle to John Jarndyce. Like so many of his relatives since, this uncle became so entangled with a Chancery lawsuit over a will made by a rich relative that he and his house fell into ruin, falling from peaks to bleakness. The cause of such debacle is none other than monetary greed, the very evil from which the inhabitants were to be protected by this home. Crawford Kilian understands the novel to be about broken family relationships and isolation of individuals (1974), a subject that certainly is symbolized by this description of Bleak House:

> It was one of those delightfully irregular houses where you go up and down steps out of one room into another, and where you come upon more rooms when you think you have seen all there are, and where there is a bountiful provision of little halls and passages, and where you find still older cottage-rooms in unexpected places with lattice windows and green growth pressing through then.
>
> (46)

Despite its claim to be "delightful," its disorder runs counter to the Victorian propensity for order. Its depiction of a labyrinth is similar to the workings of Chancery: seductive but with its ups and downs and halls and passageways that lead to bleakness.

However, when Bleak House becomes a home due to the selfless efforts of John Jarndyce and Esther, the house is no longer bleak but provides sanctuary to an extended family of odd souls such as Richard, Ada, Skimpole, Allan, Charley, and to a lesser extent, Jo. Then the house is a standing testament to the bleakness of the world that surrounds it, but it cannot protect the inhabitants from the evils of materialism that is as ubiquitous and confounding as the fog: That feckless child Skimpole ensnares Richard into financial intemperance, Richard goes mad and alienates from his benevolent guardian as he desperately expects a judgment that will make him rich, the poverty-stricken Jo infects Esther with smallpox, Richard and Ada's marriage lacks domestic bliss and certainty, and Mr. Jardyce hides out in the growlery. Janet Larson interprets this disorder as "paradoxical"; "it is at once a source of stability, with its familiar conventions of order, and a locus hermeneutical instability reflecting the times of Victorian religious anxiety in which Dickens wrote" (1983, 134). What she means is that Dickens "secularized sacred plots" in his novels and particularly in *Bleak House* reveal his struggles with what he perceived to be "contradictions" within the Bible (134). As he extracted biblical stories and concatenated them with his fiction, like the meandering, organic structure of Bleak House, they "arrange themselves in patterns of contradiction and dissonance" (134).

In contrast to Bleak House, Chesney Wold is not susceptible to the lure of money, for it is a house of great wealth and prestige. As grand as it is, it is no home. The Dedlocks enjoy very little happiness in their marriage, and the manor house is haunted by dark secrets. Dickens had intended to call the novel *Tom-All-Alone's: The Ruined House* or *The Solitary House* (Whipple 1894, ix). Regardless of an ending that promises a happy future for its survivors, *Bleak House* "is a world of signs and marks, where fragments make a linguistic puzzle that is never quite successfully solved and where mystery becomes a semiology" (Ragussis 1979, 275). The signs say that the houses in Victorian times, no matter how delightful and desired, are mostly broken homes. Just as Bleak House and the house at Chesney Wold meander with their fragments hallways, walkways, rooms that lead to other rooms, and just as both are haunted by the past and buckle under the new stresses of capitalism, these two houses illustrate a failure to abide by biblical precepts that prioritize such spiritual treasures as love and compassion over "the love of money," which is, as 1 Timothy 6:10 says "is the root of all evil: which while some coveted after, they have erred from the faith, and pierced themselves through with many sorrows."

Another very unhappy house is *Great Expectation's* Satis House. Ironically, the name of the house means "enough," as Estella tells Pip because "Whoever had this house could want nothing else" (1881 [1861], 77). To young Pip whose homelife, aside from the love for Joe, is not "enough," Satis House comes to represent all that he wants in life, namely status, but Pip is conscious that the house has "heavy air" and "heavy darkness that brooded in its remoter corners" that threaten Estella and himself to cause them to "presently begin to decay" (112).

Years later Pip is charged to chaperone Estella to Richmond where she is to become a companion to an old friend of Miss Havisham, a Mrs. Brandley. Pip thinks that when he dies, his ghost will haunt her house because of the "unquiet spirit within [him] that haunted that house when Estella lived there!" (332). He has no peace. "Every Englishman's home was his castle," H. L. Beales mused about the Victorians,

> In its sanctities and privacy a man might escape from the trials of the outer world and be safe from its prying eyes. The family was indeed a kind of estate, like, say the British Empire, and subject like it to the benevolent despotism of its lord and master, for it *had* a lord and master, and his ways were expected to be authoritarian.
> (1949, 344)

In the heaving, callous business world in which Pip attempts to establish himself as a gentleman, he discovers Wemmick's Castle, "a consolatory accommodation to a world of alienating separations," a home that "embodies the private, human values which cannot be brought into the ruthless business world of Jaggers's office" (Milbank 1992, 134) and one that contrasts to the death that inhabits the upper-class mansion called Satis House. The Castle was kept separate from the perverse society of criminals with which Wemmick and Jaggers associate; one could access it only through a lowered drawbridge. Although small and a mere facsimile of a real castle, "it brushes the Newgate cobways away" (234), and its top was "painted like a battery mounted with guns" (323), a veritable bulwark against the world.

The houses in *Little Dorrit* are destructive prisons, fabrications of unwholesome times from which no one can escape. When Mr. Dorrit is finally released from the Marshalsea, imprisonment is not just a physical structure; it is a psychological state. Although he dreams of living in a castle (480 and 491), it is only a castle in the air (the title of Chapter 18).

The House of Clennam and Company is another example of the misguided Victorian notion of mixing business with home when home should be a sanctuary away from business. Cottage industries were once the norm in the previous centuries in England, but separation of home and business was the proper order for the Victorians. John Ruskin taught this in his famous "Of Queens' Gardens" lecture:

> This is the true nature of home—it is the place of peace; the shelter, not only from all injury, but from all terror, doubt, and division. In so far as it is not this, it is not home; so far as the anxieties of the outer life penetrate into it, and the inconsistently-minded, unknown, unloved or hostile society of the outer world is

allowed by either husband or wife to cross the threshold, it ceases to be home.

(1865, 136)

The "outer world" was the public domain of business, "his rough work in the open world" fraught with "peril and trial" (136).

At the beginning of *Little Dorrit*, Arthur Clennam is returning to England after having spent 20 years with his father in China. Most likely they were independent merchants who sold India cotton to China (Xu 1997, 56). In Chapter 3 titled "Home," once Clennam arrives at the home of his unhappy childhood, he is aware that it is "a Sunday evening in London, gloomy, close and stale. Maddening church bells of all degrees of dissonance, sharp and flat, cracked and clear, fast and slow, make the brick and mortar echoes hideous" (21). The bells seem to say, "Come to church, Come to church, Come to church!" (22); their "doleful" sounds as if also saying "the Plague were in the city and the dead-carts were going around" (21). "Miles of close wells and pits of houses, where the inhabitants gasped for air, stretched far away towards every point of the compass" as Clennam arrives in London on the Dover coach (21). Dickens vents for several paragraphs in his anti-sabbatarian campaign,[4] but clearly the house of God and the Calvinistic legalism of his mother reminded Arthur of "a legion of Sundays, all days of unserviceable bitterness and mortification" (22).

Clennam "crossed by Saint Paul's" (22)[5] and made his way to Clennam and Company. The house, personified, is broken:

> It was a double house, with long, narrow, heavily-framed windows. Many years ago, it had had it in its mind to slide down sideways; it had been propped up, however, and was leaning on some half dozen gigantic crutches: which gymnasium for the neighbouring cats, weather-stained, smoke-blackened, and overgrown with weeds, appeared in these latter days to be no very sure reliance.
>
> (23)

He will explain to his mother that their business is on the decline (33–34), but everything about her and his home have been on a decline throughout her marriage, her mothering, her health, and her house.

Just as Miss Havisham is imprisoned by the suspension of time in her house, so is Mrs. Clennam. Both have become vindictive women who attempt to destroy all those around them. Both are paralyzed in their own ways. Finally, both are killed by their houses in a demise of their own making that nearly kills the very people who try to save them. Just as Pip tries to rescue Miss Havisham from the fire so, too, Little Dorrit tries to rescue Mrs. Clennam from the collapsing house:

> As they looked up, wildly crying for help, the great pile of chimneys, which was then alone left standing like a tower in the whirlwind,

rocked, broke, and hailed itself down upon the heap of ruin, as if every tumbling fragment were intent on burying the crushed wretch [Rigaud] deeper.

(600)

Although every novel by Dickens spares no detail in delineating houses versus homes, the one that makes the contrast the clearest is *Nicholas Nickleby* (1839). The Nicklebys have taken rooms in a boarding house run by an artist of miniatures, Mrs. La Creevy. Uncle Ralph arrives there to resentfully meet the relatives who have turned to him for help. He knocks on the door that is answered by "a servant girl with an uncommonly dirty face" (15). He asks, "Is Mrs. Nickleby at home, girl?" The girl corrects him by saying "La Creevy." The landlady overhears and lets them know that "Mrs. Nickleby" is on the second floor and asks this Hannah, "Is the second floor at home?" to which the maid responds, "Somebody went out just now, but I think it was the attic which had been a cleaning of himself" (15–16). The house is not just personified here as a narrative technique, and it is not just a place. As a home, it has become one with the residents so that it has metamorphosed into the personalities of its residents. Yet, Miss La Creevy has made it a very comfortable home for herself and her boarders. Ralph warns her that although the Nicklebys suppose that the uncle will pay their rent, he has no intention to do so and therefore they should be evicted (17). Kate says, "Oh! Think of all the happy days we have had together, before these terrible misfortunes came upon us; of all the comfort and happiness of home, and the trials we have to bear now" (191).

The opening of *Nicholas Nickleby* does illustrate an ideal home with highly functional families that prioritize biblical principles, but they are unable to keep the world out. A smoking chimney was an exterior sign of an inviting hearth inside. "Every effort should conduce to make the hearth the rallying spot of the home," Lucy Orrinsmith wrote in 1878, "to collect around it the richest rugs, the softest sofas, the cosiest chairs, the prettiest treasures" (33–34). Once the Nicklebys relocate to London, however, they find:

The very chimneys appear to have grown dismal and melancholy, from having had nothing better to look at than the chimneys over the way. Their tops are battered, and broken, and blackened with smoke; and here and there some taller stack than the rest, inclining heavily to one side, and toppling over the roof, seems to meditate taking revenge for half a century's neglect, by crushing the inhabitants of the garrets beneath.

(120)

Unheavenly and Broken Homes 181

Figure 9.3 Hablot Knight Browne (Phiz), "Mysterious appearance of the Gentleman in small clothes," *Nicholas Nickleby* (London: Chapman and Hall, 1839), 486
Source: https://books.google.com/books?id=GlgJAAAAQAAJ

Instead of providing comfort to their residents, they seem to be exacting revenge for being neglected.

Furthermore the chimney allows the insane world to invade the home as evident when the crazy "old gentleman"—yes, the same one that courted ladies by tossing cucumbers and other vegetables over the wall (363 and 402)—suddenly appears, or at least his feet do, from the chimney (486–91), wreaking havoc in that Mrs. Nickleby faints and then confesses she has disrupted everyone's peace by becoming the *objet de désir* of the neighbor.

Even if one has a mother like Mrs. Nickleby who seems to constantly unsettle the home (it was her advice that led her husband to make a bad investment that resulted in his demise), Dickens encourages heroic characters like Nicholas, against all financial odds, to reconstruct it. After installing his mother and sister in Mrs. La Creevy's boarding house, he then tells Smike that he is going to take him home. Smike says that he always "longed for home till [he] was weary," but now asserts, "I could not part from you to go to any home on earth" (334). Knowing that he has not long to live (he is dying of consumption), as long as he can see Nicholas' kind smile, he will be able to "go to that home [in heaven] almost without a tear" (334). Nicholas says that his home is not "any particular four walls and a roof." Instead, it is a "place where—in default of a better—those I love are gathered together; and if that place were a gipsy's tent or a barn, I should call it by the same good name notwithstanding," meaning "home" (334).

The last scene in the novel returns to the old cottage in Devonshire, which the Nicklebys still own. It has not changed at all, and around it are children of Kate and Nicholas, and Newman Noggs who was adored by the children. Up the hill overseeing the home are two graves of their father and "their poor dead cousin" (624). The last illustration is a pastoral scene with Madeline and Kay taking care of their children. Rising high above the leafy trees in the background is the parish church. The ending of the novel depicts Dickens' ideal "home," one that is nurturing, inclusive, church-going, and overseen by a good country church, and full of love; and yet, the grave markers for Nicholas' father and cousin are reminders that the only home one can be sure of is on the other side of the grave.

Dickens faults his time for sacking domestic castles in *The Old Curiosity Shop* (1841). According to Malcom Andrews' introduction:

> The destruction of an illusory world is a key concern in the novel, and the city itself is an agent in this destruction. Nell clings to her childhood, her beauty and her innocence against the onslaughts of the city's creatures and environment—Quip's lechery, the Brasses' avarice, the influence of the grotesque curiosity in the shop.
> (1972, 17)

The shop itself is "one of those receptacles for old and curious things which seem to crouch in odd corners of this town and to hide their musty treasures from the public eye in jealousy and distrust" (82). Its residents are a grandfather who is like a child and is addicted to gambling, always hoping that he will secure a better home for his granddaughter. The other resident is Little Nell who is often described as a fairy and a spirit, as if

Unheavenly and Broken Homes 183

Figure 9.4 Hablot Knight Browne (Phiz), "The children at their cousin's grave," *Nicholas Nickleby* (London: Chapman and Hall, 1839), 627
Source: https://books.google.com/books?id=NdYNAAAAQAAJ

she does not belong to this world. Children like Little Nell, Paul Dombey, and Oliver Twist are extremely vulnerable in the modern world when they lack parentage and a nurturing home.

On the first page, the narrator meets Little Nell who is lost. He speculates that the "night is kinder in this respect than the day, which too often destroys an air-built castle at the moment of its completion, without the smallest ceremony or remorse" (79). Despite the grandfather's confidence that once they are away from the city and evildoers, they will be safe (102), it is there, in an ancient chapel, that she dies but "sorrow was dead indeed in her and perfect happiness were born" only possible, not by any home on earth, but by her home in heaven (209–10). The Old Curiosity Shop, with all its domestic discards that nobody wants, its items of the past, and its loss of family, is pulled down and replaced by a broad road (223).

As for Swiveller, he, like the grandfather, is a financial schemer. Not always distinguishing fiction from reality, he fantasizes that his bedstead is a bookcase (120), boiling water is sirloin (296), and he calls the Brasses' servant the Marchioness and a Genie, and later Sophronia Sphynx. Unlike the grandfather, he takes responsibility for someone more broken than himself. He and the Marchioness marry, set up housekeeping in a little country cottage, and live happily ever often entertaining friends and playing lots of cribbage, but not for money (220–22).

Kit also has a family who are intact and happy. He tells them about Nell, that she was taken to heaven where good people go (223). This is not exactly a biblical doctrine in that the New Testament says more than once that it is faith that saves us and not good works (Ti 3:5) and that no one is good or righteous (Rom 3:10); however, the New Testament also asks that if one has faith but does not do good works, can faith save him (Jas 2:14)?

Despite Little Nell's innate goodness, Dickens does question how children are supposed to learn to be good if they are victims of urban blight, living in a workhouse or Folly Ditch or Fagin's Den. In 1848, *The Times* reported that 90% of the children who were released from the workhouses at age 14 lived on the streets and mostly lived lives of crime (Pritchard 47). Younger children were often sent to the North to work in factories six days a week (144). Irate with the Poor Law Amendment of 1834, intended to make sure that the poor did not get spoiled by free handouts, Dickens wrote with acrimonious satire:

> The poor people liked [the workhouse]! It was a regular place of public entertainment for the poorer classes; a tavern where there was nothing to pay; a public breakfast, dinner, tea, and supper all the year round; a brick-and-mortal Elysium, where it was all play no work.
>
> (25)

Yet the orphaned Oliver had to pick oakum at six in the morning and his diet consisted of "three meals of thin gruel a-day, with onion twice a week and a half a roll on Sundays" (25). In the year 1876, 14,073 people died "within the walls of public institutions, including 8174 in workhouses" (English Registrar 1877, 415). Children who were farmed out to work in factories and mines, beginning at the age of six worked 12 hours a day (Pritchard 144).

Life in the slums was not any better than the workhouse; the houses were squalid and broken as were the lives of the tenants: The houses had

> holes from which to look upon the slime beneath; windows broken and patched, the poles thrust out on which to dry the linen that is never there; rooms so small, so filthy, so confined, that the air would seem too tainted even for the dirt and squalor which they shelter; wooden chambers thrusting themselves out above the mud, and threatening to fall into it—as some have done; dirt-besmeared walls and decaying foundations, every loathsome indication of filth, rot, and garbage—all these ornament Folly Ditch.
> (240–41)

This "Jacob's Island" is "near to that part of the Thames on which the church at Rotherhithe abuts" (238–39) as Dickens once again indicts the failure of the church to provide for the poor. The description continues:

> where the buildings on the banks are dirtiest and the vessels on the river blackest with the dust of colliers (coal ships) and the smoke of close-built low-roofed houses, there exists, at the present day, the filthiest, the strangest, the most extraordinary of the many localities that are hidden in London, wholly unknown, even by name, to the great mass of its inhabitants.
> (238)

Sikes

> walks beneath tottering house-fronts projecting over the pavement, dismantled walls that seem to totter as he passes, chimneys half rushed half hesitating to fall, windows guarded by rusty iron bars that time and dirt have almost eaten away, and every imaginable sign of desolation and neglect.
> (239)

"The houses have no owners; they are broken open, and entered upon by those who have courage, and there they live and there they die" (241); this is where the Artful Dodger brings Oliver to live, and it is also the site of Sikes' residence where the chimney of the house hangs him and not the crossbeams outside of Newgate (260–61).

The Victorian hearth was supposed to be a place of refuge for the family from the world (Welsh 144). Its warmth was to gather people together. Its significance and power to do good in an evil world reached almost religious and spiritual importance (Armstrong 1990, 38–41). But people like Sikes did not associate the chimney with family or warmth or religion; it was only an instrument of death.

186 *Brenda Ayres*

Broken houses abound in *Barnaby Rudge*. The novel begins with the Maypole, a very old establishment that knew better days in the age of Henry VIII:

> The Maypole was an old building, with more gable ends than a lazy man would care to count on a sunny day; huge zigzag chimneys, out of which it seemed as though even smoke could not choose but come in more than naturally fantastic shapes, imparted to it in its tortuous progress; and vast stables, gloomy, ruinous, and empty.
>
> (229–30)

Personified, the Maypole represents a nostalgic view of past when a man on his journey could at least find hospitality at an inn, but such places of respite have not endured into the nineteenth century: The Inn

> looked as if it were nodding in its sleep. . . . The bricks of which it was built had originally been a deep dark red, but had grown yellow and discoloured like an old man's skin; the sturdy timbers had decayed like teeth; and here and there the ivy, like a warm garment to comfort it in its age, wrapt its green leaves closely round the time-worn walls.
>
> (230)

At the beginning of the century there were 260,000 paupers in London. In 60 years, that number tripled (Brown 24). Most of the homeless were stashed away and out of sight in workhouses or were huddled together in slums where they resorted to crime in order to survive. *Barnaby Rudge* narrates the consequences of the modern world where moral contagion could and would not stay within the slums but, like smallpox carried by Jo to Esther Summerson, infected the upper classes. Violence spread like Rudge's murder of Geoffrey Haredale, Hugh's attempted rape of Dolly, and the roasting of canaries. Homes were destroyed, including private homes, homes of innocent children, ancient homes of nobility like Warren House, houses of justice, and correction institutions like Newgate. When Gabriel Varden breaks his wife's bank that is in the shape of a little house meant to collect contributions to the Protestant Association, it signifies Dickens' rejection of the hypocritical stance of Christians who did not take care of their own families much less the family of God. Gabriel (who shares the name of the biblical angel in the annunciation and in Daniel's apocalyptic vision) is the quintessential good, middle-class man of England, who breaks the house of the misguided religious miscreants in favor of his own home, one that he provides for Mrs. Rudge. His is the Christian who works for his living. is honorable, and takes care of those less fortunate. After all, he is a locksmith who refuses to unlock Newgate but holds the key to his own house, one that is modest, odd in its construction, clean, and open to all sorts of people who want and need a home once Varden is able to establish order within it.

This is Dickens' lesson to the middle class as to what they are to do in following Christ's call to love one's neighbor. Nowhere does Dickens make clear his concerns that such a lesson is imperative as he does in portraying instable homes and families in *Dombey and Son* (1848). The original title, *Dealings with the Firm of Dombey and Son, Wholesale, Retail, and for Exportation*, signals the immediate problem of the supplanting of commerce over the sanctity of the family. Sol's shop and house, the dysfunctional Dombey family, the abandonment of Dombey's second wife, the death of Carker who is run over by a train, the death of little Paul—all signify the destruction of the family brought on by industrialization, symbolized by the train, and capitalism, represented by Dombey's worship of money.

England had no railroads as of 1825 (Reader 2). Thirteen years later, there were 500 miles of railroad; by 1843, there were 2000; and by 1855, 8000 (Boyle 1989, 211). The novel was first serialized from 1846 through 1848. The displacement of homes, neighborhoods, and community by the railroad is illustrated in this passage:

> The first shock of a great earthquake had, just at that period, rent the whole neighborhood to its centre. Traces of its course were visible on every side. Houses were knocked down; streets broken through and stopped; deep its and trenches dug in the ground; enormous heaps of earth and clay thrown up; buildings that were undermined and shaking, propped by great beams of wood . . . Everywhere were bridges that led nowhere; thoroughfares that were wholly impassable; Babel towers of chimneys, wanting the most unlikely situations; carcasses of ragged tenements, and fragments of unfinished walls and arches, and piles of scaffolding, and wildernesses of bricks, and giant forms of cranes, and tripods straddling above nothing. . ., wholy chang[ing] the law and custom of the neighborhood . . . upon its mighty course of civilization and improvement.
>
> (31)

Modern times and their inherent dissolution of the home are also central to *Our Mutual Friend*. The story's houses are broken because they are built out of the dust of human misery. Boffin's Bower sits on dustheaps. Dust and rubbish have gained the price of gold, that is, providing a place for refuge has made Harmon and now Boffin rich. Boffin's dust house, Mr. Venus' trade in human bones, Boffin's study of *The Rise and Fall of the Roman Empire* (1776–1789), and the dust mounds themselves full of human discard and dung obviously symbolize a deteriorating civilization. That wealth and social position could be based upon human refuse is a major theme in this book. That society of full of broken people is another. That modern times are characterized by decay and brokenness is still another. That excessive materialism forms waste as the byproduct is also one of Dickens' indictment of the broken Victorian home.

Because of space constraints, not studied in this chapter are *Hard Times* (1854) with houses, like Stone Lodge, that are void of the human heart; *A Tale of Two Cities* (1859) and its storming of homes; and Dickens' last novel that was incomplete when he passed, *The Mystery of Edwin Drood* (1871 [1870]), with its houses that are tombs. As for his first novel, *The Pickwick Papers* (1840 [1837]), with its many houses in which the innocuous Mr. Pickwick finds himself in trouble, it appears that early enough in his writing career, Dickens feared that the house as icon for home, the God-ordained sanctuary, could not stand against the ungodly onslaughts of his own century. "There's no place like home" appeared in a comic opera in 1832, a year that is often used to signify the beginning of the Victorian period because it was the date of the first Reform Bill that gave much of the middle class the right to vote. Yet, for the Victorian, the house as center could not hold. Progress, evolution, industrialization, materialism, colonization, scientific inquiry, discovery, invention, and materialism—all came at a great price paid in broken house, broken homes, broken lives, broken spirits, and a broken time that still has not mended.

During nearly every Christian funeral, both Victorian and modern, one of the most frequent passages mentioned to assure the living that when they die, they "will not perish, but have everlasting life" (Jn 3:16) is John 14:2, "In my Father's house are many mansions: if it were not so, I would have told you. I go to prepare a place for you." This reassurance seems to be the only true hope for modern times unless people follow Christ's teaching and make a heaven on earth by providing homes of love that took care of the otherwise homeless.

Notes

1. A list of all his homes can be found at www.victorianweb.org/authors/dickens/gallery/25.html.
2. In a letter of February 9, 1871 to a medical student, Mr. Robert Lawson, at Edinburgh in answer as to the admission of females to the medical university (Wylie 1881, 100–1).
3. Quoted in Marlow (1994, 13) from Creevy (1983, 63).
4. See Norris Pope's chapter on Dickens' fight for the right of citizens to be allowed to drink and enjoy entertainment on their only day off from work (1978, 42–95).
5. Dickens often refers to St. Paul throughout his novels as a constant reminder of the failure of the house of God in taking care of all the inhabitants of the city.

Bibliography

Altick, Richard. *Victorian People and Ideas: A Companion for the Modern Reader of Victorian Literature.* New York: W. W. Norton, 1973.

Andrews, Malcolm. Introduction to *The Old Curiosity Shop* by Charles Dickens, 11–31. London: Penguin, 1972.

Armstrong, Frances. *Dickens and the Concept of Home*. Ann Arbor: UMI Research Press, 1990.

Barton, William E. "Old Plantation Hymns." *New England Magazine* 19, no. 4 (December 1898): 443–56. https://books.google.com/books?id=eHZPAQAAMAAJ.

Beales, H. L. "The Victorian Family." In *Ideas and Beliefs of the Victorians: An Historic Revaluation of the Victorian Age*, 343–50. London: British Broadcasting Corporation, 1949.

Boyle, Thomas. *Black Swine in the Sewers of Hampstead: Beneath the Surface of Victorian Sensationalism*. New York: Viking, 1989.

Brown, Julia Prewitt. *A Reader's Guide to the Nineteenth-Century English Novels*. New York: Collier Books, 1985.

Brumley, Albert E. "This World Is Not My Home." 1936. In *The Complete Book of Hymns*, edited by William Petersen and Ardythe Petersen, 461. Carol Stream, IL, 2006.

Creevy, Patrick. "In Time and Out: The Tempo of Life in *Bleak House*. *Dickens Studies Annual* 12 (1983): 63–80. https://www.jstor.org/stable/44371730.

Cumming, Charles E. "Fetichism." *The Metaphysical Magazine* 22, no. 4 (April 1908): 212–20. https://books.google.com/books?id=-Lw7AQAAMAAJ.

Davidoff, Leonore, and Catherine Hall. *Family Fortunes: Men and Women of the English Middle Class, 1780–1850*. Chicago, IL: University of Chicago Press, 1987.

Dickens, Charles. *Barnaby Rudge: A Tale of the Riots of Eighty*. London: Chapman and Hall, 1841. https://books.google.com/books?id=rmgOAAAAQAAJ.

———. *Bleak House*. London: Bradbury, 1853. https://books.google.com/books?id=KlsJAAAAQAAJ.

———. *Dombey and Son*. Philadelphia: Lea and Blanchard, 1848. https://books.google.com/books?id=dibZQA_tGLIC.

———. *Great Expectations*. 1861. Boston: Estes and Lauriat, 1881. https://books.google.com/books?id=fhUXAAAAYAAJ.

———. *Hard Times*. London: Bradbury, 1854. https://books.google.com/books?id=X9RVAAAAcAAJ.

———. *The Life of Our Lord: Written for His Children During the Years 1846 to 1849*. 1934. Introduction by Gerald Charles Dickens. New York: Simon and Schuster, 1999.

———. *Little Dorrit*. London: Bradbury and Evans, 1857. https://books.google.com/books?id=XvpcAAAAcAAJ.

———. *Martin Chuzzlewit*. 1844. London: Chapman and Hall, 1868. https://books.google.com/books?id=V7zgTtWMj5IC.

———. *The Mystery of Edwin Drood*. 1870. New York: Hurd and Houghton, 1871. https://books.google.com/books?id=YGUVAAAAYAAJ.

———. *Nicholas Nickleby*. London: Chapman and Hall, 1839. https://books.google.com/books?id=NdYNAAAAQAAJ.

———. *The Old Curiosity Shop*. London: Chapman and Hall, 1841. https://books.google.com/books?id=2dUNAAAAQAAJ.

———. *Oliver Twist*. London: Bentley, 1838. https://books.google.com/books?id=Vz8JAAAAQAAJ.

———. *Our Mutual Friend*. 1865. New York: D. Appleton, 1876 https://books.google.com/books?id=5dkGcb-MGhsC.

———. *The Personal History of David Copperfield*. London: Bradbury and Evans, 1850. https://books.google.com/books?id=NcsNAAAAQAAJ.

———. *The Posthumous Papers of the Pickwick Club*. 1837. New York: J. Van Amringe, 1840. https://books.google.com/books?id=r2ooAAAAMAAJ.

———. *A Tale of Two Cities*. Philadelphia: T. B. Peterson and Brothers, 1859. https://books.google.com/books?id=4VQOAAAAQAAJ.

Ellis, Mrs. Sarah Stickney. *The Wives of England, Their Relative Duties, Domestic Influence, and Social Obligations*. 1843. London: Fisher, Son, and Company, 1846. https://books.google.com/books?id=GzVkAAAAcAAJ.

"The English Registrar-General's Annual Summary." *Medical Press and Circular* 73 (May 23, 1877): 415–17. https://books.google.com/books?id=NhcCAAAAYAAJ.

Forster, John. *The Life of Charles Dickens*. London: Chapman and Hall, 1892. https://books.google.com/books?id=T21IAQAAMAAJ.

Harrod, Samuel, ed. "This World Is Not My Home." In *The Peculiar People's Hymn Book*, 590–91. London: A. Chalk, Daw's Heath, 1891. https://books.google.com/books?id=KCYPAAAAIAAJ.

Henry, Maura A. "The Making of Elite Culture." In *A Companion to Eighteenth-Century Britain*, edited by H. T. Dickinson, 311–28. Malden, MA: Blackwell Publishers, 2002.

Kilian, Crawford. "In Defense of Esther Summerson." *Dalhousie Review* 54 (1974): 318–28.

Larson, Janet L. "The Battle of Biblical Books in Esther's Narrative." *Nineteenth-Century Fiction* 38, no. 2 (September 1983): 131–60. www.jstor.org/stable/3044787.

Marlow, James E. *Charles Dickens: The Uses of Time*. Selinsgrove, PA: Susquehanna University Press, 1994.

Milbank, Alison. *Daughters of the House: Modes of the Gothic in Victorian Fiction*. Basingstoke: Macmillan Press, 1992.

Mingay, Gordon. "Agriculture and Rural Life." In *A Companion to Eighteenth-Century Britain*, edited by H. T. Dickinson, 141–47. Malden, MA: Blackwell Publishers, 2002.

Orrinsmith, Lucy. *The Drawing-room: Its Decorations and Furniture*. London: Macmillan and Company, 1878. https://books.google.com/books?id=ww1BAAAAYAAJ.

Patmore, Conventry. *Angel in the House: The Betrothal*. 1850. London: John W. Parker and Son, 1854. https://books.google.com/books?id=Ot0NAAAAQAAJ.

Pope. Norris F. *Dickens and Charity*. London: Macmillan Press, 1978.

Pritchard, R. E. *Dickens's England: Life in Victorian Times*. Westport, CT: Praeger, 2003.

Ragland, Charles J. *The Raglands: The Ragland Family of Granville County, North Carolina Including Its Origin* . . . . Winston-Salem, NC, Ragland, 1978.

Ragussis, Michael. "The Ghostly Signs of *Bleak House*." *Nineteenth-Century Fiction* 34, no. 3 (December 1979): 253–80. https://doi.org/10.2307/2933328.

Reader, William Joseph. *Life in Victorian England*. New York: G. P. Putnam's Sons, 1964.

Reed, John R. *Victorian Conventions*. Vol. 10. Athens, OH: Ohio University Press, 1975.
Ruskin, John. "Of Queens' Gardens." In *Sesame and Lilies*. 1865. Philadelphia: Henry Altemus, 1892. https://books.google.com/books?id=mp85AQAAMAAJ.
St. George, Andrew. *The Descent of Manners: Etiquette, Rules, and the Victorians*. London: Chatto and Windus, 1993.
Whipple, Edwin Percy. Introduction to *Bleak House*. In *The Writings of Charles Dickens*, ix–xxv. Cambridge, MA: Houghton, Mifflin and Company, 1894.
Woodward, Sir Llewellyn. *The Age of Reform, 1815–1870*. Oxford at the Clarendon Press, 1962.
Wright, Julia McNair. *The Complete Home: An Encyclopaedia of Domestic Life and Affairs*. 1870. Brantford, ONT: Bradley, Garretson and Company, 1879. https://books.google.com/books?id=NhJARQagcL4C.
Wylie, William Howie. *Thomas Carlyle: The Man and His Books*. London: Marshall Japp and Company, 1881. https://books.google.com/books?id=zWkqAAAAMAAJ.
Xu, Wenying. "The Opium Trade and *Little Dorrit*: A Case of Reading Silences." *Victorian Literature and Culture* 25, no. 1 (1997): 53–66. https://www-jstor-org.ezproxy.liberty.edu/stable/25058373?seq=9#metadata_info_tab_contents.
Young, George Malcolm. *Early Victorian England, 1830–1865*. Vol. 2. 1934. London: Oxford University Press, 1951.

10 Ghosts of Dickens' Past

The Death of Judaism in *Oliver Twist* and *Our Mutual Friend*

Lindsay Katzir

Charles Dickens is perhaps best known for his humanitarianism. The most mistreated members of the society inhabit his fiction, and he spent his life critiquing the institutions that victimized them. His sympathy in *Oliver Twist* (2003 [1838]), *A Christmas Carol* (1843), and *Bleak House* (1853) is unmistakable. But he is also known for the anti-Semitism that resounds through his writing, a contradiction especially embodied by *Oliver Twist*'s Fagin. A masterful personification of Victorian London's underworld, Fagin is also an enduring anti-Semitic stereotype. Avaricious, mendacious, and treacherous, he has haunted the world's imagination since his inception. Because readers have long loved Dickens, there has been an equally longstanding attempt to excuse his anti-Semitism; thus, it has been argued that Dickens redeemed himself by creating Riah, the virtuous, duteous, and conscientious Jew of *Our Mutual Friend* (1997 [1865]). Having observed that Fagin and Riah are not so different, though, I offer a new view of Dickens and Jews by reading the two characters as orthodox Jews.

Dickens' conception of Judaism was clearly shaped by Christian history. As Michael Scrivener explains, "What makes antisemitism different from innumerable other instances of insensitive majorities treating their minorities badly . . . is the long history, especially in a Christian society" (2011, 25). Dickens was a committed Christian who famously scorned the Hebrew Bible, the cornerstone of Judaism, but as Susan Meyer points out, "When Dickens's Christianity is discussed, it is almost never considered in conjunction with Dickens's representation of Jews" (2005, 241). According to Deborah Nord, he "shared the tendencies . . . to see the Jew as incapable of achieving spiritual or moral transcendence while retaining his fundamental Jewishness" (2011, 28). Because Dickens considered Christ to be the foundation of spiritual life, he consigned the Jews to spiritual death. Dickens portrays the death of Judaism through both Fagin's and Riah's estrangement from Jewish community and, thus, from Jewish continuity.

DOI: 10.4324/9781003156611-11

Eliza Davis and Dickens

Most scholars believe that Dickens harbored at least some animus toward Jews until he sold his London residence to James and Eliza Davis in August 1860. Although he complained to Thomas Mitton that "the purchaser of Tavistock House will be a Jew Money-Lender," he afterward complimented them as "satisfactory, considerate, and trusting."[1] From these comments, Gary Levine surmises, "[Eliza] Davis and her husband . . . evidently made a good impression on a previously prejudiced man" (2003, 23), and Harry Stone assumes, "The incident brought home to Dickens the irrationality of some of his feelings about Jews" (1959, 243). Davis seemed doubtful of Dickens' "conversion," so in June 1863, she wrote to him and pointed out, "It has been said that Charles Dickens . . . has encouraged a vile prejudice against the despised Hebrew" (quoted in Roth 1938, 304–305). Dickens replied by enclosing a charitable donation to the Lady Montefiore Memorial Fund, which was meant to show "that [he] ha[d] no feeling towards the Jewish people but a friendly one" (quoted in 306). As Deborah Heller observes, "It seems clear that Dickens definitely did not wish to be thought of as anti-Semitic" (1990, 42). Still, his writings are replete with anti-Semitic imagery, and so Murray Baumgarten claims that, by admonishing Dickens while he was drafting *Our Mutual Friend* (1865), Davis "made a major difference in his understanding of [Jews]" (2015, 50). According to these scholars, Davis inspired Dickens to reevaluate his own anti-Semitism.

Dickens is said to have written *Our Mutual Friend* in part as an atonement for the anti-Semitism of *Oliver Twist* (1838). In her letters, Davis laments that Fagin "admits only of one interpretation," and so she implores Dickens "to atone for [this] great wrong" (quoted in Roth 305). She later praises the introduction of "the Jew, Riah, in the 7th No. of *Our Mutual Friend*," and she ascribes it to her intervention (quoted in 307). Beginning with these letters, the so-called atonement narrative contends that Dickens meant for the benevolent Riah to contravene the malevolent Fagin. In 1886 the Anglo-Jewish writer Amy Levy suggested that in *Our Mutual Friend*, Dickens "tries to compensate for his having affixed the label 'Jew' to one of his bad fairies by creating the good fairy Riah" (176). Rabbis David Philipson (1889, 96–97) and Edward Calisch (1909, 128) also interpreted *Our Mutual Friend* as apologetic. Writing in 1958 and 1959, respectively, Lauriat Lane, Jr. and Harry Stone argued, "Dickens put the character of Riah into *Our Mutual Friend* in answer to Mrs. Eliza Davis" (Lane 1958, 98) and "Mrs. Davis . . . forced him to reevaluate what he had written about Jews and helped him to formulate what he would yet write" (Stone 243). In 1978 Lionel Trilling concurred that "when Eliza Davis took him to task for maligning her race, he . . .

strove to make amends with the character of Riah, a creature as impossibly good as Fagin was impossibly bad." Baumgarten and Heller revived the atonement narrative in the 1990s, and since then, countless others have retold it.[2]

Most also point to Dickens' revision of *Oliver Twist* as evidence of his rehabilitation. In 1867 Chapman and Hall decided to publish a special edition of Dickens' collected works, offering him the opportunity to revise his earlier writings (Anthony Julius 2010, 203). Whereas Fagin is derisively called "the Jew" throughout the original text, Dickens excised almost all instances of this epithet in the revision, calling him "Fagin" instead. According to Maria Cristina Paganoni, Dickens meant "to further disprove [claims of] anti-Semitic prejudices" (2017, 308), and for Susan Meyer, it "lessen[ed] the heaviness of the novel's antisemitism" (2005, 240). Scholars especially appreciate the revision in Chapter 52, "Fagin's Last Night Alive," which explores Fagin's emotional state before he is hanged for his crimes. As Lane remarks, it "emphasizes the real individual rather than the archetypal racial villain" (99–100). The revision supposedly answers Davis' complaint by softening *Oliver Twist*'s anti-Semitism.

Though most continue to uphold the atonement narrative, it has been challenged by some. For Jonathan Grossman, the narrative is unconvincing because "Dickens does not make a mimetic attempt to construct a Jew, as George Eliot does in *Daniel Deronda* by 'realistically' depicting multiple Jewish personalities and milieus" (1996, 49). For Efraim Sicher,

> It is not . . . that Dickens is in some way making up for Fagin in his depiction of Riah in *Our Mutual Friend*, but that . . . the Romantic reading of 'the jew' was characterized by simultaneous and contradictory impulses of philo-Semitism and anti-Semitism.
>
> (2002, 141)

And for James D. Mardock, "These assumptions [about atonement] neglect the wider context of the novel's engagement with *The Merchant of Venice*, and that rather than simply serving as an apology for Fagin, Riah functions explicitly as an anti-Shylock" (2005 n.p.). I also question the atonement narrative, in part because it seems too simplistic, perhaps even too convenient.

For one, *The Jewish Chronicle* accused Dickens of anti-Semitism long before Davis. In fact the publication regularly reproached famous figures such as Thackeray, Ruskin, and Dickens for fueling anti-Semitism (Cesarani 1994, 27, 39). The editors were particularly offended by Dickens' *Bentley's Miscellany* (1837–1839) and *Household Words* (1850–1859), both of which circulated anti-Semitic stereotypes (Stone 231–32; Cesarani 27). In 1854 the *Chronicle* declared, "Jews alone [are] excluded from 'the sympathizing heart' of this great author and powerful friend of the oppressed" (quoted in Baumgarten 1996, 51). Dickens refused to countenance such accusations. He responded to the *Chronicle*, "I know of no reason the Jews can have for regarding me as 'inimical' to them," and later claimed the same to Davis (quoted in 51).

Additionally, these accusations appear to have evoked neither remorse nor reform in Dickens. His response to Davis is "polite, albeit vaguely insulting" (Hirsch 2003, 318); he wrote "that if Jews felt that he had done them 'a great wrong,' then 'they are far less sensible, a far less just, and a far less good-tempered people that I have always supposed them to be," making his victims into victimizers (quoted in Roth 306). Dickens assured Davis that "I always speak well of [Jews], whether in public or in private, and bear my testimony . . . to their perfect good faith in such transactions as I have ever had with them" (quoted in Roth 306). During the Tavistock transaction, though, he seemed suspicious of "the Jew Money-Lender," confiding to Mitton, "I shall never believe in him until he has paid the money."[3] James Davis was a solicitor, not a banker, but Dickens easily associated him with the stereotypes he replicated in his writings, which, in 1864, still contained traces of anti-Semitism.[4]

In general, Dickens did not defend the Jews as he did others. Throughout the Russian Empire, for instance, Jews thought of Britain as a model democracy and of Dickens as a great humanitarian (Morgentaler 2017, 87–88). Still, Sholem Aleichem, who admired Dickens greatly, wrote to a Russian newspaper, decrying how, "when Charles Dickens . . . needed to describe a thief who founds a school for thieves, he could find no other candidate in all of England but a Jew" (quoted in 93). Davis believed that "Dickens, the large hearted, whose works plead so eloquently and so nobly for the oppressed of his country," stoked anti-Semitism with his writings (quoted in Roth 304–305). Calisch lamented that "the writer who wrought so sturdily for the oppressed and downtrodden . . . took occasion to place a stigma upon a people who were in the midst of a struggle for the native rights of citizenship" (127). Indeed, Dickens never apologized for Fagin, a figure who was born again and again in characters like Ebenezer Scrooge, Uriah Heep, and Riah himself.

Ultimately, scholars have overstated the creation of Riah. For them, Dickens "intended to plead the Jewish case" (Stone 246); was "conscious that he had been guilty of a great injustice" (Philipson 95–96); "was genuinely contrite and strove to make amends" (Trilling); "had some sense of his own injustice" (Meyer 240); and was "aware of the implications of his portrayal of Jews" (Endelman 2002, 104). But "Dickens himself, however, gives us no evidence, in the novel or elsewhere, that he intended Riah to serve simply as atonement for Fagin" (Mardock n.p.). Rather, "It is Mrs. Davis who understood Riah to be a correction of Fagin" (Sicher 147). In 1867, she sent him a Hebrew Bible that was inscribed, "To Charles Dickens, in grateful and admiring recognition of his having exercised the noblest quality man can possess—that of atoning for an injury, as soon as conscious of having inflicted it" (quoted in Lane 99). In fact, the atonement narrative obscures significant similarities between *Oliver Twist* and *Our Mutual Friend*.

Anti-Semitic Stereotypes

As part of the neat narrative of Dickens' contrition, scholars see Fagin and Riah as representing two contrasting myths of "the Jew." According to Trilling, the nineteenth century responded "to the myth of the Jew as a degraded inferior . . . with an assertion of his natural goodness." If, as Heller claims, Fagin is villainous while Riah is virtuous, then "an examination of Fagin and Mr. Riah, the embodiments of opposing Jewish stereotypes, may possibly reveal something of Dickens's shifting attitudes toward Jews" (40). But, as Levine suggests, "Both the villainous Jew and the saintly Jew emerge. . . [as] an essentially stable [stereotype]" (24). Thus, I compare Fagin and Riah as examples of equivalent anti-Semitic stereotypes, revealing Dickens' largely unchanged attitude toward Jews and Judaism from one work to the next.

First, both resemble the stage Jew of medieval and Elizabethan drama. Stone describes this stock character as "a rapacious moneylender, or perhaps later, a thieving peddler or old-clothes dealer. . . [who] usually shuffled about the stage in black gabardine and a broadbrimmed hat, [with] his red hair, red whiskers, and hooked nose" (228). Fagin's face is "villainous-looking and repulsive," veiled by "a quantity of matted red hair" (Dickens 2003 [1838], 64). He has a hooked nose and shuffling gait. Riah's face is obscured by long hair and a beard. He stands with "his head bowed and his eyes cast down" (Dickens 1997 [1865], 275), wearing "a shovel-hat and gaberdine" (525). Both old men dress shabbily and speak cringingly. Fagin is grotesque (Sicher 146), and Riah is "grotesquely virtuous" (Mardock n.p). Scholars see these traits in Fagin, but only Mardock observes that "Riah functions in Dickens's novel . . . as a stage Jew," though he sees Riah as a reversal of the stereotype, not as a recurrence of it (Mardock (n.p).[5]

Second, both are associated with the buying and selling of old clothes, a common vocation among Victorian Jews. In 1837 most were impoverished, unskilled, and uneducated, undertaking various street trades to survive (Endelman 44). By 1864 their situation had improved, but many continued to hawk clothing, rags, and rubbish in the streets (79). As an old-clothes dealer, Fagin is well known at Rag Fair, a market where Jews purchased secondhand clothing to sell (82). Brownlow spurns Fagin for his disreputable associates, including the old-clothes dealer who helps him abduct Oliver, and Fagin becomes "dangling heaps of clothes" upon his death (445). When meeting Riah, Eugene Wrayburn dismisses him as "an old clothesman" and endeavors to separate him from Lizzie Hexam (398). Because "the Old Clothes Man in particular locates 'the jew'

Ghosts of Dickens' Past 197

Figure 10.1 George Cruikshank, "Oliver introduced to the respectable Old Gentleman," *Oliver Twist* (London: Richard Bentley, 1838), 133.

Source: https://books.google.com/books?id=Vz8JAAAAQAAJ.

within the larger anxieties of contamination of nationhood, class, and domesticity" (Sicher 139–40), both characters are ostracized as a result of this association.

Third, both are portrayed as criminals, coinciding with an "increase in the incidence of Jewish criminal activity in London" (Endelman 82). Defending himself against Davis, Dickens insists, "It unfortunately was true of the time to which [*Oliver Twist*] refers, that that class of criminal almost invariably *was* a Jew" (quoted in Roth 306). This "criminal class" largely comprised Jewish peddlers dealing in stolen property (Scrivener 47). Old-clothes sellers acquired their poor reputation from those who, like Fagin, worked as professional thieves with connections to criminal organizations and outlets (Endelman 44). Most scholars believe that Fagin was at least partially inspired by Ikey Solomon (1785–1850), the notorious fence from Houndsditch who dealt in stolen goods and stood trial at the Old Bailey in 1830.[6] They denounce Fagin for his villainy while celebrating Riah for his integrity, but Riah willingly misrepresents himself as the corrupt moneylender behind Fledgeby's firm. Riah is not the criminal that Fagin is, but he is characterized as one, and by appointing Riah himself as his only advocate, the novel does not entirely vindicate him.

Thus, both resemble Shylock, the miserly Jew of Shakespeare's *The Merchant of Venice*. Fagin jealously guards his stolen treasures and purposefully withholds money from his associates, excusing himself as "only a miser" (Dickens 69). Riah is not miserly, but because of his professional arrangement, he must act so toward Fledgeby's victims. For most scholars, Riah represents a profound reversal of the Shylock stereotype, though Dickens did not invent this motif.[7] In 1794, Richard Cumberland's *The Jew* introduced a Jewish character who performs the part of "a bloodsucker, an extortioner, a Shylock" but is "at heart a person of generosity and gratitude" (quoted in Trilling 24). In the case of *Our Mutual Friend*, such "subversion" seems immaterial. Characters readily identify Riah with Shylock because of his stereotypical appearance, which, for Fledgeby, makes him "a good'un . . . for the part" (Dickens 276). Mortimer Lightwood tells Eugene that he "had an interview . . . with a Jew [Riah], who seems determined to press [them] hard. Quite a Shylock, and quite a Patriarch" (525). Most believe "Dickens uses the unnaturally benevolent Riah not only to answer the charge of anti-Semitism but to give a study of anti-Semitism in action" (Lane 98). But Dickens merely projects the Shylock stereotype onto Fledgeby rather than dismantling it through Riah. Although Riah leaves Fledgeby's firm repentant, he later reprises his role as Shylock when lending money for John Harmon.

Next, both cultivate inappropriate relationships with children, "a disturbing connection that has stirred sensitivities to this day" (Paganoni 307). For one, their relationships recall the medieval blood libel, a legend in which Jews kidnapped Christian children for use in unholy rites, draining their blood to make matzah for Passover. In Dickens' "modernized version of the blood libel" (Litvak 1998, 43), Fagin abducts and corrupts orphans, sending them to the gallows in his stead. By amusing and "nurturing" Oliver, "the wily old Jew . . . prepared his mind, . . . slowly instilling into his soul the poison which he hoped would blacken it and change its hue forever" (Dickens 152). Anthony Julius calls *Our Mutual Friend* "a negative imprint of the blood libel" (203), but Riah essentially "abducts" Lizzie when he finds her on the streets and takes her to a hideout, causing others to fear she has been "corrupted" (converted) by the Jews.

They also function as perverse schoolmasters. Fagin houses and educates orphaned children, and "his methods are admirably progressive: strictly learning by doing" (Mardock n.p.). He teaches Oliver to pickpocket and orders him to become "deeply involved in his new study" (Dickens 72). Riah also houses and educates orphaned children, and "Lizzie and Jenny learn to read and write with the help of a tutor he provides" (Baumgarten 1996, 53).[8] He schools them on the rooftop of Fledgeby's firm, where "they both pored over one book; both with attentive faces; Jenny with the sharper; Lizzie with the more perplexed" (Dickens 276). Scholars typically contrast Fagin and Riah as educators, noting that Fagin abuses Oliver and prostitutes Nancy, whereas Riah nurtures Jenny and protects Lizzie.[9] But as with the other stereotypes, Riah is still *perceived* as perverse. Fledgeby accuses Riah of desiring Lizzie, pressing him to "out with [his] reason for having [his] spoon in the soup," that is, for guarding her against Eugene's attentions (Dickens 425).[10] Riah rebuffs the implication, but "Eugene realizes that Riah stands steadfastly between him and Lizzie" (Nord 37), as though Riah were responsible for her chastity, not unlike a pimp controlling a prostitute. During this period, "Jews were also to be found keeping brothels and working as prostitutes" (Endelman 58), so this association is not farfetched.

Last, and most concerning, both are religious caricatures. Dickens describes Riah as "professing [the Jewish] faith," and he points out "that [Fagin] is called 'The Jew,' not because of his religion, but because of his race," so most scholars assume that Fagin is irreligious (quoted in Roth 306). According to some, "Dickens seems to be reasoning, 'the Jew' is not a definition of religion, but a definition of race" (Sicher 146), and "For Dickens, Fagin's Jewishness was a matter of race and not religion" (Weltman 2011, 375). According to others, "Dickens makes it clear that Fagin has long since rejected the Jewish religion" (Lane 96), and "Dickens separates Judaism as a religion from Fagin's character" (Grossman 38). However, Dickens never claims that Fagin is not religious but rather that Judaism is not the source of his animus toward Jews.

Moreover, Victorian Jews did not think of "religion" and "race" as distinct. Some were merely more remiss in their religious observance than others. Todd Endelman explains that during the eighteenth and nineteenth centuries, "[most] were not Orthodox in the usual sense of the term . . . despite belonging to congregations whose ritual and religious leadership were Orthodox" (114). Only some practiced Judaism faithfully by observing kashrut, attending synagogue, studying Torah, and celebrating Shabbat (54). The rich often rejected the regimented and segregated nature of traditional life, and the poor became more casual in their observance of religious rituals and customs, with some ceasing to practice Judaism entirely (57). Even those who regularly attended Shabbat services might later be found at theaters, concerts, exhibitions, races, restaurants, and pubs, in violation of Sabbath laws (114–115). Philipson insists that Fagin "is no Jew; he is a villainous criminal," though he was "born into the Jewish religion" (92).[11] Linda Gertner Zatlin believes, "Had he been characterized as a believer in God, Fagin would have been less credible as a soulless, inhuman criminal" (1981, 124). When discussing Judaism, most scholars equate the term "religious" with pious, overlooking the historical fact that some were either bad people or "bad Jews," those who considered themselves orthodox but were not meticulously observant. This stereotype, in particular, dominates Dickens' depiction of Jews.

When assessing Fagin's religiosity, scholars generally first examine his diet. It is important to understand that most Victorian Jews did not follow Judaism's dietary laws precisely. Many purchased unsalted and unpurged meat and ate unkosher foods in public (Endelman 115). Even Sir Moses and Judith Montefiore ate unkosher meat when traveling in 1823, though they were observant and traveled with a shochet (kosher slaughterer) in 1838 (Lipman and Lipman 1985, 10). Scholars tend to hold Fagin to more stringent standards, arguing, as Steven Marcus does, "When we first see him, he is cooking sausages for his boys, and it is clear throughout that such matters as the dietary laws and the customs of the Jewish community mean nothing to him" (1962). For Grossman, "the sausages distance Fagin from kosher Judaism" (38), and for Weltman, "Fagin is not religious: he doesn't keep kosher, as is obvious from the sausages he eats when Oliver first meets [him]" (375). Indeed, Fagin cooks sausages, boils coffee, and toasts bread for his gang. He "[sits] down [with them] to breakfast off the coffee and some hot rolls and ham" (Dickens 69) and later holds "a saveloy and a small loaf in his hand" (96). But Fagin never actually eats anything, whereas Oliver "ate his share" of sausages (66), Charley spat "the coffee he was drinking" (70), and Noah "took a series of large bites" of bread (377). Fagin does not keep kosher, strictly speaking, but neither did most of his historical coreligionists.

Scholars also scrutinize Fagin's dress. Medieval and Renaissance Jews were known for wearing gabardines, and in the eighteenth century, Polish Jews also began wearing caftans.[12] By the mid-nineteenth century, orthodox immigration to Britain had increased, making religious men more visible, a contrast to the unobservant who had already sartorially assimilated (Endelman 51–58, 81). Riah wears "a large brimmed low-crowned hat, and a long-skirted coat" (Dickens 396), which Dickens and his characters identify as "a shovel-hat and gaberdine" (525), the traditional ensemble of the Polish orthodox. Contrary to Baumgarten, Mardock insists that Fagin and Riah dress differently.[13] However, Fagin is introduced "in a greasy flannel gown" (Dickens 64), which Paganoni describes as "a sort of debased caftan" (308). Later, Fagin dons "an old patched great-coat" (145), and Cruikshank's illustrations show him wearing a gabardine and broad-brimmed hat. Davis told Dickens that "people [like Riah] dress as their neighbors do, and before the present fashion of beards prevailed, did not wear theirs unless, indeed, they are Polish [orthodox] Jews" (quoted in Roth 308). Dressing and looking like Riah, then, indicates that Fagin has at least a nominal relationship to traditional religiosity.

Finally, and most commonly, scholars point out that condemned Fagin rejects religious intercession. Before Fagin is hanged, "Venerable men of his own persuasion had come to pray beside him, but he had driven them away with curses. They renewed their charitable efforts, and he beat them off" (Dickens 445). Most see this passage as significant evidence of Fagin's irreligiosity. Indeed, "at one time he raved and blasphemed," but "at another howled and tore his hair" (445). However, in the Tanakh, tearing of the hair is often symbolic of repentance; for example, when Ezra contemplates the great sins of the Israelites, he is recorded as having rented his garment and his mantle "and plucked off the hair of [his] head and of [his] beard and sat down appalled" (Ezr 9:3, *Tanakh: The Holy Scriptures*). Notably, Fagin's erratic and blasphemous prayer service occurs on Shabbat.[14] As Davis observes, Riah also utters blasphemies, being "made to say 'they curse me in Jehovah's name,'" and she points out, "No Jew ever utters this appellation of the 'Creator,' even in his prayers" (quoted in Roth 307). Likewise, Morgentaler notes "that an observant Jew would never appear in public bear-headed, as [Dickens] has Riah do" (151), making a hypocrite of him, too. I am not suggesting that Fagin is pious or that Riah is evil but rather that Dickens relied on all the same stereotypes in his creation of both characters.

The Death of Judaism

By portraying Fagin and Riah as hypocrites and legalists, Dickens marshals stereotypes from Christian theology. The stage Jew, old clothesman, moneylender, and blood libel stereotypes originated with medieval Christianity, and the tropes of falseness, avariciousness, and abusiveness come directly from the New Testament. Likewise, Christianity has long equated Judaism with death, and the New Testament vividly elaborates this metaphor (Newman 1993, 456). Calling Jews hypocrites, Jesus likens them to "whitewashed tombs, which on the outside look beautiful, but inside they are full of the bones of the dead and of all kinds of filth" (Mt 23:27 *New Oxford Annotated Bible*) and "unmarked graves, and people walk over them without realizing it" (Lk 11:44). These passages represent Jews as outwardly pure but spiritually dead by comparing them to sepulchers. Jesus also dubs them the children of Satan (Jn 8:44), being synonymous with death (Heb 2:14). Because the New Testament is supposed to have superseded the Hebrew Bible, the birth of Christianity has been seen as the end of Judaism. Dickens famously scorned the Hebrew Bible, deriving his religious views exclusively from the New Testament (Sable 1986, 67–68; Meyer 250), and like the New Testament, he proclaims the death of Judaism in several ways.

To start, Fagin and Riah are perceived as ghosts, vampires, and devils, all avatars of death. Scholars have noted that Jenny Wren refers to Riah as her "fairy godmother" (Dickens 429), but Riah is more specter than sprite.[15] He "ascend[s] to a prophet's tomb" (276), haunts a churchyard in his "long-skirted coat" (398), and "steal[s] through the streets in his ancient dress, like the ghost of a departed Time" (400). Similarly, Fagin is envisioned as an "ugly ghost just rose from the grave" (2003, 154), a "hideous phantom, moist from the grave" (390), and an "old carcase" that belongs in a grave (154). Riah "come[s] out of his grave" like vampire (279), and Fagin's home, which resembles a coffin, is "as dark as the grave" (212). Like vampires, Riah is supposed to be a "bloodsucker," and Fagin is nocturnal, roaming only at night. Scholars know Fagin as the "merry old gentleman," a euphemism for Satan, but few know Riah as "devilish" (560). Bill Sikes assumes that "[Fagin's] father . . . is singeing his grizzled red beard by this time, unless [Fagin] came straight from the old'un without any father at all betwixt [them]" (371). According to Sikes, Fagin is the son of "the old'un," and according to Fledgeby, Riah is the "old'un," himself (419). Riah disappears "into the fog, and was lost" to onlookers (417), just as Fagin disappears from Oliver's window, leaving "not even the traces of recent footsteps" (285).[16] As Zatlin asserts, "Demonic power resides in Fagin's ability to change the appearance of others for his own benefit and in his disappearance from the Maylies" (125). Likewise, Jenny imagines Riah to be a shapeshifter, "look[ing] so unlike the rest of people, and so much as if [he] had changed [himself] into that shape" (429). In both novels Dickens underscores the Gospels' perspective on Judaism by depicting Jews as unredeemed fiends that haunt the faithful.

Next, Dickens characterizes Jewish texts as spiritually dead by endowing Jews with so-called Old Testament traits. The "God of the Old Testament," a common signifier among those who repudiate the themes of the Hebrew Bible, has been pronounced harsh and unforgiving. Accordingly, Fagin punishes Nancy for a single infraction, encouraging Sikes to kill her for betraying the gang, and Riah calls Lizzie's brother a "thankless dog," exhorting her to "let him go" after a bitter argument (396). The Talmud, the compendium of Jewish laws, has also been described as harsh and unforgiving, and so Talmudists are seen as elevating the "letter of the law" over the "spirit of the law." Therefore, Riah is called a "methodical . . . scribelike figure" (435), suggestive of Jesus' admonishment of the "scribes and Pharisees" who resemble graves, and Fagin is fittingly destroyed by a legal system that shows him no mercy.

Ghosts of Dickens' Past   203

In fact, Dickens critiques Jewish thought as legalistic by comparing Judaism to materialism. Specifically, Fagin and Riah approach work as orthodox Jews would approach ritual, with strict meticulousness. Oliver trains with Dodger, who "understands the catechism of his trade," having been taught by Fagin himself (151). Dodger and Bates, Fagin's standout pupils, practice thievery according to the gang's "little code of laws," abandoning Oliver to the authorities to protect themselves (94). These two "renowned and learned sages"

> evince great wisdom and foresight in providing against every possible contingency which can be supposed at all likely to affect themselves. Thus, to do a great right, you may do a little wrong; and you may take any means which the end to be attained, will justify; the amount of the right, or the amount of the wrong, or indeed the distinction between the two, being left entirely to the philosopher concerned, to be settled and determined by his clear, comprehensive, and impartial view of his own particular case.
>
> (95)

Like the stereotype of the Talmudist, Fagin and his gang interpret laws to suit their whims, a practice that has disastrous consequences for Oliver. Likewise understanding his trade, Riah recalls Twemlow's loan, reminding him that he is "invested with no authority" to show mercy (560). Riah meticulously observes all the laws of Pubsey and Co., causing Jenny to claim, "[he's] not the godmother at all" but "the wicked Wolf" (562), just as Paul likens Jews' "obsession" with ritual to the behavior of canines (Phil 3:2–3 *New Oxford Annotated Bible*).

In both examples Jews are believed to value wealth over truth, much like Judas, "the ancient foe of the Christian redeemer" from the Gospels (Sicher 141). For Victorian Christians "Jews bore the guilt of Judas' betrayal and the collective guilt attributed to the Jews in the Christian scriptures," especially in relation to Judas' betrayal of Jesus for 30 pieces of silver (142). Indeed Fagin and Riah both trade in money, but they resemble Judas in other ways, too. Fagin's red hair corresponds to diabolical images of Judas, and Riah is repeatedly called Judah, the Hebrew name of Judas, a generic insult made more significant by Jenny's accusation that "if ever [her] dear Lizzie is sold and betrayed, [she] shall know [Riah] sold and betrayed her" (Dickens 562). According to Martin H. Sable, Dickens rejected the "religious cruelty" of the Old Testament, trusting instead that "the God of the New Testament is . . . the God who forgives, who asks in return the willing and loving obedience of man, and who transforms death from a condemnation into a paradoxical condition for eternal life" (69). Dickens believed that the New Testament promised life while the Hebrew Bible ensured death, a conviction revealed through

Fagin, who worries he will "shake and tremble" (Ps 77:18) when he approaches the gallows (Dickens 449).

Finally, Dickens declares the death of the Jewish faith, the real "ghost of a departed Time," as he called Riah. For Dickens, Judaism has no place in modernity, and he illustrates this idea in three major ways. First, ritualism is represented as morally dead. Fagin explicitly worships wealth. In fact, he holds a short ceremony that resembles a Torah service, but the object of his piety is a box containing gold and jewels. Solemnly approaching the "ark," a trapdoor in the floor, Fagin removes the box, "which he placed carefully on the table," as though he meant to open and read the contents (67). While revering each item, Fagin utters "prayers" for the dead, the children, "clever dogs" and "fine fellows," who obtained the items at the expense of their lives (67). After reading the inscription on one item in particular, Fagin gives a "sermon" on the merits of capital punishment. His service is interrupted by Oliver, and Fagin is angry to have been observed at prayer by an outsider. Marcus points out that "the trinket which Fagin pores over in the previous scene, is never explained," but considering that the scene takes place from Oliver's perspective, it is understandable that he would not recognize an object with ritual significance only to Fagin. Later, after Oliver escapes, Fagin plans to "shut up [his] shop" (104). Since Oliver carries a potential payout for Fagin, he closes his business to find him, as though he were shutting up shop for Shabbat. According to Jesus, "man cannot serve both God and Mammon [wealth]" (Mt 6:24 *New Oxford Annotated Bible*), and Fagin's devotion to wealth leads to his death.

Riah holds a worship service that Jenny literally describes as being dead. Riah invites Fledgeby to observe this service, which takes place on his firm's rooftop. There, they find Jenny and Lizzie, who are "thankful to come . . . for rest" (Dickens 279). Jenny remarks that Fledgeby does not "know what the rest of this place is to us; does he, Lizzie? It's the quiet, and the air" (279). As an outsider, Fledgeby is "much perplexed" at the description of their Shabbosdik service, which is "so tranquil . . . so peaceful and so thankful" that they "feel as if [they] were dead" (279). Jenny reminds Fledgeby of his outsider status, that he is "not dead" and should "get down to life," meaning that he should leave (279). Like Jewish ceremonies, the rooftop service contains repetitious chanting. When Riah leaves with Fledgeby, Jenny

> called out to the Jew in a silvery tone, "Don't be long gone. Come back, and be dead!" And still as they went down they heard the little sweet voice, more and more faintly, half calling and half singing, "Come back and be dead, Come back and be dead!"
>
> (279)

To Jenny, Riah belongs to this purgatory, and he experiences a moment of spiritual ecstasy as he returns: "the call or song began to sound in his ears again, and, looking above, he saw the face of the little creature looking down out of a Glory of her long bright radiant hair, and musically repeating to him, like a vision: 'Come up and be dead! Come up and be dead!'" (280). Although the congregants feel strengthened by this service, the rooftop is available to them only because Riah sold his soul to Mammon. Neither Riah nor Fagin is seen observing Jewish rites, but they *are* shown worshipping death, a practice that is incompatible with Dickens' concept of morality.

Second, Christianity is presented as the only path to life. At the close of *Oliver Twist*, Dickens contrasts Fagin's death with Oliver's rebirth. Fagin never "held any defined or positive hopes of mercy" (Dickens 446), whereas Oliver shows "gratitude to that Being whose code is Mercy" (453–54). Meyer observes that Cruikshank's drawings of these moments "are visually parallel . . . with a stained glass window replacing the barred window of Fagin's dark prison cell" (249), suggesting a "connection between Fagin's death and the restored Christianity of the novel's conclusion" (249). Dickens refuses him redemption, so his death

> purges the novel's representative of the absence of Christianity by killing off Fagin, preparing the way for a vision of a purified England in the idyllic village, with the church at its moral center, to which Oliver, Mr. Brownlow, and the Maylies retreat in the novel's final pages.
> (Meyer 241)

Meyer argues that here, the "inhabitants practice a true Christianity, characterized by mercy and benevolence" (249), the antithesis of Dickens' harsh and unforgiving Judaism. Heidi Kaufman explains that "progress in mid-century novels drew heavily from a number of related strands, including the Christian Bible . . . and the view that Christian conversions were a sign of moral or spiritual improvement" (2009, 99). According to Kaufman, "while Oliver progresses to become a Christian, Fagin . . . suffers because he refuses to develop" (104). Fagin's death indicates that Dickens saw Judaism as spiritually insufficient unless "fulfilled" by Christianity.

Thus, Riah is figuratively converted. Throughout *Our Mutual Friend*, Eugene calls him "Aaron," knowing his name is Riah. Heller argues that "Eugene uses the name of a venerable Hebrew forefather to deprive Riah of his human individuality and replace it with a collective racial designation, a standard anti-Semitic ploy" (58). Indeed, Eugene is anti-Semitic, but the name also serves a conversionary function. Eugene tells Lightwood, "It comes into my mind that—no doubt with an instinctive desire to receive him into the bosom of our Church—I gave him the name of

Aaron" (Dickens 525). Even though Aaron is the high priest of Judaism, Eugene means to baptize Riah by renaming him. Unlike Fagin, who speaks in Hebrew verse, Riah echoes the Gospels, telling Lizzie to "shake the dust from [her] feet," an allusion to Matthew 10:14. Nord claims that "Though Riah is never overtly or literally converted to Christianity, he emerges as one of the best, truest Christians in *Our Mutual Friend*, in the sense that true Christianity consists here of goodness [and] selflessness" (40). Fiedler describes the "the old story of the bond and the pound of flesh" as "a parable, from the Christian point of view, of the Jews' stubborn invocation of that greater Covenant whose literal meaning seems to be their salvation, the Gentiles' exclusion, but in the end proves to mean just the opposite" (1949, 411). By abandoning his vocation, Riah embraces the "greater Covenant" of Christianity. Dickens "atones" for Fagin by "making Riah a decent man and a good Christian" (Nord 42), redeeming his "bad Jew" by making his "good Jew" profess his Christian beliefs.

Finally, and most critically, neither one enlivens Judaism by joining communities or building families. Scholars tend to agree that both characters are outsiders to British society. Baumgarten claims they are intentionally isolated, that labeling Fagin "the Jew . . . ensures that Fagin is alone" (1996, 48) and that "to keep Riah separate, to make him the only Jew, is to scapegoat him as a Jew" (52). Heller argues that "both are outcasts from the dominant society," where Fagin is a villain and Riah is a victim (55, 60). According to others, Fagin is alienated because of his "improbable and purebred English" (Marcus), and Riah because of his "anachronistic dress and Oriental exoticism" (Mardock n.p.). But more glaringly, neither has meaningful relationships with the Jewish community. Some see Fagin as part of "a Jewish peddling network" (Paganoni 310) because he knows a Jewish bartender and an old clothesman (Scrivener 46). Others see Riah as "part of a 'networking' Jewish community" (Heller 55) because he has "Jewish acquaintances in the countryside" (Nord 37). Indeed, both know a few Jews, as well as the Jewish areas of London. Fagin takes Oliver to his Whitechapel residence, keeping "on his course, through many winding and narrow ways, until he reached Bethnal Green; then, turning suddenly off to the left, he soon became involved in a maze of the mean and dirty streets which abound in that close and densely populated quarter." The Jew was evidently too familiar with the ground he traversed to be at all bewildered, either by the darkness of the night, or the intricacies of the way (Dickens 153).

Riah lives in St Mary Axe, which "is in the heart of London's Jewish district" (Lane 97). But Fagin realizes "he would be the only mourner in his own funeral train" (Dickens 446), and Riah does not "[turn] to the Jewish community for help in his poverty—the same invisible Jewish community 'in the country'" (Levine 28). Both are outsiders to Jewish society, destroying Jewish traditions by neglecting them.

Dickens denies both characters the chance to participate in Jewish world-building by having families. Scholars have argued that Fagin seems feminine, "violating valued Victorian gender boundaries" by behaving "both paternal and maternal, . . . both masculine and feminine at once. As a surrogate father he provides a home for the orphaned boys, as a surrogate mother he cooks for and plays with them" (Paganoni 308). He is seen as "effeminate" (Meyer 239), wearing "feminized garb" (Paganoni 308). Likewise, Riah "is described as the girls' 'fairy godmother'; when the abusive father dies, his daughter 'hid[es] her face in [Riah's] Jewish skirts.' The Gentile father is the persecutor; the feminized Jewish father ('godmother,' 'skirts') is the fairytale rescuer" (Julius 203). His gabardine is seen as feminine (Baumgarten 1996, 53) and androgynous (Heller 52). Although they come across as mothers (and fathers), they have no Jewish children, serving as surrogates to Christians instead. In fact, scholars describe them as "unmanned" (Baumgarten 1996, 53), "desexualized" (Levine 28), and lacking "sexual self-interest" (Heller 52), placing them apart from other denizens of Dickens' novels, who usually form traditional families. Fagin has no familial origins or context, treating his treasures "as he would a favored child" (Nord 30), which is an insult to important Jewish world-building institutions like marriage and family. And even worse, Riah tells Jenny, "Some beloved companionship fades out of most lives. . . . That of a wife, and a fair daughter, and a son of promise, has faded out of my own life" (Dickens 430). Riah lost his family and limps on toward his own death. Both characters represent the brokenness of Judaism, a religion Dickens believed to be anachronistic, comprised of a people he believed to be malevolent. Discounting the spiritual aims of Judaism, Dickens interprets Jews' adherence to ritualism as focused not on divine law, but instead on self-serving criminality. Ultimately, Fagin and Riah are rootless and childless. Unlike Abraham, they have no calling from God, no promise of generations of Jewish descendants, and no inheritance in this world or the world to come.

Conclusion

Indeed, Dickens is known as a humanitarian. I have not meant to suggest that he was anti-Semitic or that the Jews were uniquely excluded from his humanitarianism; rather, I have argued that his perspective on Judaism conformed to stereotypes that were created by Christianity and persist to this day. These stereotypes have harmed real Jews throughout history. Because Dickens is greatly beloved by readers the world over, and because they would rather not think badly of him, they have decided that he must have had a change of heart. This impulse is understandable. I also love Dickens, and I credit him with my early interest in pursuing a career in the professoriate, which has allowed me to write about my true love: Judaism. But we readers, students, and scholars of Dickens cannot know how he really felt or what he truly believed, so we must turn to his work for answers. His work indicates that, at the very least, he harbored some anti-Semitic prejudices. Dickens was haunted by the specter of Fagin throughout his career. We are still haunted by the ghosts of Auschwitz. So, we must continue to confront anti-Semitism, wherever we may find it.

Notes

1. See Murray Baumgarten (2015, 45); Maria Cristina Paganoni (2017, 307); Harry Stone (1959, 242); quoted in Lauriat Lane (1958, 98).
2. See Baumgarten (2015, 50–57); Deborah Heller (1990, 42–51); Joseph Litvak (1998, 37); Todd M. Endelman (2002, 104); Susan Meyer (2005, 240); Gary Levine (2003, 24); Anthony Julius (2010, 203); Paganoni (307); Michael Scrivener (2011, 5); and Deborah Nord (2011, 42).
3. Letter to Thomas Mitton 16 August 1860 (Storey 1997, 9:286).
4. See Stone (237).
5. See also Zatlin (124), Stone (233), Paganoni (308), Scrivener (4–5), and Lane (95).
6. See Endelman (82); Zatlin (72); Scrivener (4–5); Lane (95); Stone (226); and Heller (40).
7. See Edward Calisch (1909, 129); Jonathan Grossman (1996, 45); Stone (246); Levine (24); and Mardock.
8. Heller points out that "the opportune death of Jenny's alcoholic father opens the way for Riah to move in with the orphaned girl. In Jenny's last appearance, she explains to a visitor, underscoring again Riah's androgynous and mythic status, '[I] live here with my fairy godmother' (881)" (1990, 59), but this comment causes me to question the appropriateness of an older (unrelated) man living with a young girl. See also Baumgarten (1996, 53); Julius (203); Levine (18); and Mardock.
9. See Heller (52) and Nord (38).
10. Heller claims that "[Riah's] role as protector of both Jenny and Lizzie, [is] particularly crucial in his relation to Lizzie, whose 'virtue' and 'innocence' are threatened" (52), which, again, causes me to question Riah's role in protecting Lizzie's "virtue," considering that he is a virtual stranger to her.
11. Ephraim Sicher notes that Fagin was probably circumcised, like most boys born into Jewish families (2002, 140).
12. See Eric Silverman (2013) and Leonard Jay Greenspoon (2013).
13. Mardock claims, "Riah is clothed, after all, as Fagin is not (except perhaps by Cruikshank's illustrations), in Shylock's 'Jewish gaberdine'" (n.p.), whereas Baumgarten observes, "the traditional Jewish garb [Riah] wears . . . Fagin too wears them" (1996, 51).
14. Dickens writes, "The day passed off. Day? There was no day; it was gone as soon as come—and night came on again; night so long, and yet so short; long in its dreadful silence, and short in its fleeting hours. At one time he raved and blasphemed; and at another howled and tore his hair. Venerable men of

his own persuasion had come to pray beside him, but he had driven them away with curses. They renewed their charitable efforts, and he beat them off. Saturday night. He had only one night more to live" (446).
15. See Stone (247–8); Julius (203); and Heller (52).
16. Both are also like figures from dreams. Harry Maylie tells Oliver that his sighting of Fagin "must have been a dream" (285), and "Miss Abbey had her doubts whether she had not dreamed" Riah (417).

Bibliography

Baumgarten, Murray. "The Other Woman." *Dickens Quarterly* 32, no. 1 (March 2015): 44–70.

———. "Seeing Double: Jews in the Fiction of F. Scott Fitzgerald, Charles Dickens, Anthony Trollope, and George Eliot." In *Between "Race" and Culture: Representations of "the Jew" in English and American Literature*, edited by Bryan Cheyette, 44–61. Stanford, CA: Stanford University Press, 1996.

Calisch, Edward. *The Jew in English Literature: As Author and as Subject*. Richmond, VA: The Bell Book and Stationery Company, 1909. https://books.google.com/books?id=NXqEdDHGj2oC.

Cesarani, David. *The Jewish Chronicle and Anglo-Jewry, 1841–1991*. Cambridge: Cambridge University Press, 1994.

Cumberland, Richard. *The Jew, a Comedy in Five Acts*. London: Longman, Hurst, Rees, and Orme, 1808.

Dickens, Charles. *Bleak House*. London: Bradbury, 1853. https://books.google.com/books?id=KlsJAAAAQAAJ.

———. *A Christmas Carol. In Prose. Being a Ghost Story of Christmas*. London: Chapman and Hall, 1843.

———. *Oliver Twist*. 1838. Edited by Philip Horne. New York: Penguin, 2003.

———. *Our Mutual Friend*. 1865. Edited by Adrian Poole. New York: Penguin, 1997.

Endelman, Todd. *The Jews of Britain, 1656 to 2000*. Berkeley: University of California Press, 2002.

Fiedler, Leslie A. "What Can We Do About Fagin? The Jew-Villain in Western Tradition." *Commentary Magazine* 8 (January 1, 1949): 411.

Greenspoon, Leonard Jay. *Fashioning Jews: Clothing, Culture, and Commerce*. West Lafayette, IN: Purdue University Press, 2013.

Grossman, Jonathan. "The Absent Jew in Dickens: Narrators in *Oliver Twist*, *Our Mutual Friend*, and *A Christmas Carol*." *Dickens Studies Annual* 24 (1996): 37–57.

Heller, Deborah. "The Outcast as Villain and Victim: Jews in Dickens' *Oliver Twist* and *Our Mutual Friend*." In *Jewish Presences in English Literature*, edited by Derek Cohen and Deborah Heller, 40–60. Montreal, QC: McGill-Queens University Press, 1990.

Hirsch, David A. H. "Dickens's Queer 'Jew' and Anglo-Christian Identity Politics: The Contradictions of Victorian Family Values." In *Queer Theory and the Jewish Question*, edited by Daniel Boyarin, Daniel Itzkovitz, and Ann Pellegrini, 311–33. New York: Columbia University Press, 2003.

Julius, Anthony. *Trials of the Diaspora: A History of Anti-Semitism in England*. Oxford: Oxford University Press, 2010.

Kaufman, Heidi. *English Origins, Jewish Discourse, and the Nineteenth-Century British Novel: Reflections on a Nested Nation.* University Park, PA: Pennsylvania State University Press, 2009.
Lane, Lauriat, Jr. "Dickens' Archetypal Jew." *PMLA* 73 (March 1958): 95–101.
Levine, Gary Martin. *The Merchant of Modernism: The Economic Jew in Anglo-American Literature, 1864–1939.* New York: Routledge, 2003.
Levy, Amy. "The Jew in Fiction." *Jewish Chronicle* (June 1886): 13.
Lipman, Sonia L., and Vivian David Lipman. *The Century of Moses Montefiore.* Oxford: Littman Library of Jewish Civilization, 1985.
Litvak, Joseph. "Bad Scene: *Oliver Twist* and the Pathology of Entertainment." *Dickens Studies Annual* 26 (1998): 33–49.
Marcus, Steven. "Who is Fagin?" *Commentary Magazine* 34, no. 1 (July 1, 1962): 48.
Mardock, James D. "Of Daughters and Ducats: *Our Mutual Friend* and Dickens's Anti-Shylock." *Borrowers and Lenders: The Journal of Shakespeare and Appropriation* 1, no. 2 (2005): n.p.
Meyer, Susan. "Antisemitism and Social Critique in Dickens's Oliver Twist." *Victorian Literature and Culture* m33, no. 1 (2005): 239–52.
Morgentaler, Goldie. "When Dickens Spoke Yiddish: Translations of Dickens into the Language of East European Jews." *Dickens Quarterly* 34, no. 2 (2017): 85–95.
Newman, Amy. "The Death of Judaism in German Protestant Thought from Luther to Hegel." *Journal of the American Academy of Religion* 61, no. 3 (1993): 455–84.
Nord, Deborah Epstein. "Dickens's 'Jewish Question': Pariah Capitalism and the Way Out." *Victorian Literature and Culture* 39, no. 1 (2011): 27–45.
Paganoni, Maria Cristina. "From Book to Film: The Semiotics of Jewishness in *Oliver Twist*." In *Dickens Adapted*, edited by John Glavin, 307–20. London: Routledge, 2017.
Philipson, David. *The Jew in English Fiction.* Cincinnati, OH: Robert Clarke, 1889.
Roth, Cecil. "The Genesis of Riah." In *Anglo-Jewish Letters, 1158–1917*, 303–8. London: The Soncino Press, 1938.
Sable, Martin H. "The Day of Atonement in Charles Dickens' *A Christmas Carol*." *Tradition: A Journal of Orthodox Jewish Thought* 22, no. 3 (1986): 66–76.
Scrivener, Michael. *Jewish Representation in British Literature, 1780–1840.* New York: Palgrave Macmillan, 2011.
Sicher, Efraim. "Imagining 'the Jew': Dickens' Romantic Heritage." In *British Romanticism and the Jews: History, Culture, Literature*, edited by Sheila A. Spector, 139–55. New York: Palgrave Macmillan, 2002.
Silverman, Eric. *Cultural History of Jewish Dress.* London: Bloomsbury, 2013.
Stone, Harry. "Dickens and the Jews." *Victorian Studies* 2, no. 3 (March 1959): 223–55.
Storey, Graham, ed. *The Letters of Charles Dickens.* Vol. 9. 12 vols. Oxford: Clarendon Press, 1997.
Trilling, Lionel. "The Changing Myth of the Jew." *Commentary Magazine* 8 (August 1978): 24.

Weltman, Sharon Aronofsky. "'Can a Fellow Be a Villain All His Life?': *Oliver! Fagin,* and Performing Jewishness." *Nineteenth-Century Contexts* 33, no. 4 (2011): 371–88.

Zatlin, Linda Gertner. *The Nineteenth-Century Anglo-Jewish Novel*. Farmington Hills, MI: Twayne, 1981.

11 Theological Shifts in Dickensian Narratives Before and After Darwin's *Origin*

Little Dorrit and *Our Mutual Friend*

Aaron K. H. Ho

Charles Darwin alone did not kill God. Chartist churches in the 1830s and 1840s, Christian socialists in 1848 who argued that the Bible was used as a tool for political oppression, urbanization, industrialization, population growth, economic stability, the Oxford Movement led by John Henry Newman who eventually converted to Catholicism, influences from the German Higher Criticism and philosophy from the Enlightenment, a growing number of closeted *and* morally exemplary atheists including Harriet Martineau, all slowly chipped away at the sway of the Established Church of England. Furthermore, the torpid Church had not reformed its diocesan and parochial structures for more than 500 years until the Convocations of Canterbury and York in 1852, a year after the 1851 Census Report on the declining church attendance. This report was generally taken as an indication of the Victorian crisis of faith, especially of the working class who did not feel represented in the Established Church. It was under such conditions that Charles Dickens wrote his novels, essays, and short stories.

As the publisher and editor of the journals *Household Words* (1850–1859) and *All the Year Round* (1858–1870) and having to keep abreast of changes in Victorian culture and society, Dickens was familiar with the evolutionary theories of his time according to Philip Allingham (2014) and George Levine (1988, 120–24). Although there is no concrete evidence that Dickens had read Darwin's *On the Origin of Species* (1859), the book, along with other notable evolutionary studies such as Charles Lyell's *Geological Evidence of the Antiquity of Man* (1863), Comte de Buffon's (Georges-Louis Leclerc's) *Natural History* (1797–1807 [1749–1788]), Georges Cuvier's *Animal Kingdom* (1840 [1817]), and George Henry Lewes' *The Physiology of Common Life* (1859), was found on the shelves of his country home, Gads Hill Place (Ackroyd 1990, 663). In addition, *All the Year Round*, in which Dickens personally sanctioned every story and review (Allingham), published three anonymous reviews based on Darwin's book on evolution: "Species" (June 2, 1860), "Natural

Selection" (July 7, 1860), and "Transmutation of Species" (March 9, 1861). Levine posits that the complimentary tone in the reviews suggests that Dickens approved and endorsed the evolutionary theories (1988, 129). Using *Little Dorrit* (1857), written before the publication of *Origin*, as a foil to *Our Mutual Friend* (1865), the lapse between the two novels would have given Dickens enough time to ruminate on Darwinian evolutionary theories and how they would play out in his literary narratives.

As many scholars such as Dennis Walder and Norris Pope (1978) point out, Dickens' religious beliefs were amorphous and difficult to pinpoint; he grew disgruntled with and eventually rejected the hermeneutic teachings of the high church to vacillate between broad church and Unitarianism. He eschewed the Old Testament and espoused the New, execrated institutionalized religion (Evangelicalism and Roman Catholicism) but still clung onto a Christian belief, preferring private moments of devout communions. In 1846, reviewing *Martin Chuzzlewit* (1844), William Howitt remarked, "No man . . . cared to inquire after [Dickens'] religion; he has stood amongst us belonging to us all; of our creed, of our party, of our way of thinking" (1971 [1846], 205). It is fair to conclude, as Hai Na does, that "Dickens's concern transcends the boundaries of sects: he is in a quest for the core and common bond of all true religions" (2018, 132). In general, Dickens believed in the fundamental morality of religion: benevolence, humility, faithfulness, forgiveness, compassion, sympathy, and philanthropy to the oppressed and suffering. Dickens believed in the Works more than the Faith (House 1942, 109–111; Holbrook 1993, 30).

Darwin's book challenges implicitly basic theological framework of Christianity such as aspects of theodicy, providentialism, Creator, natural theology, and eschatology. Simply put: If humans are made in the image of God, what does it mean when evolution states that we descend from a primate, sharing a common ancestor with apes, lemurs, and monkeys? At which stage of the evolutionary process did God add souls to humans? Given the randomness of evolution, that is dependent on suitable conditions of time and space, requiring a future that is not fated or set in stone, how does divine providence function? Was evolution a part of God's will? If God's creations are perfect, then why do they go extinct? Since humans evolved from primates and did not descend from Adam and Eve, who were expelled from the Garden of Eden for their original sin, does theodicy exist? Although it must be stressed that Darwin did not intend his theories to be applied on humans (that is, Social Darwinism), what happens to a society when morality is defined in survivalist, sublunary values instead of the transcendental? Since humans are animals, why not behave like them? Victorians exhibited a spectrum of attitudes toward these contestations which Darwinian evolution brought to Christianity. The extremely pious were indignant, others defended Darwin, and the rest of the eminent Victorians including George Mivart, James

Clark Maxwell, William Thomson (Lord Kelvin), Charles Kingsley, the Archbishop of Canterbury Frederick Temple, and Richard Owen asseverated that they saw no contradiction in terms between the two competing ideologies.

Darwinian scholars Gillian Beer (2000) and George Levine (2006) have famously compared narrative strategies between Dickens and Darwin: Both Victorian thinkers utilized chance, random entanglements, death, and survival over a period of time at a specific environment in their narratives. But Beer's and Levine's analyses pose serious chronological problems since most of Dickens' *oeuvre* (except his last three novels) was completed before the publication of Darwin's *Origin*. Levine explained away this analytic limitation by claiming that the two Victorians tapped into a moment of shared cultural *Zeitgeist* (5). Although this chapter concerns itself with the two Victorians' narrative strategies as signposts that lead to their beliefs, it also examines how Darwinian evolutionary theories affect Dickens' works and theological thinking by inspecting his pre- and post-*Origin* novels. Darwin professed to be agnostic in his autobiography (2005 [1958], 71–80) although Levine in a later book, *Darwin Loves You: Natural Selection and the Re-Enchantment of the World*, shows that he could not come out as an atheist in the cultural climate he was in, or his theories would not be as widely accepted as it was; by following Victorian norms and protocols, Darwin manipulated the system so that his theories could be acknowledged (2006, 235–37). If Darwin's theories propagated an ambiguity over the existence of God, then did Dickens accept the evolutionary science that would cast doubt on his Anglican beliefs or was he unaffected?

Robert Butterworth, author of *Dickens, Religion, and Society*, opines that Dickens was "utterly untroubled" about the clash between Christianity and evolution (2016, 13), whereas Levine demonstrates that not only did Dickens find the two ideologies compatible but he, being amenable to science, also revealed an ambivalence about God (1988, 121–128). Before *Origin*, Butterworth's supposition may ring true as Dickens writes in the last paragraph of the first chapter in *Martin Chuzzlewit*:

> Firstly, that it may be safely asserted, and yet without implying any direct participation in the Monboddo doctrine touching the probability of the human race having once been monkeys, that men do play very strange and extraordinary tricks. Secondly, and yet without trenching on the Blumenbach theory as to the descendants of Adam having a vast number of qualities which belong more particularly to swine than to any other class of animals in the creation, that some men certainly are remarkable for taking uncommon good care of themselves.
>
> (1986 [1844], 56)

The "Monboddo doctrine" refers to Lord Monboddo's *The Origin and Progress of Language* (1773–1792) in which he suggested that humans and orangutangs share a close biological bond. The Blumenbach theory emanates from J. F. Blumenbach who was a pioneer in the science of comparative anatomy. (Although Darwin avoided human beings in *Origin*, he would expand, explain, and carefully exemplify ideas similar to Monboddo's and Blumenbach's to prove the theory of natural selection.) Here, Dickens employs a jocular tone to satirize evolutionary science but does not dismiss it completely. However, after the meticulous argument laid out in *Origin*, which caused a public furore in the Victorian society, it is highly unlikely that Dickens was "utterly untroubled" by the sociocultural implications of Darwinism. Thomas Hardy, George Eliot, and Elizabeth Gaskell were all affected; few writers were not. More scholars agree with Levine than Butterworth: Janet Larson argues that "all around [Dickens] far reaching cultural dislocations were shaping a world that seemed no longer to fit the Bible's concordant design of history" (1985, 9). Vincent Newey views Victorian literature, including Dickens' works, as "the provider of a new canon, a substitute bible, a secular scripture informed by and disseminating . . . 'an alternative set of liberal-humanist values'" (2004, 3). Barry Qualls traces Dickens' increasing disenchantment with the "supernatural" (1982, 89), a euphemism for Christianity, such that by the time of *Our Mutual Friend*, "All effort to suggest a God above 'the prison of this lower world' has been abandoned" (1997 [1865] 110). Situating the nexus of Dickens' disenchantment between *Little Dorrit* and *Our Mutual Friend*, sandwiching the release of Darwin's *Origin*, allows us to discern how social and scientific forces impacted the novelist's style of storytelling.

Little Dorrit, thought by Levine to be "the most religious of Dickens' novels," reproduces the structure of Old and New Testaments in publishing the book in two parts "Poverty" and "Riches," instead of the usual format of the triple decker, that the first part prefigures and brings to fruition in the latter half (1988, 155). Early on in the process of writing, on October 29, 1855 Dickens informed his publishers about his decision to bifurcate the book. In the Old Testament, Adam sins, condemning humankind to suffering, and Jesus redeems humanity in the New. The Tree of Knowledge of Good and Evil in Genesis becomes the cross Jesus bears. *Little Dorrit*'s second chapter, "Fellow Travellers," connects and introduces the characters quarantined on an ark, kickstarting their intertwined lives. Book the Second's first chapter shares the same title, "Fellow Travellers," and documents the beginning of some characters' decline. At the end of Book the First, the Dorrits, eager to leave and disavow any connections to the debtors' prison, forget about Amy who has fainted from being overwhelmed. Arthur Clennam carries her out of the Marshalsea. This scene prefigures the denouement in the second book that shows Arthur and Amy leaving the prison to marry in the nearby church where she was baptized. Unlike evolution that is random and linear, *Little Dorrit*'s structure of parallels and mirroring supports a providential godly world.

The second part is titled "Riches," despite Arthur and Amy both losing their individual money because he gains her hand in marriage. Modern readers may find this mawkish and saccharine, but Dickens means it without any irony. He emphasizes that she "pour[s] out [her] inexhaustible wealth of goodness upon [Arthur]" (2003 [1857], 791). Affluent characters in the Dickensian world are usually cheats or villains but here he appropriates the language of economy and uses it for Christian virtues of the Angel in the House. Amy is "Angelically comforting," with an emphatic capital A, to Arthur during his bankruptcy (790). In a novel that bludgeons the reader on the head with the symbolic significance of light and shadows, the angelic Amy is often associated with the sun and light. The sun, observes Carolyn Oulton, is "a token of divine mercy" (2003, 74). Amy's association with light is often meant to prefigure events that happen later in the book such as when Arthur makes a rare confidence in his "Fellow Travellers" onboard the ship in the first book: "I have no will. That is to say . . . next to none that I can put in action now . . . What is to be expected from *me* in middle-life? Will, purpose, hope? All those lights were extinguished before I could sound the words (35; emphasis in original). Arthur is thus characterized so that later Amy would inspire and shine a light on him; she would save him and imbue him with purpose and will. Such female figures of redemption in Dickens' fiction may emanate from his personal history. Walder (2007, 28) suggests that the untimely death in 1837 of the 17-year-old Mary Hogarth, Dickens' sister-in-law, and his perpetual bereavement for her subjected him to a life-long yearning of a female figure of spirituality and salvation, a figure that Lionel Trilling (1955, 57) calls "the female paraclete." In Genoa in 1844, Dickens dreamed of asking her what true religion was; in his mind, he had already linked innocent female figures with salvation.

The symbolism of light and shadow plays out most significantly when Mrs. Clennam asks Amy for forgiveness, as Stephan Wall (2003) and Oulton have examined in detail:

> In the softened light of the window, looking from the scene of her early trails to the shining sky, [Amy] was not in stronger opposition to [Mrs. Clennam] the black figure in the shade, than the life and doctrine on which she rested were to that figure's history.
>
> (826)

Layered onto this imagery is the representation of Old versus New Testament personified by Mrs. Clennam and Amy, respectively. Although Mrs. Clennam professes her love for her adopted son to Amy, she could not escape her stern and cold upbringing. She prays that "her enemies . . .

might be put to the edge of the sword, consumed by fire, smitten by plagues and leprosy, that their bones might be ground to dust," images of vengeance taken from the Old Testament (826). In contrast, Amy pleads with Mrs. Clennam to let go, to forgive, and to be guided by "the patient Master who shed tears of compassion for our infirmities," quoting from John 2:35 (826).

But Mrs. Clennam cannot change and is punished (by Dickens? by the Creator?) to suffer a paralytic life of a long confinement. In a predetermined, deterministic world where God has ordained every individual's path, nobody can change. Mrs. Clennam cannot, neither can Rigaud or Fanny or Miss Wade. Knowing that she could enjoy a blissful relationship with a man who worships her, Fanny refuses to change: "I cannot submit. I should not be able to defer to him enough," she says (617). She echoes Rigaud's justification for murder. He confesses to his cellmate, "It is . . . my character to govern. I can't submit; I must govern" (23). Changing is beyond their natures; character is fixed in most of Dickens' pre-*Origin* fiction. Walder observes that Rigaud's immutability reminds us of "Dickens' continuing belief in the possibility of absolute evil" (171); this is a Godly world of good battling evil. Fred Kaplan also notes that Dickens' villains seem always unredeemable, giving readers a cathartic release when villains inevitably meet their just deserts, usually leading to a predestined punishment of horrible death (1987, 69). Not only are the natures of Dickens' villains intractable, unyielding, and recalcitrant, but also protagonists in this deterministic world cannot change their natures. Amy and Arthur behave consistently throughout the novel, whether they be rich or poor. In this world, there can be no character development, just static characters coping with different circumstances.

Essentialism in characters lends itself easily to allegories, and in Dickens' case, the good people find support and love in one another and the bad face dire consequences. Essentialism draws rigid moral boundaries among characters, separating the good from the evil (Levine 1988, 142–47). Darwinism opposes such essentialism. Evolution works by the slowly changing, generations by generations, based on the natural selection of a species that best suits the environment. Each generation differs from the previous one ever so slightly, inferring that there is no Platonic blueprint, no essential element of what a certain individual should be. In this world, the best may not be rewarded. If a quick animal lives in a dense forest with no space to run, its speed is not an advantage and may even be an impediment. In Darwinism, change is necessary. In comparing Dickens' and Darwin's narrative strategies, Levine (1988, 121) laments that the novelist's characters are essentialists. While this is true for *Little Dorrit*, people do change in *Our Mutual Friend*. Scam artist Mrs. Lammle saves a girl from entering a disastrous marriage while Mr. Venus confesses his blackmailing plans so that the victim can take precautions against his partner-in-crime. Repentant criminals are rare in Dickens' fiction, but readers encounter at least two in *Our Mutual Friend*. With shifting identities as a starting point, readers enter a world affected by Darwinism, a world that differs from previous Dickens' novels, a world where you can be John Harmon or John Rokesmith or Julius Handford or even George Radfoot.

That *Our Mutual Friend* presents a different theological perspective from *Little Dorrit* can be easily seen in the female protagonists. Unlike the unwavering, stalwart Amy Dorrit, the Angel in the House who is patient and kind and constant, Lizzie Hexam and Bella Wilfer are in constant danger of degenerating into someone else with moral laxity and animalistic instincts, one undone by avarice and greed, the other by sexual transgression. "A decent character moving towards real evil is something new in Dickens's work," observes Brian Cheadle (2001, 87). Victorians' fear of regression and degeneration manifests itself in the novel. Bella's initial competitiveness for material resources—not only to survive in the animal kingdom but also to thrive—could have corrupted and degraded her like many other money-minded characters in Dickens' fiction. Lizzie's inability to resist Eugene Wrayburn's seduction could have made her follow the footsteps of Little Em'ly in *David Copperfield* (1850). In one more day, had Eugene not been mutilated, Lizzie would have succumbed to her animalistic, ungovernable desires. The Darwinian women not only have to be vigilant against the tide of degeneration but they also need to be heedful against men. For Darwin, sexual selection, lightly touched upon in *Origin*, signifies male sexual predators' constant seduction. But for Dickens, the danger of men to women extends further socially. Despite Old Harmon knowing about Bella's avarice, he still places her in a position where she could be easily corrupted. Attempting to atone for her origin, Lizzie must first fight off the sexual attention of men in their sexual prime, Eugene and Bradley Headstone. Unlike Amy and Arthur, who develop their relationship by knowing each other over time, their attraction in *Our Mutual Friend* is instantaneous and visual and animalistic, for Eugene, for Lizzie, for Bradley, and even for John who does not know the reason why he loves a petulant woman except that she is exceedingly beautiful (207). The non-deterministic world of *Our Mutual Friend*, where criminals can now make an effort to get back on the straight and narrow, predicates on the Darwinian laws of constant mutability and sexual desires.

The help that the women need to prevent their own degradation comes not from divine intervention but from mortal means. Two competing geological concepts fought for dominance in Victorian evolutionary theories: uniformitarianism (a gradual change from generations to generations) and catastrophism (a sudden change). Darwin believed in the former because changes in a species require generations to occur and because the latter would suggest the existence of a Creator who magically makes sudden changes. Levine (1988, 119) complains that Dickens' fiction often adopts catastrophism as a way to indicate divine punishment. Rigaud, for instance, is killed in an apocalyptic fashion, Mrs Clennam's house crushing him is reminiscent of the fall of the Tower of Babel according to Oulton (140). But here, in *Our Mutual Friend*, the women's salvation does not come from any divine intervention. Dickens carefully plots how they are to be saved: Bella by an elaborate and long-drawn plan involving the Boffins and John Harmon to make her gain self-awareness about her worship for Mammon; and Lizzie by Bradley's assault on Eugene. This assault should not be seen as catastrophism; it is carefully detailed over the course of the novel ever since Eugene and Bradley meet, evident by Bradley's ungovernable rage, his intense libidinal urges for Lizzie, his stalking Eugene, his sexual jealousy of Eugene, his avowal to murder Eugene, his association with another villain Rogue Riderhood, and Lizzie warning Eugene to be cautious. Astute readers know that the murder attempt would come sooner or later from the clues gradually released throughout the novel. The question is would the attempt be stopped by an act of divine intervention? No. This is not that kind of world. Help can only arrive in mortal form. Lizzie doesn't hear Eugene's cry for help from miles away as Jane Eyre heard Rochester's (Brontë 2001 [1847], 357). Lizzie is nearby, having just left Eugene, and besides, there is a scientific reason: "sound travelling far with the help of water" (682). Lizzie saving Eugene is not an act of divine intervention because she does not receive super divine strength from God. Her strength and boating skills come from her experience and training with her father, fishing corpses out of Thames.

Many critics, including Daniel Scoggin (2002, 99), Thomas Vargish (1985, 158), and Michael Wheeler (1990, 282), note that the river is a symbol for baptism. Dickens could not escape using theological language of his time nor could Darwin in *Origin*, as Gillian Beer and George Levine observe, because theological language abounds in Victorian currency, impossible to avoid. Larson demonstrates that Dickens' use of religious allusions is perfunctory and conventional, serving only to draw "automatic reactions for certain kinds of novelistic occasions, such as the child's deathbed or the exaltation of the heroine's virtues" (6). Following Larson, it is perhaps more important to examine how literary baptism works for Dickens' characters. Before Eugene is dumped into the river, left to die, there is a possibility that he, like Lizzie and Bella, would fall into moral turpitude, despite that his name means "well-born" from the Greek εὐγενής (*eugenēs*), a combination of εὖ (*eu*), "well," and significantly γένος (*genos*), "race, stock, kin." In Dickens' stories of predestination, names are your destiny; readers would quickly identify characters with names like Merdle, Murdstone, and Headstone as antagonists of the stories. But for Eugene, even with a positive name, he is flippant, languid, cynical, condescending, and insouciant. He calls Mr. Riah by a derogatory slur, refusing to acknowledge the Jew by his name/identity.

He saunters. All these traits and behaviors exist in Dickens' bad boys previously: James Steerforth in *David Copperfield* and James Harthouse in *Hard Times*. When his good friend Mortimer Lightwood asks him what his "designs" are for Lizzie, he cannot say but he insists that he will not marry her (283, 292). A Victorian reader would recognise the loaded word, "design." Dickens also uses the phrase "the intention of its existence" (184) earlier in the novel, a phrase which would remind Victorian readers about arguments revolving the presence of design in creation in the 1860s. There is a real chance that Eugene may seduce, desert, and ruin Lizzie. Dickens himself had an affair with actress Ellen Ternan and at the time of writing *Our Mutual Friend*, they would have been together for about half a decade. After Lizzie hauls him out of the river, Eugene changes his mind and marries her, thinking that he may die soon. Some critics such as Poole (1997, xxiii) and Oulton (158) read this scene as the river baptizing him, transforming him into a new person. But a secular reading would work as well. People often make drastic changes to their characters after they experience life-and-death situations. Julie Melnyk posits that although Dickens was "most religious when he portrays the possibility of redemption through 'conversions' . . . these conversions, however, seem much more psychological than spiritual, and they are effected not by God or the Church but by human love and sympathy" (2008, 111). Furthermore, after marriage, Eugene says that he prefers to die because there is a chance that he may revert to his old self (735). In this anti-essentialist world where permanence is not ensured, regression is a possibility regardless of baptism.

Baptism does not necessarily signal a turning over of new leaf in this new world. There is no guarantee that baptism will lead to salvation. Rogue Riderhood falls in the river, nearly dies, revives, and remains to be the same villain. He does not receive the absolution Eugene does. His near-death episode is strange in itself because it is unnecessary and redundant; it does not advance the plot in any way and if it is to show that he is malevolent and hateful, readers already know his character well. The episode, to contrast with Rigaud's demise, serves to demonstrate how Dickens was no longer seeking a catastrophic ending. If there is a God, then Riderhood should have perished here but Dickens saves Riderhood in order for him to be killed by a human being, Bradley, whom Riderhood inveigles into committing a murderous act and then blackmails. All Riderhood's despicable deeds cumulate for him to receive retributive punishment in the hands of another human.

In between Eugene who receives absolution from the symbolic baptism and Riderhood who does not, John Harmon after being dumped in the river changes his identity to Julius Handford and John Rokesmith, from a wealthy heir to a penurious secretary. He is neither absolved nor condemned; his resurrection does not change him for good nor does he remain the same. Some Victorians found Darwinism disquieting because humans, if not created by God, lose their unique identity among animals. Boundaries of identities are blurred as humans become cousins to apes. This concern for shifting fluid identities is reflected in John. In this world, any male can be John Harmon, including George Radfoot's cadaver fished from the river, mistaken for John, and a baby whom the Boffins adopted to replace the presumably deceased heir of dust. "There is no such thing as I," John says (363). Eugene, John, and Riderhood are dead and reborn through baptism, but baptism means differently for different characters. Eugene's Lazarus-like rebirth seems closest to Christian theology, being a completely changed man, invigorated and moral. John, using different identities to fulfill different needs, represents a Darwinian mode of thinking. The difference in their fates when put in similar situations suggests that each person is accountable for their actions and that they are no longer trapped in a predestined world. Since choice, not God's divinity, is the operative function for an individual's change, the river itself has lost its meaning of baptism. Dickens has secularized the river and baptism.

Another implication of Darwinism on identities is the question on morality. Darwinian evolution does not depend on morality and laws; only survival and propagation matter. Although Darwin did not coin the term "survival of the fittest"—Herbert Spencer did—he approved of it (Letter to A. R. Wallace, July 5, 1866) and inserted the phrase in the fifth edition of *Origin*. This survivalist mantra, however, breeds aggressive individualism and immorality. While Darwin intended his theories to be applied in the animal kingdom, it was not a far leap for Victorians to adapt them to their society. As a result, morality is blurred in Dicken's fiction. Even the Angel in the House has transformed into fallible women like Bella and Lizzie. Like Eugene before his near-death experience, John behaves in a morally ambiguous manner such that readers couldn't read him. He is "dark" and has "a very bad manner . . . diffident, troubled." He avoids eye contact and hesitates to sign a legal document to rent the Wilfer's apartment. He looks at Bella "stealth[i]y" (46–47). He lies to her about his identity for a very long time, even after they have a child together. The four protagonists are no longer the essentialist moral characters of light, pure from the beginning till the end. One may even argue that Bradley, in his attempt to murder Eugene, has saved Lizzie from perdition; he is not that bad. Mr. Riah, a moral person, manages Mr. Fledgeby's money-lending business and thus does hateful deeds by proxy, causing Jenny Wren to be confused on whether he plays the part of a fairy godmother or a wolf. Mr. Boffin appears temporarily to be a cruel miser. With few exceptions (Riderhood, Mr. Lammle, and Mrs. Boffin, for instances), main characters in *Our Mutual Friend* exist on a morally ambiguous spectrum.

Darwinism impacted not only Victorians' way of thinking about morality or how best to live one's life but also the value of human lives and deaths, evident by the metaphors of river and dust, and by Eugene's, John's, and Riderhood's deaths and revivifications. In a world where John Harmons are interchangeable and recyclable, Dickens interrogates the value of life. Individuals who are suited for the environment survive and propagate; those who are not die. Unlike Christianity and the hope of an afterlife, death has no higher purpose in nature. Deaths, for Darwinism, could sometimes be beneficial for the population as Francis Galton, Darwin's cousin, showed in his book, where the term "eugenics" first appears (1883). Death holds little meaning for Darwinism. Not only was Dickens affected by Darwinian notions of death but his personal life might also have seeped into the narrative. As Adrian Poole notes, around the time of writing *Our Mutual Friend*, Dickens' mother and his son Walter passed away within months of each other (1997, ix–x). He also grieved for the loss of his old friends, Frank Stone, Arthur Smith, W. H. Thackeray, John Leech, and Augustus Egg. Having passed the age of fifty, "his body was beginning to protest at the strains of it" (x) and he was laid up for several months in the spring of 1864. Then, on June 9th, 1865, when Dickens was travelling with Ternan, they were nearly killed in the Staplehurst rail crash. He helped to rescue the survivors and later told his friends about the horror of working "for hours among the dying and the dead" (quoted in Poole x). He managed to retrieve *Our Mutual Friend* manuscript from wreckage. Under these circumstances, his personal life, and debates surrounding evolution in the 1860s, he ruminated about death in *Our Mutual Friend*.

Poole, in an introduction to *Our Mutual Friend*, remarks that most of the life in the novel tends to "a state of suspended animation":

> Nothing seems certainly dead nor entirely alive. The wood that upholds the riverside tavern remembers the forests from which it derives. Silas Wegg's leg forgets that it is a "timber fiction" and behaves like a more fleshly member. At his friend Mr Venus's shop the skeletons, studded animals and bottle babies make an attentive audience to the scenes they witness. The dolls dressed by Jenny Wren out of scraps and remnants are hard to distinguish from her models and patrons . . . All matter has been used before and will be used again. Every thing and every body is partly composed of the dead-but-not-gone, which will in turn decompose and be shaped into new forms of matter.
>
> (ix)

The reusability and recyclability of people and things suggest Dickens' struggle with Christian theology in the face of Darwinism. Social decay in a society of intense economic competition between individuals—"survival of the fittest"—is metaphorized into decaying bodies in the novel. Eugene's and John's bodies are mutilated and dumped in the river to fester and decompose. Characters lose their essential nature since they are changeable and can be transformed into something new. The renewal and reincarnation are closer to Buddhist philosophy than Christianity. In Buddhism, the soul reincarnates for various lifetimes in different animal forms. But here, following Christianity, Dickens seems to question if there is a soul. Where does the soul lie when receptacles change constantly? Wegg commits a crime because he wants to buy back his leg to be whole again. Some Victorians believed in reassembly on Judgement Day when the dead would resurrect, reuniting bodies and souls. This belief may have stemmed from Jesus' resurrection: if his body was neither whole nor entombed, there was no possibility that he would have risen up. Although Wegg's reason to buy back his leg is class-based, that he "wish to collect myself like a genteel person" (88), Victorian readers would have sympathized with or at least recognized Wegg's desperation to be whole in connection to the resurrection on Judgement Day. Dickens, by plotting Wegg to blackmail and fail to redeem his leg, indicates that the importance of morality in this life outweighs a consideration for the afterlife. Living a moral life in this world is better than hankering for eternity in the next.

The other disabled person in the text, Jenny Wren, has reveries about death and visions of angels. For Jenny, as for other characters in the text (Lizzie, Eugene, and Betty Higden), death provides a release from the pain of living. "Living amidst such unreality and disorder," Qualls explains, "Dickens' decent people inevitably find death attractive, a release from the dunghill earth" (108). Victorians had exuviated the horrific Dantean version of the inferno and adopted a version of a pleasant afterlife buoyed by social movements such as Darwinism, the preference of the loving God in New Testament over the vengeful in the Old, the Oxford Movement, and Utilitarianism (Rowell 1974, 13 and 153). Although Dickens, in "Some Recollections of Mortality," described a suicide victim in the Thames as being "dragged down to perdition" (1997 [1863], 107), in the novel suicide is a holy release. The river speaks to Betty:

> Come to me, come to me! When the cruel shame and terror you have so long fled from, most beset you, come to me! I am the Relieving Officer appointed by eternal ordinance to do my work; I am not held in estimation according as I shirk it. My breast is softer than the pauper-nurse's; death in my arms is peacefuller [*sic*] than among the pauper-wards. Come to me!
>
> (497)

The words mirror Christ's in Matthew 2:28: "Come unto me, all ye that labour and are heavy laden, and I will give you rest." Where suicide was a mortal sin before, Dickens realized how suicide, or death in general, can be a release and victims should not be punished in the afterlife. Although

Dickens might not have Darwinism completely in mind, this line of blasphemous thinking, reading against the grain of the Bible, could be enabled partly because of the evolutionary theory, for if death serves no higher purpose and no higher meaning, then it is not a sin to kill oneself.

The description of Betty's death by self-incurred exhaustion is loaded with Christian imageries. She sees light (mentioned several times) and supports herself against "the tree," reminding her of "the Cross." Her pass over is assisted by "an Angel" (505), who is Lizzie even though at this time Lizzie is not out of danger of committing an extramarital affair. For Qualls, when discussing *Dombey and Son*, the "luxuriant" and religious prose surrounding Little Paul's death "calls attention to divine love and . . . comforted his readers in a religious way. But the excess of the prose and the very conventionality of the rhetoric indicate . . . Dickens' fear that he does not know what he can believe" (96). Similarly, the over-the-top melodrama of Betty's death seems to imply Dickens is giving his readers what they wanted but he was not sure of what he believed in. Betty's salvation is suspended for a moment, she does not die immediately when she reaches "the foot of the Cross" (505). It is Lizzie who finds Betty on her way from work at the paper mill as they connect through their working-class ethics. "What work, deary?" asks Betty despite being on her last breath. Betty then tasks Lizzie to send a letter and tells her not to let the Parish touch her, or so much as look at her. In the end, Lizzie "lifted her as high as Heaven" (506). While religious imageries abound, it is the human connection that gives Betty her salvation. Oulton argues that "The loving interaction between characters is not a substitute for the neglected order of an absent God. Rather salvation is freely offered through the love of God, either directly or as represented by another character" (159). But if God is absent and negligent, then what evidence is there to indicate that God use a character to deliver salvation? Unlike other Dickens' novels, the salvation in *Our Mutual Friend* comes from human love, in finding joy in small mundane incidents: keeping kind and loyal friends, marrying, having children. On their wedding day, Bella "leaning on her husband's arm, they turned homeward by a rosy path which the gracious sun struck out for them in its setting. And O there are days in this life, worth life and worth death" (656). This echoes Darwin's thoughts about evolution in the last paragraph of *Origin*, that although natural selection seems amoral and perhaps even callous, he implied that the beauty in the world makes life worth living (1859, 490). For Dickens, this beauty refers to human love and connection.

In *Our Mutual Friend*, Dickens eradicates sin from suicide and death. John R. Reed observes: "From the outset of his career Dickens was deeply concerned with the need for withholding judgement, extending compassion, and, with evidence of repentance, assuring forgiveness. But he was equally convinced that transgressions required retributive punishment"

(1995, 71). In other words, Dickens as the Creator was behaving like the vengeful God in the Old Testament. Reed's assertion is true for most of Dickens' *oeuvre* except *Our Mutual Friend*. Oulton demonstrates that villains are let off lightly and Dickens does not judge them (147–55). Merdle and the Veneerings go bankrupt but only the *Little Dorrit* character suffers and kills himself. The Lammles escape any punishment except that they leave the country and the narrative. Mr. Fledgeby is flayed to an itch of his life by Mr. Lammle but this has less to do with divine intervention than revenge and a personal grudge. Although Riderhood and Bradley die in the end, the authorial treatment "leaves the question of future judgement and damnation open" (Wheeler 1990, 295). Oulton presents an even more optimistic interpretation to their deaths: Bradley's "abandonment at the bottom of the lock links his end to annihilation of Gaffer Hexam and spares him the threat of hell" (157). In the Darwinian universe where morality is blurred and there is no divine punishment, Dickens defers his judgment on his characters such that even the serial murderer Bradley is shown compassion by the author.

In *Victorian Religion*, Melnyk writes, "Dickens's novels do endorse an individual morality based on humanistic values that are consistent with and possibly derived from Christianity, but the moral content is largely secularized" (111). The secularization of morals is most obvious in his last completed novel. As this chapter has shown, the theological chasm between *Little Dorrit* and *Our Mutual Friend* is vast before and after Dickens knew about Darwinism. In *Little Dorrit*, Dickens uses a Christian framework of the prefigural, light versus dark metaphors, Old versus New Testaments, and divine punishment on malefactors. However, in *Our Mutual Friend*, although there are some Christian elements here and there, the novel basically follows a Darwinism structure that includes anti-essentialism, a blurring of moral boundaries, fluid identities, human choice, and salvation not by Providence but by human connections and love, elements that aren't found in his previous works but all the more created more interesting and complex characterization on human nature.

Bibliography

Ackroyd, Peter. *Dickens*. London: Sinclair-Stevenson, 1990.
Allingham, Philip. "Darwin's *On the Origin of Species* Reviewed in *All the Year Round*—an Introduction." *Victorian Web*. January 2, 2014. www.victorianweb.org/science/darwin/dickens.html#:~:text=Since%20Dickens%20sanctioned%20every%20single,and%20approved%20of%20the%20three.
Beer, Gillian. *Darwin's Plots: Evolutionary Narrative in Darwin, George Eliot and Nineteenth-Century Fiction*. Cambridge: Cambridge University Press, 2000.
Brontë, Charlotte. *Jane Eyre*. 1847. New York: W. W. Norton, 2001.
Butterworth, Robert. *Dickens, Religion, and Society*. London: Palgrave Macmillan, 2016.

Cheadle, Brian. "The Late Novels: *Great Expectations* and *Our Mutual Friend.*" In *The Cambridge Companion to Charles Dickens*, edited by John O. Jordan, 78–91. Cambridge: Cambridge University Press, 2001.

Cuvier, Jean Léopold Nicolas Frédéric (Georges). *Cuvier's Animal Kingdom.* 1817. London: William S. Orr and Company, 1840.

Darwin, Charles. *The Autobiography of Charles Darwin.* Edited by Nora Barlow. 1958. New York: W. W. Norton, 2005.

———. "Letter no. 5145." July 5, 1866. Darwin Correspondence Project. March 12, 2021. www.darwinproject.ac.uk/letter/DCP-LETT-5145.xml.

———. *On the Origin of Species.* London: John Murray, 1859.

Dickens, Charles. *David Copperfield.* London: Bradbury and Evans, 1850. https://books.google.com/books?id=NcsNAAAAQAAJ.

———. *Little Dorrit.* 1857. Harmondsworth: Penguin, 2003.

———. *Martin Chuzzlewit.* 1844. Harmondsworth: Penguin, 1986.

———. *Our Mutual Friend.* 1865. London: Penguin, 1997.

———. "Some Recollections of Mortality." 1863. In *Charles Dickens: Selected Journalism*, edited by David Pascoe, 102–11. Middlesex: Penguin, 1997.

Galton, Francis. *Inquiries into Human Faculty and Its Development.* London: Macmillan and Company, 1883. https://books.google.com/books?id=V91CAQAAMAAJ.

Holbrook, David. *Charles Dickens and the Image of Women.* New York: New York University Press, 1993.

House, Humphry. *The Dickens World.* Oxford: Oxford University Press, 1942.

Howitt, William. "Charles Dickens." *The People's Journal* (June 3, 1846): 8–12. In *Dickens: The Critical Heritage*, edited by Philip Collins, 205. New York: Barnes and Noble, 1971.

Kaplan, Fred. *Sacred Tears: Sentimentality in Victorian Literature.* Princeton, NJ: Princeton University Press, 1987.

Larson, Janet. *Dickens and the Broken Scripture.* Athens, GA: University of Georgia Press, 1985.

Leclerc, Georges-Louis. *Comte de Buffon. Buffon's Natural History: Containing a Theory of the Earth, a General History of Man, of the Brute Creation, and of Vegetables, Minerals, &c &c.* 1749–1788. Translated by James Smith Barr. 10 vols. London: H. D. Symonds, 1797–1807.

Levine, George. *Darwin and the Novelists: Patterns of Science in Victorian Literature.* Cambridge, MA: Harvard University Press, 1988.

———. *Darwin Loves You: Natural Selection and the Re-Enchantment of the World.* Princeton and Oxford: Princeton University Press, 2006.

Lewes, George Henry. *The Physiology of Common Life.* 2 vols. Edinburgh: William Blackwood and Sons. 1859.

Melnyk, Julie. *Victorian Religion: Faith and Life in Britain.* Westport, CT: Praeger, 2008.

Na, Hai. "Grammar of Choice: Charles Dickens's Authentic Religion." *Dickens Quarterly* 35, no. 2 (June 2018): 127–42.

Newey, Vincent. *The Scriptures of Charles Dickens: Novels of Ideology, Novels of the Self.* Aldershot: Ashgate, 2004.

Oulton, Carolyn W. de la L. *Literature and Religion in Mid-Victorian England: From Dickens to Eliot.* Basingstoke: Palgrave Macmillan, 2003.

Poole, Adrian. Introduction to *Our Mutual Friend* by Charles Dickens, ix–xxiv. London: Penguin, 1997.

Pope, Norris. *Dickens and Charity*. New York: Columbia University Press, 1978.

Qualls, Barry. *The Secular Pilgrims of Victorian Fiction: The Novel as Book of Life*. Cambridge: Cambridge University Press, 1982.

Reed, John R. *Dickens and Thackeray: Punishment and Forgiveness*. Athens, OH: Ohio University Press, 1995.

Rowell, Geoffrey. *Hell and the Victorians: A Study of the Nineteenth-Century Theological Controversies Concerning Eternal Punishment and the Future Life*. Oxford: Clarendon Press, 1974.

Scoggin, Daniel. "A Speculative Resurrection: Death, Money, and the Vampiric Economy of *Our Mutual Friend*." *Victorian Literature and Culture* 30, no. 1 (2002): 99–125.

Trilling, Lionel. *The Opposing Self*. New York: Viking Press, 1955.

Vargish, Thomas. *The Providential Aesthetic in Victorian Fiction*. Charlottesville: University Press of Virginia, 1985.

Walder, Dennis. *Dickens and Religion*. London: Routledge, 2007.

Wall, Stephen. Introduction to *Little Dorrit* by Charles Dickens, xi–xxvii. Harmondsworth: Penguin, 2003.

Wheeler, Michael. *Death and the Future Life in Victorian Literature and Theology*. Cambridge: Cambridge University Press, 1990.

12 Teeming City, Tangled Web
Dickens' Affinity With Darwin

Tony Schwab

When Charles Dickens' journal *All the Year Round* posted its first of the three reviews of Charles Darwin's *On the Origin of Species* (1859), it must be seen as an important day in the history of both religion and science. The first review was published on June 2, 1860 and focused on species. The second was published on July 7, 1860 and focused on natural selection. The last review was on March 9, 1861 and focused on transmutation of species (Anstead 1861).[1] At that moment the popular journal, owned and operated by one of the foremost chroniclers of Victorian life, weighed in on what was soon to become the age's most influential scientific theory of life. Darwin's theories were already stirring up worry and angry debates among Victorian Christians who believed in a literal interpretation of the Bible that God created Earth and its inhabitants in six days fewer than 10,000 years ago. When Darwin published his ideas, he knew that they would unsettle people's faith in God and the Bible, for they already disturbed his wife who was a devout Christian as well as himself, adding illness to his infirmities. The reviews in Dickens' journal added more tinder to the fire.

The reviews were published anonymously as was usually the case when nonfiction pieces appeared in Dickens' journals (Schelstraete 2013, 154). The recent discovery of the identity of the reviewers is, in itself, an example of scholarly evolution. Philip Allingham, the first contributing editor to *The Victorian Web* and author of several articles on Dickens, reported that for a century the authors were unknown, but he came to think that Richard Owen was the author (2014). Owen, who was Dickens' friend and Britain's leading paleontologist at the time, came up with the word "dinosaur" (1841, 103), and soon became superintendent of the natural history departments of the British Museum. Owen admired Darwin's evidence but, at the time, he was arguing for an explanation of development that had a more theistic stance than Darwin's theory. He published an emphatically anti-Darwinian review in the *Edinburgh Review* (1860) that same year, and its tone shows enough of a contrast with the more open-minded *All the Year Round* reviews that many scholars rejected him as the author of the reviews in Dickens' journal.

DOI: 10.4324/9781003156611-13

Then a breakthrough came in 2015 when Allingham read Jeremy Parrott's announcement at a conference in Belgium "that he had discovered Dickens' own annotated set of *All the Year Round*, with a key annotating all the contributors. A full guide to the magazine is being prepared."[2] As reported in *The Guardian* at the time (Flood 2015), the resolution of authorship has a nice resemblance to evolutionary theory in that it came from a random event: Parrott's purchase of a bound set of the journal from an online bookseller in north Wales that turned out to have "pencil annotations in the margin." Interestingly, the newspaper notes that, "the lucky incident would not look out of place in a Charles Dickens novel" (Flood). Parrott, Honorary Research Fellow at The University of Buckingham, has established definitively that the first two reviews are by Edmund Saul Dixon and the third is by Thomas David Anstead. Parrott reports that "their names are clearly legible in the marginal notes next to the respective pieces."[3]

Although one cannot be certain that Dickens endorsed the views of his writers, Allingham makes this assertion:

> Since Dickens sanctioned every single story, article, and serial instalment in his weekly journals, often offering editorial embellishments to make the entire number jump to the same tune called by the 'Conductor,' the only named contributor, Dickens himself, it is indeed likely that he read and approved of the three anonymous reviews of Darwin's work.
>
> (2014)

"Dickens himself," so Victor Sage reports,

> is well known to have been an extraordinarily careful and attentive editor, not an editor in fact, but a 'conductor' as he put it later, explicitly creating the impression that everything that was printed in the magazine was his own opinion, ruthlessly expunging and actively rewriting material which was apparently inconsistent with his known public image.
>
> (2001, para. 17)

Sage adds this statement from *All the Year Round* which is quoted in Engel's *The Maturity of Dickens*: "The statements and opinions of this Journal generally are, of course, to be received as the statements and opinions of its Conductor" (1958).[4]

Dickens was a micromanager when it came to editing articles for his journals. Jasper Schelstraete therefore deduces that the nonfiction pieces "can be read as at least maintaining Dickens's central editorial voice." In a letter to Elizabeth Gaskell written in 1850, Dickens explained that the use of anonymity in *Household Words* allowed all the contents to 'seem to express the general mind and purpose of the Journal" (154).[5] Schelstraete also asserts:

> Within the context of the *All the Year Round*, Dickens's name absorbs all of the "exchange value" that might otherwise have gone to the individual nonfiction contributors. Dickens, then, is the real literary adventurer, trail-blazing a new kind of presence, blending his authorial and editorial personas.
>
> (155)

If Schelstraete is correct, then one may assume that Dickens approved of the reviews and may even have agreed with them. Regardless, as a hands-on editor who was trusted to conduct to his large audience news of the day from many fields, Dickens knew the influence these articles would have as an introduction to Darwin's ground-breaking thinking.

Certainly, there is evidence that at the time of the reviews, when *All the Year Round* had been in existence for a little over a year, Dickens was giving high priority to the content of his new journal. It was "the point in its editor's career when the fate of his journal mattered the most to him, and his role as magazine owner-editor-writer was at the forefront of all his professional activities" (Mackenzie, Winyard, and Drew 2012, 251).

The *Origin* was published in November 1859, and "given the potential of evolution to undermine the ideological foundations of Victorian society" (DeCoursey 1997), the first book reviews had particular impact. Dickens' liberal publishing principles, which he had presented to the public when he started the *The Daily News* in 1846, suggest his commitment to new ideas like Darwin's:

> Principles of Progress and Improvement; of Education, Civil and Religious Liberty, and Equal Legislation; Principles such as the Conductors believe the advancing spirit of the time requires, the Condition of the country demands, and Justice, Reason, and Experience legitimately sanction.
>
> (quoted in Grubb 1945, 813)

Aspects of Dickens' editorial stance clarify what he would have been looking for in the reviews, starting with his commitment to delivering his readers science news in a style that was layman friendly. George Levine, author of *Darwin and the Novelists*, the groundbreaking work on the connections between Victorian scientists and novelists, praises Dickens' articles on science, calling them "surprisingly sophisticated despite their popularizing strategies" (1991, 124). For even the most serious topics, Dickens demanded an approachable tone and told contributors to combine their facts with imaginative touches or fancy. Shu-Fang Lai corroborates Dickens' "earnest wish to study and understand the universe and to catch up with new ideas" (2001, 50) along with his requirement that articles had to be "well directed to the interests and capacity of the general reader" (49). Lai uses the example of the well-received *Household Words* article based on lectures by the physicist and science writer Michael Faraday. Paul Halpern, an authority on popular science, describes how in 1850, Dickens wrote to Faraday, whom he had never met, and asked for his lecture notes which were probably the scientist's only copy (2017). Dickens wrote:

> Sir, I take the liberty of addressing you as if I knew you personally; trusting that I may venture to assume that you will excuse that freedom. It has occurred to me that it would be extremely beneficial to a large class of the public, to have some account of your late lectures on the breakfast table.
>
> (quoted in Halpern n.p.)

Faraday sent them, and Dickens turned them into a humorous, charming article, "Chemistry of the Candle," in which a teenager interprets Faraday's concepts for his family. Dickens wrote to his fellow philanthropist Miss Burdett Coutts that he did not like topics "difficult to approach in pages that are intended for readers of all classes and all ages of life" (quoted in Lai 46). He aimed for "the familiarity of friendly talk," which Wilkie Collins evidently mastered (256). Dickens told his contributor Henry Morley: "You know as well as I do how severe the struggle is, to get the publication down into the masses of readers" (quoted in 47). These principles would have been crucial when it came to the journal's response to evolution which so clearly challenged beliefs in divine power. From the start of the Victorian controversy over theories of species development, "one gets a sense of the fence on which editors of popular magazines had to sit" in regard to "contemporary fears about human origins and the danger of atavism" (Mackenzie, Winyard, and Drew 270).

In the middle of the first review is a summary of the journal's stance on Darwin that strikes a remarkable balance between science and religion and then concludes by subtly emphasizing self-development and so reinforcing the possibility that Darwin's theories were correct. Darwin opened the possibility for such a statement when he added the "Creator" to the *Origin*'s last paragraph under outside pressure and perhaps anxiety of his own (2012 [1860] 490). Thus the "Species" review reads:

> This view is not necessarily irreligious, as it seems to be at the outset; for it does not deny the existence of a Supreme Overruling Power, although acting in a manner to which the minds of men in general are little accustomed; nor of a Sustaining and Regulating Influence, although the desired ends are brought about by contrivances which unthinking persons might call accident. But God is Continuous and

Unyielding Law, and Incessant Energy, and All-pervading Life; and all those we behold around us wherever we direct our eyes. Whether we conceive many successive creative acts, or few, or only one, a creation once in existence must be sustained, not from day to day, and from hour to hour, but from half-second to half-second, without the intermission of the smallest imaginable fragment of time. But the creation which we see around us is so complicated and perfect, that it can only be sustained by an All-wise, Almighty Divinity. The greater the complexity of the machinery which is kept in action, the greater must be the energy and the untiring power of the eternal mainspring. It may be just as noble a conception of the Deity to believe that he created a few original forms capable of self-development into other and needful forms, as to believe that He required a fresh act of creation to supply the voids caused by the action of His laws.

(Dixon 1860b, 176)

This endorses life as an all-pervasive process of change, but in the same breath it expresses awe that development is so continuous that it does not stop for any amount of time, conjuring a vision of "incessant energy" that the journal is compelled and presumably quite happy to call "divine."

Harvey Peter Sucksmith made this statement that is widely quoted in Dickens scholarship: "Dickens does in fact seem to have been receptive to biological facts throughout his life" (1970, 171). What Dickens did with these biological facts and how he reconciled them with his theological beliefs are evident in *Oliver Twist* (2003 [1838]) and *Bleak House* (1993 [1853]).

The second review in *All the Year Round* characterizes natural selection as "Malthus's doctrine applied to the whole animal and vegetable kingdoms, with increased force . . . a grain in the balance will determine which individual shall live and which shall die" (1860a, 297). In 1798, economist Thomas Malthus published his principle that, "the power of population is indefinitely greater than the power in the earth to produce subsidence for man" (1798, ch. 1). Darwin credited Malthus for solidifying his idea of natural selection as the process through which species fail to adapt and become extinct or survive to propagate. Malthus's idea started dialogue across disciplines not only about the inevitability of the human fight for survival but also about the chances that it can be ameliorated by human ingenuity and altruism. At the time of the second review, this allusion to Malthus, as Sage explains, is "very close to [Herbert] Spencer's 'struggle for existence'" (para. 30), a concept which was fomenting a debate among social thinkers and business leaders about whether the harsh realities of Victorian social and economic struggle were almost a biological necessity driven by self-interest and laissez-faire economics. Self-interest certainly is Fagin's philosophy in *Oliver Twist*—at any cost, to be "number one" (2003 [1838], 373)—and it drives important characters in Dickens like Mr. Smallweed (the miser) and the elite lawyer Tulkinghorn of *Bleak House*. Although most Victorians endorsed laissez-faire and capitalistic competition, Dickens portrays these men in a negative light, and they are always impediments to the characters whom Dickens treats with unmistakable affection, from Esther and Jarndyce to Caddy Jellyby and fragile Miss Flite. Certainly, as Nicola Bown shows, by the time of *Our Mutual Friend* in 1865, Dickens is consciously bringing into his work this harsh interpretation of Darwinian natural selection that is being promulgated around him, and he is accentuating the ill effects of a "reptilian world of mid nineteenth-century capitalism fueled by . . . waste, greed and ruthlessness" (2010, 10). Bown finds that "For all Dickens' best efforts, the world that is shaped by natural selection is one in which life is sometimes wasted and love is not enough" (15). But Bown also emphasizes another view of evolution and shows that, in the same novel, Dickens "counterposes the world conceived by natural selection with the redeeming power of love" (2).

Darwinian natural selection would have melded with Dickens' view of human life as a struggle between good and evil. In Dickens' view of Christianity, the human contest pitted the humility of the persevering majority against power in the hands of the greedy. It is the contention of this chapter that Dickens was implicitly fighting for the evolution of England with the goal of a good and benevolent society. There is a remarkable similarity between Darwin and Dickens when, from within their own fields, they each assert optimistically their adherence to the principle of the Good. Darwin announces that "natural selection works solely by and for the good of each being" (2012 [1859], 489). He counts it as a positive that the evolutionary process is an interconnected "grand natural system" (478) of living and dying, starting with "organized beings of the simplest class" that "produce something more nearly and more highly organized; and of these again, the best only would survive, to be the parents of something still nearer perfection" (Dixon 1860b, 175). Philosopher and cognitive scientist David Dennett notes Darwin's "conviction that life does have meaning, that goodness matters" (1995, 16). This is Dickens' sentiment too, in his 1841 preface to *Oliver Twist* where he announces that he will "show . . . the principle of Good surviving through every adverse circumstance" (13). It can seem odd to speak of an agreement on moral principle between a creative artist and a natural scientist. In fact, for most contemporary biologists, the process of natural selection is more straightforward. Seen strictly from the natural scientific viewpoint, as philosopher of science Michael Ruse puts it, "The key to evolutionary success is adaptation—the development of features that help their possessors to survive and reproduce" (2017). This is how the paradigm is taught to new scientists. The moral interpretation of the process as good or bad, harsh or noble, designed or random has become a separate philosophical discussion for many scientists but one that is robust.

As for Darwin's attachment to the moral significance of natural selection and even of the war of nature with all its casualties, he was sufficiently close to the time when the religious argument for design was dominant to weave moral terms into the *Origin*, usually in order to extol the beauty of the process in its entirety. In the work of both the scientist and the novelist, the details that flow from this idea of the Good play out in myriad ways, but the venerable concept is the same. Though there is no record of correspondence or meetings between Dickens and Darwin, as they study life in their own ways, they circle back consistently to this value concept. In the final paragraph of the *Origin*, Darwin emphasizes natural selection's "progress toward perfection" and that "the most exalted object we are capable of conceiving' is 'the production of the higher animals" (2012 [1859], 490). He then becomes poetic: "Whilst this planet has gone cycling on according to the fixed law of gravity, from so simple a beginning endless forms most beautiful and most wonderful have been, and are being, evolved"; he ends by emphasizing the "grandeur" of his vision (490). There is convincing evidence in *Oliver Twist* and *Bleak House* that Dickens would have agreed with the view Darwin expresses that the life cycle—from the individual to the species to all living things—is a transcendent Good. In other words, life itself is the Good, whether over the eons since the "Silurian epoch" (2012 [1859], 489) or in the life of the infant watched over by the bricklayer's wife in *Bleak House* even as it dies (1993 [1853], 95).

The three reviews of *On the Origin of the Species* attempt to convince skeptical readers that times are changing, and they pointedly appreciate truth not as static law but as a process. "Truth is a bugbear which is fast losing its terrors," Dixon's first review declares, "and we are getting more and more accustomed to it, and are less and less afraid to look it in the face" (1860b, 293). The review then underscores this advice by using evolution itself as a metaphor:

> Timid persons, who purposely cultivate a certain inertia of mind, and who love to cling to their preconceived ideas . . . may be reassured by the reflection that, for theories, as for organized beings, there is also a Natural Selection and a Struggle for Life. . . . If Mr. Darwin's theory be true, nothing can prevent its ultimate and general reception, however much it may pain and shock those to whom it is propounded for the first time. If it be merely a clever hypothesis . . . its failure will be nothing new in the history of science.
>
> (299)

As for Dickens' openness to the idea that life is evolving, this probably arose in him intuitively and from the influence of Victorian scientific thinking that was moving toward acceptance of the origin of living things as a natural and not a divine phenomenon. From the beginning of his career, he had always presented his own version of what Darwin came to call "the war of nature," which causes "famine and death" because he felt keenly the human damage caused by England's conflicts and inequality. It seems that he would have agreed with Darwin's vision of what can be called progress: that evolution moves toward a type of "perfection," especially in terms of "the most exalted object," the human being (Dixon 1860a, 299; Darwin 2012 [1859], 490). The plot of *Bleak House*, for example, is driven by Dickens' impatience at the strained and combative state of England. His displeasure is emphatically expressed by the omniscient narrator and also by Esther through her pity (not least for herself as a victim of emotional abuse) for what they both see: from the deathly conditions in Tom-all-Alone's, to the middle-class suitors in Chancery pleading for a verdict that will set them free for social mobility, to the alienated routines at Chesney Wold that sap vitality and honesty. So, though believers scoffed when Darwin made room chronologically in the *Origin* for his war of nature and for life's long "progress toward perfection" (Dixon 1860a, 299; Darwin 2012 [1859], 490) by expanding Earth's age to hundreds of millions of years, one can imagine Dickens drawn to this long view of history and seeing divinity in it.

Darwin's ultimate image in the *Origin* is "an entangled bank" (2012 [1859], 489) of interdependent species that complements Dickens' vision. As Gillian Beer says of *Bleak House*, the "'fifty-six named—and many more unnamed—characters all turn out to be related by way either of concealed descent . . . or of economic dependency. . . . The work demonstrates the terrible redundancy of human kind and shows all the interconnections" (2000, 42). For Dickens, the tangle of London lives is essential, and it gives rise to one of his essential questions, a religious one: in any human population will the dominant dynamic be self-interest and individual survival or love and altruism? In *Oliver Twist* the question comes up as Oliver is shuttled back and forth by powers beyond his control between the thief Fagin and Brownlow, who wants to become his moral mentor. In *Bleak House*, will Lady Dedlock reach out to her estranged and disgraced daughter or bury her maternal feelings in fear and snobbery? Will anyone who passes Jo, the sickly and alienated street sweeper, on his corner notice that he needs attention and care? In his book for his children, *The Life of Our Lord*, Dickens gives an answer: "It is Christianity TO DO GOOD," he says, "to be gentle, merciful, and forgiving, and . . . to never make a boast . . . of our love of God, but always to show that we love Him by humbly trying to do right in everything" (1996 [1934], 32). Darwin's bank also depicts a combination of confusion and order among living things: "an entangled bank, clothed with many plants of many kinds, with birds singing on the bushes, with various insects flitting about, and with worms crawling through the damp earth ... elaborately constructed forms, so different from each other, and dependent upon each other in so complex a manner" (2012 [1859], 489). Levine appreciates the beauty both men see in forms of life developing in awful proximity which he says is captured by the image of the entangled bank (1986, 275). Dickens and Darwin seem awestruck by the profound struggle happening before them. The Court of Chancery in *Bleak House*, where the case of Jarndyce and Jarndyce holds centerstage, is a tangle of life and death, and the lawyer who knows it best, who "is famous for it—supposed never to have read anything else since he left school" (7)—is named Tangle.

After Darwin describes his bank, a kind of belief fills him: "When I view all beings not as special creations, but as the lineal descendants of some few beings which lived long before the first bed of the Silurian period was deposited, they seem to me to become ennobled" (2012 [1859], 489). George Levine states that "Dickens' preoccupation with discovering connections links him ... with the Judeo-Christian insistence that we are our brothers' keepers" (1991, 120). Dickens' picture of the Chancery suitors tangles despair and hope; some suitors languish and die, but Miss Flite, who has been in court since childhood, hopes for the day when she can set her caged birds free. For Levine, in both Dickens' and Darwin's worlds "there is an almost uncontrollable energy of life" (1991, 149). This energy in Dickens, bound up as it is in characters' contradictory and individualistic adaptations to their common environment, leads to theological questions: What part does the transcendent play in these lives? What do these people live for and why? In another affinity with Darwin, Dickens' life experience led him to find nobility in the law of a beneficent power overseeing this urban tangle and providing a way out of the labyrinth.

Dickens did not declare himself an evolutionist, but he must have intuitively appreciated the concept as it had developed. The Latin *evolutionem*, "an opening of what was rolled up," would mean by 1640 "to unfold, open out, expand," and by Victorian times "to develop by natural processes to a higher state" (*Online Etymology Dictionary* 2017), meanings he would have woven into his hope for a higher state promised in the Bible with its prophesy of the Heavenly Jerusalem (Gal 4:26; Heb 11:10, 12:22–24, and 13:14; and Rv 21. In the last Book of *A Tale of Two Cities*, he writes of the future, "I see a beautiful city and a brilliant people rising from this abyss, and in their struggles to be truly free, in their triumphs and defeats, through long years to come, I see the evil of this time and of the previous time of which this is the natural birth, gradually making expiation for itself and wearing out" (2015 [1859], 313; bk 3, ch. 15). *Oliver Twist* garners additional theological and Darwinian nexus when compared to *Pilgrim's Progress* (2008 [1678]): Dickens' characters, especially children, are on perilous journeys through Victorian London toward a reward. Demons like Fagin and Tulkinghorn throw up snares for their victims while heroes like Oliver and Esther find ways to enhance their survival. In line with Dickens' moral outlook, these villains die desperate deaths while Esther and Oliver become well-adjusted examples of Dickens' version of the survival of the fittest. Survival in Dickens' novels is often dependent on the miraculous, the phenomenon he described for his children as "something wonderful which cannot be done without God's leave" (1996 [1934], 6). His novels are full of miracles, but they are not overtly delivered by a supreme divinity; they occur through human means: kindness, perseverance, and luck. If one combines the dire predicaments in which Dickens found his fellow citizens with the promise of Christian love and his hope for the evolution of Londoners, one can appreciate that Dickens could have felt sympathy with Darwin's epic story that brought evolution to the planetary level.

Dickens perceived London as a primeval quagmire of sloshing mud and thick fog where one could "meet a Megalosaurus, forty feet long or so, waddling like an elephantine lizard up Holborn Hill" (3) This dinosaur was inspired by Dickens' paleontologist friend, Owen (Levine 1991, 122), whose work anticipated today's developmental biology which compares the developmental processes of organisms and infers their ancestral relationships. The first scene of *Bleak House* strikes us as a swamp from which Londoners might have evolved thus far, where at the "heart of the fog, sits the Lord High Chancellor in his High Court of Chancery" (3), the novel's central symbol where bureaucratic man—call him London Man or *Homo londinium*—slowly grinds out right and wrong, dispensing and withholding justice, giving shape to lives.

As the novel opens, three participants in this endless legal tangle are unknown to each other and seem to have nothing in common, but Dickens will reveal their intimate bond—as all humans are interconnected. Lady Dedlock and Esther Summerson are a mother and her illegitimate daughter estranged since Esther's birth, their bond destroyed by the prejudice and shame that altered their life paths. Esther accompanies a detective to uncover the secret of her mother's life and finds her lying dead by smallpox at the gate of the cemetery where Esther's father is buried, having run from her estate with the same aim as Esther's, to understand their past. Dickens also reveals the wealthy lady's other connection, to Jo who is from the lowest rung of the hierarchy who sweeps mud from the street corner. Jo, whom no one takes notice of when he is alive, dies of smallpox too after the lady enlists him to show her the grave of her lover. So as Esther faces her mother, now "distressed, unsheltered, senseless" like the street sweeper (686), class difference, lust, shame, and the virus mix. Dickens foreshadows this epiphany as Jo is dying: "What connection can there have been between many people in the innumerable histories of this world who from opposite sides of great gulfs have, nevertheless, been very curiously brought together!" (189). The trio's equal susceptibility to infection—Esther survives but is disfigured from the same disease—makes London one family. Levine calls the idea that humans are one family "one of the great Christian metaphors" (1986, 272). In evolutionary terms, Dickens' characters share the same genes and can die the same death. This is Dickens' revelation of London's community of souls, and it is wonderfully similar to Darwin's "hidden bond of community of descent . . ." from a common parent, the bond he says he and his fellow "naturalists have been unconsciously seeking" (2012 [1859], 420).

In the earlier novel *Oliver Twist*, Oliver's adventure is drawn in broader strokes and shows Dickens' schema more easily. The subtitle is intriguing in light of an evolutionary focus: "The Parish Boy's Progress." At first just a scream in a public birthing room, his mother dead the moment he arrives, Oliver is akin to a one-celled organism swimming in the waters of the System. But Dickens plans a miracle to deliver him from "ill-usage and violence" to asylum in the countryside where a reconstructed family of relatives and benefactors will nourish the boy's "youthful energies," "priceless treasures . . . the Creator bestows but once" (399). Oliver's mentor speaks in evolutionary terms about the benefits that will come the boy's way: his nature is going to develop itself and show "the thriving seeds of all he wished him to become" (466).

Goodness is a pure phenomenon for Dickens, almost otherworldly; goodness floats above the fray, embodied by law-abiding, modest men and women, and Dickens rarely brings this down to earth by having these characters show confusion or anger that they live in a world where their goodness is easily passed over. Still, being a man driven by a mission to urge social reform that would relieve the impoverished, Dickens emphasized realism, conducting Oliver's journey and his salvation without mentioning God. In an article subtitled "The Evolving Form of *Oliver Twist*," William T. Lankford discusses the scene when Oliver's young and kind aunt Rose is ill and Oliver protests that "Heaven will not let her die so young." Rose's foster mother gives a realistic check to this simple hope: "You think like a child, poor boy," she says, and adjusts her own attitude to accept that death and "the agony of separation" may be near (1978, 282). Lankford says, "In effect, Dickens is here removing Providence from the surface of his created world, making it more distant from the development of plot" (25). Dickens knew that the plot needed to revolve around a miracle but that his narrative must cleave to realism, so rather than the hand of God, Oliver's well-being depends on his survival instinct, on coincidence, and on luck.

Luck and randomness are another link between Dickens and Darwin. Each wondered if there was a pattern behind chance events. Through natural selection over time, a species and its environment will interact in powerful but random ways that can enhance life or end it seemingly with no reason or purpose, and Darwin worried over this finding. R. A Varghese reports that Darwin wrote to his friend, T. H. Farrer, "If we consider the whole universe, the mind refuses to look at it as the outcome of chance. . . . The whole question seems to me insoluble" (quoted in 2013, x). Levine also notes this commonality between the two men but insists that in Dickens, chance is different because it is very much under Dickens' control and is inserted to make a moral point—in fact an old-fashioned point which Levine says points backward to the pre-Darwinian argument for Design by the Creator (2006, 267). John Robert Reed argues that coincidence in novels was a Victorian convention, one understood by Victorian readers to imply the invisible but absolute "hand of God" (1975, 132). But it should be considered that Dickens' use of a convention like a stroke of luck leading to the triumph of goodness is a more modern choice than Levine or Reed allow. Dickens' novels often reflect society so realistically—as in his depiction of a London slum or Bill Sikes' grotesque death before a bloodthirsty mob—that the survival of goodness becomes a striking narrative choice and can strike readers in a decidedly unconventional way.

Dickens provides contrast to Oliver's lucky journey in the scene between the prostitute, Nancy, and Oliver's benefactors under London Bridge. Here Nancy refuses the same offer that Oliver accepts—in effect, an adaptation—to escape "the very air which is pestilence and death to you" by moving away from the city (400). In evolutionary terms, Nancy's decision is an example of her lifelong maladaptive behavior in London's war of nature. Her reasons for refusing are a good explanation of the environmental and psychological factors that block her path: "I am chained to my old life. I loathe and hate it now, but I cannot leave it. I must have gone too far to turn back" (400). In this novel, while intuitively deploying an evolutionary theme, Dickens also employs his religious one which is best explained in his children's book, *The Life of Our Lord* which retells the Gospel of Luke and which emphasizes life and love over evil, pain, and death. When Oliver sets off by himself to London, he says goodbye to his friend the orphan Dick at the workhouse who is ill, and Dick's innocent but knowing presence takes on the roles of both the angel who told the shepherds to seek out the Child and the shepherds themselves when they blessed Him, divine moments that Dickens highlighted for his children (1). Dick intuits the mysterious possibilities in Oliver's exodus and blesses him: "The blessing was from a young child's lips, but it was the first that Oliver had ever heard invoked upon his head; and through the struggles and sufferings, and troubles and changes, of his after life, he never once forgot it" (79). When readers despair that as a fledgling criminal the boy is losing his innocence, Nancy's lover, Sikes, forces him to take part in a robbery. Part of the plan is for the housebreakers to pass him through a tiny window to unlock a door and allow the gang access.[6] When the robbery is foiled and the crooks gone, the boy is literally left in the cold, but—and this is the miracle—he has in effect left the bad world and entered the good. More extraordinary, he is delivered to his family; in the house to be robbed live his aunt and her foster mother, and without knowledge of this coincidence, they instinctively take the boy in. Half of Dickens' readers may reject this as sentimentalism, but the other half will find joy in the primitive reunion. This is Oliver's second safe house, one of three that constitute the route Dickens invents for him so that he can progress toward personal freedom. The final destination will be a parsonage in the country where Oliver will be protected by his new blended family of devout Christians.

After the aborted robbery, when the thieves leave Oliver in the snow, he embodies the central contradiction that always attracted Dickens. At the moment he is abandoned, he also is on the threshold of deliverance. What drives the thieves who desert him is to serve themselves, but what drives the family inside is to care for Oliver. Dickens' adolescent trauma, which stemmed from when he was 12 and his impoverished family had him live alone and earn his living at a warehouse (Forster 1875, 51), revolved around the absence of care, so he was devoted to loving units and intimate, mentoring relationships. It can be argued that the Good is Dickens' main contribution to what Darwin characterizes as life's "progress towards perfection" (2012 [1859], 489) and Dickens' benevolent society is an evolutionary adaptation he demanded. Dickens' views matured as the world evolved. As he rode the fantastic new railroads across Europe, he described the world Darwin helped create, one without a traditional center. His observations revealed to him that the new world would be different, always changing, but viable. Imagine him while writing *Bleak House*, studying the designs for the huge concrete Megalosaurus planned for London's Great Exhibition of 1851,[7] readying himself to accept Darwin's extension of the age of Earth and that creation was an ongoing process, while remaining adamant that the love of God would remain. He felt keenly the loss of the traditional center and sympathized with Londoners. For Dickens, it compared to the loss of a parent, and there would be consequences; love would survive but it would be experienced differently, seem chaotic, a question without a complete answer.

Dickens' question was always, how will Londoners survive? What modifications and adaptations will prove the most beneficial? Darwin's optimism about natural selection is pertinent here: it is always "working, whenever and wherever opportunity offers, at the improvement of each organic being in relation to its organic and inorganic conditions of life" (2012 [1859, 84]). Dickens sought an answer: For him, a certain balance always came to mind. Evolutionary biologists today would call it "equipoise" (Torday 2015, 575). These scientists are now modifying the harsh reputation of Darwin's survival of the fittest by observing that within organisms, homeostasis, the process of adapting the internal environment to the external environment through a feedback loop like a thermostat, continually promotes balance for the individual and the species (573). Emphasis is shifting from the few hard hits a living thing might take to the ongoing process of minute adaptations within the organism to restore its balance and enhance its survivability. The triumphant denouements of both *Oliver Twist* and *Bleak House* are a prescient touchpoint with this new science. Oliver and Esther establish conditions to foster their own homeostasis and find optimal environments to live healthily in spite of the disturbances of modern life. Dickens must have understood this evolutionary fact intuitively because the novels appeared before the *Origin*. He knew from his observation of Londoners that "reduced entropy is the driving force behind evolution" (Torday 577), that it was necessary for his protagonists to reduce their susceptibility to the lack of order and predictability around them in order to achieve the highest levels of physical and mental well-being.

Oliver and Esther discover the Dickensian version of homeostatic adjustment, and they both balance their internal environments with the demands of the external by moving away from the city to what Dickens describes in *Oliver Twist* as "a little society whose condition approached as nearly to one of perfect happiness as can ever be known in this changing world" (2003 [1867], 462). The words "nearly" and "changing" are critical because they allude to the long arc of evolution and also of progress toward the Good. The need to create balance by homeostasis goes in the other direction too and creates the peculiar adaptations that animate Dickens' oddballs. But what makes a hero for Dickens—the highest stage of Dickensian Man—is the ability to find inspired homeostatic solutions. Look at Oliver and Esther in their final homes to see these beautiful adaptations. Esther and her blended family build a new house outside London to surround her with good memories and personal meanings, an evolutionary achievement that promotes her survival. Oliver will be brought up in a community designed for his benefit. To Dickens these are blessed occurrences, but he will not say they are directed by the hand of God. They are choices. Something wonderful in these two seeks a higher life beautiful in form and content.

The need for positive adaptation is made explicit by Esther's guardian and Oliver's benefactor, older men who keep to a small circle of family and friends and make them conscious that environmental dangers can be met by meditative attention to good faith. Consciousness is a factor in this highest level of Dickensian adaptation—knowing who one is and what the world is. This is clear in the guardian Jarndyce's contention that when the wind changes direction and starts blowing from the east, anxiety is about to threaten his circle (57). He then teaches Esther how to look for workarounds in the name of health and survival. The minister who heads Oliver's reconstructed family chooses a place in the country anchored by his parsonage for Oliver to develop as a whole person. The parson expresses a plan to "level all fancied barriers" (2003 [1867], 451) and reminds us that the higher purpose behind Dickens' coincidences and alliances is awareness of the interconnection of all.

Oliver's "little society" (462) will promote Dickens' Christian values, "mercy to others and mutual love . . . strong affection and humanity of heart," but perhaps most importantly, "Benevolence to all things that breathe" (466), and this emphasis on the environment is in line with *Bleak House* which ends with Esther's enraptured description of the gardens that will sustain her little society. The interior of her new home has been designed by Mr. Jarndyce to remind her of her journey to self-actualization: "*my* little tastes and fancies, *my* little methods and inventions . . . my old ways everywhere" (721; emphasis in original); outside is radiant sun, "a rich and smiling country with water sparkling . . . woodbine, jasmine, and honey-suckle" and of course, a "sweet west wind" (721). For Esther and Oliver, born outside social norms, Dickens has engineered a second chance.

Speaking to her reader, "the unknown friend to whom I write" (738) Esther explains the value of her new environment. She compares it to the old one in terms of money, that main measure of success back in London. Though she and her husband "are not rich in the bank" (740), she reports they are prospering. She has children and close friends, and the good works of her and her husband are appreciated and returned. She has "never known the wind to be in the East for a single moment" (739) and so concludes, "Is not this to be rich?" (740). In the life of a Dickens' character, the achievement of poise and balance may be the greatest evolutionary accomplishment.

Notes

1. I wish to than Brenda Ayres, coeditor of *The Theological Dickens*, for her help and encouragement in tracking down the latest scholarship on the writers of the three Darwin reviews and for editorial changes and reference recommendations throughout.
2. Per Allingham's emails of January 29 and 30, 2021.
3. Per Jeremy Parrott's personal correspondence of February 3, 2021.
4. Quoted in Sage (para. 17n11) from Dickens' Note in the *All the Year Round* (December 26, 1863, 419).
5. The letter to Gaskell was dated January 31, 1850, printed in Storey, Tillotson, and Burgis (1988, 21–22).
6. Sarah E. Maier, coeditor of *The Theological Dickens*, points out that "Oliver's tiny stature is a poor adaptation to the survival skills needed for the streets (versus Sikes' massive size) but is a demonstration of how he is evolving past physical survival to salvation" (personal communication, 2021).
7. Herb Moskowitz of the Dickens Fellowship writes that "Artist Benjamin Waterhouse Hawkins was commissioned in 1852 to create 33 concrete prehistoric animals for a sculpture garden outside of the Crystal Palace. . . . He worked with Sir Richard Owen on what the animals may have looked like" (2011). Adelene Buckland notes that for these exhibition replicas, "Owen directed the sculptor that the dinosaurs he had named, including the megalosaurus . . . were accurately created" (2007, 683). Moskowitz continues: "It has been suggested that Dickens saw the dinosaurs as they were being constructed and that it was

the concrete megalosaurus that inspired him to include one while describing the primordial atmosphere of London in *Bleak House*" (2011).

Bibliography

Allingham, Philip. "Darwin's *On the Origin of the Species* Reviewed in *All the Year Round*—an Introduction." *The Victorian Web*. 2014. www.victorianweb.org/science/darwin/dickens.html.

[Anstead, Thomas David]. "Transmutation." *All the Year Round* 98 (March 9, 1861): 519–21. www.djo.org.uk/all-the-year-round/volume-iv.

Beer, Gillian. *Darwin's Plots: Evolutionary Narrative in Darwin, George Eliot and Nineteenth- Century Fiction*. Cambridge: Cambridge University Press, 2000.

Bown, Nicola. "What the Alligator Didn't Know: Natural Selection and Love in *Our Mutual Friend*." *Interdisciplinary Studies in the Long Nineteenth Century* 19, no. 10 (2010): 1–17. https://doi.org/10.16995/ntn.567.

Buckland, Adelene. ""The Poetry of Science': Charles Dickens, Geology, and Visual and Material Culture in Victorian London." *Victorian Literature and Culture* 35, no. 2 (2007): 679–94. www.jstor.org/stable/40347182.

Bunyan, John. *The Pilgrim's Progress*. 1678. London: Penguin Classics, 2008.

Darwin, Charles. *On the Origin of Species*. 1859. 1st ed. *Online Variorum of Darwin's "Origin of the Species*," edited by Barbara Bordalejo, 2012. http://darwin-online.org.uk/Variorum/1859/1859-1-dns.html.

———. *On the Origin of Species*. 1860. 2nd ed. 1859*Online Variorum of Darwin's "Origin of the Species*," edited by Barbara Bordalejo, 2012. http://darwin-online.org.uk/Variorum/1859/1859-1-dns.html.

DeCoursey, Christina. "Darwin and Dickens 1860–65." *Cultural Studies Study Group*. 1997. warlight.tripod.com/CHRISTINE.html.

Dennett, David. *Darwin's Dangerous Idea*. New York: Simon and Shuster, 1995.

Dickens, Charles. *Bleak House*. 1853. Hertfordshire: Wordsworth Editions Limited, 1993.

———. *The Life of Our Lord*. 1934. *Our Favourite Books*. 1996. www.ourfavouritebooks.co.uk/downloadindiv/dickens/The%20Life%20of%20Our%20Lord.pdf.

———. "Note." *All the Year Round* 10 (December 26, 1863): 419.

———. *Oliver Twist*. 1838. New York: Barnes and Noble Books, 2003.

———. *A Tale of Two Cities*. 1859. Overland Park, KS: Digireads Publishing, 2015.

[Dixon, Edmund Saul]. "Natural Selection." *All the Year Round* 63 (July 7, 1860a): 293–99. www.djo.org.uk/all-the-year-round/volume-iii.

———. "Species." *All the Year Round* 58 (June 2, 1860b): 174–78. www.djo.org.uk/all-the-year-round/volume-iii.

Engel, Monroe. *The Maturity of Dickens*. Harvard, CT: Harvard University Press, 1958.

"evolution." *Online Etymology Dictionary*. 2017. www.etymonline.com/search?q=evolution.

Flood, Alison. "Dickens Marginalia Reveal Famous Contributors to His Journal." *The Guardian*. July 13, 2015. www.theguardian.com/books/2015/jul/13/dickens-marginalia-famous-contributors-journal-wilkie-collins-elizabeth-gaskell.

Forster, John. *The Life of Charles Dickens.* Vol. 1. Boston: James R, Osgood, 1875. www.gutenberg.org/files/25851/25851-h/25851-h.htm#51.

Grubb, Gerald Giles. "Dickens' Influence as an Editor." *Studies in Philology* 42, no. 4 (1945): 811–23. www.jstor.org/stable/4172737.

Halpern, Paul. "Forget 'A Christmas Carol,' Charles Dickens and Michael Faraday Created 'A Chemistry Carol'." *Forbes Magazine.* December 20, 2017. www.forbes.com/sites/startswithabang/2017/12/20/forget-a-christmas-carol-charles-dickens-and-michael-faraday-created-a-chemistry-carol/?sh=5db9d4901347.

Lai, Shu-Fang. "Fact or Fancy: What Can We Learn about Dickens from His Periodicals *Household Words* and *All the Year Round*?" *Victorian Periodicals Review* 34, no. 1 (2001): 41–53. www.jstor.org/stable/20083777.

Lankford, William T. "The Parish Boy's Progress: The Evolving Form of *Oliver Twist.*" *PMLA* 93, no. 1 (1978): 20–32. https://doi.org/10.2307/461817.

Levine, George. *Darwin and the Novelists: Patterns of Science in Victorian Fiction.* 1988. Chicago, IL: University of Chicago Press, 1991.

———. *Darwin Loves You: Natural Selection and the Re-enchantment of the World.* Princeton; Oxford: Princeton University Press, 2006.

———. "Dickens and Darwin, Science, and Narrative Form." *Texas Studies in Literature and Language* 28, no. 3 (Fall 1986): 250–80. www.jstor.org/stable/40754801.

Mackenzie, Hazel, Ben Winyard, and John Drew. "*All the Year Round*, Vol 1: 30 April—22 October 1859 Nos. 1–26." *Dickens Quarterly* 29, no. 3 (2012): 251–77. https://doi.org/10.2307/45292594.

Malthus, Thomas. *An Essay on the Principle of Population.* London: J. Johnson, 1798. gutenberg.org/files/4239/4239-h/4239-h.htm

Moskowitz, Herb. "Dickens and the Dinosaur." *The Charles Dickens Page.* September 10, 2011. www.charlesdickenspage.com/dickens-and-the-dinosaur.html.

[Owen, Richard.] "ART. VIII.—1. *On the Origin of Species by Means of Natural Selection, Or the Preservation of Favoured Races in the Struggle for Life.*" *The Edinburgh Review, 1802–1929* 111, no. 226 (April 1860): 487–532. http://ezproxy.liberty.edu/login?qurl=https%3A%2F%2Fwww.proquest.com%2Fhistorical-periodicals%2Fart-viii-1-on-origin-species-means-natural%2Fdocview%2F6417174%2Fse-2%3Faccountid%3D12085.

———. "Report on British Fossil Reptiles." Part 2. In the *Report of the Eleventh Meeting of the British Association for the Advancement of Science; Held at Plymouth on July 1841,* 60–204. London: John Murray, 1842. https://babel.hathitrust.org/cgi/pt?id=njp.32101076796059&view=1up&seq=102.

Parrott, Jeremy. Personal Correspondence. February 3, 2021.

Reed, John Robert. *Victorian Conventions.* Vol. 10. Athens, OH: Ohio University Press, 1975.

Ruse, Michael. "Darwin Made Me Do It." *The New Atlantis* 52 (Spring 2017): 57–69.

Sage, Victor. "Dickens and Professor Owen! Portrait of a Friendship." *Sillages Critiques,* 2 (2001): 87–101. https://doi.org/10.4000/sillagescritiques.3865.

Schelstraete, Jasper. "'Literary Adventurers': Editorship, Non-Fiction Authorship and Anonymity." In *Charles Dickens and the Mid-Victorian Press, 1850–1870,* edited by Hazel Mackenzie and Ben Winyard, 147–56. Buckingham: University of Buckingham Press, 2013.

Storey, Graham, Kathleen Tillotson, and Nina Burgis, eds. *The Letters of Charles Dickens, 1850–1852*. Vol 7. Oxford: Clarendon Press, 1988.
Sucksmith, Harvey Peter. *The Narrative Art of Charles Dickens: The Rhetoric of Sympathy and Irony in His Novels*. Oxford: Clarendon Press, 1970.
Torday, John. "Homeostasis as the Mechanism of Evolution." *Biology* 4, no. 3 (2015): 573–90. www.ncbi.nlm.nih.gov/pmc/articles/PMC4588151/pdf/biology-04-00573.pdf.
Varghese, Roy Abraham, ed. *The Missing Link: A Symposium on Darwin's Framework for a Creation-Evolution Solution*. Plymouth, UK: University Press of America, 2013.

13 Theology of the Street
Dickensian Characters for the Twenty-First Century

Sarah E. Maier

> Cheap Literature is not behind-hand with the Age, but hold its place, and strives to do its duty. I trust the series in itself may help much worthy company to show.
> Charles Dickens, Preface to *The Pickwick Papers* (1986 [1837], xii)

Perhaps no one novelist is read with as much nostalgia as Charles Dickens; he has his own wistful nickname—the Inimitable. If a kind of prophet of the people, then Dickens' writings give us insight into his theological position in relation to the many creeds of Victorian culture. In *The Pickwick Papers*, there is a telling discussion between Same Weller and Mr. Weller:

> "I know'd a 'ostler o' that name," said Mr. Weller, musing.
> "It warn't him," said Sam. "This here gen'lm'n was a prophet."
> "Wot's a prophet?" inquired Mr. Weller, looking sternly on his son.
> "Wy, a man as tells what's a goin' to happen," replied Sam.
> "I wish I'd know'd him, Sammy," said Mr. Weller. "P'raps he might ha' throw'd a small light on that. . . ." (361)

Dickens seeks to throw some light on the plight of the common people—the vastly overcrowded, forgotten communities of characters—where he believes the divine is found in the kindness of the everyday. Dickens does not believe the dogma put forward by the Anglican Church, Anglo-Catholics, Evangelicals, or the shaming techniques of the Sabbatarian or Temperance movements, to be of any use to the downtrodden. To that end, it seems inevitable that his views on family, women, children, criminality, usury, and justice that abound in the *Dickensian* (2015–2016) reflect both the contextual views of Victorian time and our postmodern, neo-Victorian relation to the characters—like Oliver Twist, Fagin, the Barbary and Cratchit families, the Bumbles, Little Nell, Jaggers, and Miss Havisham—who intermingle in one street under the watchful eyes of Inspector Bucket as they reflect to us

DOI: 10.4324/9781003156611-14

the theological and ethical questions of the Victorian past and neo-Victorian present.

At a time of yearly spiritual reflection, it is fitting that on the day after Christmas in 2015, and running until February 21, 2016, the *Dickensian*—created by Tony Jordan for Red Planet Pictures/Netflix—aired to mixed reviews and confusion as to whether a viewer had to "know" Dickens or his works to understand the show. The question under consideration here is two-fold: first, what theology exists on the streets of Dickens' world, especially if the characters represent such a vast array of persons; and second, what part of that theology—a theology of the street—is then reflected on to the post-modern, neo-Victorian viewer? *Dickensian* is, in itself, created as a collection of fragmented stories recombined for the modern viewer. Critical to the series is the revelation of inherent need for individuals to act upon the theological virtues—"And now abide faith, hope, love, these three; but the greatest of these is love"[1]—found in Corinthians 13:13. Dickens' theology of the street is to love one's neighbor and, as such, is exemplified on *Dickensian*.

Dickensian is a neo-Victorian work that cannot be merely dismissed as "mimicry or pastiche" (Heilmann and Llewellyn 2010, 27) especially since Marie-Luise Kohlke encourages the reader/viewer to see such pieces as "suitably elastic" (2014, 27). The producer, David Boulter, says it is a "reimagining of the world of Dickens" ("101," 00:12), an "alternative view of the nineteenth century for the modern audience" (Heilmann and Llewellyn 7), and Jordan is clear that the "Richness of *Dickensian* is founded in the richness of Dickens" (extra "101,"56), including his ideas on theological questions. Jordan articulates his desire to "take all of Dickens' iconic characters, build a world, a Dickens world, and put the characters in and mix them all and mix all the stories up" ("101," 16) to show his admiration for Dickens' imaginative creations without a straightforward adaptation which lean toward the academic. The intent of his creation of *Dickensian* was to give a "authentic" and "truthful" Dickens back to a popular audience (01:24). Mark Stanley, the actor who plays Bill Sikes, describes the excitement of a show with "very well known, often iconic, characters placed into circumstances and situations that aren't necessarily always following your typical plotline that Dickens wrote" (25); without question, there is clearly a sense of reverence in this production for the man and for his views on the importance of the theological virtues as they are embodied on the street in *Dickensian*.

Any neo-Victorian "critique [is] of the less admirable Victorian values and practices—those attitudes, institutions or social conditions commonly described as 'Dickensian'" but more often than not, "Dickens seems to hover over the neo-Victorian like an avuncular but reticent deity" (Kaplan 2011, 81). It is in the everyday where he finds the godly; it is on the street where people interact with other people and should invest in the improvement of the common good. These many afterlives of Dickens' characters people "the archontic (the continual archival expanding) of cultural memory" of what it means to be Dickensian (England 2020, 313). To be Dickensian is, of course, to be lesser than or derivative of Dickens; the very definition is clear on that point. The educated, serious creation of the mid-nineteenth century world and its codes of behavior in the *Dickensian* not only clearly demonstrates all these factors but also exemplifies a neo-Victorian stance in relation to many of the issues of the day including the moral obligation to care for the social welfare of the less fortunate, and crucially, on the questions of virtue and sin.

Transmedia serial representations are "the Victorian novel's legitimate heir, carrying on its traditions of realist and reformist social understanding, borrowing its strategies, and even learning from it modes of circulation" (Caroline Levine 2013 para. 4). In addition, they present a kind of "macrorealism" that by revealing "the depth of social interconnectedness" through which Dickens' novels such as *Bleak House* (1853), "and its heirs," in the modern age use engage the moral imagination, as well as "the webs of causality and responsibility that render all of us complicit" (Maynes-Aminzade 2013, para. 25). Here, the investigation lies on just how such a presentation represents Dickens' views on theological questions. Ann Heilmann and Mark Llewellyn have pointed out, "it is a long-standing trope that Dickens equates to the Victorian and that much of the mainstream public perception of the nineteenth century is, in fact, rooted in a Dickensian sense of the period" (214), and that an author/creator of a show like *Dickensian* might "collude with readers" who already know what will happen to the characters that we are reading (15) but might be struck by moral and ethical questions not quite as easily apparent in a lengthy novel. If the viewer already knows where the characters will end up from cultural memory, then the interactions between various characters or the implications of their actions can be the focus of the narrative. In this case, the core question is how theological virtues inform our "reading" of the characters—both virtuous and sinful—as well as what neo-Victorian awareness can be brought to bear on that transmedial depiction.

The characters chosen to be illustrative of the spectrum of morality and/or ethical reasoning are a conglomeration of characters from *Oliver Twist* ([2000] 1838), *The Old Curiosity Shop* (1841), *A Christmas Carol* (1845 [1843]), *Bleak House* (1853), and *Great Expectations* (1861) as well as a few characters from seven other of Dickens' novels, to create "referential rather than reverential" (England 315) prequels to the stories found in Dickens' novels. Just as London becomes a character of sorts—or many characters—in Dickens' novels, here the character of the street itself is created by its people. The streetscape reflects the spaces and graces of the people who live there. It is in their successes and failures, or in their potentialities, that a theology of the street becomes clear as a reflection of Dickens' social gospel. In *The Life of Our Lord* (1999

[1934]) written for his children, Dickens makes clear that the Apostles are of the people:

> He chose them from among poor men, in order that the poor might know—always after that in all years to come—that Heaven was made for them as well as for the rich, and that God makes no difference between those who wear good clothes and those who go barefoot and in rags. The most miserable, the most ugly, deformed, wretched creatures that live will be bright Angels in Heaven if they are good here on earth, Never forget this when you are grown up. Never be proud or unkind, my dears, to any poor man, woman or child.
> (28)

Further, these actions of positive interaction are to be ongoing because "you may always do good, no matter what the day is" (38).

Dickensian makes possible this same microcosm of social interaction wherein the characters interact in one neighborhood bounded at one end by Satis House and the other by The Three Cripples. The street is lined with the Old Curiosity Shop, Mantalini's, Scrooge and Marley's Office, and the Cratchit home. Offshoot streets and alleys provide the taxidermy space of Mr. Venus, the offices of Mr. Jaggers, the home of Barbarys, the workhouse where the Bumbles reside, the lair of Fagin's crew, and the police station out of which Inspector Bucket works. The social hierarchy of the spaces runs from upper class mansion to dockyard slum; as a result, the people vary in class, gender, race, and creed, but one consistent thread justifies having them all together: they are a wide spectrum of humanity who represent or defy conventional expectations seen through their expression of the theological virtues in their actions.

On this Dickensian street, Jacob Marley sadistically walks this street; Miss Amelia Havisham inherits a business, Merriweather Compeyson wreaks havoc, Peter Cratchit is sweet on Little Nell Trent, Honoria Barbary suffers greatly, and Bill Sikes saves Nancy from Fagin.

This multifaceted street is where the characters bump against each other, interact cautiously, and share moments; it is also a shared space to consider the morality of individuals and the stories now brought together, to see whether there is a lesson to be learned from how well they do or do not adhere to the Golden Rule: "For all the law is fulfilled in one word, even in this; Thou shalt love thy neighbour as thyself" (Gal 5:14), or as expressed by the Apostle Paul,

> Owe no man any thing, but to love one another: for he that loveth another hath fulfilled the law. For this, Thou shalt not commit adultery, Thou shalt not kill, Thou shalt not steal, Thou shalt not bear false witness, Thou shalt not covet; and if there be any other commandment, it is briefly comprehended in this saying, namely, Thou

shalt love thy neighbour as thyself. Love worketh no ill to his neighbour: therefore love is the fulfilling of the law.

(Rom 13:8–10)

In *Bleak House*, the narrator asks, "What connexion can there have been between many people in the innumerable histories of this world, who, from opposite sides of great gulfs, have, nevertheless, been very curiously brought together?" (Dickens 1853, 156). *Dickensian* shows us these very connections with characters who have been curiously brought together on a common street. The viewer sees a collective with "unity ... provided by the camera movements that, like an omniscient narrator glide from one set of characters to another" (Parey 2017, para. 15) to create a sense of a shared charitable community of neighbors.

Writing to Reverend R. H. Davies on December 24, 1856, Dickens is clear that he has a "veneration for the New Testament" not based on "obtrusive professions of and tradings in religion" but on "real Christianity" that avoids "squabbles about the letter which drive the spirit out of hundreds of thousands" (Hartley 2012, 315). Dickens advocates for a "practical Christianity grounded in the sublime simplicity of the New Testament versus mere professions of religion and the audacious interposition of vain and ignorant men" (315). These theological leanings are articulated as a novelist within the elements of his medium; according to Dennis Walder, they are "rarely explicit, they are embodied in the texture of his work" (1981, 3) including his characters and their circumstances.

The Irish author George Moore (1852–1933) believed Dickens was a "true Christian without great profession" (quoted in Collins 1981, 2:320); in other words, Dickens was keenly non-dogmatic. More recent critics see Dickens' theological leanings as non-doctrinal but part of the Church of England's Broad-Church movement; as such, he placed greatest emphasis on the New Testament and where "Working to remedy social ills and caring for the needy were seen as the most important part of Christ's teaching and these were exactly the aspects emphasised in person and in the fiction by Dickens" (Smith 2008, 14).[2] Dickens' religious sentiments were very "broad church," even though the term was not in vogue at the time of his writing of novels prior to 1840[3]; however, he used the word "broad" in the epigraph he wrote in his will: "I commit my soul to the mercy of God through our Lord and Saviour Jesus Christ, and I exhort my dear children humbly to try to guide themselves by teaching of the New Testament in its *broad* spirit, and to put no faith in any man's narrow construction of its letter here or there" (quoted in Forster 1870, 301; emphasis added). Walder argues strongly that Dickens held that "Religious beliefs need not be abstract" if they are "to move our feelings" (16). More recently, Karl Ashley Smith is persuasive on the point that Dickens does not write tracts; therefore, "in dramatizing a dimension of religious experience, the author is not obliged to exemplify a theological truth naturalistically, but may rather provide images that make the reader feel the reality of it in other ways" (20).

In an 1861 letter to Reverend David Macrae, Dickens says of his theological exemplars—his characters—that "all my good people are humble, charitable, faithful, and forgiving" (Storey 1997, 9.556). *Dickensian*, following Dickens, makes the viewer feel the reality of the characters and their world, not abstractly, but in a series of considerations of the characters' characters and the dilemmas in which they find themselves. Gary Colledge admits that while these virtues are not the whole of "real Christianity" (2012, 118), they certainly are key to Dickens' social gospel. The storylines and characters of *Dickensian* demonstrate that they are exactly the virtues that measure the population of the street. Be it Scrooge, Mr. Venus, Inspector Bucket, or Mrs. Cratchit, the theological virtues of faith, hope, and love are applied to all with characters who are then found to be righteous or wanting. Even the streetscape of *Dickensian* shows a kind of deterministic frame, a "conjuring of an organic chain, within which all living things are set" (Cerutti 2000, 45). The setting demonstrates just how Dickens was "interested in human welfare more than in transcendental doctrines" as well as how his "fiction is pervaded by a profound human compassion and an enlightened social dimension" (46) in the "ethics of his imaginary world" (47).

In the reality of *Dickensian*, the paradigm of these virtues is the Cratchit family. Central to Dickens' theological example is the concept of family, whether given or denied by birth or, alternatively, a family of choice. The Cratchits are located in the middle of the street, a kind of locus of stability that counters the extremes of the individuals who spend time together at the public house and the well-off family, the Havishams, of the street's far end. In *A Christmas Carol*, the poverty of the Cratchits is emblematic of the graceful poor, those individuals for whom Dickens, according to George Levine, "attempts to imagine a place for decency and love in a world that promises no rewards for them" (2009, 16). Father of six with a young son-in-law who joins them, Bob Cratchit works hard for unkind men who withhold both money and support at every opportunity. Virtuous in every way, he happily provides for his family even if it means going to the street fair to scrounge after it has closed to see if any fruit or nuts have been left behind (ep. 1, 27:36) to supplement their meager but joyous Christmas dinner. Mrs. Cratchit bakes meat pies for sale at The Three Cripples and their eldest daughter works alongside Honoria at Mantalini's. The family is rewarded with the happy marriage of the next generation and they all congregate in gratitude at the Church, bells ringing, to witness the exchange of vows (ep. 5, 26:20). Camera shots through dusty windows of the family home often reveal love and caring within the family unit.

The Cratchits are significant to the neo-Victorian narrative to show the positive effects of the mobilization of the virtues. According to Karen

Hansen, *A Christmas Carol* is a "hypotext of a neo-Victorianism characterised by a nostalgia for—and sometimes fetishisation of—an *imagined* Victorian/ Dickensian past, a past that can best be seen in the cosy family" (2011, 185–86) of the Cratchits as an exemplar of comfort and security. In addition, the sensitive relationship between kindly "Bob and the tough and protective Mrs. Cratchit represents a subtle shift in domestic norms" (Hansen 176). One such moment where we see the kindness and understanding between the *Dickensian* Cratchits is when she takes the gift of a necklace and repays the debt it incurred so the family would not be beholden to Scrooge. Dickens' family structure "reinforces and contributes to the cult of domesticity, but—although often covertly—also alters that representation" (Ayres 1998, 6). The Cratchits believe that their children will benefit from the example from their hard work just as Dickens thought that "Whilst denying the necessity of expiation for original sin, Dickens uses work as a sign of inner worth" (Oulton 2003, 31). Their children are "a daily blessing" (ep. 5, 27:02). The goodness of the individual is crucial in *Dickensian* when Mrs. Cratchit stoically withholds her personal trauma as a victim of attempted rape and her subsequent murder of Marley. Rather than being peripheral to the story of Scrooge and Marley, in *Dickensian* the Cratchits here remind the modern viewer that happiness was possible even among the poor if they dealt with each other as set out by the theological virtues, particularly faithfulness, each unto the others, like for Tiny Tim who is the receiver of much compassion from others like care from Mrs. Gamp and a crutch from Mr. Venus when they realize the Cratchits need help.

Although Dickens was generally a New Testament man, the fourth commandment "Thou shalt not steal" (Ex 20:15) is only one of several commandments broken in his works and it is embodied by Fagin, his criminal family's children, and by the men Marley and Scrooge. Any reader of Dickens knows that he is not above "moralizing of money matters"; certainly, money is "the key emblem of that corrupt and depressing secularity that Dickens describes so powerfully and with a quite awful grasp of living detail. It is the circulating material that makes for moral decay" (George Levine 27). *A Christmas Carol* begins with Marley seven years dead and Scrooge is described as "a squeezing, wrenching, grasping, scraping, clutching, covetous, old sinner! Hard and sharp as flint" who thrives in "secret, and self-contained, and solitary as an oyster" (stv. 1); the neo-Victorian series seeks to fill in the backstory for these men to understand what leads to Marley's death and to Scrooge's miserly personality. Marley preys upon Nancy, beating her as he uses her, and denies dignity in his avarice to those like Little Nell's grandfather when they must beg for more time to pay while Scrooge is nearly an automaton in his inability to see beyond himself, misanthropically retorting "Hum bug" (ep. 20, 43:56) against any proffer of inclusion by his neighbors.

Theology of the Street 253

While the Victorian underworld of thievery and stolen goods, prostitution and muscle-for-hire is represented by Fagin and Bill Sikes, it is the socially legitimate—but callous—businessmen, Marley and Scrooge, who are less forgiving in their demands of repayment. Dickens has "nothing against Scrooge's being rich It's not whether you have it; it's not even how you get it, exactly: the post-ghost Scrooge, for instance, doesn't give up his business. . . . No, it's what you do with your riches that really counts" (Atwood 2008, 98–99). Neither Marley nor Scrooge participate in any way willingly in the community but prey upon their needs, reminding the reader of the warning, "In thee have they taken gifts to shed blood; thou hast taken usury and increase, and thou hast greedily gained of thy neighbours by extortion, and hast forgotten me, saith the Lord GOD" (Ez 22:12).

Even Scrooge sees the depravity of his partner because the *Dickensian* Marley is sadistic and cruel, a man who attacks women and disdains all. Here, "what the contemporary text does is to 'speak' the unspeakable of the pre-text by very exactly invoking the original and hinting at its silences or fabrications" which then sets the *Dickensian* as a "recast . . . itself a 'new' text to be read newly" (Widdowson 2006, 503–504) about Scrooge's partner. Marley is the exemplar of a man of means who has turned away from the theological virtues in his lust for sexual and monetary gratification warned against where "Thefts, covetousness, wickedness, deceit, lasciviousness, an evil eye, blasphemy, pride, foolishness: All these evil things come from within, and defile the man" (Mk 7:22–23). Marley embodies most of the seven deadly sins without a single virtue. At the end of the series, when Scrooge hears Marley's voice and chains, the viewer wonders what such a material man might have to "teach" Scrooge in his spectral form that he did not embody in life versus the compassion professed by Dickens' ghostly Marley.

The importance of the consideration of money, and its relation to righteous virtue, is two-fold: First, it is clear that to the monetary discrepancy between the have and have-nots on the street is massive. The Havisham fortune could, in itself, provide for the inhabitants of the street. Second, the extensive fiscal dealings—be it by Marley and Scrooge or Fagin, raise the issue whether "Taking money literally, as a good and an end in itself, leads to the literal commodification of human beings" (Poovey 1995, 166). On this question, the juxtaposition of Dickens' texts on the street shows it is imperative, according to Jesus in the parable of the Good Samaritan, to "Be compassionate to all men. For all men are your neighbours and brothers" (Dickens 1934, 69). Class is irrelevant where money is exchanged for human beings, be it Honoria in exchange for title and money for the Barbary family or Nancy's body and the orphan children's unpaid criminal labor for Fagin; on all cases, it is against the biblical word and to act against another is to fail in both love and faithfulness to a fellow human being.

Perhaps if the Church and the workhouse provided as they should for the poor and the abandoned, then such exchanges might not occur. If faith can be seen in good works, then an interesting contrast occurs in the series between the purposes of the non-involved church on the street and the active, involved community in the pub. Dickens has a well-known lack of faith in churchmen, exposing their hypocrisies on many occasions. The hypocrisy of those persons who profess, but do not necessarily practice, religion and/or Christian principles like the Bumbles are, in *Oliver Twist*, "nominally, not authentically, religious" (Na 2018, 137) become ludicrous in *Dickensian*. In an alteration to the original text, Mrs. Bumble is present and has been married to Mr. Bumble for a fair length of time; her benevolence is questionable. She harangues Mr. Bumble— "act Bumble!" to "Win the Board. Raise us up—gain the position we deserve" (ep. 6, 10:15)—so that she might have a new house and a maid. The children must be deloused and washed after having corrections screamed at them by Mrs. Bumble when they misspeak the Lord's Prayer or when she laments the hard work it will take to "mould those wretched children into young adults ready to take their place in society" (ep. 11, 19:40). Street children must be educated into a higher place in society, and Dickens felt strongly this endeavor should be undertaken by the workhouse and the ragged Schools which were, like at the Bumbles, children "too ragged, wretched, filthy, and forlorn, to enter any place" need somewhere to "find some people not depraved, willing to teach them something, and show them some sympathy."[4] The Bumbles are oblivious to the hardships and abuses of the children's previous lives on the street. Rather than tend to their pupils' needs and teach them that hard work is virtuous, they put on a show for the Board. The food is embellished with dumplings which are not the usual fare for the children, the house is reappointed with paint and a founder's portrait while a new too-small, button-popping suit is bought for the gluttonous Bumble, and new china are intended to reimagine Mrs. Bumble's gentility. None of these changes involve a sense of love or charity toward the children, or compassion for their circumstances; they certainly are not indicative of any understanding of theological virtue but act as a counter-example full of hypocrisy.

Ironically, rather than virtue, Mrs. Bumble exudes potential vice including various titillating comments to ensure Bumble's cooperation and to tempt Superintendent Gradgrind (originally from *Hard Times*) to their social-climbing cause. When Bumble suggests that, no matter what occurs, his wife will find her reward in heaven, she replies, "I have no intention of waiting that long" (ep. 20, 02:40). In another moment exemplary of a false shepherd, Reverend Chadband visits Dodger in jail, ostensibly bringing a Bible to comfort him; however, one assumes Dodger cannot read. The viewer realizes that it is not the intention; with the Bible, the Reverend includes a match so that the word of God can be sacrificed in fire to facilitate escape, both for Dodger from jail and the Reverend from the public exposure (promised by Nancy and Sikes) of his physical use of Nancy (ep. 14, 17:20).

The *Dickensian* evokes the author's fondness for authentic social interaction that encompasses a sense of community and social responsibility over religious guilt or performance, over conventional ideas of social hierarchies, and over the places where these gatherings should occur. Although the series opens with Havisham's well-appointed funeral procession, it does not proceed from the church but outside their home; on another occasion, only Barbary with Frances, the Bumbles, Mathew Pocket with Miss Havisham, and Bucket emerge from the church after a Sunday service (ep. 8, 04:00). The small, subdued post-church crowd is juxtaposed with how the pub is a gathering place without judgment of the people of the street proving that the mid-Victorian "public house [was of] vital importance as a social centre" (Schlicke 1988, 4). While not particularly a place equated with love, hope, or charity, The Three Cripples is such a place for family of choice. Most characters at one point or another move through the pub, from upper-class Arthur Havisham, the confidence man Compeyson, as well as all the usual suspects, both literally and figuratively. Mrs. Cratchit makes meat pies for the pub which catch the fond attention of Inspector Bucket while Wegg's infected leg is nursed by Mrs. Gamp, as her "Christian duty" to look after him in exchange for gin and his companionship (ep. 9, 11:19) which she often shares in the camaraderie of Biggelywitch and the Bumbles as they commiserate over their plights. In another show of compassion, Mrs. Gamp visits a sickly Little Nell because she believes "There's something circular in it all. I seen little Nelly into this world, and so I am disposed to see her out again" (ep. 1, 01:08:15). Without money to give, the characters rely on each upon the other's care and loyalty to keep them sheltered from life's cruelties.

Cerutti points out that "the Christian precept 'love your neighbour' is practised by amiable good-living people, who may happen to be good Christians. For Dickens, solidarity is rooted in natural sentiment rather than in religious practice" (50). In two particularly moving scenes which allow the viewer to witness the sentimentality of several characters, Nancy sings for the crowd in one and, another time, for Sikes. Bucket joins with his baritone voice in church because it is "good for the soul, singing, don't you find?" (ep. 8, 05:30), a parallel with Nancy's higher voice raised across the street in the pub (ep. 20, 27:30) between gathering places seemingly supports Dickens believe in non-Sabbatarian restrictions[5] given joy and love can be found of a day in the neighborhood pub among friends.

Dickens "refused overtly to target one faith system in his novels, aware that his audience comprised a diversity of believers (Christian and Jew)" (Mason 2011, 320); there has been a great deal of discussion of his anti-Semitic caricatures in his novels.[6] Dickens' advocation of kindness to all sometimes fails in his treatment of historically othered persons as in his anti-Semitic portrait of Fagin as "The Jew." *Dickensian* makes inclusive moves regarding race—Little Nell is biracial, and Mr. Venus is Iranian, and Dodger is South Asian—and all three exemplify concern for their neighbours or compatriots. The portrait of Fagin is still within the construction of Dickens' criminality but not necessarily tied to his Jewishness symbolized only by his head covering. Fagin's backstory, too, is reconsidered. Known in *Oliver Twist* as a criminal fence who runs a gang of pickpockets, scares children, and gets Nancy killed by Sikes; here, *Dickensian* implies that Fagin has, perhaps, come down in life and has created his criminal family in the slum of the docks as a means of survival for all of them even if his self-interest remains paramount. Dickens' novels contain criminal behavior, lawyers, and in/justice through the legal courts and, like other fiction writers, he emphasizes "the idea of child criminality and images of children as victims when left to the mercies of the streets or of strangers posing as surrogate family pervade representations of crime" (Vlasopolos 2011, 300). Dickens makes clear that in order to succeed in life, these children need to be given an education and he supported heartily the "principle of reforming education of the poor rather than blaming them for their condition" (Oulton 168). In some ways, the *Dickensian* lost boys of Fagin's gang are taught self-worth; when one boy comes back saying that a man who "calls himself a gentleman [Marley]" but only paid a farthing, Fagin tells him, "insist upon a penny" (ep. 1, 03:16) and then gives him food. Dodger is embraced as Fagin's right hand and "very best boy" (ep. 20, 33:28) when he returns to the family. Nancy, in particular, challenges his miserly ways with "You're an old rogue Fagin, but there's a heart in there somewhere, I know there is" to which he says, "Well, keep it to yourself my dear. A hear is very bad for business" (ep. 20, 09:54). He sees Nancy as "the daughter I never had" (15.19:48); those whom he holds to his heart are, to a certain extent, his family and his responsibility. Nancy tells him, "you're the nearest thing I've had to a parent, so, I want to say thank you" (ep. 16, 21:00) in gratitude and constancy.

Although orphans abound in Victorian novels, Dickens has a particular fondness for the pitiful, discarded children who live on the street, creating portraits of them in *Great Expectations, David Copperfield* (1850)*, Oliver Twist,* and others. Perhaps, in *Dickensian* too, it is a salient point that "at the core of Dickens's Christian humanism is a child" (Cunningham 2008, 265) and that Dickens makes "us think better than society customarily does of moral outsiders—by getting them to show a saving kindness to little ones" (266). His narratives express concern for how unprotected children are, particularly poor children, "at the lack of mercy and charity" (Walker 53) of society unless they are within a family unit like the Cratchits or as brought into a family unit by choice.

While the objectivity of the law sees no need for compassion, Bucket expresses the simplicity of the golden rule. Bucket stands in for Dickens'; they seemingly share the belief that "at the last, acts of individual love, sympathy and goodwill may provide for the suffering poor, if not the thoroughly wicked, and that it is the duty of good Christians to carry out such acts" (Walder 44). In *Nicholas Nickleby*, Dickens defines charity as, in fact, the greatest "cardinal virtue, which, properly nourished and exercised, leads to . . . all the others" (1839, 161).

In ugly contrast, one of the most provocative ideas in *Dickensian* is that Fagin's criminality extends to the trafficking of children. Like Dickens, Bucket uses common sense to express his extreme disgust at the very idea of shipping starving children across the world but Jaggers reminds him "It is entirely within the law" (ep. 12, 17:42), a horror not lost on the twenty-first-century audience. Robert Newsom argues that the good, for Dickens, is "not, very clearly, in religious or moral thought, but rather in immediately and self-evidently useful actions" (2000 n.p.) like when Bucket takes immediate action to comfort one child. His instant belief us reminiscent of Luke 10:29: that it is up to virtuous individuals to care for those who "fell among thieves" and to provide, where "there is little to be hoped for from public charity, at least . . . signs of private sympathy and aid" (Walder 56). In the very last scene of the series, a young boy is discovered in the warehouse who captivates the childless Bucket and is later revealed to be Oliver, cast out on to the street by the Bumbles and found by Dodger who takes him into the warmth of the pub as he speaks to him of Fagin. Where public institutions fail, children of the street become prey.

Aside from the need for charity to children, in *Dickensian* in the portraits of the street's inhabitants and misused persons includes a prostitute, a fallen woman, a jilted woman, and a closeted queer man, all of whom suffer in some way from a lack of charity from their neighbors. Dickens' books are replete with conversations and evocative descriptions of social conventions that repress rather than seek to reform; in like manner, the series confronts double standards of social condemnation.

Nancy is between a child and a woman—child by age and woman by trade—whose heart is full of charity, and she acts with kindness; for example, she refuses to hear any denigration of Fagin and remembers he saved her from starvation. Dickens did not condemn such a woman as fallen beyond charity; it is well-documented that Dickens worked tirelessly with philanthropist Miss Angela Burdett-Coutts for over a decade and established Urania Cottage, a home for prostitutes and destitute women who sought change through service or emigration. *Dickensian* reminds us that she, too, is an orphan taken in by Fagin, but here, they have a relationship aside from an exploitive one. She comments to Sikes that she owes Fagin her life, but that does not mean Nancy is without hope for a life of her own. Even Bill still aspires to be "the best cracksman in London" (ep. 6, 17:30) and to be with Nancy if he can raise the 50 pounds Fagin demands. Fagin has played a pivotal part in Nancy's emotional life. When Nancy tells him that she wants to live with Sikes, he is saddened by the change, asking if this is what she really wants. Fagin desperately warns her of Sikes' temper and reminds her it's not the same if she is down the road but that she "always has a home to come back to" (ep. 20, 42.15) where they "take care of each other because no one will do it for us" (32:30). The viewer now wonders if the 50-pound marker was set because it was thought to be out of reach rather than as exchange value. The interaction between Nancy and Fagin shows his concern because he believes her to deserve better but warns her to be careful with Bill's temper. This prehistory leaves out any preconception of Sikes' as his character is informed by his murder of Nancy in *Oliver Twist*. Here, always acting as her protector, Sikes cleans up for Nancy with soap and a shave, then "like a proper gent" (ep. 7, 06:00) brings her flowers and a picnic. Eventually, Sikes quite cleverly buys out Nancy's future with Fagin's own money because he cares for her as "a good girl" (ep. 9, 23:50) in spite of her profession and addresses her as "my Nancy" (24:05). Cynicism and our foreknowledge of Sikes cries out for a reading of his behavior as possessive; within the context of Dickens' theological values of the street, he promises her his love and faithfulness as an alternative to a life where she is sent out to any man who will pay, like the abusive Marley, at Fagin's behest. Nancy, talking to Bucket, is clear that she cares for Bill and that "although the men buy the time, they don't buy me" (ep. 9, 14:00). Bucket finds her a contradiction (13:48) and promises, unlike many mid-Victorian men, to "listen without judgement" (11:55) to her life story of sleeping rough outside before Fagin and true hunger. He asks her "What about love?" (15:53), but Nancy is clear that those are "just the words you get in fairy tales ... love don't put food in your belly" so there will be no such ending for her. (16:15).

Dickens believed that to "embrace and not reject the magdalen is to raise the fallen" (Cunningham 274). On more than one occasion, Dickens shows empathy for Nancy, as does the series, particularly in the opening episode where she sees a beautiful doll in a shop window that also reflects her own image which emphasizes her youth and loveliness (ep. 1, 21:49). Although her innocence has been robbed from her, Nancy's child-like wonder remains even while she recognizes the doll will never be for her. Perhaps one day it will be for a child of her own. The vindication of Nancy's character as a soul of goodness is clear when, through helping Bucket, she demonstrates Dickens' belief of "offering Christian charity" and in "exposing the difference between the more hopeful and optimistic form of Christianity he believes in" versus the "evangelical stress upon the innate depravity of sinners which calls down retribution on their heads" (Walder 59).[7]

The middle-to-upper classes are equally victimized by those who cease to follow the theological virtues and positive social action. Frances and Honoria Barbery in *Bleak House* are loving sisters. The elder sister, Frances, is full of guilt, feeling that she has let down the family, and she suffers for it because she knows she has failed the family. In the past, her fiancé left her, but she has been blamed by her family and their social circle as the guilty party who refused to marry and, because of her pride, refuses to admit the truth. Always under control, Frances' quiet moments are spent cross-stitching the text of "The Lord's Prayer" for a picture. She was left after her mother's early death to manage the household that included her extravagant sister and economically incompetent father. Her quiet strength is signified by the small gold cross she always wears. Recognized within the community as a woman of charity, Fagin comments when he passes her on the street, "May God smile on you, Christian lady" (ep. 5, 09:07), and she is considered a "good Christian lady" by Bucket (ep. 8, 17:40). Within the Barbery family, Frances is the only one who understands the social risks in their lack of virtue, as well as the toll it will have on their family name should their secrets be discovered. Honoria is beautiful, vivacious, fallen, and oblivious while their father owes massive debts held by Scrooge, including the house as collateral. The sisters must save the family. In *Dickensian*, Honoria comes to understand her familial responsibilities. She is aware, like Frances, that a sense of duty "is compelling as one's obligation to the community—the more immediate the better" (Newsom n.p.) but in *Bleak House*, Lady Dedlock's belief is that she has failed in her role as a wife in spite of Sir Leicester's forgiveness. She dies now barren, desolate, and alone reaching out to her once-lover's grave. Sadly, Lady Honoria Dedlock denies herself the theological virtues of hope and faithfulness she has so willingly extended to others.

Logan's portrait of not-yet Lady Dedlock—when she is still Honoria—is more tragic than even the fate of Miss Havisham. In love with a solider, Captain James Hawdon, both her father and sister emphatically disapprove of him as a suitable match based on his class and his character as a known gambler (ep. 9, 05:00). Reckless and defiant, Honoria becomes pregnant and is then forced to see that the love she desired was not without theological virtue but physical virtue is demanded by the strict social expectations of a proper young woman. Honoria gives premature birth with the help of Frances and a medical book to guide them. Terrifying for the sisters, the birth scene evokes Genesis 3:16, "Unto the woman he said, I will greatly multiply thy sorrow and thy conception; in sorrow thou shalt bring forth children." Frances demonstrates her Christian spirit in the love and compassion she has for her sister's pain and despair; Honoria finally grasps that "this is my ruin" (ep. 16, 24:40). When the girl-child, Esther Frances, appears to be stillborn, the effect on both the repressed Frances and the distraught Honoria is devastating. Afterwards Honoria tells Hawdon that the death is "a judgement on us" because now Esther is "a little girl in the dark" and "we are ghosts of the people we used to be" (ep. 17, 14:25). As in *Bleak House*, *Dickensian*'s Esther is alive; here, the child is found to be alive the next morning, but Frances makes the wrenching decision to not tell Honoria and to place the child with Jaggers for adoption. Seeking to protect and save her sister's reputation, Frances hopes to let Honoria move on.

Barbery is without concern for faith or spirituality; his materialism results in a lack of adherence to altruism or theological principles. In a repayment for Barbery's sinful pride and his envy of the riches of others, any attempts to keep Scrooge at bay—with money from ancestral items pawned at the Old Curiosity Shop and promises of merchandise that never arrives—fail. As the patriarch, Barbery moves without conscience to secure his family's good name and future with another trade: Honoria to Sir Leicester Deadlock. The traumatic experience has brought the sisters together in a recognition of family comfort; in his solipsism, their father lacks any comprehension or empathy because his only concern is for his business. The neo-Victorian conception of this arrangement as usurious is voiced by the younger sister who demands, at the very least, honesty about the exchange that is to occur (ep. 19, 06:36). This conception of how to form a family, while not based on desire is not disparaged as means to marriage because, as Newsom reminds, "Dickens's rather domestic conception of heaven—the goods of a kindly companionship: healing, teaching, loving. They can be summed up in one word (one of Dickens's favorites): 'comfort'" (n.p.). In *Dickensian*, although seemingly a ridiculous old man, Sir Leicester Dedlock is factually the embodiment of the theological virtues of love, hope, and faithfulness with a clear sense of devotion to provide domestic life of kindness and comfort for Honoria.

The jilted Miss Havisham suffers the lack of charity, hope, and faithfulness at the hands of the two men, her half-brother and her fiancé. One of the most captivating women in the Dickens' *oeuvre*, it is at least partly because the reader is left wondering why, as Claire O'Callaghan says, "we do not get [to] see how Miss Havisham 'became' Miss Havisham, so to speak" (2020, 84). Enmeshed but without a Christian name in Pip's story in the original text, there is little space for her own; neo-Victorian narratives, seek "to give voice to vanished or silent elements of the past" (Mitchell 2010, 123) including characters or authors theological positions. *Dickensian* bookends the series with the rise and fall of the now-named Amelia Havisham, upper-class heiress, at the hands of her covetous, illegitimate brother, Arthur, while Compeyson breaks her heart with his greed leading to her humiliation and alienation from social interaction. Amelia's naiveté is excruciating to watch as her virtuous character becomes entrapped by Havisham's self-hatred and Compeyson's manipulation. She is physically man-handled by her half-brother and seduced out of her chastity by the other's professions of love;[8] the two men's failure to provide love and faithfulness is punished in her half-brother's suicide but Compeyson escapes with his "thirty pieces of silver" (Logan ep. 20, 19:00).[9]

Logan does create a potential reason why Havisham believes he has been, for all intents and purposes, disinherited by his father from his assumed patrilineal assumption of position, money, and power; perhaps it is because of his difference as the bastard son of a cook, both of whom were in but not of the family because in *Great Expectations*, he is described "not as being so christened but as a surname. He was in a Decline, and was a shadow to look at" (379) and is jealous of his half-sister. It is strongly suggested in *Dickensian* that Havisham is homosexual; his effeminacy, his overwhelming sense of shame, and his fearful submission to the overtly male-dominant behavior of Compeyson all complicate his own sense of self-worth. Compeyson mocks and sinfully warns Havisham, asking "Why did your father stop loving you Arthur? Why? [pause with sneer and epiphany] Oh" (ep. 5, 03:08) and "I'm not the one who is desperate to gain back his dignity though, am I. Just remember: I know your secret" (ep. 8, 13:23) in a threat of social exposure.

No love, charity, or loyalty would save Havisham's upper-class social ruin. His queerness provides immediacy to his desperation; without the money he may have to enter into a heteronormative marriage to retain his position and his secrecy. Like his sister, Havisham is physically, emotionally, and financially abused by Compeyson; he is whipped (ep. 10, 27:53) until he, much later, enlists the brutality of Sikes to hold the abuser at bay (ep. 20, 15:20). Noticeably, Sikes is unmoved by the revelation he is asked to pass on. The trauma Havisham suffers makes clear that the viewer is to feel empathy as witness. The interaction between the two men is a homoerotic relationship of rivalry, triangulated around a woman—Amelia—which Holly Furneaux, following Eve Kosofsky Sedgewick (1985, 1990), identifies as the "violent break that modern culture imposes onto the homosocial continuum, so that male bonding is prescribed at the expense of male homosexuality, which must be aggressively repudiated" (2007, 158) and points out how "Sedgewick's most extended readings of Dickens conflate male-male desire with brutal attacks, perceiving positive representations of intimacy between men as 'much less tinged with the sexual' than the male-male bonds expressed through persecution and murder" (Furneaux 2007, 158n12). The neo-Victorian perspective makes clear that the persecution of Havisham for his sexuality should be uncomfortable even while it may demonstrate a conservative nineteenth-century that lacked acceptance of non-heteronormative sexualities.

It is not until Jaggers, the family lawyer, tells Havisham his father wished him to be a self-made man that Havisham gains a sense of confidence try for a questionable if reaffirmed allegiance with his sister to regain his family. Betrayed, Amelia Havisham refuses her brother, repaying his deceitfulness with coldness, and his suicidal thoughts return when he is permanently cast out of Satis House, now knowing what it is to be poor and alone. Havisham's death fall from a building's rooftop to the muck of the street does reaffirm William Howitt's contemporary declaration that Dickens advocated "no party or prejudices, but treated human interests as they belonged to man and not to classes" (quoted in NA 132).[10] Havisham and Compeyson, like Marley, are men without any of the theological virtues, without a sense of community, and without compassion, all theological failures on all counts.[11]

Mr. Venus from *Our Mutual Friend* is on the right side of justice; a taxidermist by trade, in *Dickensian* he acts as a second and as a moral compass for Inspector Bucket. He is engaged by Bucket to "read" clues in a learned, if not yet forensically scientific, manner and he is respectful of the new profession and Bucket's methods. Together, they work through difficulties in burgeoning forensics as well as ethical questions of interest. In *Bleak House*, Bucket "is fully enmeshed in familial and social relations of all kinds and achieves his extraordinary knowledge by dint of labor and experience" (Yousef 2009, 62); part of that experience teaches him that sometimes justice is best met by a righteous exchange. The improvement needed in ragged schools was not only an important cause in Dickens' sense of charity but is also linked to his hope for the poor and the disenfranchised. When Bucket discovers that Wegg has lifted brandy from a shipment, rather than send him to a magistrate, Bucket informs Wegg that a donation, rather than the law, will do; he says "You can make a donation to the local ragged school. About the same amount as a crate of Brandy" an exchange of "like for like" (ep. 8, 02:45) where a non-violent offence based on a vice is met with an act of social good through theology of the street where the charitable benefit is given to those closest to home.

Inspector Bucket, in *Dickensian*, embraces the creation of the "Detective" and his position as the first of his kind which means he must, in part, define the role as one of persecution or one of compassionate understanding. With the new method of criminal investigation, Bucket feels strongly that he will find the criminal "devil in the details" (ep. 17, 11 30). As the first Inspector of the Detective, he knows there is a burden he—not the abstraction of the law—carries to be correct. In one telling discussion, Venus and Bucket discuss the evidence of Marley's murder. There are a great many potential suspects given the inhumanity of Marley. As he closes in on a particular subject, Bucket ponders an ethical and moral question of the killer being ordinary:

VENUS: "An honest killer?"
BUCKET: "Jacob Marley was by all reports a bad man. His killer could well be a good one."

(ep. 6, 15:55)

Then later, in a conversation with Mr. Venus, they discuss his confusion; Bucket admits he knows who Marley's killer is, but "Suffice to say discovering their identity has brought me no pleasure. None at all." while the "the new Detective has been an unqualified success" he fears " 'justice may well not be best served" as he acknowledges, "I am neither judge nor jury. I am simply an instrument of the law" (ep. 18, 20:20). Unhappily, Bucket arrests Mrs. Cratchit and casts her among the criminals who wait at the station and as he watches, he sees the loss to her family and community if he equates her necessary action with their crimes. Bucket sees his eventual action—to allow a different, violent, five-time murderer to hang for Marley's murder and to allow Mrs. Cratchit to live free—as a chance to rectify the indifference of a system and serve the people of the street directly by his active participation in the lives of others as a force for good as well as with a progressive understanding of self-defence (07:44) by a victim escaping her own imminent rape and murder.

Dickens' idea of "authentic religion hinges on the central idea of choice-making" (Na 128) but it is rarely found in church nor is it exemplified in clergymen; rather than "the study of theology or adherence to forms; religion for him is embedded in the characters' choices at every moment of every day" (132) because choice is what determines character.[12] In *Dickensian*, Inspector Bucket must make the biggest choice with the largest theological implications when he discovers the identity of the person who killed Marley. Dickens knows there is rarely an ease of identification of a criminal; while certain people may stereotypically appear to be of a criminal disposition, he understands that "the all-inclusiveness of his imaginary world incorporates ambiguities and contradictions as fundamental notions in his fictive construction" (Cerutti 63). For the virtuous Inspector Bucket, who works the street and cares for its people, is content in that the "rewards of religion are replaced with a sense of moral satisfaction and inner peace" (Taft 2015, 661).

Notes

1. All biblical citations in this chapter are from the King James Bible, which would have been the version familiar to Dickens.
2. Aside from Dennis Walder (1981), see Humphrey House (1942), Jennifer Gribble (2018) and Janet Larson (1985).
3. Benjamin Jowett, Master of Balliol, heard it from poet Arthur Hugh Clough in 1848 ("Broad" 2021).
4. Dickens letter to *Daily News*, February 4, 1846.
5. Dickens was staunchly against the restriction of activities on Sundays, arguing that the seventh day was often the only day the poor had for any recreational activities.
6. See Katzir in this collection.
7. Other fallen women who are presented without judgment by Dickens are Alice Marwood in *Dombey and Son* (1848) and Emily and Martha in *David Copperfield*.

8. O'Callaghan is right to speak of the extensive gendered violence against and traumatization of Miss Havisham as witnessed by the *Dickensian* audience; misogyny, domestic abuse are reworked by Jordan to emphasize "these abject states and embellish—rather than critique—scenes of gendered violence" (86). As a neo-Victorian critical engagement should demand an investigation of this discourse of trauma, *Dickensian* fails to do so, exploiting the voyeurism of Miss Havisham's traumas.
9. A reference to Matthew 26:15 when Judas betrayed Jesus to the chief priests.
10. First published in *The People's Journal* 1 (June 3, 1846): 8–12.
11. Compeyson's many failures parallel Zechariah 7:10, "And oppress not the widow, nor the fatherless, the stranger, nor the poor; and let none of you imagine evil against his brother in your heart."
12. See Na (132n3) on Aristotle.

Bibliography

Atwood, Margaret. *Payback: Debt and the Shadow Side of Wealth*. London: Bloomsbury, 2008.

Ayres, Brenda. *Dissenting Women in Dickens' Novels: The Subversion of Domestic Ideology*. Westport, CT: Greenwood Press, 1998.

Boulter, David. "101." *Dickensian*, DVD.

"Broad." *Oxford Reference*. In *Oxford Dictionary of Phrase and Fable*. Oxford University Press, 2021. www.oxfordreference.com/view/10.1093/oi/authority.20110803095528510?rskey=GJaqlI&result=5.

Cerutti, Toni. "The Lay World of Dickens." In *Athena's Shuttle: Myth Religion Ideology from Romanticism to Modernism*, edited by Franco Marucci and Emma Sdegno, 45–67. Milan: Cisalpino, 2000.

Colledge, Gary. *God and Charles Dickens*. Grand Rapids, MI: Baker Publishing Group, 2012.

Collins, Philip. *Dickens Interviews and Recollections*. Vol. 2. London: Palgrave Macmillan, 1981.

Cunningham, Valentine. "Dickens and Christianity." In Paroissien 2008, 255–76.

Dickens, Charles. *Bleak House*. London: Bradbury, 1853. https://books.google.com/books?id=KlsJAAAAQAAJ.

———. *A Christmas Carol. In Prose. Being A Ghost Story of Christmas*. 1843. London: Chapman and Hall, 1845. https://books.google.com/books?id=MlMHAAAAQAAJ.

———. *David Copperfield*. London: Bradbury and Evans, 1850. https://books.google.com/books?id=NcsNAAAAQAAJ.

———. *Great Expectations*. 1861. Boston: Estes and Lauriat, 1881. https://books.google.com/books?id=fhUXAAAAYAAJ.

———. *The Old Curiosity Shop*. London: Chapman and Hall, 1841. https://books.google.com/books?id=2dUNAAAAQAAJ.

———. Letter to Editors of *The Daily News*, February 4, 1846, 4. *Charles Dickens Letters Project*. https://dickensletters.com/editors-daily-news-4-feb-1846.

———. *The Life of Our Lord*. 1934. New York: Simon and Schuster, 1999. https://archive.org/details/lifeofourlordwri011897mbp.

———. *Nicholas Nickleby*. London: Chapman and Hall, 1839. https://books.google.com/books?id=NdYNAAAAQAAJ.

———. *Oliver Twist*. 1838. Oxford: Oxford University Press, 2008.

———. *The Posthumous Papers of the Pickwick Club*. 1837. London: Chapman and Hall, 1847. https://books.google.com/books?id=UR0GAAAAQAAJ.SCY B0YQ6AEwAnoECAYQAg#v=snippet&q=was%20a%20prophet&f=false

———. Preface to *The Pickwick Papers*. 1837. Edited by James Kinsley, 883–88. The Cheap Library and Charles Dickens Editions. 1858 and 1867. Oxford: Clarendon Press, 1986.

Dickensian. Written by Tony Jordan et al. Directed by Harry Bradbeer et al. Produced by Red Planet Pictures. 20 episodes. December 16, 2015–February 21, 2016, DVD.

England, Maureen. "Dickens's Afterlife: Character and Cultural Memory." *Victoriographies*. 10, no. 3 (2020): 311–31.

Forster, John. *The Life of Charles Dickens*. Vol. 2: 1842–1852. London: Chapman and Hall, 1870. https://books.google.com/books?id=olkDAAAAYAAJ.

Furneaux, Holly. "Charles Dickens's Families of Choice: Elective Affinities, Sibling Substitution, and Homoerotic Desire." *Nineteenth-Century Literature* 62, no. 2 (2007): 153–92.

Gribble, Jennifer. "Dickens and Religion." In *The Oxford Handbook of Charles Dickens*, edited by Robert Patten, et al., 581–96. Oxford: Oxford University Press, 2018.

Hansen, Karen. "The Cratchits on Film: Neo-Victorian Visions of Domesticity." In *Neo-Victorian Families: Gender, Sexual and Cultural Politics*, edited by Marie-Luise Kohlke and Christian Gutleben, 175–96. Amsterdam: Rodopi, 2011.

Hartley, Jenny, ed. *The Selected Letters of Charles Dickens*. Oxford: Oxford University Press, 2012.

Heilmann, Ann, and Mark Llewellyn. *Neo-Victorianism: The Victorians in the Twenty-First Century, 1999–2009*. Basingstoke: Palgrave Macmillan, 2010.

House, Humphrey. *The Dickens World*. London: Oxford University Press, 1942.

Kaplan, Cora. "Neo-Victorian Dickens." In Furneaux and Ledger 2011, 81–87.

Kohlke, Marie-Luise. "Mining the Neo-Victorian Vein: Prospecting for Gold, Buried Treasure and Uncertain Metal." In *Neo-Victorian Literature and Culture: Immersions and Revisitations*, edited by Boehm-Schnitker, Nadine, and Susanne Gruss, 21–37. New York: Routledge, 2014.

Larson, Janet L. *Dickens and the Broken Scripture*. Athens, GA: University of Georgia Press, 1985.

Levine, Caroline. Introduction: "Television for Victorianists." *érudit* 63 (April 2013). www.erudit.org/en/journals/ravon/2013-n63-ravon01450/1025613ar/.

Levine, George. "Dickens, Secularism, and Agency." In Gillooly and David 2009, 13–34.

Logan, Tony, creator. *Dickensian*. Red Planet Pictures and BBC One. December 26, 2015–February 2016.

Mason, Emma. "Religion." In Furneaux and Ledger 2011, 318–25.

Maynes-Aminzade, Liz. "You're Part of Something Bigger: Macrorealist TV." *Romanticism and Victorianism on the Net*. no. 63 (April 2013): n.p. www.erudit.org/en/journals/ravon/1900-v1-n1-ravon01450/1025617ar/.

Mitchell, Kate. *History and Cultural Memory in Neo-Victorian Fiction: Victorian Afterimages*. Basingstoke: Palgrave Macmillan, 2010.

Na, Hai. "Grammar of Choice: Charles Dickens's Authentic Religion." *Dickens Quarterly* 35, no. 2 (June 2018): 127–42.

Newsom, Robert. "Religion." In *Oxford Reader's Companion to Dickens*, edited by Paul Schlicke and Simon Callow. Oxford: Oxford University Press, 2000. www.oxfordreference.com/view/10.1093/acref/9780198662532.001.0001/ acref-9780198662532-e-0369?rskey=PUeTr3&result=369

O'Callaghan, Claire "'Awaiting the Death Blow': Gendered Violence and Miss Havisham's Afterlives." In *Dickens After Dickens*, edited by E. Bell, 83–100. York: White Rose University Press, 2020.

Oulton, Carolyn W. de la L. *Literature and Religion in Mid-Victorian England: From Dickens to Eliot*. Basingstoke: Palgrave Macmillan, 2003.

Parey, Armelle. "Confluence and the Neo-Victorian in *Dickensian*." *Revue de la Société d'études anglaises contemporaines*. 2017. https://journals.openedition.org/ebc/3607

Paroissien, David, ed. *A Companion to Charles Dickens*. Hoboken, NJ: John Wiley and Sons, 2008.

Poovey, Mary. *Making a Social Body British Cultural Formation, 1830–1864*. Chicago, IL: University of Chicago, 1995.

Schlicke, Paul. *Dickens and Popular Entertainment*. Abingdon-on-Thames: Taylor and Francis Group, 1988.

Sedgewick, Eve Kosofsky. *Between Men: English Literature and Male Homosocial Desire*. New York: Columbia University Press, 1985.

———. *Epistemology of the Closet*. Berkeley: University of California Press, 1990.

Smith, Karl Ashley. *Dickens and the Unreal City: Searching for Spiritual Significance in Nineteenth-Century London*. Basingstoke: Palgrave Macmillan, 2008.

Storey, Graham, ed. *The British Academy/The Pilgrim Edition of the Letters of Charles Dickens, Vol. 9: 1859–1861*. Oxford: Oxford University Press, 1997. www.oxfordscholarlyeditions.com/view/10.1093/actrade/9780198122937.book.1/actrade-9780198122937-book-1.

Taft, Joshua. "Disenchanted Religion and Secular Enchantment in *A Christmas Carol*." *Victorian Literature and Culture* 43 (2015): 659–73.

Walder, Dennis. *Dickens and Religion*. London: Allen and Unwin, 1981.

Widdowson, Peter. "'Writing Back': Contemporary Re-Visionary Fiction." *Textual Practice* 20, no. 3 (2006): 491–507.

Yousef, Nancy. "The Poverty of Charity." In Gillooly and David 2009, 53–74.

Notes on Contributors

The Editors

Brenda Ayres and Sarah E. Maier coedited and contributed chapters to the following: *Neo-Victorian Madness: Rediagnosing Nineteenth-Century Mental Illness in Literature and Other Media* (Palgrave, 2020); *Neo-Gothic Narratives: Illusory Allusions from the Past* (Anthem, 2020); *Animals and Their Children in Victorian Culture* (Routledge, 2020); and *Reinventing Marie Corelli for the Twenty-first Century* (Anthem, 2019). The two cowrote *A Vindication of the Redhead: The Typology of Red Hair Throughout the Literary and Visual Arts* (Palgrave, 2021) and will be publishing *Neo-Victorian Things: Re-Imagining Nineteenth-Century Material Cultures* with Palgrave in 2021 (adding Danielle Dove as coeditor).

Contributors' Biographies

Brenda Ayres, now retired from full-time residential teaching, currently teaches online for several universities. Her additional works can be found at Amazon, and they include her first book on Dickens *Dissenting Women in Dickens' Domestic Novels: Subversion of Domestic Ideology* (Praeger, 1998). She published two other books by Routledge: *Victorians and Their Animals: Beast on a Leash* (2019) and *Animals and Their Children in Victorian Culture* (2020).

Lydia Craig is finishing her dissertation at Loyola University Chicago. Her most recent publications are "What Charles Dickens Never Said: Verifying Internet 'Quotes' and Accessing the Works with Online Resources"; "A Horrid Female Waterman' in *Dickens Quarterly*; "The Contentious Legacy of Grace Darling in Charles Dickens's *Our Mutual Friend*" in *Dickens and Women Re-observed*, edited by Edward Guiliano (Edward Everett Root Publishers, 2020), and "The

Devastating Impact of Lord Wharton's Bible Charity in *Wuthering Heights*" in *Victorians: A Journal of Culture and Literature* (2018).

Julie Donovan is Associate Professor of Women's Leadership Program and University Writing at Columbian College of Arts and Sciences at George Washington University. She has published *Sydney Owenson, Lady Morgan and the Politics of Style* (2009). Her most recent publications are " 'Grossly Material': Jesuit Material Culture in *Villette*" in *Charlotte Brontë, Embodiment and the Material World*, edited by Justine Pizzo and Eleanor Houghton (Palgrave Macmillan, 2020); "Elizabeth Gaskell's *North and South*" in *The Palgrave Guide to Women's Writing*, edited by Lesa Scholl (Palgrave Macmillan, 2020); and "For Ireland or Against Woman?: The Irish Riposte to Harriet Martineau" in *Nineteenth-Century Prose* (Spring 2020).

Marie S. Heneghan has recently completed her doctoral thesis at the University of Southern Queensland entitled "Re-Forming Faith: Idolatry and the Victorian Novel." She taught English Literature at universities in Spain and Australia. Her publications include "The Post-Romantic Way to God: Personal Agency and Self-Worship in *Wuthering Heights*" in *Australasian Journal of Victorian Studies* (2018) and " 'I believe in Willie Hughes': *The Portrait of Mr. W.H.*" in *Critical Insights: Oscar Wilde*, edited by Frederick S. Roden (Salem Press, 2019).

Aaron K. H. Ho has taught at universities in New York, China, and Singapore for more than ten years. His research interest lies in intersectional minority studies (gender, sexuality, race, and disability) with an emphasis on Victorianism and Asian cultures. He recently edited an academic collection titled *The New Witches* (McFarland) in which he wrote on the representation of disabilities.

Susan Johnston is Associate Professor of English at the University of Regina. She has published on Victorian literature, adaptation, and popular culture, including articles on fantasy and theology such as "Harry Potter, Eucatastrophe, and Christian Hope" in *Logos: A Journal of Catholic Thought and Culture* (2011) and "Grief Poignant as Joy: Dyscatastrophe and Eucatastrophe in *A Song of Ice and Fire*" in *Mythlore* (2012). Recent work includes chapters on Canadian fantasist Guy Gavriel Kay (2019) and on time and the Victorian factory in *The Rail, the Body, and the Pen* (McFarland, 2021), and a forthcoming chapter on theology of the body and *Game of Thrones*. She returns here to subjects she took up in her first book, *Women and Domestic Experience in Victorian Political Fiction* (Greenwood, 2001).

Lindsay Katzir is Assistant Professor of English at Langston University where she teaches British literature and composition. Her research centers on issues of race, religion, and gender in nineteenth-century

British literature, generally, and in particular, she focuses on Victorian Jewish literature and culture. Recent publications have appeared in *Jewish Studies Quarterly*, *Nineteenth-Century Prose*, *Animals and Their Children in Victorian Culture* (Routledge, 2019), and *Victorians and Their Animals: Beast on a Leash* (Routledge, 2018). She lives in Oklahoma City with her husband, Brandon Katzir, and sons, Avigdor and Yonatan.

Sarah E. Maier is Professor of English and Comparative Literature at the University of New Brunswick. She has published extensively on the Brontës; edited special issues on *Sir Arthur Conan Doyle*, *Neo-Victorian Considerations* and *Charlotte Brontë at the Bicentennial* as well as published articles on biofiction, neo-Victorian vampires, *Penny Dreadful*, transmedia adaptations; Anne Lister, and neo-Victorian narratives.

Christine Schintgen is Associate Professor and Chair of Literature at Our Lady Seat of Wisdom College in Barry's Bay, Ontario, Canada, where she has been a faculty member for 17 years. Her research interests include Dickens, Dante, prisons, criminals, and the relationship between faith and literature. Her most recent publications are "Goodness, Truth, and Beauty in Dante's *Inferno*" for *Fellowship of Catholic Scholars Quarterly* (2020) and "The Fullness of Mercy: Western Literature and the Illumination of a Divine Attribute" for *Touchstone Magazine: A Journal of Mere Christianity* (2017).

Tony Schwab writes on topics in English Literature, specializing in Jane Austen and Dickens. His essays have appeared on *The Victorian Web*. He has taught at Rutgers University and Bergen Community College. Since 1988 he has been an educator in alternative secondary school settings, recently retiring as principal of a therapeutic high school for teens with anxiety and depression. He has contributed essays on disaffected youth to The Research Lab for Children's Relationships, Emotions and Social Skills, University of Sussex, England. Schwab's career, thought, and writing are informed by studies in phenomenology and qualitative understanding of the whole person.

Mary-Antoinette Smith is Associate Professor of Eighteenth- and Nineteenth-Century British Literature at Seattle University. Her pedagogy promotes race, class, gender, and sexuality theory which moves toward praxis. Among her scholarly publications are "Of Human Bondage: Recurrent Replications of Supplication, Enslavement, and Appeal from Antiquity through the Nineteenth Century" in *Adaptation Before Cinema: Literary and Visual Convergence from Antiquity through the 19th Century* (2021) and *Thomas Clarkson and Ottobah Cugoano: Essays on the Slavery and Commerce of the Human Species* (Broadview Press, 2010).

Daniel Stuart recently received his PhD in English from the University of North Texas where his dissertation focused on the issue of predatory behavior in the novels of Charles Dickens. His current research involves surveillance studies and new historical approaches to Victorian literature along with emerging topics in the nineteenth-century print culture. He is also a librarian and, since 2017, has been a clinical faculty associate with the School of Medicine at Texas Tech University. His most recent work can be found in *Victorian Review* as well as the information science journals *Medical Libraries Reference Quarterly* and *Journal of Resources in Electronic Medical Libraries*.

Index

Allingham, Philip, 12, 62, 212, 228–229
All the Year Round 12, 64–65, 67, 70n1, 104, 120, 212, 228–230, 232, 242n4
America 7–8
American Notes 7
Angel in the House 161, 216, 221
angels 29, 100, 118, 176, 223
Anglicanism: broad church 1, 13n3, 110, 112, 213, 250; high church 27, 112, 130, 213; low church 112
anti-Catholicism *see* Catholicism
anti-Evangelicalism *see* Evangelicalism
anti-Semitism 10, 192–195, 198, 208

Barnaby Rudge 5, 70n2, 70n5, 91, 95–96, 98–104, 104n1, 105n8, 174, 186
bells 5, 31, 59–60, 70n5, 91–97, 99–104, 105n4, 105n12, 116, 130, 179, 251
Bentham, Jeremy 130, 144n7
Bible 11, 18, 21, 23–25, 29–30, 32–33, 39, 149, 177, 205, 212, 215, 224, 228, 236, 254; general 39, 212; New Testament 22; Old Testament 2, 22, 105n13
bildungsroman 9, 39, 149–153, 159
Bleak House 3, 6, 12, 30, 32, 38, 40, 42, 47, 51–52, 52n1, 119, 176–177, 192, 232–237, 240–242, 248, 250, 259–260, 262
Browne, Hablot Knight 98, 171, *172–173*, *181*, *183*

Calvinism 30
capitalism 129, 132–133, 135–136, 177, 187, 233
Carlyle, Thomas 3, 9, 57, 59, 62, 69, 70n6, 130, 174

Catholicism 4, 8, 11, 27, 56, 70nn2–3, 75, 95–97, 112, 129, 212–213
cemetery *see* graveyards
Child's History of England, A 26, 96
Chimes, The 59, 60, 63, 64, 67, 70n4, 101, 105n11
Christmas books 4, 55–57, 59–60, 62, 64, 69, 70n1
Christmas Carol, A 4, 6, 37, 57, 67, 70n3, 75–78, 81, 87–88, 111, 192, 248, 251–252
Church of England *see* Anglicanism
churchyard *see* graveyards
clerics *see* ministers
Colledge, Gary 13n1, 25, 30–31, 73, 112, 124n1, 154, 161, 163n5, 164n9, 251
Collins, Philip 24, 30–31, 128
Cricket on the Hearth, The 62, 70n1
Cruikshank, George *197*, 201, 205

damnation *see* hell
Darwin, Charles 212–214, 218–219, 221, 233–236, 238–240, 242n1
Darwinism 11–12, 215, 217–218, 220–225
David Copperfield 9, 40–41, 105n3, 149–152, 154, 156, 159, 161, *172–173*, 218, 220, 256, 263n7
devil 6, 21, 56, 121–123, 262
Dickens, Catherine Hogarth 41
Dickens, Charles: biographical 59; correspondence 11, 37, 234
Dickens, Henry Fielding 13n5, 30, 34n8
Dickens, John 10, 170
Dickensian 4, 12–13, 74–75, 80, 85, 96, 141, 149–150, 152–154, 159, 216, 241, 248, 249, 252
dissenting 120, 124n3

Index

Dombey and Son 34n12, 42, 170, 187, 224, 263n7
domesticity 197, 252
doppelgänger 62, 80, 87

Edwin Drood 42
Established Church *see* Anglicanism
Evangelicalism 113, 115–116, 120–122, 124, 213
evil 2, 4, 8, 10, 12, 28, 61, 64, 76, 79, 139, 141, 176–177, 185, 201, 217–218, 233, 236, 239, 253, 264n11
evolution 11–12, 188, 212–214, 216–217, 221–222, 224, 228, 230–231, 233–235, 237, 241

Forster, John 2, 7, 13n2, 30, 41, 46, 59, 70n3, 75, 99, 101, 103–104, 170, 240, 250

Gaskell, Elizabeth 7, 112, 215, 229
George Silverman's Explanation 6, 110, 120, 124
ghosts 4, 55–57, 59, 62, 65–70, 100, 202, 208
Gordon Riots 5, 91, 95–97, 102
Gospel *see* Bible, New Testament
graveyards 48, 51
Great Expectations 9, 39, 105n3, 149–152, 154, 158, 162–163, 175, 248, 256, 261

Hard Times 5–6, 57, 73, 114–116, 119, 122, 124, 128–131, 134, 137, 140, 143, 144n7, 188, 220, 254
Haunted Man, The 62, 64, 70n1
heaven 20, 24, 26, 30, 53n2, 57, 67, 118, 144nn12–13, 169, 174–176, 184, 188, 254, 260
Hebrew Bible *see* Bible, Old Testament
hell 2, 24, 30, 225
Hogarth, Mary 3, 41, 42, 44, 56, 70n3, 216
Household Words 26, 64–65, 67–68, 70n1, 104, 113, 194, 212, 229, 231
hypocrisy 23, 30, 96, 99, 119, 129, 254

Ignatius of Loyola 76, 78, 82, 83, 86
Italy 7, 56, 68

Jesus Christ 2, 6, 18, 20, 25, 28, 34n12, 73–75, 87–88, 110, 112, 164n6
Judaism 8, 10–11, 192, 196, 199–208
judgment 2, 18, 24, 30, 34n11, 102, 121, 123–124, 177, 225, 255, 263n7

latitudinarianism *see* Anglicanism, broad church
legalism 179
Levine, George 11–12, 212–215, 217–219, 230, 236–239, 251–252
Life of Our Lord, The 2, 4, 7, 13n1, 13n5, 19, 20, 25–26, 28, 30, 33n2, 73, 77, 154, 163n5, 168, 235, 239, 248–249
Little Dorrit 12, 31, 40, 105n3, 175, 178–179, 213, 215–218, 225
Lyell, Charles 12, 212

Malthus, Thomas 232
Martin Chuzzlewit 105n3, 119, 174, 213–214
Martineau, Harriet 112, 212
Marxism 132
Master Humphrey's Clock 5, 91, 93
materialism 55, 57, 59, 62, 69, 70, 177, 188, 203, 260
mesmerism 25
Methodism 28
ministers 119, 121

natural selection *see* Darwinism
neo-Victorian 1, 13, 246–248, 251–252, 260–261, 264n8
Nicholas Nickleby 3, 19, 37, 40, 52n1, 69, 180, *181*, *183*, 257
nonconforming *see* dissenting

Old Curiosity Shop, The 3, 38, 43, 46, 47, 52n1, 182, 248
Oliver Twist 7, 10–12, 37, 39, 42, 137, 192–194, 196, *197*, 205, 232–236, 238, 241, 248, 256, 258
orphans 10, 48, 198, 256
Oulton, Carolyn W. de la L. 30, 216, 219, 220, 224–225, 252, 256
Our Mutual Friend 3–4, 10–12, 14n10, 40, 69, 70n6, 105n3, 175, 187, 192–194, 196, 198, 205, 206, 213, 215, 217–222, 224–225, 233, 262

Owen, Richard 214, 228, 242n7
Oxford Movement 96, 112, 130, 212, 223

Parliament 5, 49, 59, 91, 93, 95, 116, 144n3
Phiz *see* Browne, Hablot Knight
Pickwick Papers, The 13n2, 39, 52n1, 64, 69, 119, 188, 246
Pictures from Italy 56, 96, 101
Pilgrim's Progress, The 4, 39, 43, 52–53n2, 75, 153, 159, 236
Poor Law 7, 137
prison 3, 8, 102, 162, 170, 175, 178, 215
Providence 31, 138, 225, 238
Puritan 43, 52n2, 93, 95, 121
Pusey, Edward *see* Oxford Movement

redemption 9, 29–31, 38, 50, 110, 118–120, 153–154, 159–163, 205, 216, 220
Ruskin, John 9, 26, 28, 95, 178, 194

Sabbatarianism 111, 120
salvation 24–26, 28, 44, 78, 81, 88, 99, 118, 131, 152, 160–161, 164n8, 206, 216, 219, 220, 224–225, 238, 242n6
Satan *see* devil

science 12, 23, 67, 138–139, 214–215, 228, 230–231, 233–234, 241
Scripture *see* Bible, general
séances 68, 69
Shakespeare 67, 70n3, 198
signal-man 67
Sketches by Boz 1
Slater, Michael 33, 105n11, 112, 155, 160
Spencer, Herbert 11, 221
spiritualism 25, 69

Tale of Two Cities, A 19, 40, 188, 236
Temperance 13, 246
Ternan, Ellen 33, 220, 222
theosophy 110, 114, 116, 123–124
Tractarianism *see* Oxford Movement

Uncommercial Traveler, The 37
Unitarianism 1, 8, 9, 112, 213
utilitarianism 9, 129, 133, 134, 142

Walder, Dennis 13, 31, 38, 46, 96, 102, 104n1, 116–117, 153, 163n2, 163n5, 213, 216, 217, 250, 257, 258, 263n2
workhouse 3, 37, 168, 170, 184–186, 239, 249, 254

Milton Keynes UK
Ingram Content Group UK Ltd.
UKHW031502071224
451979UK00020B/230